JOSEPHUS

AND THE NEW TESTAMENT

Second Edition

JOSEPHUS
AND THE NEW TESTAMENT
Second Edition

STEVE MASON

Hendrickson Publishers, Inc.
P. O. Box 3473
Peabody, Massachusetts 01961-3473

Printed in the United States of America

First Edition—1992

Second Edition—July 2003

Library of Congress Cataloging-in-Publication Data

Mason, Steve, 1957–
Josephus and the New Testament / Steve Mason.— 2nd ed.
p. cm.
Includes bibliographical references and index.
ISBN 1-56563-795-X
1. Josephus, Flavius. 2. Jewish historians—Biography. 3. Bible. N.T.—Biography. 4. Bible. N.T.—Criticism, interpretation, etc. I. Title.
DS115.9.J6M38 2003
933′.05′092—dc21
2003013535

For Cara and Ian

Contents

Preface to the Second Edition ix

Abbreviations xiii

Introduction: The Purpose of This Book 1

Chapter 1: The Use and Abuse of Josephus 7

Chapter 2: The Career of Josephus 35

Chapter 3: The Writings of Josephus 55

Chapter 4: Who's Who in the New Testament World? 147

Chapter 5: Early Christian Figures Mentioned by Josephus 213

Chapter 6: Josephus and Luke-Acts 251

Conclusion: The Significance of Josephus for New Testament Study 297

Index of Subjects 303

Index of Ancient Sources 309

Preface to the Second Edition

The first edition of *Josephus and the New Testament* (1992) was a pleasure to write. It has been gratifying to see it reach just the sort of audience for which it was intended. Letters from readers show the ways in which it proved useful (all of them dignified as far as I know, though some unexpected), but they also raise challenges on a few points. It may help readers of this new edition to know what is different here.

A great deal has happened since 1992, when "Josephus studies" was the exotic preserve of a few diehards. In that year most of the world's active Josephus specialists converged on San Miniato, Italy; those invited numbered no more than fifty. Few book-length studies of Josephus, much less of his individual works, existed at the time. In a 1988 survey, however, Per Bilde observed a perceptible "buzz" in the written scholarship of the field: Helgo Lindner (1972), Harold Attridge (1976), Shaye Cohen (1979), Tessa Rajak (1983), and Louis Feldman (1984 plus dozens of lengthy articles). Since 1992, international commentary and translation projects, professional and graduate seminars, essay collections, monographs, and doctoral dissertations devoted to Josephus have proliferated. Some of the most important developments include the German text, translation, and commentary project of the *Life, Against Apion,* and *Antiquities,* which is based in Münster, Germany, and directed by Folker Siegert, along with the related international Josephus-Kolloquium that meets annually in European centers; the French text, translation, and commentary project beginning with *Antiquities,* directed by Étienne Nodet of the École biblique et archéologique in Jerusalem; the Brill Josephus Project (full commentary and English translation), which I edit; and the Society of Biblical Literature's Josephus Seminar, which meets annually. New books and essay collections from the past decade are too numerous even to list here. It is a thrilling time to be involved in the study of Josephus. His extensive writings have only now begun to receive the attention we lavished on other ancient texts for centuries.

So a new edition of *Josephus and the New Testament* required some degree of revision at least. The main stimulus was provided by Dr. Manuel Vogel of Münster. During our memorable tour of Galilee's archaeological sites in 1998, he graciously offered to translate the book for an audience in Germany, where the study of Josephus has a distinguished history. Given the developments since 1992, and my own evolution in thinking, it was necessary to provide a revised English text as a basis for the German (Tübingen: Francke, 2000). Translations into Italian (2001) and Korean (2002) did not, alas, benefit from these changes. However, they were incorporated into this new English edition, and because things moved so quickly—even since 1999 when I finished the revisions for the German—quite a few more have been added.

The result is a book that retains the format and logic of the original, but in which the content has changed in significant ways. Chapter 1 is the least affected, for I have little new to say about the use (and abuse) of Josephus through Western history. Changes there are limited to corrections and possibly improved phrasing. At the other extreme, chapter 3 has been completely rewritten and expanded because this is where the main action has occurred in the reassessment of Josephus's writings. The field continues to explode with new ideas and approaches, through a range of international projects and conferences that simply did not exist a decade ago. The other chapters fall somewhere between these two poles: chapter 2, though making the same basic points as before, places a new emphasis on the rhetorical character of the evidence for Josephus's career; chapter 4 puts Josephus's discussions of the Herods, high priests, Pharisees, and others into modified contexts; in chapter 5 the section on James is rewritten and other parts lightly revised; and in chapter 6 I have significantly adjusted my readings of both Luke-Acts and Josephus. Josephus's environment in Rome and the importance of that context for his first audiences is a new emphasis in general. I have tried to show restraint in making changes and have tried not to confuse this book with the more formal introduction to the writings of Josephus that I am also preparing. Still, I think that this book marks a generational change from its parent. What has not changed is my goal of providing an accessible door to Josephus for the New Testament reader.

Finally, I must thank many agencies, groups, and individuals for their support over the past few years, while I have been doing the background work reflected in the changes observable here: York University, for research support and for sponsoring me as their Canada Research Chair (in Cultural Identity and Interaction in the Greco-Roman World) from 2003; the Canada Council for the Arts, for the enviable Killam Research Fellowship, 2001–2003; All Souls College, University of Oxford, and its fellows for a salubrious Visiting Fellowship in 2002–2003; the Social Sciences and Humanities Research Council of Canada, for research support through most of the past decade; my colleagues in things ancient at York, a remarkable fellowship of inspired scholars and decent human beings; the members of the SBL Josephus Seminar from around the globe, always a delight to see; James Ernest and Dawn Duncan of Hendrickson Publishers, consummate professionals; and my parents, siblings, and children (Cara and Ian), who are my mainstays.

Abbreviations

Ancient Sources

1 Cor	1 Corinthians
1 En.	*1 Enoch*
1 Kgs	1 Kings
1 Pet	1 Peter
1 Sam	1 Samuel
1 Thess	1 Thessalonians
1QH[a]	*Thanksgiving Hymns*
'Abot R. Nat.	*'Abot of Rabbi Nathan*
Acts Jas.	*Secret Book of James*
Aristotle	
Eth. nic.	*Nicomachean Ethics*
Pol.	*Politics*
Rhet.	*Rhetoric*
Cicero	
Cat.	*Catilinarians*
De or.	*On the Orator*
Div.	*Divination*
Fat.	*On Fate*
Flac.	*For Flaccus*
Inv.	*On the Classification of Rhetoric*
Leg.	*On Laws*
Leg. man.	*On Pompey's Command*
Rep.	*Republic*
Rosc. Amer.	*For Sextus Roscius Amerianus*

Col Colossians

Dan Daniel

Deut Deuteronomy

Dio Cassius
Hist. rom. *History of Rome*

Diogenes Laertius
Vit. phil. *Lives of Eminent Philosophers*

Dionysius of Halicarnassus
Ant. rom. *Roman Antiquities*

Epictetus
Diatr. *Discourses*

Eusebius
Dem. ev. *Proof of the Gospel*
Hist. eccl. *Ecclesiastical History*

Exod Exodus

Ezek Ezekiel

Gal Galatians

Gen. Rab. *Genesis Rabbah*

Git. *Gittin*

Gos. Heb. *Gospel of the Hebrews*

Gos. Thom. *Gospel of Thomas*

Heb Hebrews

Herodotus
Hist. *Histories*

Hesiod
Op. *Works and Days*

Hippolytus
C. Jud. *Against the Jews*

Homer
Il. *Iliad*
Od. *Odyssey*

Horace
Carm. *Odes*

Isa Isaiah

Isocrates
Antid. *Antidosis*

Jas James

Jer	Jeremiah
Josephus	
Ag. Ap.	*Against Apion*
Ant.	*Jewish Antiquities*
Life	*Life of Josephus*
War	*Jewish War*
Justin	
1 Apol.	*Apology*
Dial.	*Dialogue with Trypho*
Juvenal	
Sat.	*Satires*
Lam	Lamentations
Lev	Leviticus
Livy	
Hist. rom.	*History of Rome*
Lucian	
Men.	*Menippus*
Nigr.	*Wisdom of Nigrinus*
Matt	Matthew
Martial	
Ep.	*Epigrams*
Melito	
Pascha	*Passover Sermon*
Minucius Felix	
Oct.	*Octavius*
Neh	Nehemiah
Num	Numbers
Origen	
Cels.	*Against Celsus*
Comm. Matt.	*Commentary on Matthew*
Fr. Lam.	*Fragments on Lamentations*
Phil	Philippians
Philo	
Embassy	*On the Embassy to Gaius*
Hypoth.	*Hypothetica*
Philostratus	
Vit. Apoll.	*Apollonius of Tyana*

Plato
- *Resp.* — *Republic*

Pliny the Younger
- *Ep.* — *Epistles*

Plutarch
- *Cat. Maj.* — *Cato the Elder*
- *Flam.* — *Titus Flamininus*
- *Mor.* — *Moralia*
- *Num.* — *Numa*
- *Phil.* — *Philopoemen*
- *Superst.* — *On Superstition*

Polybius
- Polybius — *Universal History*

Porphyry
- *Abst.* — *On Abstinence*

Pre. Pet. — *Preaching of Peter*

Ps — Psalms

Pseudo-Clement
- *Rec.* — *Recognitions*

Sallust
- *Bell. Cat.* — *Catilinarian Conflict*
- *Bell. Jug.* — *Jugurthine War*

Seneca the Elder
- *Contr.* — *Controversies*

Seneca the Younger
- *Ep.* — *Epistles* or *Moral Epistles*

Silius Italicus
- *Pun.* — *Punica*

Suetonius
- *Claud.* — *Claudius*
- *Dom.* — *Domitian*
- *Tit.* — *Divus Titus*
- *Vesp.* — *Vespasian*

Sulpicius Severus
- *Chron.* — *Chronica*

Syb. Or. — *Sybilline Oracles*

Ta'an. — *Ta'anit*

Tacitus

Agr.	*Agricola*
Ann.	*Annales*
Hist.	*Histories*

Thucydides

Hist.	*History of the Peloponnesian War*

Valerius Flaccus

Arg.	*Argonautica*

Virgil

Aen.	*Aeneid*

Technical Abbreviations

b.	ben (son of)
b.	Babylonian Talmud
B.C.E.	before the Common Era
BJRL	*Bulletin of the John Rylands University Library of Manchester*
CBQ	*Catholic Biblical Quarterly*
C.E.	Common Era
d.	died
h.p.	high priest
HTR	*Harvard Theological Review*
IDB	*Interpreter's Dictionary of the Bible.* 4 vols. Edited by G. A. Buttrick. Nashville: Abingdon, 1962
JBH	*Josephus, the Bible, and History.* Edited by Louis H. Feldman and Gohei Hata. Leiden: Brill, 1989
JBL	*Journal of Biblical Literature*
JJC	*Josephus, Judaism, and Christianity.* Edited by Louis H. Feldman and Gohei Hata. Detroit: Wayne State University Press, 1987
JJS	*Journal of Jewish Studies*
JMS	*Josephus and Modern Scholarship (1937–1980)* Berlin: de Gruyter, 1984
LCL	Loeb Classical Library
m.	married

MGWJ	*Monatsschrift für Geschichte und Wissenschaft des Judentums*
NJPS	*Tanakh: The Holy Scrpitures: The New JPS Translation according to the Traditional Hebrew Text*
NPNF[2]	*The Nicene and Post-Nicene Fathers,* Series 2
NT	New Testament
OT	Old Testament/Hebrew Bible
PW	Pauly, A. F. *Paulys Realencyclopädie der classischen Altertumswissenschaft.* New edition G. Wissowa. 49 vols. Munich, 1980
TDNT	*Theological Dictionary of the New Testament*
ThQ	*Theologische Quartalschrift*
y.	Jerusalem Talmud
ZNW	*Zeitschrift für die neutestamentliche wissenschaft und die Kunde der älteren Kirche*

Introduction

The Purpose of This Book

When I first became interested in Josephus, I was discussing my new passion with a lawyer friend who also had a strong, though not professional, interest in the New Testament world. He said, "I must sit down some time and read Josephus right through, from cover to cover." We have since lost touch and I don't know whether his ambition was ever fulfilled, but I doubt it. "Reading Josephus through" is a daunting task and probably not the most efficient way to come to terms with the ancient author. When visiting a new city, we first buy a map of the place in order to orient ourselves, so that we get some idea of the "big picture." This book is intended as a kind of map to the world of Josephus—his life, thought, and writings—for readers of the New Testament. I offer it to all those who have bought or borrowed the works of Josephus out of a keen interest in the New Testament world, only to feel frustrated at the obscurity of his writings.

Every scholar in the area understands the importance of Josephus for the serious study of the New Testament. He was born in 37 C.E., just a few years after Jesus' death and very soon after Paul's conversion to Christianity. He grew up in Jerusalem and was intimately acquainted with the religion of Israel, its temple and its feasts, at one of which Jesus had been arrested. He knew a lot about the important background figures in the gospels—King Herod and his sons, Roman governors such as Pontius Pilate, the Pharisees and Sadducees—and he was a priest himself. Having lived for a time in Jesus' home region of Galilee, he knew intimately its geographical and social conditions. Josephus was reaching maturity at about the time that the apostle Paul was imprisoned and sent to Rome; he even moved to Rome within a decade of Paul's execution there, though under circumstances very different from Paul's.

This means that when Josephus undertook his literary career in Rome, from about about 70 to 100, he was an exact contemporary of the gospel writers, whose work is usually assigned to the same period. His compositions, about which we shall have much more to say in the coming chapters, are four: *Jewish War* (seven volumes), *Jewish Antiquities* (twenty volumes), *Life* (one volume), and *Against Apion* (two volumes). Further, Josephus did not write only about political and social life in Judea and the Eastern Mediterranean; he reached back to begin the story of the *Antiquities* from creation with an extensive paraphrase of the Bible. Thus his writings provide abundant examples of the ways in which a first-century Jew read the "Old" Testament.[1]

So, Josephus's works offer us a potential gold mine for understanding the world of the New Testament. They are a resource whose value for New Testament study is not even remotely paralleled in another contemporary author. If his writings had not survived, Bible dictionaries would all be pocketbook size, and textbooks on the background of the New Testament would have little to tell us. We would still have the considerable archaeological work of the last forty years, to be sure, but physical remains do not speak for themselves; even here, Josephus has been the archaeologist's constant companion, suggesting where to look and how to interpret what is found.

Here is where the problems begin. Although everyone realizes the *value* of Josephus's writings, not many are able to sit down and read through them with profit. I confess to having fallen asleep a few times

---

[1] I use quotation marks because for Josephus, as for Jesus and the early Christians, there was no "Old" Testament. What we call the Old Testament was, of course, their Bible. The Christian writings that would later come to be collectively called the "New" Testament were being written about the time of Josephus, but he seems not to have known of them. In any case, even for Christians they were not considered "Scripture" until at least a century after they were written.

I have assumed that the reader has a copy of both the NT and Josephus's writings alongside this text. That assumption excuses me from quoting extensively from either collection, which would have made this book a considerable burden to carry. References to classical authors, including Josephus, follow the Loeb Classical Library (LCL) scheme wherever possible. Readers using the Hendrickson Publishers edition of Josephus will find these section numbers in parentheses, supplementing Whiston's chapter divisions. In those places where I have quoted from the NT, the translations are mine. In the case of Josephus, I have translated shorter segments—to bring out some particular nuance; otherwise, I have deferred to the LCL standard, as the references indicate.

while working through some lengthy digression—and Josephus likes to digress. So I suspect that, in spite of the fact that his collected works continue to sell in the tens of thousands every year, they mainly gather dust on the shelves of the ministers, rabbis, seminarians, and interested lay people who purchase them.

The reasons for this neglect are clear enough. First, his writings are extensive—somewhat longer than the Old Testament and more than four times the size of the New. Second, they often seem to ramble endlessly, especially the lethargic *Antiquities*, which paraphrases the entire Old Testament story in its first half and then continues with subsequent Jewish history. Readers looking for immediate enlightenment on the background of early Christianity are apt to find much in Josephus that is annoyingly trivial, irrelevant, or opaque. Third, the most popular English text of Josephus today was translated in 1737 by William Whiston. Although Whiston's translation and accompanying essays were a tremendous achievement in the early eighteenth century, today's reader gets the feeling that they are themselves "period pieces" from the remote past. To make matters worse, Whiston's Josephus is usually printed in double columns, and with the books arranged out of order (*Life* first, *Antiquities* second, *War* third, *Against Apion* last). Even the less accessible twentieth-century translation in the Loeb Classical Library is quickly becoming dated. And no matter how good the translation, the substance of Josephus remains a challenge to the most curious investigator. The result is that Josephus's works often suffer the same fate as the King James Version of the Bible—a perennial best-seller, much loved, occasionally quoted, but hardly ever read.

Professional analysts of Josephus are aware of these problems and, in the past few years, have taken some important steps to provide students with the necessary "maps." Some have reissued portions of his works in attractive formats that include scholarly commentaries, such as the Penguin edition of the *Jewish War* (trans. G. A. Williamson, 1981) and the beautifully illustrated edition by Gaalya Cornfeld and others (1982).

Two authors have written very useful introductions to Josephus. Tessa Rajak, a classical historian, published *Josephus: The Historian and His Society* in 1983. And Per Bilde's *Josephus Between Jerusalem and Rome: His Life, His Works, and Their Importance* appeared in 1988. We would not be academics if we did not disagree on minor points, but these two books are exemplary introductions. Both are quite readable, and I recommend them to interested students. They serve to update a series of lectures given by H. St. John Thackeray in the 1920s, published as *Josephus: The Man and the Historian* (1927), which are themselves still worth reading, even though some of Thackeray's distinctive views have not proven durable.

More adventurous readers might also want to tackle two collections of essays on Josephus edited by Louis H. Feldman and Gohei Hata. Titled *Josephus, Judaism, and Christianity* (1987) and *Josephus, the Bible, and History* (1988), respectively, these two volumes provide an outstanding survey of recent research by the world's leading scholars. The project was commissioned by a Tokyo press to accompany Professor Hata's translation of Josephus's writings into Japanese, to apprise Japanese readers of the "state of the art" in Josephan studies. These English originals of the translated essays are sometimes heavy going for the general reader, with sprinklings of untranslated Latin, Greek, and Hebrew, but they will reward the patient student. When I refer to particular essays from these volumes, I shall cite them as *JJC* and *JBH*, to avoid repeating the full titles of each book.

Heniz Schreckenberg and Louis Feldman have compiled a series of extremely useful annotated bibliographies to Josephus. Schreckenberg's main work runs chronologically, from the end of the Middle Ages to the 1960s, and cites books that deal substantially with Josephus (*Bibliographie zu Flavius Josephus;* Leiden: Brill, 1968). His *Supplementband* (1979) fills in some gaps and includes a special section on editions of Josephus in various languages. Feldman's thousand-page *Josephus and Modern Scholarship (1937–1980)*, published by W. de Gruyter of Berlin in 1984, has a narrower chronological focus but a broader reach and fuller annotation. A valuable summary is provided by Feldman's article, "A Selective Critical Bibliography of Josephus," in *JBH*, pp. 330–448. In 1986 Feldman published a bibliography to supplement Schreckenberg's (*Josephus: A Supplementary Bibliography;* New York: Garland).

Recent years have seen a proliferation of essay collections on Josephus. Among the more accessible of these are Fausto Parente and Joseph Sievers, eds., *Josephus and the History of the Greco-Roman Period: Essays in Memory of Morton Smith* (Leiden: Brill, 1994); and Steve Mason, ed., *Understanding Josephus: Seven Perspectives* (Sheffield: Sheffield Academic Press, 1998). The Münster team is also publishing an annual collection of scholarly essays on Josephus (Münsteraner Judaistische Studien; LIT Verlag), resulting from their ongoing project and related international colloquia. And Louis Feldman's studies of Josephus's biblical paraphrase (*Josephus's Interpretation of the Bible;* Berkeley: University of California, 1998) go far beyond their stated brief to give much insight into Josephus's thought and language.

The book in your hands was not written because of any deficiency in the materials just mentioned. It simply has a different focus. This book is for students of the New Testament and its world who want to know how to approach Josephus so that he will throw light on the New Testament texts. It will draw heavily from recent research on Josephus's life and writings, especially in chapters 2 and 3. But whereas that research forms the core of the studies mentioned above, we shall focus our attention on matters of direct relevance to New Testament interpretation.

Chapter 1, "The Use and Abuse of Josephus," sets the stage by sketching out how Christian readers have usually read Josephus, arguing that this method is inappropriate. Scholars, too, come in for some criticism in their use of the ancient writer. I argue that the best approach is to try to meet Josephus as a writer from the first century, to enter his world of thought and language, and to deal with the issues that were of importance to him. Only then can we understand him.

This does not mean that we cannot ask him about things that interest us as readers of the New Testament, but only that we should read his answers in the context of his own thought-world, and not manipulate his statements for our purposes. So chapters 2 and 3, while discussing his life and writings, outline some major features of his thought-world, especially his assumptions about writing history and his view of religion. We shall look also at key words in his vocabulary to get a feeling for his "worldview."

Chapter 4 applies this approach to some prominent groups in the background of the New Testament: the family of King Herod, the Roman governors, the Jewish high priesthood, and the Pharisees and Sadducees. Our goal is not, in the first instance, to learn the historical truth about these issues; rather, we need first to ask how Josephus, a real person with his own biases, understood them. Chapter 5 continues in the same direction, but now with the major figures of the early Christian world who are mentioned by Josephus, namely: John the Baptist, Jesus, and Jesus' brother James.

In chapter 6, I take up the fascinating question of the relationship between Josephus's works and the two NT volumes known as the "Gospel of Luke" and the "Acts of the Apostles." There I demonstrate some striking parallels of structure, aim, and vocabulary between Josephus and Luke-Acts and then ask how those parallels are best explained.

A concluding chapter draws together the main lines of the book and reflects on the "Significance of Josephus for New Testament Study." It is my contention that, if we try to understand him as a real person from the first-century Jewish world, our reading of the Christian Scriptures will at least be greatly enriched, if not radically changed.

To avoid the appearance of making false promises, academics often like to state in advance what they are *not* intending to do. The ritual is meant primarily for the eyes of specialist readers (and reviewers!). First, this book does not seek to provide an objective summary of the current state of scholarship on the issues it touches, much less a history of scholarship. Since every account is also an interpretation, such objectivity is neither possible nor desirable. In any case, my goal is to help the beginning student encounter Josephus. I shall certainly draw on those scholarly insights that seem helpful in this project, but I make no attempt at either systematic presentation or rebuttal of others' arguments. Interested readers will find that sort of thing in the journal articles and monographs mentioned.

Likewise, I have tried to use the footnote sparingly, so that the reader is not faced with reading two books at the same time—the one in the text and the one in the notes. My goal has been to reserve the notes for essential explanations of unusual terms and for crediting scholars with absolutely peculiar ideas. Otherwise, the scholarly works will be cited *en bloc* at the end of each chapter (under "For Further Reading"). Although a vast amount of modern scholarship on Josephus is in languages other than English, I have usually referred only to English titles. The few exceptions are some truly seminal works written in other languages, which informed readers should know about even if they cannot consult them at the moment.

In short, the book before you is not the "last word" on Josephus; it is intended to be more of a *first* word. It will be a success, in this writer's view, if it provides some shape and contour to what might otherwise seem bewildering terrain, and thereby stimulates the reader to explore more fully the writings of Josephus.

Chapter 1

The Use and Abuse of Josephus

In modern English, when we speak of "using" people, we often mean abusing them—exploiting them for some selfish benefit while disregarding their personal integrity. I believe this is precisely what has happened to the legacy of Flavius Josephus in the nineteen hundred years since he lived: he has been widely *used* but little understood and seldom appreciated as an intelligent author. And this exploitation has come at the hands of both religious and scholarly communities. The last four decades have brought some welcome changes, however, and a major goal of this book is to convey the significance of those changes to the NT reader. Let me explain.

Most of the thousands of books that were written in the ancient world did not survive into the Middle Ages, let alone into the modern world. In the absence of paper, printing presses, and photocopiers, it was not a foregone conclusion that any given book would live beyond its author's own generation. Publication of books was in general the prerogative of a small and literate elite. Books were often published ("made public") in oral form, by recitation before a group of interested friends. Book manuscripts, on papyrus or occasionally parchment[1] rolls, were relatively rare because they had to be copied individually by hand—usually the hand of a wealthy man's slave. Libraries and booksellers existed, but they, too, were few and far between. Therefore, only those books that enjoyed a lively readership or some sort of official

---

[1] Paper made from wood pulp was not introduced into the Western world until the late Middle Ages. Papyrus, its ancient precursor, was made from strips of the papyrus reed, laid side by side and pressed together in double thickness.

sponsorship could remain accessible. Only such committed readers would invest the necessary effort to have lengthy manuscripts copied and recopied.

Initially, Josephus owed his literary survival to sponsorship by the ruling family: the Flavian emperors Vespasian (69–79 C.E.), Titus (79–81), and Domitian (81–96). Although his *Jewish War* was probably not commissioned by them, as we shall see, after its completion Titus endorsed it and arranged for it to be made public (by copying? *Life* 360–362; *Ag. Ap.* 1.50). Since Josephus's favor appears to have continued throughout Domitian's reign (*Life* 428–429), we may suppose that his later works enjoyed the same friendly treatment. Eusebius knows a statue of Josephus in Rome (*Hist. eccl.* 3.9.2), which might confirm Josephus's continuing imperial support. In any case, this initial boost from the ruling family would have ensured that his works were copied in public *scriptoria*[2] and maintained in imperial libraries for some time, perhaps until the decline of the empire.

What, then, enabled Josephus's works to persevere beyond the collapse of the empire? The decisive factor was the Christian church's appropriation of the Jewish historian's writings. Two famous church leaders in particular, Origen (d. 254) and Eusebius (d. 340), cited Josephus extensively in their writings and thus popularized his works in Christian circles. By the time the structures of the Roman empire were seriously faltering in the late fourth century, Christianity had risen to become the predominant religion in the state, and Christians had long since adopted the Jewish historian Josephus. It was the church, with its own infrastructure, that would rise from the ashes of the empire to preserve the Greco-Roman heritage. So the church's attachment to Josephus assured him an ongoing role in Western tradition.

---

[2] A scriptorium was an ancient copying room for the mass production of books. A reader would stand in front of a group of scribes and read aloud, slowly, from the master text. The scribes would listen carefully and copy what they heard. Needless to say, this technique, which remained in effect until the invention of the printing press in 1454, could result in all sorts of errors, because of sound-alike words or sleepy scribes. That is why the first stage in the scholarly study of any ancient work—Josephus, the New Testament, or Plato—is the "reconstruction" of what the author really wrote, based on a careful comparison of the various scribal copies that have come down to us.

WHY JOSEPHUS'S WRITINGS WERE PRESERVED

But why were Christian authors so attached to Josephus? Already by the late second century C.E., some Christian writers had become interested in the famous Jewish author for several reasons. First, his writings provided extraordinary background information for the reader of early Christian writings, especially the gospels. Many of the characters and places mentioned incidentally in those works are described by Josephus at some length, for example: King Herod and his descendants (Archalaus, Antipas, Agrippa I, and Agrippa II); the high priests Annas and Caiaphas; the temple in Jerusalem, where Jesus was arrested; Jesus' home region of Galilee; the Samaritans and their relations with Judea; and the Pharisees and Sadducees, whom Jesus encountered. For second-century Christians far removed from tiny Judea and its politics, Josephus's writings had much the same fascination as they have held for every subsequent generation of Christian readers. They filled in a vast amount of history between the close of the Old Testament and the birth of Christianity.

Especially valuable for Christian readers were Josephus's discussions, brief though they were, of John the Baptist, Jesus' brother James, and Jesus' own career. As we shall see, it is almost certain that Josephus's paragraph on Jesus has been edited by Christian copyists, but the editing was done early on, by about 300 C.E. Later Christian readers assumed, therefore, that the glowing account of Jesus in our versions of Josephus had been written by the Jewish historian himself. Josephus's descriptions of the Baptist and of James's death seem to have remained intact. Naturally, these short passages were also highly valued. Since Christianity had not made a major impression on either the Jewish or larger Greco-Roman worlds in the first century, and since no other writers before 100 mention the Christians,[3] Josephus's few brief notices became important independent testimony to the historical foundations of the church.

It is one of history's paradoxes that Josephus enjoyed a surge of popularity at the time of the Christian "crusades" in the twelfth century, because of his detailed information about Palestinian geography.

---

[3]The first Roman authors to mention the Christians were Pliny the Younger, Tacitus, and Suetonius, all of whom wrote in the second decade of the second century.

Beginning in 1096, Christian soldiers marched from all over Europe to wrest Jerusalem from the Muslims, who had administered the city since the seventh century. (The crusaders were ultimately unsuccessful.) Many crusaders took copies of Josephus's writings with them as a kind of tour guide to the Holy Land. Yet for many of these Josephus-reading crusaders it created no dissonance for them to stop en route and butcher Josephus's coreligionists—the men, women, and children of Europe's Jewish communities—for being "Christ-killers." They were evidently not reading Josephus himself as much as the church's Josephus, a quasi-Christian. This contradiction between a high valuation of Josephus for his historical and geographical detail and an utter disregard for what he actually says in explanation and defense of Judaism is a consistent feature of the Christian misuse of Josephus.

A second reason for the early church's interest in Josephus was that he seemed to offer help with the Christians' pressing social-political predicament. That predicament stemmed from the novelty of Christianity. In a culture that respected what was old and established, Christianity seemed to be a new religion—a contradiction in terms for Roman thinking!—for it worshiped as Lord someone who had been quite recently executed by the Roman authorities, in the humiliating way reserved for trouble-making provincials (crucifixion), and in a backwater province no less. Strangest of all, this new faith had neither a national center nor an ethnic character, unlike the familiar religions of Greece, Egypt, Phrygia, Persia, and Syria. In what seemed to be a most antisocial stance, it even prohibited its members from participating in local festivals on the grounds that those celebrations inevitably involved sacrifice to the traditional gods. And because Christians met in private homes, at night, where men and women greeted each other with kisses and then partook of "body and blood," all sorts of lurid rumors circulated about their behavior. Just as medieval Christians would later accuse the Jews of sacrificing children at Passover, so the early Christians were charged with promiscuity and cannibalism.[4]

---

[4]The earliest surviving reference to Christianity by a Roman comes in Pliny's letter to Trajan concerning the Christians (10.96). Writing in about 111 C.E., Pliny assumes that Christians practice cannibalism and other crimes. A full description of the vices attributed to Christians is given by the character Caecilius in the *Octavius* of Minucius Felix, 8–10 (early third century). See the first three items under "For Further Reading."

Josephus was indirectly helpful to the young church on this score because he had faced something of the same animosity toward his nation and religion. Although Judaism did have a national and ethnic base, and though most Greco-Roman authors seem to have recognized the antiquity of the Jews, there was still a fair amount of misinformation about Jewish origins and customs. A large part of Josephus's concern had been to defend Judaism against charges that it was merely a corrupt derivation of Egyptian religion and that it practiced immorality, including human sacrifice. Especially in his *Jewish Antiquities* and *Against Apion,* he had sought to demonstrate his nation's long and noble history, to show that its "constitution" espoused the highest standards of morality, and to explain the Jewish belief in "one God only" (monotheism) in a way that would both deflect charges of antisocial propensities and appeal to philosophically minded readers.

All of this apologetic effort was extremely useful to Christian spokesmen. Many early Christians tended to see themselves as the "true Israel," as heirs to the biblical tradition. The church's apologists, therefore, were quick to see the value of Josephus's *Against Apion,* which sharply refuted Greco-Roman attacks on monotheism and abstinence and in turn criticized common morality while eloquently arguing the superiority of biblical ethics and "philosophy." This work became something of a model for Christian self-representation to the outside world, especially with Origen's *Against Celsus* (though the title itself was not patterned on Josephus; see chapter 3).[5]

Without question, however, the most compelling source of Josephus's appeal to early Christians was his detailed description of the Roman siege and destruction of Jerusalem in 70 C.E. Of all the Christian references to Josephus that have survived from the ancient world and Middle Ages, the passage most commonly cited from his works, next to his reference to Jesus, is one that describes a horrible act of cannibalism during the Roman siege.[6] A formerly wealthy woman named Mary, he claims, took refuge with her infant son in Jerusalem during its final days. Faced with starvation because of the scarcity of food within the besieged city, this aristocratic woman took her son and ate him (*War*

[5] Cf. Wataru Mizugaki, "Origen and Josephus," *JJC,* 334.

[6] In Heinz Schreckenberg, *Die Flavius-Josephus-Tradition in Antike und Mittelalter* (Leiden: Brill, 1972), 186–203, there is a list of known references to Josephus through the Middle Ages.

6.201–213). It may seem peculiar to modern Christians that this grisly episode should have so awakened the church's interest, but it did. Christian authors cited it even more often than Josephus's important references to John the Baptist or to Jesus' brother James. This little story was chosen for illustration in medieval editions of Josephus's works and was reenacted in Christian plays.[7] Largely because of this brief episode and a few others, Josephus's book on the unsuccessful Jewish revolt, the *Jewish War,* was much more interesting to early Christians than his *Jewish Antiquities,* which contains the references to Jesus, John the Baptist, and James. Some explanation is necessary.

It has been a standard feature of Christian preaching through the ages that the Roman destruction of Jerusalem in 70 was really God's decisive punishment of the Jewish people for their rejection of Jesus, who had died around the year 30. The earliest Christian sermon that we possess, outside of the NT, is largely a tirade against the Jews for their treatment of Jesus. Melito, bishop (apparently) of Sardis in the mid-100s, declares that the Jewish people and its Scripture became an "empty thing" with the arrival of Christianity and the gospel (*Pascha* 43); only those Jews who believe in Jesus have any ongoing religious validity. Melito accuses the Jews as a nation of having "murdered" Jesus and asserts that their current suffering (after 70 and a further failed revolt in 132–135) is a consequence: "You cast the Lord down, you were cast down to earth. And you, you lie dead, while he went up to the heights of heaven" (*Pascha* 99–100).

In the same vein, a work *Against the Jews* credited to bishop Hippolytus (d. 235 C.E.), declares:

> Why was the temple made desolate? Was it on account of the ancient fabrication of the calf? Or was it on account of the ancient idolatry of the people? Was it for the blood of the prophets? . . . By no means, for in all these transgressions, they always found pardon open to them. But it was because they killed the Son of their Benefactor, for He is coeternal with the Father. (*Against the Jews* 7)

Origen, who taught in the early 200s, pointedly restated the theme:

> I challenge anyone to prove my statement untrue if I say that the entire Jewish nation was destroyed less than one whole generation later on ac-

[7] Cf. Guy N. Deutsch, "The Illustration of Josephus' Manuscripts," *JJC,* 408–9.

> count of these sufferings which they inflicted on Jesus. For it was, I believe, forty-two years from the time when they crucified Jesus to the destruction of Jerusalem. . . . For they committed the most impious crime of all, when they conspired against the Savior of mankind, in the city where they performed the customary rites which were symbols of profound mysteries. Therefore, that city where Jesus suffered these indignities had to be utterly destroyed. The Jewish nation had to be overthrown, and God's invitation to blessedness transferred to others, I mean to the Christians, to whom came the teaching about the simple and pure worship of God. (*Cels.* 4.22)[8]

Eusebius, a Christian author of the early 300s, made the same sort of claims in his *Ecclesiastical History,* which became an extremely influential document for subsequent generations of Christians; his history fixed many aspects of the Christian understanding of history until the modern period. Speaking of the fall of Jerusalem in 70, he asserts that Christians fled the city so that "the judgement of God might at last overtake them for all their crimes against the Christ and his Apostles, and all that generation of the wicked be utterly blotted out from among men" (*Hist. eccl.* 3.5.3, [Lake, LCL]). Similar sentiments are found in such authorities as Minucius Felix, John Chrysostom, and Augustine, not to mention many lesser figures.

Obviously, Christian fascination with the destruction of the temple and the fate of the Jews was not a matter of merely antiquarian interest. As we have seen, Christians typically—though not universally: there were varieties of Jewish Christianity—saw the "death" of the Jews as the necessary condition for the birth of Christianity. These authors leave no doubt that the church took over the heritage of God's covenant from the Jews, who then more or less disappear from the scene. This theological interpretation of Jerusalem's fate explains why Christian authors tended to view the events of 70 as a total or near-total destruction of the Jews, whereas in fact most Jews lived outside of the Jerusalem region by the first century.[9] The large Jewish communities of Rome, Alexandria, Greece, Asia Minor, and Babylonia were not physically affected by the events of 70. In those places, and even in Palestine itself after the war, Judaism continued to thrive; hence its vigorous existence today. But the church fathers conjured up the destruction of the Jews for symbolic reasons: to support their contention that God's grace had passed from

---

[8] Origen, *Contra Celsum* (trans. and ed. H. Chadwick; Cambridge: Cambridge University Press, 1965), 198–99.

[9] Cf. Albert A. Bell Jr., "Josephus and Pseudo-Hegesippus," *JJC,* 354.

Judaism to the church. Far from being an incidental event in history, the fall of Jerusalem to the Romans provided a critical foundation for Christian self-understanding.

The common interpretation of Jerusalem's fall as God's punishment of the Jews continued to flourish throughout the Middle Ages. By then it had become part of popular Christian culture and not just the property of theologians. From the ninth to the fifteenth centuries, a recurring theme of plays and novels was "The Revenge of Our Lord," in which the Roman conquest was triumphantly reenacted. Several French communities produced such plays on a regular basis, to complement their "passion" plays, in which the Jews were charged with Jesus' death. By the time of Martin Luther (1483–1546), the great reformer who initiated what would become Protestant Christianity, the Christian interpretation of Jerusalem's capture had long been fixed. His tract on "The Jews and Their Lies" reflects the common view: the Romans were God's instruments, punishing the Jews for their "delusions regarding their false Christ and their persecution of the true Christ."[10] In that same tract, Luther advocates that Jews be deprived of normal civil rights, that their property and books be burned, and that they be herded together in forced labor camps.

This brief sketch of traditional Christian attitudes toward the Jews and the destruction of Jerusalem in 70, which could easily be expanded, helps to explain why Josephus's writings, and especially his *Jewish War,* were so popular among Christian theologians. Although the Jewish historian did not make any connection between Jesus' death and the fall of Jerusalem, his writings provided detailed corroboration of the horrors that befell Jerusalem in the war, which happened to follow Jesus' death by a few decades. The episode of Mary's cannibalism was so popular because for Christian apologists it showed the depths to which "the Jews" as a body had fallen as a consequence of their rejection of Jesus.

It was perhaps inevitable that, once Josephus's works were known, his *Jewish War* would be exploited for details of the Jewish catastrophe. Melito of Sardis probably already knew something of Josephus, for he includes a reference to the cannibalism episode to illustrate the de-

---

[10] *Luther's Works* (56 vols.; ed. Helmut T. Lehmann and Jaroslav Pelikan; St. Louis: Concordia, 1955–1986), 47:233; cited in Betsy Halpern Amaru, "Martin Luther and Flavius Josephus," *JJC,* 418. Compare also Luther's "Lectures on the Psalms," *Luther's Works,* 13:258.

pravity of non-Christian humanity (*Pascha* 52). But the pivotal figures in the Christian adoption of Josephus were Origen and Eusebius. Both of these men had traveled extensively throughout the Roman world; both had visited the city of Rome itself, where Josephus's works were maintained in the libraries; and both lived for some time in Caesarea, the coastal city of Josephus's native Palestine. Because of these unusual opportunities, both men were able to read Josephus first hand, so they both saw the potential in his works for Christian adaptation.

In addition to borrowing from Josephus for *Against Celsus,* Origen cites him in his Bible studies on Lamentations, in which he discusses among other things the fall of the Jewish temple. In that discussion, he claims that Josephus had researched the cause of the debacle and attributed it to the Jews' execution of Jesus' brother James around the year 62 C.E. This is a considerable distortion. In reality, Josephus's writings are peppered with various reasons for the city's fall; any conspicuous violation of the Mosaic law or Jewish custom is a candidate. He does express horror at the unlawful treatment of James (*Ant.* 20.200–201) but does not isolate this episode as a reason for the destruction. Rather, it is one of a number of infractions, including the bestowal of unprecedented privileges on the Levites (!), that he lists as causes of the later punishment. So Origen significantly misleads his readers in claiming that Josephus attributed the fall of Jerusalem to James's mistreatment.

In any case, Origen himself pointedly disagrees with Josephus. He criticizes the Jewish historian for not realizing that it was the Jewish role in Jesus' death, not that of James, that brought about the "annihilation" (as he says) of the Jewish people: "If, therefore, he says that the destruction of Jerusalem happened because of James, would it not be more reasonable to say that this happened on account of Jesus the Christ?" (*Cels.* 1.47). Evidently Origen distorted Josephus's account because Josephus's real explanation of Jerusalem's fall would not have served his purpose (see below). By pretending that Josephus had isolated James's execution as the cause, he pulls the Jewish historian into the Christian orbit: at least, Josephus is "not far from the truth" (*Cels.* 1.47).

It is in support of his claim that Jerusalem fell in retribution for Jesus' death that Origen cites Josephus's account of the horrors suffered by the Jews during the war. He dwells in particular on the cannibalism episode, which he sees as fulfilling Lam 4:10 (*Fr. Lam.* 105). But he also mentions Josephus's claim that, some months before the destruction, strange voices were heard in the temple saying, "We are departing from here" (Josephus, *War* 6.299–300). Origen interprets these voices as those of the angels who supervised the temple activities. He sees their departure as the definitive moment of collapse for the whole temple regime and for Judaism itself (*Fr. Lam.* 109).

In a similar way Eusebius, who knew Origen's writings well, used Josephus to bolster his theological interpretation of the fall of Jerusalem. His thesis is that the Jews compounded their guilt after Jesus' execution by persecuting Jesus' followers: Stephen, James the son of Zebedee, and others (*Hist. eccl.* 3.5.2). As a result, he asserts, they suffered increasing calamities. His proof of this claim? "Those who wish can retrace accurately from the history written by Josephus how many evils at that time overwhelmed the whole nation, . . . how many thousands of youths, women, and children perished by the sword" (*Hist. eccl.* 3.5.4).

Significantly, Eusebius decides to focus his account on the starvation faced by the Jews who were trapped in Jerusalem during the siege, "in order that those who study this work may have some partial knowledge of how the punishments of God followed close after them for their crime against the Christ of God" (3.5.7). To substantiate this very Christian claim, he quotes verbatim several pages from Josephus concerning the misery faced by the Jews during the Roman siege. His concentration on the starvation of the Jews allows him to bring up Josephus's heart-rending story of Mary's cannibalism (3.6.20–28). Immediately after this climactic episode (for Eusebius), he concludes: "Such was the reward of the iniquity of the Jews for their crime against the Christ of God" (3.7.1). Here Josephus is thoroughly domesticated to Christian use.

But if the destruction of Jerusalem was punishment for the Jews' treatment of Jesus, why did it not occur until forty years after the crucifixion? Aware of the problem, Eusebius responds that God suspended his justice for forty years both because of the presence of the apostles, who protected the city by their presence, and in order to provide the Jews with a suitable opportunity for repentance (3.7.8–9). God even sent warnings of the coming catastrophe if the Jews did not repent. These warnings are the omens mentioned by Josephus (*War* 6.288–309), and Eusebius confidently refers the reader to the Jewish author as his external witness. Of course, Josephus does not connect the omens with Jesus of Nazareth, who does not even appear in the *Jewish War.*

Eusebius takes over Origen's distortion about Josephus's attributing the destruction of Jerusalem to the death of James, but he is bold enough to manufacture the missing passage. We have seen that Josephus did not link the fall of Jerusalem specifically to James's death, although Origen implied that he did. Eusebius, however, actually quotes Josephus: "Of course Josephus did not shrink from giving written testimony to this, as follows: 'These things happened to the Jews to avenge James the Just, who was the brother of Jesus' " (*Hist. eccl.* 2.23.20). Here we witness an astonishing phase in the Christian adoption (and corruption) of Josephus.

Eusebius's other noteworthy distortion of Josephus arises from his desire to parallel Jesus' death at Passover with the destruction of Jerusalem at the same time:

> It was indeed right that on the same day on which they had perpetrated the passion of the Saviour and Benefactor of all men and the Christ of God they should be, as it were, shut up in prison and receive the destruction which pursued them from the sentence of God. (3.5.6)

The problem with this neat scheme is that Josephus carefully dates the various stages of the war and makes it plain that the temple finally fell in late September (by our calendar, *War* 6.392, 407), whereas the Passover feast was in the spring. Josephus does note that those who had come for Passover in the spring were trapped in the city when the Jerusalem phase of the war came to a head, and some had to stay for the duration. But several months elapsed between Passover and the final battles, so Eusebius appears to have collapsed the dates in order to strengthen the symbolic connection that he wants to make between Jesus' death and the destruction of the temple. In his hands, we see Josephus already well on the way to becoming a kind of quasi-Christian because of the support he seemed to offer for Christian claims.

The need to Christianize Josephus becomes most obvious in a free Latin paraphrase of his works written around 370 C.E.[11] An unknown author, erroneously thought by some medieval commentators to be the second-century Hegesippus, created a work in five volumes on the destruction of Jerusalem *(De excidio Hierosolymitano)* out of relevant material in Josephus's *War* and *Antiquities.* But his motive for doing so was that Josephus's own accounts were not Christian enough. He would

[11] See especially Bell, "Josephus and Pseudo-Hegesippus," 354.

rewrite Josephus to bring him into closer accord with the church's position. In his preface, he acknowledges Josephus's usefulness but claims that he was too Jewish in his outlook. He was:

> an outstanding historian, if only he had paid as much attention to religion and truth as he did to the investigation of facts and moderation in writing. For he shows himself to be sympathetic to Jewish faithlessness even in the very things he sets forth about their punishment. (1.1)[12]

In other words, although Josephus wrote the *Jewish War* to explain the causes of the temple's destruction, he failed to see the true (i.e., Christian) interpretation. Pseudo-Hegesippus will not make such a mistake:

> And so that no one will think I have undertaken a useless task, or one of no value to the Christian faith, let us consider the whole race of the Hebrews embodied in its leaders. . . . (1.3)

The Jewish race, he wants to demonstrate, is "depraved" and has lost its place in the story of salvation. He intends to use Josephus's account to show what Josephus had not shown, namely, that in the fall of Jerusalem the Jews "paid the penalty for their crimes, because after they had crucified Jesus they persecuted his disciples" (2.12).

A telling example of the way in which Pseudo-Hegesippus's Christian outlook determines his subsequent narrative is his rendering of a scene in which Cestius Gallus, the Roman governor of Syria, withdraws his troops from the attack on Jerusalem in the autumn of 66, after the very first Roman attempt to quell the revolt.[13] Josephus had expressed wonder at this withdrawal because (a) if Cestius had pressed the attack, the whole war could have been won then and there, and (b) the Jewish rebels' victory over the withdrawing Roman troops (whom they successfully ambushed and massacred) gave them a false sense of strength, which emboldened them to prosecute the war more vigorously. As to why Cestius decided to retreat when he was not in peril, Josephus hints that the Syrian commander had been bribed by the governor of Judea, who wanted to see the Jews utterly annihilated (*War* 2.531). His more religious explanation is that "God, I suppose, because of those miscreants [i.e., the relatively few rebels, whom Josephus despises], had already turned away even from His sanctuary and ordained that that day should not see the end of the war" (*War* 2.539).

---

[12] From Bell, "Josephus and Pseudo-Hegesippus," 352–53.

[13] I owe this example to Bell, "Josephus and Pseudo-Hegesippus," 354.

Pseudo-Hegesippus, however, transforms this account by introducing a Christian theological explanation for Cestius's withdrawal:

> The will of God delayed the imminent end of the war until the ruin could involve much—almost all—of the Jewish race. God expected, I think, that the enormity of their [the Jews'] crimes would increase until, by the heaping up of impropriety, it would equal the measure of his supreme punishment. (2.15)

We find here once again the erroneous claim that virtually all of the "Jewish race" was in Jerusalem during the siege. This assertion can be explained only on theological grounds, for it permits the Christian writer to dispense with Judaism as an ongoing reality. God wiped out the heart and soul of Judaism in 70; the few who remain witness to the truth of Christianity by their homeless suffering. Whereas Josephus himself had spoken from within Judaism, as its passionate spokesman and defender *after 70,* Pseudo-Hegesippus mined Josephus's account in order to depict the Jews as a destroyed nation.

To summarize thus far: Josephus's writings were preserved from antiquity by the Christian church for several reasons. They provided a lot of useful background information, a paraphrase of the Old Testament, a valuable model for apologetics, and even some brief references to key figures in the birth of Christianity. Their greatest attraction, however, seems to have been their detailed descriptions of the atrocities that accompanied the fall of Jerusalem to Rome. Josephus's account of the war could be used as apparent proof of the Christian belief that the Jews had become God's enemies *by rejecting Jesus* and the claims of his followers. Eusebius was critical to the preservation of Josephus for these purposes, for he made the Jewish historian the key external witness for his theological interpretation of history. Other accounts of Judean history and geography were in circulation, such as those by Nicolaus of Damascus and Justus of Tiberias, and some of these survived as late as the ninth century. But when decisions were made then, in part by the patriarch Photius, as to which ancient texts should continue to be copied, it was apparently Eusebius's glowing endorsement of Josephus that secured him a privileged position.[14] His competitors, who lacked the endorsement of such an imposing figure, are known today only in fragments quoted by others (such as Josephus!).

---

[14] Cf. Stephen Bowman, "Josephus in Byzantium," *JJC*, 365–68.

PROBLEMS WITH THE TRADITIONAL USE OF JOSEPHUS

I hope that the foregoing survey of how and why Josephus's works were preserved will explain what I mean when I say that the ancient author has usually been abused. He wrote, as we shall see, in order to explain Judaism to outsiders and to demonstrate its virtues in a world that was often hostile. But Christian authors took over his most self-critical work, in which he castigates a small number of Jews for their failure to live up to the standards of Judaism, and turned that work against the Jewish people as a whole, thus exactly reversing Josephus's intention. His writings were treated not as the production of an intelligent human mind but as a mine of data that could be excerpted willy-nilly to produce a new document such as that of Pseudo-Hegesippus. In Josephus we have a vigorous defender and explainer of post-70 Judaism, and yet his Christian adapters used him to argue that Judaism had been overthrown in 70. His own analysis was barely acknowledged and, where it was, it did not move users. By making him their ally, they grotesquely distorted the very source that they prized for its witness to the truth of Christianity.

To see more clearly the incompatibility of Josephus's account with these Christian purposes, before we examine Josephus in greater detail, we must present each side in sharp relief. In effect, the Christian claim was that the Jews suffered for being so stubbornly Jewish, that is, for clinging to their ancestral traditions and not responding to the gospel concerning Jesus. Josephus argued what amounts to the opposite position: that Jerusalem fell because some Jews were not faithful enough to Jewish tradition, but rebelled against the national and external authorities ordained by God. Those few untypical and reckless men filled the sacred temple with murder and pollution. Whereas the zealous priest Josephus had been concerned with the scrupulous observance of the laws, his Christian users charged the Jews with failing to abandon those laws in favor of Christian faith.

Although he would not call himself a prophet, Josephus presents himself and his perspective in continuity with the long line of Israel's prophets—some of whom, such as Ezekiel and Jeremiah, were also priests. They, too, had threatened Israel with punishment, back in biblical times, for its laxity in keeping the divine teaching or "torah."[15] Notice how the Old Testament accounts for the fall of the first temple, which was built by Solomon. Jeremiah repeatedly warned of disaster because the people had disobeyed God's commands. Their crimes included worship of other nations' gods (Jer 17:1–4) but also, and equally grievous, carrying water jugs and lighting fires for warmth and cooking on Saturday, the Sabbath (17:21–27). In short, the people had not scrupulously maintained the terms of the covenant; these terms occupy the greater part of Exodus through Deuteronomy and include much more than the Ten Commandments. When the disaster finally came in 586 B.C.E., and Solomon's temple was destroyed, the prophets concluded that it was God's means of punishing the people for having departed from the worship of the one God of Israel. Ezekiel, Nehemiah, and Daniel all confess that ever since the divine teachings were given to Moses, the people have lapsed from their observance, and that is why Jerusalem and its great temple have been destroyed (Ezek 20:4–44; Neh 9:12–37; Dan 9:4–14). When the Jews were permitted by the Persians to return to their land and rebuild their temple in the late sixth century B.C.E., they naturally took this opportunity as a second chance from God. So they begged forgiveness for past errors and resolved scrupulously to adhere to the divine teachings. They took "an oath with sanctions to follow the Teaching of God, given through Moses the servant of God, and to observe carefully all of the commandments of the LORD our Lord, His rules and laws" (Neh 10:30, NJPS).

In explaining the fall of the second temple, Josephus has largely taken over the model provided by the Old Testament prophets. He wants to portray himself as a latter-day Jeremiah, lamenting the fall of the city and the sins that caused it. Needless to say, the prophets had not mentioned faith in Jesus as a criterion of righteousness, and neither does Josephus. It is the Christian interpretation that introduces a new claim.

This variance in explaining the fall of Jerusalem shows how difficult it is to deduce cause from sequence—to say: "Y came after X;

---

[15] The Hebrew word *torah* means "instruction" or "teaching." It is the expression used in the OT for the terms of the covenant received from God by (especially) Moses. Although often rendered "law," in English translation, the word conveys a much more comprehensive scope and positive nuance than we tend to associate with "laws." See, for example, the psalmist's exultation over the "laws" in Ps 119, which may seem strange to English readers.

therefore, Y was caused by X." There is simply no way to prove such claims to be either true or false. They will be convincing only to those who already believe the proposition being advanced. That is because any number of Xs (here, pre-70 events) might be cited as potential causes. For example, some Romans said that the temple fell because of the wrath of *their* gods, who were angry at the Jews because of their rebellion against Rome. The second-century philosopher Celsus asserted that the destruction of Jerusalem decisively proved the weakness of the God worshiped by both Jews and Christians; the Roman victory, by implication, proved that the traditional Greco-Roman gods were more powerful and worthy of worship. Note that Celsus also cited the miserable plight of the Christians, who were at that time on the extreme margins of lawful society, as evidence of futility of Christian worship—since their God was unable to create a better life for them.[16] So it was somewhat inconsistent for Christian authors, when the church had finally won imperial recognition and security in the fourth century, to cite the destruction of Jerusalem and the plight of the Jews, which had been quite deliberately worsened by the anti-Jewish legislation of Christian rulers, as proof of Jewish guilt and Christian truth.

Before leaving this matter of the early church's misuse of Josephus to bolster its interpretation of the fall of Jerusalem, we need to admit that such an interpretation also suffers from serious moral objections. It does so because it depends on a doctrine of collective responsibility, where the collective in question (Jewish identity) is involuntary and inalienable. Thus all Jews of all times and places share the guilt of a very few, who acted two thousand years ago.

First, the criterion is applied to only one party involved in Jesus' execution, some Jewish leaders. If a Jewish court was involved in Jesus' crucifixion, it may have had somewhere between twenty-three and seventy-one members—a group small enough, apparently, to fit in the high priest's home (Mark 14:53; 15:1).[17] But the Roman governor Pilate and his entourage, according to the gospels, also had a crucial share in Jesus' death. Crucifixion was a Roman (not Jewish) punishment, and

---

[16] For obvious reasons, Celsus's writings were not thought worthy of preservation during the Christian Middle Ages. They are known to us only in fragments quoted by Origen in his tract *Against Celsus.* These are conveniently accessible in Molly Whittaker, *Jews and Christians,* 185.

[17] See the Mishnah (a compendium of Jewish law compiled in about 200 C.E.), *Sanhedrin* 1:4–5.

Pilate was the one who passed and executed the sentence. His soldiers beat and mocked Jesus, and it was they who hung him on the cross. How then is it that no one has ever accused *any* Italians, of *any* generation, of being "Christ-killers," while the charge has been *relentlessly* leveled against the Jews? Where are the church fathers' sermons denouncing Romans? On the contrary, in some Christian traditions Pilate became "in his secret heart already a Christian" and he was credited with addressing a glowing account of Jesus to the emperor.[18]

Second, the whole concept of collective responsibility is repugnant because it involves indiscriminate revenge: anybody with certain religious or genetic characteristics becomes morally responsible for the actions of any others with those features. Especially in view of the average life expectancy in the first century, which was much shorter than ours,[19] it is rather unlikely that any of the Jewish judges who may have been involved in Jesus' trial were still active when the temple was destroyed in 70. If hundreds of thousands of men, women, and children died in that catastrophe to punish their fathers and grandfathers, how is that just? Although no Jewish magistrate from Jesus' day was alive when Melito of Sardis preached his *Passover Sermon* in the 160s, he addressed Israel in the second person as if it had a single corporate personality through the centuries: "You, on the contrary, voted against your Lord. The nations worshiped him. The uncircumcised [i.e., non-Jews] marveled at him. . . . Even Pilate washed his hands in this case. This one you did to death on the great feast" (*Pascha* 92). Evidently Melito and the later Fathers had forgotten the words of Ezekiel seven centuries earlier:

> The person that sins, he alone shall die. A child shall not share the burden of a parent's guilt, nor shall a parent share the burden of a child's guilt; the righteousness of the righteous shall be accounted to him alone, and the wickedness of the wicked shall be accounted to him alone. (Ezek 18:20, cf. 2–4, NJPS)

The tenacity of the claim that Jerusalem fell as punishment for "the Jews'" treatment of Jesus, the incredible energy devoted to this matter

---

[18] See Tertullian, *Apology* 21.24 (and 5.2); compare the second-century *Gospel of Peter* 1–24, 46; Eusebius, *Hist. eccl.* 2.2.1; and the apocryphal *Acts of Pilate.*

[19] See Tim G. Parkin, *Demography and Roman Society* (Baltimore, Md.: Johns Hopkins University Press, 1992); Bruce W. Frier, "Roman Demography," in *Life, Death, and Entertainment in the Roman Empire* (ed. D. S. Potter and D. J. Mattingly; Ann Arbor, Mich.: University of Michigan, 1999).

over the centuries, and the Christian lack of interest in the Roman involvement in Jesus' death call for an explanation. But that would take us too far afield. It is enough for now if we recognize the problem and resolve not to engage in the same sort of polemics.

So far we have seen that the customary use of Josephus by Christian authors has been doubly abusive: first, his material has been wrenched out of its narrative setting, so that his own story has been lost. Second, that material has been used to tell another story—one that he did not espouse. My contention is that readers of the NT need not resort to these traditional devices, which are really cheap tricks, in order to make Josephus's writings useful. They do not need to rewrite him or baptize him as a Christian. It is a sign of maturity when we stop trying to make everyone into clones of ourselves (whether they be our students, children, or employees) and begin to appreciate them for who they are. We are invariably rewarded when we make the effort to encounter another person in his or her integrity. We need to do the same sort of thing with Josephus. If we will read him as a genuine, first-century Jewish author, with his own concerns and interests, our reading of the NT will be greatly enriched.

JOSEPHUS AND JUDAISM

One would think that, if the Christian transmitters of Josephus had completely ignored his Jewish identity, Jewish readers at least would have noticed and appreciated it. But strangely enough, this did not happen much. Jewish responses to Josephus have always been ambivalent at best because of his personal history.

The key point is that Josephus seems to have abandoned his own people in their fateful hour, in the conflict that would spell the end of the temple and, ultimately (in 135 C.E.), the disbarment of Jews from Jerusalem.[20] Sent to Galilee as a regional commander in the revolt, he capitulated to the Romans when they besieged his base at Jotapata. He not only surrendered, but also gave speeches urging his compatriots in

[20] A second major Jewish revolt against Rome, from 132 to 135, resulted in the total destruction of Jerusalem and its rebuilding as a Roman colony called Aelia Capitolina, with a temple to the god Jupiter on the site of the demolished Jewish temple. The Roman emperor Hadrian forbade Jews to enter this city on pain of death.

Jerusalem to do likewise (*War* 5.114, 360–362). After the war, he was granted Roman citizenship and a generous pension by the emperor, and it was in these circumstances that he wrote his account of the revolt, which includes lavish praise of the imperial family and relentless castigation of the Jewish rebel leaders (though not of the Jews as a whole). Consequently, Jews have traditionally viewed him as a traitor to the Jewish people.

In the coming chapters we shall consider both Josephus's outlook with respect to world affairs and the difficulties involved in reconstructing his personal life from the texts he has given us. It certainly appears from his writings, however, that during the war he was constantly accused by some of his fellow fighters (e.g., *Life* 261, 284, 302), that he routinely deceived other Jews about his intentions (e.g., *War* 3.193–201; *Life* 75, 79, 128–131, 141–142), and that he knew of a principle requiring generals to die fighting (*War* 3.400; *Life* 137)—and later felt insecure about his behavior in this regard.

In any event, from the moment of his surrender until his death, Josephus faced relentless hatred from his compatriots. Some tried to have him executed, while others wrote accounts of his wartime behavior that challenged his own self-vindicating portrayal (*War* 3.438; 7.447–450; *Life* 425; cf. 40, 336). Understandably, the cozier he became with the Romans—the military conquerors of the Jews—the more detestable he became to his people. And when this Jewish historian was posthumously adopted by the church, which claimed that he had even declared Jesus to be the Messiah—the same church that immediately passed laws restricting Jewish civil rights, relegating Jews to second-class status as "Christ-killers," and using Josephus to support their claims—his fate was sealed. His name does not appear in either version of the voluminous Talmud, which was finally edited in the fifth and sixth centuries, or in any other early Jewish writing.[21]

Josephus's perceived cowardice would also prevent him from achieving respect in modern Jewish circles, particularly in the Zionist

---

[21] A possible exception is a reference in a (fifth-century?) text called Derek Ereṣ Rabba, to a wealthy Jew in Rome, at the end of the first century, identified as "FLSOFOS," which some have taken as a corruption of "Flavius Josephus." See Heinz Schreckenberg, *Rezeptionsgeschichtliche und Textkritische Untersuchungen zu Flavius Josephus* (Leiden: Brill, 1977), 49. Other Greek-speaking Jewish authors, like Philo, likewise receive no mention in rabbinic literature; other factors, therefore, may have contributed to the neglect of Josephus.

movement, which took root in the late nineteenth century and culminated in the creation of Israel in 1948. A nation built on the determination to survive against all odds had no place for someone who could so easily surrender, accept luxurious privileges from enemies, and then serve those enemies' propaganda aims. Thus Josephus has appeared to many modern Jews, and not a few Gentiles, as the classic self-serving traitor.[22]

On the other hand, the sheer wealth of historical information offered by Josephus has necessarily commanded at least grudging respect among all those who are interested in either biblical interpretation or postbiblical history. Already in the middle of the tenth century, when Jewish scholarship was flourishing in southern Italy, someone from the region was motivated to translate Josephus's writings into Hebrew. This version of his *War* and *Antiquities* 1–16 proved extremely popular and was itself recopied and translated into several languages. Known as "Josippon," from a corruption of Josephus's name, this text was used extensively by medieval Jewish commentators to illuminate their interpretation of the Bible and Talmud.[23]

In modern times too, especially since the capture of East Jerusalem in 1967 and the resultant flourishing of Israeli archaeology, Josephus has become an indispensable guide to first-century Palestinian geography. He has proven particularly helpful on the matter of King Herod's building projects, which once covered the land and now provide a major focus of modern archaeology. Since this archaeological effort is in part a function of the nationalist agenda (to demonstrate Jewish roots in the land), Josephus has paradoxically become an ally of the Zionist cause. While his personal history is deplored in some Jewish literature, his writings are still valued as unparalleled sources of history.[24]

Josephus's perceived betrayal of the Jewish people has loomed so large that his obvious devotion to Judaism and enthusiastic defense of Jews against widespread slanders in the Greco-Roman world have received relatively little attention in Jewish scholarship until recently.

---

[22] Cf. Norman Bentwich, *Josephus* (Philadelphia: Jewish Publication Society, 1914); A. Schalit, "Josephus Flavius," *EncJud* 10 (1971): 251–65; and, in general, Louis H. Feldman, *JMS*, 75–98.

[23] See David Flusser, "*Josippon,* a Medieval Hebrew Version of Josephus," *JJC*, 386–97.

[24] For a concise statement of Josephus's importance to the archaeologist, see Louis Feldman, *JBH*, 434–40.

Whereas traditional Christian readers had disregarded his Jewish perspective because they found it distasteful, Jewish readers often dismissed it as an artificial ploy meant to deflect the hostility that he faced from his own people. In both cases, his fundamental viewpoint was lost to the world.

SCHOLARS' MISTREATMENT OF JOSEPHUS

Before we discuss Josephus's writings and outlook, fairness demands a brief consideration of the *scholarly* mistreatment of Josephus, for until recently the academic community has also tended to wrench Josephus's statements out of their original context and exploit them for its own purposes.

The intensive historical study of Josephus, as of the NT and early Judaism, took flight in the middle of the nineteenth century. These branches of study were based in Germany, where there was a remarkable awakening of scholarly interest in the ancient world. Professors began to produce massive reference works in their efforts to recover as much information as possible about ancient life and language. Numerous manuals, encyclopedias, lexicons, atlases, and dictionaries appeared, and serious archaeological work was begun in the Mediterranean countries. Although scholars of preceding centuries had already tried to reconstruct the original Greek texts of the NT and Josephus, by comparing the many manuscripts that had survived, scholars of the nineteenth century pursued more disciplined projects along these lines, in the case of the NT with the aid of newly discovered manuscripts.

It was in this atmosphere that Emil Schürer wrote his magisterial text, *Lehrbuch der neutestamentlichen Zeitgeschichte* (1874), which later became *Geschichte des jüdischen Volkes im Zeitalter Jesu Christi* (1886–1890). This manual was so influential that it has been updated, translated into English, and reissued in the 1970s. For Schürer, naturally, Josephus's writings were a major source of information. Yet his method of treating the ancient author was sometimes alarming. He regularly cited Josephus's isolated statements as if they were "facts" that could be combined with other facts (i.e., statements of other writers or archaeological evidence) to produce a whole picture. For example, Schürer opens his discussion of the Pharisees with a collection of passages from Josephus, combined with fragments from other sources, and then proceeds to weld these together into a coherent whole. He fails to take into account, however, that Josephus's remarks can be understood only in the context that Josephus gave them, for words have meaning only in context. Josephus wrote lengthy stories, not digests. If we want to know what he meant to say about the Pharisees, we must read his remarks about them as part of his story, paying careful attention to his use of language. We cannot simply pull them out and combine them with statements from other people who had entirely different stories to tell and who used language in different ways.

Schürer's method is often called the "scissors-and-paste" style of history. Although everyone today realizes that it doesn't work, in principle, we all find ourselves drifting into it from time to time. We still see authors, some of whom would insist on interpreting passages from, say, the gospels, within their narrative contexts, ripping chunks out of Josephus and citing them as "raw data" or facts—as if they were the product of a robot and not a real human mind with a story to tell.

Examples abound. First, one commentator argues that, since Josephus mentions "fate" in his discussions of the Jewish groups, and since fate was generally understood in antiquity in astrological terms, as an inescapable and oppressive power, Josephus must be implying that Judaism offers deliverance from fate (as some other religions claimed for themselves).[25] A careful reading of Josephus, however, would show that he speaks positively of fate and considers the recognition of it a religious duty.

Second, if they do not pluck out bits of Josephus and assign the bits an arbitrary meaning in this way, scholars often treat Josephus's narrative as if it were a kind of continuous or at least proportional video coverage of ancient Judea. For example, some recent manuals of Judean history propose that the Pharisees must have faded *from public view* from about 6 to 66 C.E. because Josephus does not describe their activities during this period.[26] Typically, these scholars say that the Pharisees do not "appear" or "are not mentioned" for these six decades, as if there was a vast array of historical literature from which the Pharisees disappear.[27] In fact,

---

[25] So Luther H. Martin, "Josephus' Use of *Heimarmenē* in the *Jewish Antiquities* XIII, 171–73," *Numen* 28 (1981): 127–37.

[26] Lester L. Grabbe, *Judaism from Cyrus to Hadrian* (2 vols.; Minneapolis: Augsburg Fortress, 1992), 2.470; E. P. Sanders, *Judaism: Practice and Belief, 63 B.C.E.–66 C.E.* (Philadelphia: Trinity, 1992), 380–85.

[27] Grabbe, ibid., 2.476; Sanders, ibid., 386

however, they are chiefly referring to Josephus, who provides the only connected narrative. Leaving aside the question whether the Pharisees truly *are* absent from Josephus's narrative at this time, we face the problem that Josephus does not pretend to give a proportional narrative. This is clear enough from the fact that almost four volumes of the *Antiquities* (14–17) are devoted to the reign of Herod (40–4 B.C.E.). But in both the *War* (2.117–183, minus the major excursus 2.119–166) and the *Antiquities*, Josephus gives only a few paragraphs to the years 6 to 66 in Judea, although the latter has considerable material on Roman and Mesopotamian affairs at this time (*Ant.* 18–20). So there is little occasion for him to mention the Pharisees' activities here. Still, he does insist that the Pharisees remained prominent in society (*Ant.* 18.15, 17). Making deductions from his stylized, episodic narrative as if it presented Judean public annals cannot work.

In effect, then, modern scholars have perpetuated, though in different ways and for their own reasons, the traditional failure to come to terms with Josephus's narrative.

Another approach to Josephus that has effectively denied his personality is "source-critical" analysis. This method was extremely popular from about 1880 to 1920, when much of the fundamental work on Josephus was accomplished. Now source analysis is an essential part of historical study because it asks the important question: Where did this author acquire his or her information? Since most of the events Josephus discusses occurred either before his lifetime or outside of his personal experience, it is crucial for us to know where he obtained his information if we are to determine its value. But because of the widespread presence of plagiarism in ancient literature, older source critics tended to assume that Josephus took over his sources bodily, simply reproducing them with very light editorial seams.[28] For example, scholars claimed that Josephus took his paraphrase of the Old Testament (in *Ant.* 1–11) from someone else, ready-made, so they had no interest in trying to see what that paraphrase revealed about Josephus's own thought. If he wrote differently about such figures as Herod the Great in *War* and *Antiquities*, that must have been because he used different

[28] See H. Bloch, *Die Quellen des Flavius Josephus in seiner Archäologie* (Wiesbaden: Sändig, 1868); J. von Destinon, *Die Quellen des Flavius Josephus I: Die Quellen der Archäologie Buch XII–XVII = Jüd. Krieg Buch I.* (Kiel: Lipsius & Tischer, 1882); Gustav Hölscher, "Josephus," *PW* 18 (1916): 1934–2000.

sources in the two works, not because he changed his mind or had different purposes in writing the two books. Or if he sometimes expressed great admiration for the Hasmoneans, he must have found those passages in a "pro-Hasmonean source," even though he claimed in his autobiography to be a proud descendant of the Hasmoneans (*Ant.* 16:187; *Life* 2). This kind of criticism was taken to such an extreme that even Josephus's reports about things that he certainly knew firsthand—e.g., his discussions of groups like the Sadducees, Essenes, and Pharisees—were attributed to his sources.

Once again, most scholars today would repudiate such a thoroughgoing source criticism, one that ignored Josephus's own intelligence as an author; however, those early treatments still wield a considerable influence, and we occasionally find modern scholars falling into the same way of thinking. A recent book, for example, examines Josephus's descriptions of the Essenes, which have taken on great significance in light of the Dead Sea Scrolls, on the *assumption* that they are borrowed from other writers. Although he writes an entire book on Josephus's Essene passages, Roland Bergmeier does not even ask how their language, themes, and contexts contribute to Josephus's narratives. Imagining that one can identify different sources within the Essene passages on the basis of word usage—but without, by and large, consulting Josephus's own habits—he wishes only to identify those sources.

Since the late 1960s, a new and much more realistic approach to Josephus has taken root, and it seems to be reinforced with almost every new study that appears. What unifies this newer scholarship is the realization that Josephus was the author of his own literary productions. He wrote with purpose and accommodated his material (extensively borrowed from other sources, to be sure) to his own agenda. He used words, as we all do, in a distinctive way. A team of scholars led by K. H. Rengstorf has now produced *A Complete Concordance to Flavius Josephus,* which enables us to trace his characteristic vocabulary. His writings can also be searched electronically, by computer. It turns out that he had favorite phrases and themes. Recent studies of his paraphrase of the OT have shown that he carefully worked over the biblical story to serve his larger purposes. From his earliest to his latest writings, his "worldview" remains remarkably coherent.

This is not to deny that Josephus was sloppy at times, that he sometimes went off on tangents, that he contradicted himself in some places and dissembled in others. All of these things are to be expected with an ancient author of such extensive writings, who had such a controversial past. In my view, they make Josephus particularly intriguing. But none of this excuses us from taking him seriously as a person from another time and place who had something to say about his world.

CONCLUSION

We find ourselves in the peculiar position of being grateful that Josephus's works survived, while at the same time regretting the primary reason for their survival—as a rod with which to beat the Jews. Josephus himself was a Jew, an extremely energetic spokesman for his nation after 70. Paradoxically, although he was probably the most influential nonbiblical Jewish writer of all time, his intended meaning was not influential at all, with either Jews or Christians. On the contrary, it was completely inverted. Even when the religious maltreatment of Josephus subsided, the poor fellow was largely abused by the academic world, which similarly tended to fragment his writings into little bits of data. As a result it has taken us the better part of two thousand years to begin reading what Josephus actually wrote.

The new willingness to listen to Josephus's own voice has been greatly facilitated by a new academic atmosphere. Since World War II, Jewish, Christian, and other scholars have begun an unprecedented adventure in cooperative scholarship within university departments of religious studies. This cooperation has meant that we can no longer use as proof things that would convince only our own constituencies, but must discuss history in a public way—with proof that is universally compelling. If we cannot appeal to our own traditions for our interpretations of Josephus, we must finally read what he had to say for himself. When we do that, remarkably enough, we can agree to a large extent about what he was up to.

I hope that the following chapters will begin to show how truly useful Josephus can be for readers of the NT, when we try to engage him as an authentic person with something to say. The next chapter will introduce his life, writings, and world of thought. After that we shall explore particular issues in Josephus's works that are of interest to NT readers, attempting in each case to relate the passage or theme to his larger concerns.

FOR FURTHER READING

On the earliest Roman impressions of Jews and Christians, see:

- Molly Whittaker, *Jews and Christians: Graeco-Roman Views* (Cambridge: Cambridge University Press, 1984).
- Robert Wilken, *The Christians as the Romans Saw Them* (New Haven: Yale University Press, 1984).
- Stephen Benko, *Pagan Roman and the Early Christians* (Bloomington: Indiana University Press, 1986).
- Menahem Stern, *Greek and Latin Authors on Jews and Judaism* (3 vols.; Jerusalem: Israel Academy of Sciences, 1974–1984).
- Peter Schäfer, *Judeophobia: Attitudes toward the Jews in the Ancient World* (Cambridge, Mass.: Harvard University Press, 1997).

On the position of the Jews in Western (Christian) history, see:

- Peter Richardson, David Granskou, and Stephen G. Wilson, eds., *Anti-Judaism in Early Christianity* (2 vols.; Waterloo, Ont.: Wilfrid Laurier University Press, 1986).
- Marcel Simon, *Verus Israel: A Study of the Relations between Christians and Jews in the Roman Empire (135–425)* (Littman Library of Jewish Civilization; Oxford: Oxford University, 1986).
- Wayne A. Meeks and Robert L. Wilken, *Jews and Christians in Antioch in the First Four Centuries of the Common Era* (SBL Sources for Biblical Study 13; Missoula, Mont.: Scholars Press, 1978).
- Jacob R. Marcus, *The Jew in the Medieval World: A Source Book: 315–1791* (New York: Atheneum, 1975).
- Rosemary Ruether, *Faith and Fratricide: The Theological Roots of Anti-Semitism* (New York: Seabury, 1974).

On the transmission of Josephus's writings, the most complete studies are in German, by Heinz Schreckenberg of Münster:

- *Die Flavius-Josephus: Tradition in Antike und Mittelalter* (Leiden: Brill, 1972).
- *Rezeptionsgeschichtliche und Textkritische Untersuchungen zu Flavius Josephus* (Leiden: Brill, 1977).

But *JJC* includes a brief summary essay by Schreckenberg in English translation, called "The Works of Josephus and the Early Christian

Church," pp. 315–24. It also contains several important essays on the Christian use of Josephus, pp. 325–426. They deal with Origen, Josephus's passage on Jesus, Hegesippus, Josephus in Byzantium, the illustration of Josephus's manuscripts through the Middle Ages, and Martin Luther. An accessible essay on the Hebrew Josippon is:

- D. Flusser, "*Josippon,* a Medieval Hebrew Version of Josephus," in *Josephus, Judaism, and Christianity* (ed. Louis H. Feldman and Goehi Hata; Detroit, Mich.: Wayne State University Press, 1987), 386–97.

The Career of Josephus and Its New Testament Context

	Career of Josephus	Early Christian Writings and Figures	Significant Events
6 B.C.E.		Birth of Jesus of Nazareth	
6 C.E.			Census in Syria/Judea
30		Death of Jesus of Nazareth	
37	Birth of Josephus	Conversion of Paul	
38			Gaius Caligula's Statue Ordered in Temple
40		1 Thessalonians	
		d. James brother of John	
		1 Corinthians	
		Philippians, 2 Corinthians	
	Advanced	Philemon	
	Education	Galatians, Romans	
		"Q" Sayings Source	
		Gospel of Thomas(?)	
	Trip to Rome	d. James brother of Jesus	
	Galilean Commander	d. Paul	Jewish Revolt
	Aramaic *War* (?)	Peter prisoner	
70	Josephus in Rome	Gospel of Mark	Fall of Jerusalem
	Aramaic *War* (?)		Fall of Masada
	Greek *War* (1st ed.)	Hebrews	
		Gospel of Matthew	
		Gospel of John	
	Antiquities	Johannine letters	
	Life		
	Against Apion	Luke and Acts	
100	d. ca. 100 (?)		

Chapter 2

The Career of Josephus

In the preceding chapter we have seen how *not* to use Josephus for the study of the NT. That leaves me with the obligation of proving, in the remainder of this book, that there is a better way. I have argued that we need to read him on his own terms, to allow him his integrity. This is a bit of an oversimplification because, once scholars have accepted that point, they must still define what his "own terms" are. In many respects, specialists do not yet agree about what Josephus was up to. That is inevitable, but it should not hinder us from making some fundamental observations. Once again, I claim no pretense of objectivity here, since every account is an interpretation, but I can promise to introduce Josephus in a way that reflects the current insights of scholarship.

Before we get down to specific examples of how Josephus can shed light on the NT, we must get to know him a little better. This chapter and the next will take a broad view of his life and writings within their social contexts. The resulting overview will provide us with the necessary basis for interpreting specific passages in Josephus as they relate to the study of the NT (chapters 4–6).

Unlike the vast majority of ancient authors whose works have survived, Josephus tells us a good deal about himself. At first this seems like a rare treat. None of the gospel authors even divulges his name, much less the circumstances in which he is writing. Even such a prolific author as Philo of Alexandria betrays little about his own life. Those who wrote the Dead Sea Scrolls, the apocalyptic literature, and most of the so-called apocryphal texts, if they did not falsely attribute their work to some great figure from the past, were content with anonymity. That is why scholars must spend a good deal of their time weaving careful hypotheses about who wrote these texts, where, when, and why.

Josephus, however, writes a "life," an autobiography that seems to offer plenty of information about himself. Autobiographies had been written for at least three hundred years before Josephus, but most of them have survived only in name; his is one of the earliest examples of the genre we possess.[1] And his *Jewish War* also recounts many details of his career. The main problem with Josephus's self-portraits is that they are highly stylized. In the Greco-Roman world, the art of persuasion or "rhetoric" was the central feature of education, preparing the elite for legal and political careers. Rhetorical training required one to be able to make whatever case was necessary and therefore to make several different cases from a single set of data or texts. The rhetorical exercises preserved in the elder Seneca's *Controversies* demonstrate this skill very well. In rhetorical training, one learned both standard techniques, or patterns of argumentation, and set pieces, or *topoi* (singular: *topos*): typical scenarios that one could insert into the narrative of one's argument on the assumption that they would be familiar to one's audience. Manuals of rhetoric abounded, and the aristocrat Josephus would have become familiar with the techniques—if not in his Jewish education, then at least in his study of Greek literature (*Ant.* 20.263). Even those who lacked such educational opportunities (Paul?) were bound to have absorbed rhetorical conventions from their environment, much as we absorb a lot of popular psychology even if we lack formal psychological training. So, entering Josephus's world of thought means first of all being wise to the kinds of conventions that he used. There was a certain playfulness in ancient rhetoric, even when it was used in such serious pursuits as historical narrative, that we tend to find alien and somewhat irresponsible. We shall see that in spite of his many protestations about telling the unvarnished truth (e.g., *War* 1.3, 6, 16; *Ag. Ap.* 1.47, 53), which were also standard in works by the most accomplished rhetoricians, Josephus's own portrayals of his life are so highly stylized that it is difficult to find reliable data. Let me illustrate.

[1] The *Confessions* of St. Augustine are often cited as the first true autobiography in Western literature, but that is because of their marked interior turn. In contrast, presumably like the Roman autobiographies before him (and somewhat like Julius Caesar's rather autobiographical *Gallic War*), Josephus's *Life* lacks any real probing of the author's psyche.

THE EARLY YEARS

Josephus opens his *Life* with a pedigree of his aristocratic heritage (1–6). This genealogy is perfectly in order for an ancient "life," though it may seem strange to us. We tend to believe in individual freedom and so care little about the parents of our famous athletes, musicians, and actors. Indeed, we often expect to hear that a famous industrialist or other celebrity came from ignominious roots, that he or she escaped a web of poverty. But this is a modern Western bias. Most of the world, most of the time, has functioned under more rigidly defined class lines. In Josephus's world, social mobility—the freedom to "rise up the ladder"—was minimal. One was born into a particular social class and, unless truly extraordinary circumstances occurred, one could expect to remain within its confines. Because aristocracies controlled most societies of the Mediterranean, the indispensable condition of real prestige was a noble parentage. Although some philosophers challenged this paradigm, the ingrained prejudice of tradition could recognize nobility only in the wellborn. The bible of the Greco-Roman world, Homer's epics the *Iliad* and the *Odyssey*, plainly reflects this identification of status with lineage: Odysseus's son Telemachus, for example, is treated with great respect because of his father's prestige (e.g., *Od.* 4.60–64, 147–154; 14.264–269). The parallel Roman epic by Virgil is all about ancestry: that of the entire nation (allegedly springing from the famous Trojan war) and that of some leading Roman families (*Aen.* 6.761–895). The biographer Plutarch, Josephus's contemporary, frequently includes family pedigrees for his subjects (cf. Tacitus, *Agr.* 4.1). On the other hand, the emperor Vespasian (69–79), who was of humble origins, attracted comment because he refused to do what was expected and concoct an illustrious pedigree (Suetonius, *Vesp.* 12).

In the Jewish world, the apocryphal book of Tobit provides an example of the same social assumptions. There, even the archangel Gabriel, who is sent to help the young Tobias, must concoct a genealogy in order to be accepted by Tobias's father (Tob 5:11–14)! In later rabbinic literature, too, appropriately distinguished genealogies were necessary for certain leaders (*y. Ta'an.* 4:5; *m. Ta'an.* 68d; *Gen. Rab.* 33). And of course, two of the gospels offer genealogies for Jesus (Matt 1:2–17; Luke 3:23–38). So the provision of a suitable genealogy was an important rhetorical convention in Josephus's world.

Since an illustrious lineage was so often considered the basis of good character, it is not surprising that Josephus's *Life,* which sets out to prove his character (*Life* 430), should begin with a genealogy (*Life* 2–6). However, although he claims to transmit only what he finds in the public record, this ancestry does not inspire confidence. (a) In *Life* 2, he asserts that his royal heritage comes from his mother, who descended from the Hasmoneans (=Maccabees), who "for a very considerable period were kings, as well as high-priests, of our nation." But the genealogy that follows in support of this claim goes through his father, not his mother. He now says that it was his great-great-grandfather on his *father's* side who married into the Hasmonean line (*Life* 4); no further mention is made of his mother. (b) According to Josephus elsewhere (*Ant.* 13.301), the Hasmoneans did *not* assume the title of "king" until Aristobulus (104 B.C.E.)—well after Josephus's ancestor's marriage. (c) The dates that he gives for his ancestors do not compute. Josephus puts his great-grandfather Matthias's birth at 135 B.C.E., his son Joseph's at 70 B.C.E., and his son Matthias's at 6 B.C.E. That his forebears should have sired children at sixty-five and seventy-six years of age, respectively, is not impossible, but it would require back-to-back feats of Abrahamic proportions. It is especially problematic in view of the short life expectancy in Greco-Roman antiquity. We may leave aside such additional problems as why Simon's son Matthias was "known as the son of Ephaeus" (*Life* 4).

Most scholars would agree on the futility of undertaking heroic measures to salvage Josephus's genealogy. It seems clear enough that he was, as he claimed, both a priest and a descendant of the Hasmoneans. We know this because priestly and pro-Hasmonean biases creep into his writings in many places where he is not trying to make a case about his heritage. For example, studies have shown that in his paraphrase of the Bible, Josephus consistently reshapes the narrative so as to highlight priestly concerns.[2] Later in his story, he treats the Hasmonean John Hyrcanus as a hero, and he even names his oldest son after this ruler (*Life* 5). For historical purposes, this *unintentional* evidence is much more convincing than Josephus's formal attempt, in the genealogy, to

---

[2] Salomo Rappaport, *Agada und Exegese bei Flavius Josephus* (Vienna: Alexander Kohut Memorial Foundation, 1930); B. Heller, "Gründzüge der Aggada des Flavius Josephus," *MGWJ* 80 (1936): 237–46; Seth Schwartz, *Josephus and Judaean Politics* (Leiden: Brill, 1990), 88–90.

prove his ancestry. As for the genealogy itself, it is easiest to believe that Josephus was unclear about the details of his parentage beyond two or three generations, but that he was forced by rhetorical convention to provide an impressive pedigree. He knew very well that his Roman readers had no way of consulting the public archives of Jerusalem.[3]

Even more obviously conditioned by rhetorical convention is Josephus's account of his youth and education (*Life* 7–12). He was such a precocious youngster, he claims, that the leading dignitaries of the city used to seek out his advice when he was but fourteen years of age (*Life* 8). At the age of sixteen, he embarked on advanced philosophical training in the major Jewish schools—those of the Pharisees, the Sadducees, and the Essenes. Not content with that experience, though it required painstaking discipline and effort, he attached himself to a teacher named Bannus. This monklike figure practiced a rigorous lifestyle in the Judean desert, wearing clothes made from bark and leaves and eating only wild vegetation. Josephus was deeply committed to Bannus's way and remained with him three years, but at the appropriate age (eighteen or nineteen) he returned to the city and began his public career (*Life* 10–12). One of his major diplomatic efforts was a trip to Rome to secure the release of some fellow priests who had been summoned by Nero (*Life* 13–16).

What are we to make of this account? To begin with, it brims with rhetorical commonplaces. The image of the child prodigy, both brilliant and wise beyond his years, appears in many other famous lives. The philosopher Pythagoras, while still a youth, was a model of virtue and wisdom; Apollonius of Tyana, as a child, miraculously spoke with perfect grammar; Moses did not engage in childish pursuits but quickly surpassed his teachers in wisdom; and Jesus, according to the apocryphal Infancy Gospel of Thomas, confounded his teachers with mysterious understanding.[4]

---

[3] Josephus elsewhere claims that the Jerusalem archives had been utterly destroyed during the revolt of 66–70, first by the rebels and then by the victorious Romans (*War* 2.427; 6.354). A less certain tradition reported by Eusebius held that King Herod (reigned 37–4 B.C.E.) had already burned the genealogical registers so as to eliminate anyone else's claims to royal ancestry (*Hist. eccl.* 1.7.13).

[4] A convenient selection of such commonplaces is in David R. Cartlidge and David L. Dungan, *Documents for the Study of the Gospels* (Philadelphia: Fortress, 1980), 129–36, 261.

Equally common is the topos of broad, preferably exotic, philosophical training such as Josephus claims. Upper-class Romans were ambivalent toward philosophy. Their ideal was for a man to be engaged primarily in public affairs—first military service, to prove his mettle, and then in more prestigious government posts. Such a career left no room for protracted philosophical pursuits, which were often considered inimical to public life. Philosophical fanaticism was as abhorrent then as religious fanaticism is today. Nevertheless, since a statesman must be wise and inwardly noble, he must be well acquainted with the teachings of philosophy. Further, many Romans admired the simplicity of life associated with such philosophers as the Pythagoreans and enjoyed reading about the exploits of Eastern philosophers. The usual compromise was for a man to study philosophy in his late teens, as part of his upper-level education; he might even be forgiven for a little fanaticism arising from adolescent idealism. But the completion of one's education required a decisive transition to the serious affairs of the real world. Nero's advisor, Seneca, for example, had been a vegetarian for a while, until his father, a famous Roman orator, forbade him to continue. And Tacitus writes that his father-in-law, Agricola, as a youth, "was inclined to drink more deeply of philosophy than is permitted to a Roman and a Senator, had not his mother's discretion imposed a check upon his enkindled and glowing imagination."[5] Though a broad acquaintance with philosophical issues was commendable, one had to stop short of out-and-out "conversion" to philosophy.[6]

Josephus's account of his education deftly engages these Roman sensibilities. In accord with his social status, at the appropriate age he studied intensively the major schools of Jewish philosophy. But he also had an admirable, youthful passion for something deeper than the ordinary school teachings could offer. Finding a guru who would expose him to the most rigorous lifestyle imaginable, he became this man's zealous disciple (*Life* 10–11). Still he was sensible enough to put these youthful adventures behind him (at a suitable age) and begin his diplomatic career (*Life* 12). Although designed to impress Roman readers,

[5] *Agr.* 4.3.

[6] See Arthur Darby Nock, *Conversion: The Old and the New in Religion from Alexander the Great to Augustine* (Oxford: Oxford University Press, 1933); Ramsay MacMullen, *Enemies of the Roman Order* (Cambridge, Mass.: Harvard University Press, 1966), 46–94.

Josephus's account of his youth also manages to blend in the biblical-Jewish theme of desert-sojourn as preparation for divine service.

We cannot take this whole rhetorical construction as a plain statement of what really happened. For one thing, the numbers are a problem. Josephus claims to have begun his advanced education at about age sixteen and to have completed it in his nineteenth year. We should naturally interpret this as a three-year period corresponding to the final phase of a Roman aristocrat's training. But he then says that his life with Bannus alone lasted three years (*Life* 12). This would leave little time for his "laborious exercises" in the Pharisaic, Sadducean, and Essene schools, even if we stretched the three years to four. In another context, Josephus asserts that it took three years just to become a full member of the Essene community (*War* 2.137–142), and it is likely that the Pharisees also had degrees of initiation. So once again we run afoul of Josephus's arithmetic. Such obvious inconsistencies mean either that our text of Josephus is flawed, as some think, or that he was rather careless with numbers—a conclusion supported by many other cases.

Plainly, Josephus's presentation of his youth and education owes much to the rhetorical conventions of his day. We can assume that he did come from an aristocratic family, that he was well educated, and that he knew a good deal about the Pharisees, Sadducees, and Essenes. But these points come to light elsewhere in his narratives where he is not trying to prove them. His deliberate statements in the *Life* seem contrived to impress the reader and should, therefore, be taken with a grain of salt.

JOSEPHUS AND THE JEWISH REVOLT

The same problems face us when we turn to consider the most controversial period of Josephus's career, his six months of service in Galilee at the outbreak of the Jewish revolt. This period was already a matter of contention during Josephus's lifetime. He had already described it in *War,* but chose to give a new presentation in *Life* as a celebration of the character and authority of the man who has just completed *Antiquities.* In the later work, he assembles his material to illustrate his many virtues. So we have two accounts, each with its own rhetorical constraints, that do not entirely agree.

In *War* 2.562–582, Josephus claims that the Jewish rebels' early victories over the Romans brought over those who had initially opposed the revolt (presumably including Josephus) to the rebel cause. The Jewish leaders, he says, met at the temple and appointed "generals" to prosecute the war in the various regions of Palestine. Given command of Galilee, Josephus set about his duties with zeal. He appointed a council of seventy men to assist him in administering the region, as well as seven men in each town to handle smaller matters. He fortified all the major cities under his command, in preparation for the Roman attack; Gischala and Sepphoris were fortified by others, but still at Josephus's command (*War* 2.575). Moreover, he created a professional standing army of about 65,000, which he organized and trained along Roman lines.[7] Josephus allows that he faced some opposition while in Galilee, especially from one John of Gischala, but he dismisses this fellow as a thoroughly evil man, "the most unscrupulous and crafty of all who have ever gained notoriety" (*War* 2.585). John was a mischief-maker and a robber, who (only because of his evil nature) challenged Josephus's duly constituted authority.

In the *Life,* we get a radically different picture. Here, Josephus portrays the Jewish leadership (including himself) as consistently favoring peace, even after the rebels' initial success. They send Josephus to Galilee along with two other priests, not as a general but as part of a committee. This delegation's task was to persuade the Galileans to lay down their arms, which were to be reserved for the professional soldiery. The delegates were not to prepare for war, but to wait and see what the Romans did (*Life* 29). Their "chief concern was the preservation of peace in Galilee" (*Life* 78). Josephus was not free to act independently, but had to submit when the other two voted against him (*Life* 73).[8]

Far from having military control of Galilee, according to the *Life,* Josephus faced significant opposition from numerous quarters and often feared for his life (*Life* 141–144). Most important, his arch rival

---

[7] So *War* 2.583. But in 2.576 he had put the size at upwards of 100,000 men. For purposes of comparison, Canada's armed forces today number about 80,000.

[8] In *Life* 341, Josephus does claim to have been elected to the command of Galilee, a datum that does not fit well with the preceding narrative. In the context, it should refer to Josephus's final and grudging confirmation (*Life* 310), which came only at the end of his long struggles with adversaries. It could be that in *War* he has telescoped all of this conflict and final confirmation as if it were a single commission.

John of Gischala now appears as having originally opposed the revolt, as Josephus did; he was not thoroughly evil, but originally shared Josephus's aristocratic outlook (*Life* 43). John fortified his native town of Gischala in opposition to Josephus, not at his command (*Life* 45, 189). And John, it now turns out, was a close friend of the Jewish leaders in Jerusalem, including the high priest and the eminent Pharisee Simon, son of Gamaliel. These respected leaders sponsored his effort to remove Josephus (*Life* 189–198). Further, John's cause was supported by aristocrats such as Justus of Tiberias. So the opposition to Josephus looks much more respectable than it had in *War*. Moreover, we are shocked by Josephus's new admission that he cut off the hands of his opponents (*Life* 169–173) and recruited the Galilean "brigands" as a mercenary force (*Life* 77). In addition, we now learn the substance of published accusations against Josephus: he and his mercenaries incited the city of Tiberias to revolt against Rome (*Life* 340); he was a greedy tyrant who sought to extend his own power through deceit (*Life* 302).

It is not a simple matter to determine what Josephus was really up to during the months of his Galilean "command." Inevitably, scholars have supposed that he was lying in at least one account, to cover up aspects of his past. To explain the apparent difficulties that he had with Jerusalem and with John of Gischala, as well as the charges of tyranny leveled against him, some have argued that he actually began as a kind of warlord in Galilee, one among several, and that he only became a "general" when his faction outmatched his competitors'. On this hypothesis, his entire claim to have been commissioned from Jerusalem would be a later creation to make himself look better.[9] Others contend (following the *Life*) that he actually went to Galilee as a delegate from Jerusalem, pursuing peace, but once there saw the opportunities for personal gain and yielded to temptation, becoming a rogue leader.[10]

Although it may now be impossible to recover Josephus's personal motives and mindset, or even the bare facts of his mission in Galilee, it is not necessarily the case that he has lied to cover up his past. First, when the war against Rome erupted, someone in his position might well have been faced with real ambivalence and difficult choices. We have only to

---

[9] Richard Laqueur, *Der jüdische Historiker Flavius Josephus* (Darmstadt: Wissenschaftliche Buckgesellschaft, 1970 [1928]).

[10] Hans Rasp, "Flavius Josephus und die jüdischen Religionsparteien," *ZNW* 23 (1924): 27–47.

consider the situation of Western-educated politicians in non-Western countries today to see similar kinds of tensions: loyalty to one's own people alongside a unique awareness of the costs of conflict and the benefits of cooperation, combined sometimes with a certain local coercion to lead as one's constituents desire. All of these tensions we can reasonably posit of the aristocrat Josephus, who was both scandalized by local Roman governance and keenly aware of the need to maintain peace. In fact, we have enough evidence from the writings of other statesmen of Josephus's time to know that they faced very real tensions of just this kind. Polybius, the second-century B.C.E. Greek politician, general, and historian, whose writings Josephus admired and used as a partial model, develops exactly this kind of dilemma for local rulers under the growing world power of Rome. Leaders of weaker states have few options (as also today) but must try to maintain peace within their countries in order to forestall interference from the major power, while also preserving a sense of national dignity—and not simply kowtowing to the superpower.[11] If the nation explodes in war as in Josephus's case, the situation can become intolerable: leaders committed to their people take charge of a campaign they know is doomed to fail, even if they sympathize fully with the grievances that caused it, and try to bring it to as safe a conclusion as possible. Josephus's contemporary Plutarch also describes these tensions in his essay on *Advice to the Politician.*

So it is hardly surprising that Josephus's narratives show him moving in conflicting directions. When these social constraints are added to the rhetorical context already discussed, and we remember that Josephus describes his actions in Galilee only to illustrate his moral qualities, we must concede that reliable details about his mission in Galilee may not be recoverable. It would be a mistake, I think, to assume that in one set of passages he conceals his past, whereas in others he allows the simple truth to escape.

SURRENDER TO THE ROMANS

Josephus's surrender to the Romans is probably the most famous episode of his life. Once the Roman general Vespasian had arrived in Galilee, the outcome of the war was a foregone conclusion. Josephus's men

[11] See Arthur Eckstein, *Moral Vision in the Histories of Polybius* (Berkeley: University of California Press, 1995).

deserted him immediately, and he fled to Tiberias, as far away as possible from the conflict (*War* 3.127–131). When Vespasian moved against the fortress town of Jotapata, Josephus paid a visit to help strengthen it. With disarming apparent honesty, however, he plainly states that once he knew that the city was going to fall, he planned to leave. The citizens got wind of this and implored him to stay, fearing for their lives. He responded, with conscious duplicity, that if he escaped he could distract the Romans as well as send help (*War* 3.200). The townspeople were not convinced, but preferred to believe that "with Josephus on the spot, . . . no disaster could befall them" (*War* 3.202). They forced him to stay.

Their trust in his presence turned out to be unfounded. The Roman siege concluded, inevitably, with an attack on the city. Just before the capture, Josephus claims, "some divine providence" inspired him to run and hide in an underground cavern (perhaps a water reservoir, *War* 3.341). When his hiding spot was betrayed by a captured woman, Vespasian sent messengers to offer him safety if he would surrender. Again, he frankly admits that he was afraid to surrender because of the hardship that he had caused the Romans; he thought that he would be killed (*War* 3.346). Vespasian then sent an old acquaintance of Josephus to persuade him that he would be safe and, once again, divine intervention came to his aid. Just as he was considering the offer of safety, "suddenly there came back into his mind those nightly dreams, in which God had foretold to him the impending fate of the Jews and the destinies of the Roman sovereigns" (*War* 3.351). Only then did Josephus resolve to surrender to the Romans, now that his motives were unmistakable. He was keenly aware of an alleged law that a general must die with his men (*War* 3.400), but in this special case the law was preempted by a divine mission. Extremely sensitive to charges of cowardice and betrayal, Josephus repeatedly insists that he would have been happy to die there in the cave had not God chosen him for his divine mission, to announce to the world the coming fortunes of his Roman captors (*War* 3.137–138, 354). So he decided to surrender.

But it was not that easy. His fellow captives, unimpressed by his divine mission, drew their swords to prevent his surrender. He could die as a hero or as a traitor, but die he must. Unfazed, Josephus proceeded to reason with them on the evils of suicide (*War* 3.362–386). But this too failed to move them. Ever resourceful, he devised a plan that would satisfy everyone. He proposed that they go ahead and kill themselves, but not in suicide. They should draw lots (straws?); the one chosen first should present himself for death to the second, the second to the third, and so on. They must solemnly agree that the ones left to the end would also take their lives, for it would be unconscionable, he notes, if those left to the end were to spare their own lives. In the end, remarkably, Josephus and one other were left. He persuaded the other not to kill him, and they both surrendered.

On the one hand, given Josephus's confidence in proposing this stratagem, and given his own admissions of telling barefaced lies to save himself, it seems that here too he simply outsmarted his colleagues. On the other hand, we must remember that we are dealing with ancient literary conventions. In Homer's *Odyssey,* mentioned earlier, the hero of the story routinely fabricates stories about his past to save himself from danger. That kind of deception, when practiced by a hero in the service of his just cause, was considered scandalous only by the more severe philosophers. Within the beloved epic itself, Odysseus's ploys evoke the admiration of the goddess Athena, who compares his wily resourcefulness to her own (*Od.* 13.250–301). In Jewish literature there was a famous precedent in the apocryphal novel about Judith, who had told a fabulous lie to the Assyrian general in order to save her people. Both of these stories use the theme of deception to show the triumph of the resourceful hero(ine) over insurmountable odds. That is the kind of situation in which Josephus also found himself while defending Jewish territory against the Romans.

Josephus's frankness about his many deceptions is probably best explained as a literary device intended to prove his heroic craftiness. We may assume with some confidence that he would not deliberately retell stories to his own injury. Since his ruses may have been invented out of whole cloth, as a rhetorical artifice, it would make no sense for us to turn them against him on the basis of our own moral criteria. He will later declare against his adversaries: "nor was it in your power to ascertain the part which I played in the siege [of Jotapata], since all possible informants perished in that conflict" (*Life* 357). Although directed against others' accounts, this notice serves to remind us of the latitude Josephus had in telling about his past.

PREDICTION OF VESPASIAN'S RISE

After Josephus surrendered to the Romans, the course of his career seems easier to follow. Even here we find plenty of posturing, but since much of his subsequent life was lived before the eyes of his Roman patrons, he would have less occasion to dissemble about the past.

Once in chains, Josephus was due to be sent to the emperor Nero because he was an important prisoner. To prevent this inconvenience, he decided that this was the time to tell Vespasian about the prophecies he had earlier received concerning the general's future; it was this prophetic mission, after all, that had justified his surrender in the first place. Granted an audience with Vespasian, he reportedly addressed his conqueror as follows:

> Whereas you suppose, Vespasian, that you have simply taken Josephus prisoner, it is actually *I who have come to you* as a messenger of greater things. For had I not been sent beforehand by God, I well knew the law of the Jews, and the way in which it befits generals to die. You are sending me to Nero? But why? [Because you think that] the successors who follow Nero, before you, will remain? *You* are Caesar, Vespasian, and all-powerful *[imperator]*—you and this son of yours. So bind me even more securely and keep me for yourself [i.e., rather than for Nero], for *you* are master not only of me, but of land and sea and the whole human race. And I beg for a much harsher regime of punishment if I should be speaking frivolously even of God. (*War* 3.400–402; emphasis added)

Before we ask about its historical worth, two literary features of this passage deserve notice. The first is Josephus's extremely confident tone in addressing the Roman supreme commander. Displacing Vespasian from his evident role as conqueror, Josephus insists rather that God is in control of the whole matter and that he came only by divine command; he would not have deigned to be merely Vespasian's captive. This theme of divine (and *not* Roman) control is basic to the *War,* as we shall see. Second, it may seem that Josephus goes over the top in his praise of Vespasian's power, as he will also in praising Titus and Domitian later in the work (e.g., 5.316, 319, 409; 7.84–88). Although we can take such passages at face value, as fawning flattery, Josephus's admitted taste for deceptive speech and for persuading people of whatever they want to hear might also lead us to wonder whether this story, too, is not told in that vein. Just as the other passages mentioned may involve ironic rather than earnest flattery of the sons, this one may represent a masterful trick played on Vespasian. Nero has already flattered the general, Josephus astutely observes (3.7), to induce him to take the job. Here, in the sentences that follow, Josephus himself immediately raises the possibility of deceit by attributing the perception of deceit to many (including Vespasian) at the time (3.403). Although he dismisses this possibility by claiming that the general was gradually "drawn [possibly 'led on'] into a position of trust" because God was already stirring him for the imperial power (3.404), some ambiguity remains about Josephus's straightforwardness as narrator.

In any case, if it happened, this prediction was made in July or August 67. Just a few months later, some of the legions in Europe revolted against Nero's rule; then, facing a conspiracy by his own elite troops, the emperor committed suicide on June 9, 68. The following tumultuous year saw three Roman generals—Galba, Otho, and Vitellius—seize power in rapid succession. But in December 69, in keeping with Josephus's prediction, the people of Rome acclaimed Vespasian emperor, ratifying the earlier acclamation by his own troops (*War* 4.655). As soon as Vespasian saw that he was going to become emperor, he released Josephus from his chains and bestowed many privileges on him.

How should we evaluate this amazing prediction? Josephus's use of it to preclude questions about his behavior positively invites the suspicion that he is covering something up. A similar prediction would later be attributed to the rabbi Yohanan ben Zakkai, who fled Jerusalem during the revolt and persuaded the Roman authorities to permit his resettlement in Yavneh/Jamnia (*b. Git.* 56a–b; *'Abot R. Nat.* 4.5). In that case, too, the spectacular prophecy seems to mask some less noble pleading for survival. We might be inclined, therefore, to think that Josephus invented the episode in the interest of self-justification, and that rabbinic tradition borrowed the device to exonerate Rabbi Yohanan.

But Josephus's prediction quickly became famous in Rome, probably as a result of the new ruler's propaganda effort. Vespasian had no hereditary claim to rule and thus was in serious need of legitimation in his bid for power during the last months of 69. In a superstitious world that valued signs and wonders, it was natural that the general's supporters would pay careful attention to tales of good omens that had appeared at the time of his accession. We find lists of these marvels in several Roman authors of the period, and Josephus's prediction is included among them (Suetonius, *Vesp.* 4–5; Dio Cassius 65.1.4). Since these Roman writers do not seem to have read Josephus, the story of his prediction must have been in wide circulation among the other Flavian omens. The political need for legitimacy would have been more than sufficient reason for the Flavian emperors (Vespasian, Titus, and Domitian) to broadcast as widely as possible, with any necessary adjustments, whatever the Eastern nobleman Josephus may have said about their dynasty.[12]

This does not yet require that Josephus actually made the prediction, any more than it requires the veracity of the other omens collected in support of the Flavians. It is conceivable that Vespasian conspired with Josephus to fabricate the story in return for his life: this Jewish priest could be retained as living proof of a mysterious Eastern oracle confirming Vespasian's right to rule. But there are more likely explanations, based on clues in Josephus's own writings.

Josephus links his revelations with scriptural prophecy. Back in the cave at Jotapata, he was enabled to understand his dreams because he was "not ignorant of the prophecies in the sacred books" (*War* 3.352). What prophetic statements might have been associated with Vespasian? Josephus himself says that they are "ambiguous utterances" (*War* 3.352) that require special insight to be understood. We know that Josephus was especially fond of the book of Daniel. Although rabbinic Judaism would not ultimately include Daniel among the prophets, Josephus considered him "one of the greatest of the prophets" (*Ant.* 10.266). Josephus confirms the evidence of the NT that Daniel was widely read by first-century Jews, because that book was thought to have revealed events of their own time. That is, the four-kingdom scenario envisioned by Daniel (2:31–45), which seems to end with the reign of Antiochus Epiphanes (d. 164 B.C.E.), was understood by Jews of Josephus's time to present the Roman empire as the last world power (*Ant.* 10.276). This interpretation was doubtless enhanced by Dan 9:24–27, which counts seventy weeks of years (= 490) from the rebuilding of the temple to its final desecration and the appearance of an "anointed ruler." Since the temple had been rebuilt in about 500 B.C.E. (no one knew the exact date), speculation was rife throughout the first century that the end was near. Thus, although many biblical statements were interpreted by Jewish groups to refer to the awaited deliverer, we have good reason to suppose that Josephus was thinking of Daniel when he spoke of such prophecies.

We have one further key insight into Josephus's thinking in this matter. In *War* 6.312, he notes that the Jewish rebels had been provoked to war in part by their misunderstanding of an "ambiguous oracle in their sacred Scriptures, to the effect that at that time one from their

[12] See Rajak, *Josephus,* 185–95.

country would become king of the world." Josephus comments that, though most Jewish teachers believed this prophecy to refer to a *Jewish* leader, in reality it "signified the sovereignty of Vespasian, who was proclaimed emperor on Jewish soil" (6.313). The Roman historian Tacitus makes a similar comment on the Jews' misunderstanding of their own prophecy, which led them to oppose rather than support Vespasian (*Hist.* 5.13).

If we put all of these clues together, Josephus's recognition of a Roman ruler as divinely chosen does not seem all that remarkable. He was well aware of current Jewish interpretations of Daniel, which looked for an anointed leader to appear in his own time. Although this hope was usually interpreted in opposition to Roman power, it was natural for someone with Josephus's perspective to transfer the prediction to a Roman leader. Since Roman rule seemed inevitable anyway, such a reading would be more intrinsically probable to him than the Jewish, nationalistic one. And it had a precedent in the Bible itself, for Isaiah calls the Persian King Cyrus, benefactor of the Jews, God's "anointed" ruler (Isa 45:1). It seems plausible, at least, that such an interpretation of Daniel was current among Josephus's social circles, which opposed the revolt. He might well have had this gem in his hip pocket to be produced at an appropriate moment. Or perhaps, the link with the Romans was his own innovation.

That still leaves his personal application of the prophecy to Vespasian. There seem to be four possibilities. First, he possessed supernatural or paranormal insight. Second, he made a lucky guess, based on his knowledge of political realities at the time. It was widely known that Nero, who had ruled for fourteen years, faced substantial opposition, and Josephus might well have judged that Vespasian was the most likely of the generals to succeed him. In any case, this general was on Jewish soil and showed every intention of attacking Jerusalem in fulfillment of the prophecy (Dan 9:26). If Josephus took the prophecy seriously, there was good reason for him to associate it with Vespasian.[13] Third, he did not in fact *predict* Vespasian's rise but brought up this "oracle" only after Vespasian's soldiers had acclaimed the new emperor. We note that Josephus was not released from his bonds until after the acclamation of

[13] Notice that Dan 7:7 presents the fourth beast as ten-horned. Since many people seem to have counted "emperors" from Julius Caesar, Vespasian would have been the tenth horn in such a scheme.

Vespasian (*War* 4.623–629). Given the new emperor's need for legitimation discussed above, we can imagine that a timely word from his prisoner, even now, about this very old Eastern oracle would be seized upon and promoted vigorously. Josephus, too, had every reason to date his declaration back to the time of his surrender, to cover up his otherwise cowardly behavior. Fourth, Josephus had two encounters with Vespasian. In the first, soon after his capture, he divulged his understanding of the prophecy that *the Romans* would rule the world by God's favor. That might explain why he was not sent to Nero (if indeed Vespasian ever intended such a thing; that he remained in Judea is as easily explained by his usefulness to Vespasian as a willing informant). Then, after Vespasian's acclamation, he pointed out that the prophecy must have concerned the Flavian general personally.

In any case, it is worth noting that Josephus came to regard himself as endowed with predictive abilities (*War* 3.406; 4.629). Although this self-concept may have been entirely delusional, it is perhaps easier to understand if he had made one or two predictions that had actually come to pass. Yet Josephus concedes that others considered his prediction concerning Vespasian "a nonsensical invention of the prisoner to avert the storm which he has raised" (*War* 3.406). Although this was said in story time before the prediction came true, we may suppose that it remained the view of Josephus's opponents that he somehow manufactured a prediction to serve Vespasian's public relations needs.[14]

CAPTIVITY AND LITERARY CAREER

The sequel may be presented briefly. Josephus makes much of his involvement in the war, but it turns out that he spent most of it in captivity. The war began in earnest only in March or April of 67, when Vespasian and his son Titus gathered their legions in Ptolemais. By July of the same year, Jotapata had fallen and Josephus was in chains. Jerusalem would not fall until September 70, and the war would not end completely until the fall of Masada in 73. In all of this, Josephus was an onlooker.

---

[14] See J. Blenkinsopp, "Prophecy and Priesthood in Josephus," *JJS* 25 (1974): 239–62.

For most of the period he was imprisoned in the Roman headquarters at Caesarea. There, he was permitted to marry a captive, presumably Jewish, from Caesarea (*Life* 414)—his second marriage (cf. *War* 5.419). He would later insist that priests were not permitted to marry captive women, who were assumed to be impure (*Ag. Ap.* 1.35); that is probably why he insists that this woman was a virgin. With the legions' acclamation of Vespasian in the autumn of 69, Josephus accompanied the new ruler to Alexandria, leaving his captive wife and finding another there. He then returned to the siege of Jerusalem with Titus, who was now in charge, to help bring the revolt to a swift end. Upon its successful conclusion with the fall of Jerusalem, he traveled with the triumphant Titus to Rome and married yet again. His third wife, who bore him three sons, he had divorced because he was "displeased at her behavior" (*Life* 426). Two of his sons by the previous marriage died prematurely. His fourth wife bore him two more.

The remainder of Josephus's life was both privileged and tormented. Everywhere in his writings, we see him under attack from fellow Jews for being a coward and a traitor. Describing the scene when Vespasian first arrived in Galilee, Josephus writes:

> As for himself [Josephus], although he might look for pardon from the Romans, he would have preferred to suffer a thousand deaths rather than betray his country and disgracefully abandon the command which had been entrusted to him, in order to seek his fortune among those whom he had been commissioned to fight. (*War* 3.137, LCL)

Here, as in the description of his divine mission considered above, he takes some trouble to head off the accusation of cowardice. In another telling passage, he writes that when the Jews of Jerusalem thought that he had died at Jotapata, they mourned him as a hero with thirty days of lamentation. But when they then learned of his survival and comfortable circumstances, "some abused him as a coward, others as a traitor, and throughout the city there was general indignation, and curses were heaped upon his devoted head" (*War* 3.439, LCL). This hostility would pursue him to the grave. After the war, one Jew accused him of having financed a revolt in Cyrene (*Life* 424). Others wrote accounts of his role in the war against Rome that pointedly challenged his accuracy and charged him with having been a petty tyrant. Josephus attributes all of this to envy of his good fortune, but his adversaries may have had nobler motives. Fortunately for him, he had the support of his imperial patrons, who silenced some of his accusers by execution (*Life* 425, 429). We should remember, though, that a claim to have many accusers was itself a rhetorical commonplace, used in part to generate sympathy with the audience (e.g., Martial, *Ep.* 3.9; 4.27; 7.72).

The new emperor Vespasian permitted Josephus to live in his own former private residence in Rome, gave him a stipend of some sort, and granted him Roman citizenship along with tracts of land in captured Judea (*Life* 423). Domitian would relieve him of taxation (*Life* 429). As his familiar name Flavius constantly reminds us, the ruling family made him their client. These privileges were not remarkable, however, and it is significant that Josephus did not receive some of the customary awards for prominent foreigners and writers: honorary equestrian status, land or a villa in Italy, or promotion of his children to Roman public office. He was not as close to the Flavians as is commonly assumed by those who regard him as a Roman pawn. But given the circumstances, as a captured general, he was privileged enough to survive in reasonable comfort. It was in these circumstances that Josephus wrote his four surviving works: the *Jewish War, Jewish Antiquities, Life of Josephus,* and *Against Apion.* To the analysis of those works we now turn.

The exact year of Josephus's death is unknown. His writings require that he lived at least to about 100 C.E., or age sixty-four, but he may have survived well into the second century.

FOR FURTHER READING

For the problems surrounding Josephus's career, see:

- Shaye J. D. Cohen, *Josephus in Galilee and Rome: His Vita and His Development as a Historian* (Leiden: Brill, 1979; repr. 2002). He includes a fine survey of previous scholarship in this area (pp. 8–23), the bulk of which was in German.

For a recent synopsis of the issues, see:

- Per Bilde, *Flavius Josephus Between Jerusalem and Rome* (Sheffield: Sheffield Academic Press, 1988), 27–60.

The classic study of Josephus in English, still worth reading, is:

- H. St. John Thackeray, *Josephus: The Man and the Historian* (New York: Jewish Institute of Religion, 1929), esp. 15–22.

A sympathetic effort to understand Josephus's outlook from within his social context is:

- Tessa Rajak, *Josephus: The Historian and His Society* (London: Duckworth, 1983; 2d ed., 2002).

On the rhetorical stylization of the *Life,* see:

- Jerome H. Neyrey, "Josephus' Vita and the Encomium: A Native Model of Personality," *Journal for the Study of Judaism* 25 (1994): 177–206.
- Steve Mason, *Life of Josephus* (vol. 9 of *Flavius Josephus: Translation and Commentary;* ed. Steve Mason; Leiden: Brill, 2001), xiii–l.

On Josephus's prediction and his view of the Flavians, see:

- Steve Mason, "Josephus, Daniel, and the Flavian House," in *Josephus and the History of the Greco-Roman Period: Essays in Memory of Morton Smith* (ed. Fausto Parente and Joseph Sievers; Leiden: Brill, 1994), 161–91.

Chapter 3

The Writings of Josephus

As a writer, Josephus was much more sophisticated than his questionable behavior might suggest. The beneficiary of a first-rate aristocratic education, he was not only intimately familiar with his native Hebrew and Aramaic traditions, but he also had achieved some basic facility in Greek language, literature, and thought even before he left Judea. Greek culture had come to permeate the Mediterranean world after Alexander the Great's conquests (335–323 B.C.E.). In the period following the Roman expansion (second century B.C.E.) local aristocracies in virtually all centers had come to share a common language, grounded in Hellenistic education and accommodated to the conditions of Roman hegemony. Josephus shared in this common cultural coin; he could speak the same language as elite citizens from Greece, Asia Minor, and Syria. Because of his obviously stormy relationship with his fellow Jews after the revolt, it is important to ask: in writing about the recent war and earlier Jewish history, what is Josephus trying to tell his Roman readers about the Jews? Has he become hostile to Jews or Judaism? Does he speak as a traitor? What is his message?

To imagine how his writings would have been understood by his initial Roman audiences, we first need to have some picture of how they perceived Jews and Judaism before Josephus came along. That will set the stage for our interpretation of each of his compositions in turn.

ROMAN PERCEPTIONS OF THE JEWS

Quite a bit of research has been done recently into Greco-Roman attitudes toward the Jews. Here we can do little more than summarize the main points, emphasizing those most relevant to late first-century Rome, Josephus's new place of residence.

Because Rome was such a major political and military power, it is easy for us to forget that religion was a central part of Roman society. The Romans are often dismissed in Western tradition as "pagans" who lived in evil darkness, trying to extinguish the light of the gospel by persecuting the young church. In popular accounts and Hollywood films, even in much scholarship, Roman religion is often ignored or relegated to an entirely marginal role. Their piety is considered merely formal and public, not heartfelt.

Increasingly, however, examination of Roman texts and social structures has revealed a deep religious foundation. We need only consider the word "inaugurate," which *we* use in a merely formal sense—with respect to the installation of our public leaders—to remember its original Latin association with concrete religious operations. Roman magistrates observed such natural phenomena as the feeding of the sacred chickens *(auspices, auspicium)* to determine "auspicious" moments, according to rules established by the college of *augures,* a vitally important subcategory of priests. The Romans tried carefully to interpret signs of divine favor or disfavor before elections, going to battle, taking a census, or other significant actions. They blamed losses in these areas on failure to read the omens properly, and they were even willing to cancel elections that had been based on misread signs. The Romans did not practice the separation of church and state.

For understanding Josephus's context it is important to note that there had always been a close connection between Rome's priesthoods and the senatorial aristocracy. The senate itself was charged with the critical religious functions of deciding which gods were to be honored and determining the regulation of cults and of oracles. It decided whether sacrilege or ritual error had taken place and what the remedy should be. By the first century, it had become virtually impossible for anyone but an upper aristocrat to hold one of the fifteen seats in each of the four main priestly colleges. Augustus had been a member of all four and from Julius Caesar onward, emperors considered it important to assume the office of high priest *(pontifex maximus),* head of the college of *pontifices,* the body responsible for guarding and interpreting the main tradition of Roman relations with the gods.

It would be hard to overstate the centrality of religion to the Roman state even though they had no single word that matches our "religion." Much of what we include here—reflection on divine-human relations, speculations about the afterlife, ethical teaching passed on from great masters—they included in "philosophy." One prominent philosopher and spokesman for the aristocracy reflected thus:

> From the start the citizens must be convinced that the gods are the lords and moderators of all things, that whatever is done is done with their authority and will, that they deserve the best from the race of mortals, that they perceive how each man is, what he does, and whatever he allows himself, with what mind and what *pietas* he observes the cults, and that they take note of the pious and impious. Minds that are imbued with these principles will scarcely shrink from useful or correct opinions. (Cicero, *Laws* 2.7; trans. David S. Potter)

In the public sphere at least, Romans regarded the favor of the gods with extreme seriousness. One of their most basic virtues was *pietas:* dutiful respect of one's family, one's fellows, and the entire social order built upon divine favor. *Impietas,* its opposite, was marked by failures of duty and ritual, at its extreme by crimes such as murder of a family member or temple robbery. It was a common assumption that the state could be held responsible for the failures of one person or group, especially for such enormities as temple pollution. Most important, many Romans held to the understandably profound conviction that their gods had brought them to their current fortune, and that these gods had to be honored in the appropriate ways if they were to retain it. Even if rulers were not pious believers themselves, they recognized the social utility of religion for keeping the masses quiescent (cf. Polybius 6.56.9–12). Several emperors, from Augustus (31/27 B.C.E.–14 C.E.) through Diocletian (284–305) and even Julian (360–363), tried to reform society to make it more observant, more careful of divine favor.

So, contrary to their bad press in Christian tradition, the Romans tended to see themselves as the champions of piety and morality. They understood that every nation had its own ancestral traditions, its own temples and gods, and these were normally inviolable to the Romans. They expected that all nations, like theirs, treated worship as an integral part of daily life. For both theoretical and practical reasons, they had no desire to convert the nations within their empire to traditional Roman religion. Most intellectuals had come to believe that there was ultimately only one God or ground of being anyway, and that the gods of Rome, Egypt, Persia, Greece, or Judea were symbolic or local representatives of this ultimate truth. It would have been foolish for the Romans to risk alienating any of these regional deities; far better to promote the local religions and even sacrifice to the various gods.

To be sure, Roman aristocrats typically looked down their noses at the "superstitions" of both common people and foreigners. We should remember, however, how easy it is also for us Westerners to dismiss unfamiliar Eastern or Middle-Eastern traditions because we fail to understand them. The Romans especially complained when the foreigners started arriving in Rome and began building temples to their native gods. But the authorities allowed all of these religions to flourish. In one famous case, the Romans even deliberately imported from Pessinus in Asia Minor the image of the Great Mother *(magna mater)* Cybele to secure her assistance in the war with Carthage (204 B.C.E.). The only time that Roman officials became upset with foreign religious groups was when they seemed to threaten the worldwide "peace and security" that had been established so carefully. The senate did move to shut down some groups, for gross immorality (cannibalism, human sacrifice, or orgiastic behavior), for plotting against the empire, or for drawing people away from normal civic loyalty. Further, emperors took a dim view of new political or religious groups, on the aristocratic assumption that "new truth" was a contradiction, and on the often justifiable suspicion that such groups were up to no good. But established national traditions usually had little to fear.

Judaism benefited from this tolerance. The Greek and Latin words for "Jew" *(Ioudaios, Iudaeus)* simply mean "Judean." Romans thought of the Jews as the people from Judea who, naturally enough, had their own traditions of worship, their own God, and their own temple where their God lived. They knew that the nation was quite old and many had heard of Moses, its founder. More than that, some educated Greeks and Romans admired the Jews for their "philosophical" view of God. Unlike other nations, whose masses worshiped symbolic representations of the true God, the Jewish tradition prohibited even its humblest members from making images of the divine. Jewish ethics, which, for example, forbade the abandonment of unwanted children (a common practice throughout the empire), were also respected. Roman interest in things Jewish had a long history, extending back at least to L. Cornelius Alexander ("Polyhistor," d. 35 B.C.E.), who apparently wrote a book on the Jews. In Josephus's day some of this interest was more personal, ranging from observance of occasional Jewish customs (such as the Sabbath) to synagogue attendance and support to an actual conversion that required distancing oneself from one's native Roman traditions (e.g., Tacitus, *Hist.* 5.5; Epictetus, *Diatr.* 2.9.20; Juvenal, *Sat.* 5.14.96–106). Interested parties may have come from all classes of society, though the names we hear are from the Roman elite (e.g., Suetonius, *Dom.* 14; Dio Cassius 67.2–3; cf. 68.1.2; Josephus, *Ant.* 18.81; 20.195).

On the political side, the Jews had established close ties with the Romans long before Josephus's time, in the era of the Maccabees (1 Macc 8:1–32), and they had cemented those ties under King Herod (ruled 37–4 B.C.E.), who was a faithful ally of a series of Roman leaders. His friendship with Julius Ceasar and then Augustus was particularly important in securing privileges and exemptions for Jews living around the empire. This long history of recognition and cooperation assured the Jews a secure place in the empire's kaleidoscope of cultures and religions.

Yet the Jews were a unique group in the empire, and their uniqueness led perhaps inevitably to conflict with other groups. The theoretical issue was their traditional commitment to "only one God," or monotheism. Whereas Roman intellectuals could be philosophical monotheists while still respecting the symbolic gods of the nations, most Jews could not. Their sacred texts demanded exclusive devotion to the God of Israel and forbade any recognition of other gods on penalty of death.

The real problem, however, was not abstract but painfully concrete. Because religion was so closely woven into the fabric of life, observant Jews living in the cities of the Greco-Roman world could not participate fully in normal civic affairs. They could not join their neighbors in celebrations of local holidays, which necessarily involved sacrifice to the local god. They could not eat their neighbors' food, for it did not meet the requirements spelled out by their God in the Scriptures. They could not engage in normal business on Friday evenings or Saturdays, because their God had commanded rest. Jewish men could not attend the public baths without exposing their circumcision, which was derided by Greeks and Romans as "mutilation" of the body. And they could not run for civic offices that would involve, as most did, some reverence for the gods of the region. All of this created the impression that they were social misfits. A Sicilian author claims that the Jews "made the hatred of humanity into a tradition" (Diodorus Siculus 34.1.2). The Roman historian Tacitus, when describing Jerusalem's fortifications, asserts that the city's founders anticipated many wars "because the ways of their people differed so from those of the neighbours" (*Hist.* 5.12; cf. Cicero, *Flac.* 28.69).

The Jewish position in the Roman world was ambiguous, and probably differed from region to region, depending on local personalities. But the dominant literary image, at least, was negative. Jews were routinely accused of "atheism," for not respecting the traditional Greco-Roman gods, and of "misanthropy," for withdrawing from normal social life. We know of several incidents in which these hostile attitudes produced or perhaps reflected actual conflict between Jews and Gentiles living in the same cities. In a major city such as Alexandria, where a substantial Jewish community had lived since about 300 B.C.E., particular social factors such as disputes over citizenship rights led to major conflicts in the 30s of the first century. There, as in many cities of Asia Minor, the Roman emperor had to intervene in order to maintain peace, and in some cases the Roman senate also passed directives *(consulta)* reasserting the privileges of the Jews (*Ant.* 14.223, 230; 16.172; 19.28–92, 310). We do not know how fully such directives were observed, and we may be sure that hostilities smoldered in several regions.

Needless to say, when the Judeans revolted against Roman rule in the war of 66–73, this was seen by much of the world as but a glaring example of their difference and "hatred of humanity." Tens of thousands of Jews living in Egypt and Syria, at least, were massacred in retaliation (*War* 2. 457–486, 559; 7.367–368). That revolt was only the final explosion of a simmering anti-Romanism among some Judeans that had already expressed itself in several smaller rebellions. From the Judean side, the revolt came because some of them could take no more of the insensitive and corrupt procurators who had been sent to govern them. But the Romans saw the revolt as an impudent challenge to their cherished world order. Sitting near the eastern edge of the empire's frontier, the Judean nation had proven an irritating thorn in their side.

Once the Romans had destroyed Jerusalem in 70, anti-Jewish sentiment came to a head throughout the Mediterranean, and the Romans interpreted their victory as the triumph of their own gods. Special coins were minted in Rome and elsewhere proclaiming "Judea Captive!" The general Titus and his father the emperor enjoyed a spectacular triumphal march through the center of Rome with the spoils and captured generals in procession. In a highly symbolic gesture, the annual contribution that Jews around the world had formerly sent to Jerusalem for

Judea Capta coin, courtesy of the British Museum

the upkeep of the temple was now redirected to support the temple of the Roman god Jupiter Capitoline. This tax was, predictably, collected in a ruthless manner at times. The Roman victory was so significant that Vespasian erected a Temple of Peace in celebration, and the treasures of the Jerusalem temple were housed in it (*War* 7.158–62). One triumphal arch, in Rome's Circus Maximus (no longer standing), memorialized Titus's complete subjugation of the Jews and destruction of their city. Another arch—the famous one that still stands today in the Forum—celebrated Titus's postmortem divinization, still portraying his triumphal procession and the capture of the Jerusalem temple's treasures as the most conspicuous credential of his whole life. It has recently been demonstrated that the yet more famous Colosseum, built by the Flavian emperors (the Flavian Amphitheater) and famous to Rome's visitors for two millennia, once bore an inscription explaining that it too was constructed "from the spoils of war" (i.e., in Jerusalem).[1] Alongside the several historians of the war in Rome mentioned by Josephus (below), poets and others also took up the glorious theme. Although the future emperor Domitian was too young to take part in the fighting, he wrote an epic poem about his older brother's feats (Valerius Flaccus, *Arg.* 1.12–14). The postwar years cannot have been an easy time, especially in Rome, for Jews and Jewish sympathizers.

Long before Titus's conquest of Jerusalem, in 59 C.E., the Roman senator Cicero was defending one Flaccus, a former governor of Asia,

[1] Geza Alföldy, "Eine Bauinschrift aus dem Colosseum," *Zeitschrift für Papyrologie und Epigraphie* 109 (1994): 195–226.

on charges of extortion. One charge was that Flaccus had diverted into his own account the Jews' contributions for the temple in Jerusalem. With characteristic force, Cicero denounces the Jews' "barbarous superstition" and alludes to Pompey the Great's recent conquest of Jerusalem (63 B.C.E.):

> Every city, Laelius, has its own religious observances and we have ours. Even when Jerusalem was still standing and the Jews were at peace with us, the demands of their religion were incompatible *[abhorrebat]* with the majesty of our Empire, the dignity of our name and the institutions of our ancestors; and now that the Jewish nation has shown by armed rebellion what are its feelings for our rule, they are even more so; how dear it was to the immortal gods has been shown by the fact that it has been conquered, farmed out to the tax-collectors and enslaved. (*Flac.* 69)

Although we should generally not take Cicero's rhetorical flourishes too seriously, the fact that this assertion of Jewish alienness and Roman conquest as proof of Roman virtue comes so readily to his lips indicates that he expects it to resonate with his elite Roman readers.

We do not have a Cicero writing in the 70s or 80s C.E., after the fall of Jerusalem to Titus, but we can certainly see echoes of similar sentiments in that period. Not long after Titus's death, when his brother Domitian was emperor (81–96 C.E.), the poet Silius Italicus recalled Titus's enemies in Judea as "the fierce race of Palestine" (*Pun.* 3.605–606). Even though the historian Tacitus's full account of Jerusalem's fall is lost to us, we have enough of the preamble (*Hist.* 5.1–13) to see where he was heading. He emphasized Jewish difference and alleged misanthropy, also retailing unkind stories about the nation's origins, as preparation for his description of Jerusalem's capture. Clearly, he wished to connect the Jewish national character with their fate at Roman hands: "The Jews regard as profane all that we hold sacred; on the other hand, they permit all that we abhor" (*Hist.* 5.4).

Several authors in the later part of the second century likewise indicate how the Romans understood their victory over the Jews. The Roman Caecilius in Minucius Felix's *Octavius* uses the example of the Jews to argue that the Christians should not confine their worship to one God; the Jews did so, and their God "has so little force or power that he is enslaved with his own special nation to the Roman deities" (*Oct.* 10; cf. 33). Celsus likewise ridicules any notion that the Jews enjoy divine favor, arguing from their obvious present state; he sees their captivity to Rome as a penalty for their having followed such antisocial laws (Origen, *Cels.* 5.41). And Philostratus has one of his characters argue that the Jews were so different from and hostile to the Romans, they should never have been joined to the empire in the first place. Their life is irreconcilable with that of the rest of humanity (*Vit. Apoll.* 5.33).

It is important for us modern readers to recognize a basic difference between Roman values and ours on the question of war. Whereas we at least profess the principles of mercy and justice enshrined in "international law," exemplified by the Geneva conventions, the Romans knew nothing of this. We insist armies target only combatants (not the elderly or young), and even then only those in active engagements, sparing also as many soldiers as possible by taking prisoners and maintaining such prisoners in humane conditions. Even the most compassionate and gentle Roman authors known to us, however, provide little evidence of such concern for enemies in war. Although clemency was certainly a general virtue among Roman aristocrats, not least toward an enemy on the march if heavy bloodshed could be avoided, when it came to rebellion against the Roman order, few seemed to doubt that the only honorable remedy was swift, sure, and comprehensive defeat. After concluding the slaughter of men, women, and children that was deemed necessary to permanently humiliate the conquered and prevent any future uprising, killing that frequently ended only because of the legionaries' exhaustion, Roman soldiers were normally set free to rape survivors and pillage as desired. Rebellion against the established order was the ultimate crime, and it called for ultimate remedies.

This means that Titus's victory over the Jews and destruction of Jerusalem would have been interpreted as indeed a major triumph of Roman arms, military virtue, and divine fortune. Josephus's vivid depiction of the triumph shows that no effort was made to spare viewers from the blood and gore; to the contrary, colorful tapestries portrayed "whole battalions of the enemy slaughtered . . . an area all deluged with blood . . . fire engulfing sanctuaries and the collapse of houses upon their owners" (*War* 7.143). Violent celebration was in the air, and Titus was particularly honored for his decisive conquest of this enemy—so much so that when it neared the time for him to become emperor, citizens reportedly began to worry about his violent side, which had seemed so praiseworthy when directed at the rebellious Jews (Suetonius, *Tit.* 1.6–7).

It was in such an atmosphere of Roman triumphalism and chauvinism that Flavius Josephus—the Judean priest, Galilean commander in the revolt, Roman sympathizer turned informant, now pensioned and housed in the emperor's own villa—wrote his four works about the Jews. What did he mean to say?

JEWISH WAR

The clearest confirmation that such anti-Jewish feeling was prevalent in Rome after the revolt is the prologue to Josephus's first work, the *Jewish War,* which he began to write soon after his arrival there in 71. In this book, Josephus attempts to counter all of the current interpretations: that the Jews espouse bizarre social values, have a belligerent nature, and are poor citizens of the Roman empire; that their revolt was an expression of this national character; and that the Roman victory represented the martial virtue of Titus, the triumph of the Roman gods, and the defeat of the Jewish God. Before we turn to the ways in which the *War* makes Josephus's contrary points, we pause to consider a red herring that has often diverted readers' attention from the book's main themes.

Josephus presented the bulk of the Greek-language *War* to Vespasian (*Life* 361; *Ag. Ap.* 1.50), who died in 79 C.E., and the latest event it mentions is the dedication of the Temple of Peace in 75 (*War* 7.158); so he must have written much of it between 75 and 79. Yet in the prologue Josephus mentions an earlier account of the conflict that he had written in his native language (presumably Aramaic) for the benefit of Parthians and Babylonians to the East of the Roman empire (*War* 1.3, 6). We no longer possess this earlier Semitic version of the *War.* Nevertheless, many modern scholars have seen it as the key to understanding Josephus's motives.

Their argument goes like this. Here is Josephus, a proven collaborator with the Romans, who provided them with much information during the war, now dashing off an account of the conflict, from Rome, it is assumed, to the nations beyond the borders of the empire. The book contains numerous passages that declare the invincibility of Rome and Rome's divine favor. The emperors Vespasian and Titus receive lavish praise for their heroic and virtuous conduct throughout the campaign. Especially telling is Josephus's enthusiastic description of Roman military procedures, which is intended, he says, to offer "consolation to those who have been conquered and dissuasion of the revolutionaries"

(3.108).[2] If we recall that the Parthians, at least, came close to war with Rome a couple of times during the first century, we might easily conclude that "Josephus was commissioned by the conquerors to write the official history of the war for propagandistic purposes."[3] That he wrote *War* as a lackey of the Romans, retained by them to help quell any further revolutionary hopes in the East, was until recently the standard scholarly view, and it still has many adherents.

In recent years, however, several commentators have raised serious objections to this theory. The main one is that our Greek *War* is not merely a translation of the Semitic account that was sent to the East. On the contrary, the Greek version is written in an original, highly literary style—not "translation Greek." It is filled with themes and vocabulary (e.g., for fate, free will, fortune, providence, and historical accuracy) that were native to Greek and Hellenistic literature. It uses Greek dramatic forms in its involved portrayal of Herod the Great, as in numerous other scenes. In the fashion of Hellenistic history-writing, Josephus creates suitable speeches for several of the important characters. And he often pauses to reflect on current issues of Hellenistic philosophy or historiography. In short, the Greek *War* fits perfectly within the Greco-Roman literary context. We need not doubt that Josephus wrote an earlier account of the revolt in a Semitic language, but there is no good reason to assume that it was written in Rome, much less as imperial propaganda. The main point, however, is that we do not possess that version of the *War,* and the one we do possess has an entirely different orientation.

It is not easy to make a compelling argument about the larger aims of a historical narrative, for we must make sophisticated deductions from what is included and excluded and from the author's tone. This is very different, for example, from an essay such as *Against Apion* (below), which contains a pointed argument. History does not lend itself easily to argumentative analysis.

Yet we know that ancient writers typically wrote history to teach lessons. And even with a narrative we are not without important clues as to what those lessons might be. First, in the case of the *War* we have a

---

[2] In the Loeb edition, Henry St. John Thackeray translates the phrase as "those *contemplating revolt,*" a translation that supports the hypothesis in question.

[3] So H. St. John Thackeray, *Josephus: The Man and the Historian* (New York: Jewish Institute of Religion, 1929), 27.

programmatic statement of the author's purpose in the elaborate prologue (*War* 1.1–30) and again in later reflections on the *War*'s purposes (e.g., *Ant.* 1.1–4). Since books were written on scrolls and lacked tables of contents, indexes, or other mechanisms by which the reader could quickly determine the book's perspective and contents, the ancient prologue became a very important (though by no means infallible) guide in this respect. The reader could unroll a small section to see where the story was headed. Second, we must consider editorial asides introduced by the author, and in particular the speeches that he creates for his characters. It was widely understood in ancient history-writing that speeches were not reproductions of what was actually said on particular occasions, but that authors had considerable freedom in crafting discourses for various characters appropriate to each situation. Since the speeches are the author's rhetorical creations (even if they also contain a reminiscence of what was actually said), we should examine them carefully for clues as to his tendencies. Great caution is needed, however, since a writer as skilled as Josephus can use speeches for all sorts of purposes, including entertainment, and can seed them with many shades of truth.

Let us consider the work's structure. Most commentators now agree that, although Josephus wrote a first draft of books 1 to 6 in the last few years of Vespasian's reign, between 75 and 79 C.E., he added book 7 at a later date. That is because his style changes noticeably in the last book and it features Vespasian's son Domitian (ruled 81–96 C.E.; cf. 7.37, 85–88, 152), though the young man had not figured significantly in the first six books. This attention seems most easily explained if Domitian had risen to the throne by the time Josephus penned this book. Some scholars have also detected new themes in book 7 that correspond more closely to those of the later *Antiquities.*[4]

Even if Josephus did write book 7 later, structural features appear to indicate that he had a plan of the whole when he began writing—much as the earlier historian Livy worked from a plan when he began each five-book segment of his massive Roman history.[5] For example,

---

[4]See especially Shaye J. D. Cohen, *Josephus in Galilee and Rome* (Boston: Brill, 2002 [1979]), 84–90; Seth Schwartz, "The Composition and Publication of Josephus's *Bellum Iudaicum* Book 7," *HTR* 79 (1986): 373–86.

[5]See T. J. Luce, *Livy: The Composition of His History* (Princeton, N.J.: Princeton University Press, 1977).

the first story in the *Jewish War* concerns the high priest Onias, who left Jerusalem to establish another temple in the Egyptian district of Heliopolis (1.31–33). Although Josephus promises to return to this temple, he does not do so until the closing paragraphs of book 7 (7.420–36). This further raises the question whether Josephus gives his book a symmetrical, concentric structure built around a central pivot or fulcrum. Such structures were common in ancient literature,[6] and all four of the canonical gospels have them, at least in broad outline—most obviously Luke-Acts, with its movement toward (Luke 9:51) and away from (Acts 1:8) Jerusalem as the place of Jesus' death and resurrection, and John, where Lazarus's raising both occupies the center (chapter 11) and also dramatically alters the direction of the narrative.

In the case of Josephus's *War,* such a structure is, I think, beyond doubt. Only in books 1 and 7 does the Parthian kingdom, Rome's perceived rival, provide a background narrative presence (1.175–182, 248–269, 288–291; 7.105, 221–224, 237). Similarly, Roman civil war, which is constantly in the background of book 1, is concluded in 7.157, marked by Vespasian's dedication of the Temple of Peace. The desert fortress Masada is introduced in book 1 (1.237–238, 264–266, 286–294), roughly the same distance as from the end of book 7 (7.255–406). Near the beginning of book 2 and the end of book 6, and only in those places, Josephus describes the Passover festival as a feast of many sacrifices and equates it with the "Unleavened" feast, described as the occasion of great human slaughter, when corpses were "piled up" as a result of civil war (4 B.C.E. and 70 C.E.; 2.10–30; 6.421–431, 259). Most impressively, Josephus has two very similar accounts of the burning of the temple colonnade's roof, once when the Romans burn it to kill defending Jews (2.229–230; cf. 405), and once when Jews burn it to attack invading Romans (6.233). In both cases, he describes in long sentences of remarkable similarity the five ways in which those on the colonnade roof died.

This movement toward and then away from a pivot isolates, as the work's central episode, the murder of the former high priests Ananus II and Jesus, who were in nominal supreme command of the war effort (4.305–365). Josephus has murderers, Idumean troops from the south who ally with the Zealots, enter the city (and narrative) only in *War*

[6] E.g., J. W. Welch, ed., *Chiasmus in Antiquity: Structures, Analyses, Exegesis* (Hildesheim: Gerstenberg, 1981).

4.224–304. Their murder of the aristocratic leaders, who had wanted to refuse the Idumeans entry, is their main function in the story. Soon after this deed, the bulk of them leave again in disgust (4.353), realizing that the Zealots have misrepresented the situation and involved them in something ignoble. Moreover, Josephus, as narrator, offers a moving eulogy on Ananus and Jesus, citing this heinous act as the beginning of the end for Jerusalem:

> The taking of the city began with the death of Ananus, and from that day, on which they saw their high priest and leader of their own rescue butchered in the heart of the city, issued the breaching of the wall and the destruction of the Judeans' republic. (4.318)

In a later summary reflection, Josephus similarly excoriates the Idumeans for their brief but singularly destructive role in the war. In their madness, "they butchered the chief priests, with the result that no aspect of piety toward God could persevere, and they uprooted whatever had remained of the nation's political form; they introduced absolute lawlessness throughout everything" (7.267). This recapitulation matches the turning point in book 4, where the rebels, now deprived of aristocratic leadership, begin to behave with the savagery of animals (4.326–327). The story about Ananus's murder not only occupies the midpoint of the narrative, but it also serves as the literary fulcrum.

Identification of that turning point prompts us to return to Josephus's purpose. Why should he feature Ananus and Jesus in this way? The most common view has been that Josephus worked in the service of Roman propaganda, using sources provided by his Roman masters to write a flattering account of their reign and a warning to others against opposing indomitable Roman power. From here derives much of Josephus's reputation as quisling, lackey, and lickspittle. More recently some scholars have argued that his main concern was to absolve himself and his class, the priestly aristocracy, from involvement in the war, blaming it instead on a handful of rebels. This is a somewhat more honorable motive than enemy propaganda, to be sure, though it still has him seeking harmony with his Roman patrons and worming out of moral responsibility.

The problem with both of these arguments is that they too simplistically explain a highly sophisticated narrative, which has many dimensions, layers, internal tensions, and rhetorical tricks. The solution is perhaps to suggest a range of coherent major interests that allow for a comprehensive reading. The work has at least four overriding themes. All of these confront the triumphalist view, sketched above, which dominated Josephus's environment, the city of Rome of the 70s. (a) Most basic is the theme of the Jewish (=Judean) ruling class, of which Josephus was a proud part, and their honorable conduct in relation both to their own people and to the Romans. (b) Second is the pervasive problem of civil war, Jewish and Roman. This was not a matter of the Jewish nation's opposing Rome, but rather of Jews differing with Jews about how to respond to nearly intolerable local provocations. (c) Furthermore, the Romans, including Titus, can take no credit for Jerusalem's destruction since this was the work of the Jews' discredited God, who merely used the Romans as his agents. (d) Finally, as a people, the widely ridiculed Jews in fact had fought with brilliant resourcefulness and courage—long after the war had lost its legitimate leadership—causing the vaunted Roman legions extreme hardship on many occasions. What unites these themes is a pronounced Judean-Jewish perspective that strives mightily to preserve the dignity of a conquered and humiliated people. Let us take them up in turn.

(a) The first theme is strange to our modern values, yet it underlies the whole logic of the *Jewish War.* Without apology, Josephus begins by identifying himself as a member of the Judean aristocracy. He appears to have felt in the company of others who spoke the same basic cultural language. They, too, were aristocrats, whether Roman, Greek, or Eastern (like Josephus). We can chart some of the key shared features of the aristocracy in Greek authors from Polybius to Plutarch and Dio Chrysostom, who were similarly subject to Roman domination. On the Roman side we find many of the same assumptions about aristocracy among upper-class writers such as Cato, Cicero, and Sallust, and among Josephus's contemporaries Pliny and Tacitus.

Aristocrats belonged to a very small class who owed their special status in society first of all to birth and bloodline. Not all of these writers had the highest sort of birth, but their writings attest the importance of the issue. What distinguished aristocrats and confirmed the inherited legacy was their education (Greek *paideia*), which emphasized skills that we would consider among the least important for social leadership: public oratory and rhetoric, the ability to convincingly argue a point. Education included training in other disciplines, but youths from Rome to Egypt to Judea mainly learned texts from their respective histories, famous sayings, moral principles, and how to employ these in effective argumentation.

Graduates of such a system were then expected to lead in all areas of public life: to serve in the military and take command as necessary, to work as lawyers and magistrates and as public officials, to function as priests in the city's various religious societies, to own large estates and ensure their successful cultivation, and possibly to write—often in retirement—poetry, philosophy, and history. Whereas we regard most of these fields as technical specialties requiring long training, in the ancient world aristocrats moved broadly across the range of public responsibilities, not because of their expertise, but because of their character. Only aristocrats had allegedly learned, somehow during their years of disciplined training, to overcome impulsiveness, emotionalism, vulnerability to changing circumstances, quick anger, violence, and sexual carelessness—all natural instincts of the uneducated masses. Adult aristocrats mastered their emotions, and it was chiefly this virtue of self-control that set them above the raging mobs and which suited them for the cool, levelheaded preservation of the state.

So it was with Josephus. After an advanced training that featured mainly philosophy and "letters," he served as a priest in Jerusalem according to a very precise regimen, as regional governor of Galilee and a general in the Jewish-Roman war, as a magistrate who tried cases of all kinds in Galilee, as a councilor in the highest levels of policy, as a landowner, and finally (in retirement) as a national historian. In this range of activity he was no different in principle from the Greeks and Romans mentioned above.

Josephus's outlook is most closely paralleled in the writings of contemporary statesmen from Greek cities under Roman rule. These writers all shared the basic dilemma of how to preserve their people's dignity, with which of course their own status was inextricably tied, while at the same time accommodating the plain fact of Roman domination. Greek statesmen had to keep the populace happy, suitably proud, and productive without exciting thoughts of rebellion, which could only be catastrophic.

The situation was never static or settled once and for all. The masses were—everyone understood—highly susceptible to emotional appeals and promises. If some charismatic figure should come along and rouse them, there could be real trouble. Such leaders included, most dangerously, young aristocrats who had not yet matured. These men were typically "hotheads," inclined to reckless behavior and violence. They were especially dangerous because of their natural influence over the masses. Polybius faced just this problem when the cities of his homeland (Achaea) joined together to resist Roman rule at the instigation of a demagogue named Critolaus, who had won the favor of the masses with a promise of debt-cancellation and then persuaded them to rebel against Rome (Polybius 38.12–13). This resulted in the devastation of the region, including the utter destruction of famous Corinth, in 146 B.C.E.

In retrospect Polybius recounts Greek leaders' debates on this issue of independence, and how it should be asserted in the context of Roman power (24.11–13). Josephus's contemporary Plutarch also writes an essay of *Advice to the Statesman.* Both authors consider it a leader's principal duty to preserve the internal peace of the city by whatever means necessary, in order to prevent Roman interference in local affairs. Both deplore as undignified those inclined to fawn over the Romans, involving them in Greek affairs, and thereby undermining all self-respect and the strength of local constitutions and internal governments. Polybius and Plutarch imagine the statesman as the helmsman of a sailing ship, who must know both when to yield to forces beyond his control and when to assert strong direction, in order to bring the ship safely to harbor (e.g.,. Plutarch, *Phil.* 17.3–4).

These Greek authors spoke much of "fortune" (Greek *tuche*) to account for Roman power over them. This was a useful term because it had no clear or fixed meaning. It could signify everything from mere chance or luck (whether good or bad) to divine control. Personal and political life was filled with unanticipated, uncontrollable, and inexplicable reversals of fortune. The only partly predictable aspect of fortune, regularly personified as female, had to do with her jealousy, for she had an observable habit of unfavorably influencing circumstances just at the point of success. It behooved the wise, therefore, not to get carried away with any momentary victory. Most famously, in Polybius's history (38.20.1–21.1) the Roman general Scipio properly feels dread rather than joy at the destruction of Carthage, Rome's powerful enemy, because he knows that one day the same thing will happen to his own city. Polybius and Plutarch attribute Rome's current power to fortune. Other nations have enjoyed their season in the sun, but their once glorious positions have been overturned in favor of Rome. These Greek writers do not need to spell out the implication—that would have been impolitic—that Rome, too, must one day yield to some other power.

All of this is also basic to Josephus's outlook and language. He routinely connects Rome's power with fortune, while at the same time emphasizing reversals and so implicitly emphasizing the temporary nature of Rome's rule. "Fortune" words appear seventy-eight times in the *War* alone. Complementing military strength, fortune has brought about the rise of Rome (*War* 7.203) and the elevation to power of Vespasian (4.622) and Titus (5.88; 6.57, 413). As Josephus acknowledges in a prayer before his surrender (3.354), the Jews must accept with every other nation that fortune has passed over to Rome, a point conceded even by the rebels (3.359). Fortune is a fickle power, however, and the prologue to the *War* emphasizes this language of reversal (1.5, 23), especially in Jerusalem's recent upheaval (1.11–12; cf. 6.408). Josephus's own character best encapsulates the catastrophe that befell his people. Near the end of book 3, when he appears as a captive before the Roman generals Vespasian and Titus, Titus reflects "how powerful was fortune, how abrupt was collapse in battle; human affairs were simply not stable" (3.396). This meditation, befitting the great-souled general at the moment of his ostensible military victory, anticipates Titus's later Scipio-like reflections at the fall of Jerusalem (6.411–413).

Just as Josephus shares with other Mediterranean aristocrats a language for understanding Rome, so also he portrays himself and his class as caught in the same general dilemma faced by others under Roman rule. His is a proud people with a glorious past, which the *War* narrates beginning with the Hasmonean state, in which he finds his own ancestry. The Hasmoneans had successfully rebelled against a much larger and interfering foreign power (the Seleucid kingdom, most notoriously led by Antiochus IV) and had carved an independent state for themselves, which lasted roughly a century (140–40 B.C.E.). But whereas many of Josephus's contemporaries looked back to this Hasmonean past as a model for rebellion against the current power, Josephus includes that history so as to reinterpret it in crucial ways. Most obviously, he has the Hasmoneans succeed in part by making alliances with the Romans. One of the first things that the renowned national hero Judah Maccabee does—apparently a deliberate anachronism on Josephus's part (cf. 1 Macc 8)—is to make such a treaty (*War* 1.38), and the first thing his brother Jonathan does is to renew it (1.48).

Contrary to rebel claims, this means that independence and freedom have never been absolute, even in the glory days. Jerusalem has traditionally found its self-rule, as do the formerly powerful Greek cities, *within* the sphere of the world power. One of the noteworthy features of the brief Hasmonean narrative (*War* 1.31–122) is the flexibility of the Jewish priestly, aristocratic leaders in accommodating themselves to any power, when it is advantageous to their own state. This is not weakness or indecisiveness but, on the contrary, practical wisdom. Josephus then moves on to a master of such shifting alliances, King Herod (ruled 37–4 B.C.E.), the most famous Judean ruler known to the Romans.

In a surprisingly detailed account of Herod's reign—considering that the book is mainly about the Judean-Roman war a century later—Josephus emphasizes both Herod's friendship with Rome and his ability to change personal loyalties at the drop of a hat during the long Roman civil wars (60s to 31 B.C.E.). The Jewish king and his father support first Julius Caesar, until his death in 44 B.C.E. (1.187), then one of Caesar's enemies and murderers, Cassius (1.221), and then after the defeat of Herod's "friend" Cassius, Marc Antony and Cleopatra (1.242–244, 282). Finally, after Octavian defeated Antony and Cleopatra, and in spite of his close alliance with that ultimate power couple, Herod manages to become an exemplary client of the general who would soon be known as the Emperor Augustus (1.386–392). The last shift was most impressive of all, and Josephus dwells on it. This dizzying movement of allegiances prevents the reader from assuming that the Judean leaders are motivated by ideological or even personal attachment; rather, they take bold and deft steps to accommodate whatever power God has allowed to rise, to ensure the survival of their state. Josephus drives home this point on several occasions culminating with his own speech before the walls of Jerusalem, in which he insists—in a rhetorical *tour de force* that cheerfully contradicts the biblical source and even his own Hasmonean story—that the Jews have never prospered in taking up arms, but succeeded only when they followed the path of peace and entrusted their affairs to God (5.399). Whereas some scholars have questioned Josephus's knowledge of the Bible in light of such claims, we should rather see him doing exactly what Plutarch recommended to statesmen (*Mor.* 814c), namely sanitizing the national history to avoid exciting thoughts of military glory.

Although Josephus makes as much as he can of Herod's exemplary relations with Rome for the purposes of the *War* (this portrait will change dramatically in the *Antiquities*), he also takes every opportunity to observe that the nation's proper leaders are people like himself, the hereditary priestly aristocracy. Monarchy, he implies, was an aberration from the nation's traditions. In making this point he subtly implies a parallel between Judean tradition and its Roman counterpart, for the Romans also had a profound distaste for monarchy, ever since their own experience of it degenerating into tyranny.

Having identified himself as an aristocratic priest in the opening sentence (1.3), Josephus points out that the heroic leaders of the nation were also priests (1.36) and assumed the high priesthood (1.53, 68). Josephus emphasizes that the Hasmoneans began to go astray with Aristobulus I (104 B.C.E.), who was the first priest to proclaim himself king, many centuries after the biblical monarchy ended. Decline was inevitable and swift (1.69). Significantly, according to Josephus it was a Roman governor (Gabinius, in about 57 B.C.E.) who restored the nation to its native priestly "aristocracy," and the Jews were greatly relieved to be thus "freed" from the rule of an individual—though of course they were part of Rome's empire (1.170). Following the experiment in client-kingship represented by Herod, the people plead with the Roman emperor not be subjected to another king, one of Herod's sons, but to be granted "autonomy" or self-rule under Roman rule (2.22, 80–92). Whereas we tend to think that Judea was inevitably oppressed by the simple fact of being under Roman rule, and that was evidently the view of some at the time, Josephus and many of his class saw it otherwise. A Roman governor both excluded tyrannical native monarchy and checked popular unrest, freeing the priestly aristocracy to exercise their traditional power without interference. Much as Polybius and Plutarch had seen the Roman general Flamininus as, paradoxically, the "liberator" of Greece from Greek tyrants and civil war (Plutarch, *Flam.* 11.7), so Josephus views the Romans as the ultimate check on civil war led by Jewish tyrants and on their pollution of the sacred priestly center in Jerusalem (5.256–257; cf. 1.9–10).

Self-rule by Jewish aristocrats under distant Roman rule is the ideal Josephus describes, from bygone days and as context for his story. What happens when popular militancy gets completely out of hand? That is the story of the rest of the *War.* Polybius had seen the disaster of Corinth's destruction, and Plutarch's advice was simply to avoid such dangerous uprisings at all costs. Essentially, Josephus's point seems to be that he and his priestly colleagues did everything they possibly could to ease the situation. As he describes it, however, the recent problems began with a series of increasingly serious provocations by Roman governors, starting with Pontius Pilate (26–36 C.E.) and culminating with Gessius Florus in 66 C.E. (2.169–277). Further incitement came from the cities bordering Judea (2.232–292). In times of such distress, as every political leader knew, there was always the potential that some persuasive speakers would arouse the populace. This had happened after Herod's death in 4 B.C.E., as Josephus explains, with quite serious consequences (2.39–79). But at that time, in spite of extreme provocation by a Roman official and with the arrival of the Roman governor and his legions, the Jewish aristocrats had successfully (and somewhat improbably) defended most of the populace against any charge of insurrection. The governor had departed shortly thereafter (2.72–79).

In the case of the recent war, however, the provocations came from various quarters, after a much longer history of abuse, and there were many more popular leaders to stir things up. To get a fair sense of the narrative, it is important to realize that the senior aristocracy are by no means pliant or sycophantic pawns of Rome. They appear genuinely torn between their aim of keeping the peace internally and their deep sympathy with the grievances of the people.

Under the governor Gessius Florus (64–66 C.E.), the Jewish leaders of Josephus's narrative face their ultimate test. This man, he claims, was thoroughly corrupt and was even willing to drive the nation to war with Rome in order to divert attention from his own misdeeds. When the leaders see what he is made of, they try to bribe him to remain on their side (2.287–288), though even this does not work. After he pillages the treasures of the sacred temple, some younger men in Jerusalem mockingly pass around a basket to take up a collection for the "poor" governor (2.295). When he becomes enraged at news of this ridicule and demands to know who is responsible, the leaders wisely (again, improbably) plead complete ignorance, citing the foolishness of youth as well as the peaceful disposition of the population as a whole (2.304). Yet Florus vents his rage, punishing by flogging and crucifixion many of the leaders, including some Jewish aristocrats who hold Roman citizenship (2.306–308). Even after such severe provocation, however, the surviving leaders implore the furious masses to remain peaceful and not to bring catastrophe on the city.

This bending over backwards does not stop Florus, however, who understands the peacemaking role of the aristocrats so well that he can exploit it. He tells them that if they persuade the people to greet his troops respectfully, all will be forgiven, but then he instructs his soldiers to ignore the friendly greeting and, if anyone complains, to charge the crowds and kill anyone in the way (2.322). Predictably, this action ignites a major riot and the war is now more or less in motion from the Jewish side.

These examples illustrate the tightrope that the Judean aristocracy walked, according to Josephus's presentation, which fits well with what we know of the challenges facing aristocrats in other regions of the empire. Addressing the people, leaders were firm in calling for peace and reason, but to the Romans they were willing to undertake even personally hazardous missions to plead the innocence of the entire populace. This attitude is best depicted in King Agrippa II, who visits Jerusalem from his territories to the northeast for a feast. Before the major speech that Josephus gives him, the leading Jews report the outrageous actions of the governor Florus. "At this," Josephus claims, "Agrippa became indignant, but he strategically transferred his anger to those whom he really pitied, the Jews, wanting to bring down their high thoughts [of rebellion]" (2.337). And they understood his good intentions, Josephus claims. In the major speech that follows, Agrippa fully sympathizes with the popular anger at the governor's behavior, which is "unbearably harsh" (2.352). At the same time he points out that the central Roman government far away knows nothing of this and that to go war with them because of the local governor is a foolish way of seeking redress (2.350).

Ultimately, however, even Agrippa is unable to restrain popular emotion, and a number of fateful things happen in quick succession. Some of the more rebellion-minded men seize the stronghold of Masada (2.408), and one of the prominent younger chief priests leads his colleagues in stopping all sacrifices from foreigners, and therefore the twice-daily sacrifice offered for the welfare of the emperor (2.409–410). Youthful hotheads, including young aristocrats such as Eleazar, appear frequently in Josephus's narrative as the agents of extreme and perilous reaction (e.g., *War* 1.109, 463, 649–651; 2.225, 286, 409, 595). In any case, though the senior chief priests favor peace, they can no longer stop those preferring revolution; they fall to the last resort of begging for help from the Romans themselves (2.418). But when the Roman governor of Syria finally comes to Jerusalem with his Twelfth Legion, he unaccountably decides, after a short siege, to withdraw. The Jewish revolutionaries pursue and trap the legion in a steep mountain pass, which allows them to destroy almost the entire force. This unexpected victory naturally fuels them with great confidence—violating the principle concerning self-congratulation in moments of triumph (2.513–555).

At this point, the Jewish aristocracy faces a clear choice: to leave the nation to its own devices or to stay and bear the people's fate even though the rebellion is doomed. Josephus describes both responses, the former disparagingly: "they swam away from the city as from a sinking ship" (2.556). This he contrasts with the image of public figures as determined helmsmen, an image that is followed by Josephus himself and by chief priests such as Ananus and Jesus. They remain to take leadership of the revolt. Now we begin to see why Josephus thinks so highly of Ananus and Jesus, making their deaths the turning point in the narrative. While they lived, Judea's historic priestly nobility were still trying to manage an impossibly difficult situation, and this was the last hope for the nation. Once Josephus had surrendered in Galilee and these great men were gone from Jerusalem, the war was exclusively in the hands of self-serving "tyrants" and no hope remained for the city.

It may seem strange that Josephus and his aristocratic colleagues should join a revolt that they did not support, and many scholars suspected that he is simply making up their opposition to the war after the fact in an effort at exoneration. But this seems to me implausible for two reasons. First, he does not hide their activity in the war, but on the contrary devotes a good deal of space from books 2 to 4 to celebrate it and his own achievements as general—achievements anticipated in the first sentence of the prologue (1.3). Second, as we have seen, it was part of the ethos of the Mediterranean aristocrat, part of the shared and well understood values, that the privileged public figure lived and died with his people, even if a catastrophe befalling the state was not of his own choosing (Plutarch, *Mor.* 815d). Although there were hints of individual freedom of conscience in antiquity, by and large the values of the aristocrat were corporate, social, and public. Josephus defined himself primarily in relation to the group.

He has nothing but praise for his own character (even when that character engages in deliberate deceit of the masses) and for his kindred spirit Ananus, the supreme commander of the revolt. Josephus points out the difficulty of the latter's position. He fortified Jerusalem and prepared as fully as possible for war, but still had "the intention to bring the insurgents and the recklessness of the so-called Zealots over to the advantageous route, as he gradually sidelined the preparations for war" (2.651). Ananus did not live to achieve this goal, because he lost the trust of other rebel leaders, who suspected that he intended to betray their cause. Josephus's editorial evaluation of this man at his death highlights their shared aristocratic values and criteria: "Along with the gravity resulting from his noble birth, status, and the honor he had achieved, he eagerly accorded equal honor to the humblest folk; unique in his love of freedom, and a partisan of democracy, he invariably placed the public advantage . . . above his private rewards" (4.319). Public figures were (at their best) committed only to what was most beneficial for their people. That is the peculiar sense in which Josephus means "democracy" here (e.g., Polybius 6.4.4). Ananus paid for his commitment to the people with his life, honorably if tragically. As Josephus constructs this narrative character, Ananus aimed at maintaining his nation's self-respect, on the one side, and preserving peace as well as possible, on the other.

(b) To look at all this from the other side, as Josephus also does, the ultimate failure of the hereditary upper class to maintain tranquility in Judea boiled down to a case of civil war. The conflict recently fought was not, as the other historical accounts and Roman public opinion commonly assumed, the uprising of an inherently rebellious people against Rome, but an internal struggle. In the prologue Josephus announces the theme:

> I have permitted my own emotions to mourn over the calamities of my native place. That it was internal sedition *[stasis]* that brought it down, and that the Judean tyrants *[tyrannoi]* drew both the Romans' unwilling hands and the fire upon the sanctuary, Titus Caesar—the very one who destroyed it—is witness. (*War* 1.9–10)

The Greek word for internal strife, *stasis* (literally, a standing), had many other applications, but in politics, sedition had been discussed for centuries as the wolf at the door of every state. Josephus makes this term his key theme in the *Jewish War.* After returning to it several times in the prologue (1.24, 25, 27), he arranges the word order at the beginning of his narrative so that the very first word is *stasis* (1.31).

He will pursue this theme chiefly in the latter half of the book, following the murder of the chief priests Ananus and Jesus. It is an assortment of illegitimate rebels who create the civil war (cf. 4.397, 401). When the Zealots first erupt in Jerusalem, Josephus claims, they make the sacred temple the headquarters of their tyranny (4.151). That tyranny is exposed by the Idumeans, whom they had brought in as allies, to kill Ananus and Jesus. The Idumeans quickly realize that their hosts, though self-appointed defenders of the city, are in fact perpetrators of a murderous "tyranny" (*War* 4.347–352). As the Idumeans leave, the Zealots decide they must now kill as many of the remaining nobles as possible in order to remove their opposition (4.356–365). One of these victims, in his dying moments, calls down upon them the curse of war, famine, and above all civil war (*stasiasantes;* 4.361–362). Tyranny has begotten *stasis.*

A few paragraphs later, Vespasian and his generals, observing the *stasis* now rampant in the city, debate whether to attack immediately, before the Jews regain their unanimity, or to allow the factions to kill each other off, the path finally chosen by Vespasian (4.366–376). Soon after, Josephus ominously cites an ancient saying to the effect that "the city would be captured and the holy sanctuary burned down by right of war whenever *stasis* should arrive and domestic hands should take the lead in polluting the sacred precinct of God" (4.388), and he begins regularly to describe the newly powerful rebel leaders as "tyrants" (4.564, 566, 569, 573). Although would-be tyrants and partial *stasis* have appeared throughout the story (e.g., 2.275–276, 433, 442, 447; 4.158, 166, 177), evidently the massacre of the nobility at the halfway point marks the definitive onset of both tyranny and factionalism *(stasis).*

After a lengthy digression on Judean geography and Roman affairs, Josephus returns at the beginning of book 5 to chart this fateful development. The *stasis* is now three-sided, he explains (5.2). "Tyrants" Eleazar son of Simon, perhaps leader of the Zealots, who had allied with John of Gischala and then the Idumeans (4.225), John of Gischala, former strongman of Galilee and Josephus's challenger there (4.208), and Simon son of Giora, recently brought into Jerusalem to check the Zealots and John (4.570–584) each command a faction (5.5–20). By *War* 5.104–105, only two factions remain, John's and Simon's. After concluding this passage by saying that he will now follow "the activities of the *stasis* in sequence" (5.20), Josephus describes the miseries inflicted on Jerusalem's populace by these leaders. His occasional references to assorted others, such as religious charlatans who deceived the pathetic masses with false hopes of salvation (6.285–287), do not detract from his main tyrant-targets. John and Simon are also the tyrants who receive attention in Josephus's final reflections on the war in book 7 (7.261).

If we ask why Josephus chose to use the familiar and highly charged, even clichéd, language of *stasis* and tyranny to describe what happened in Jerusalem, at least three reasons come to mind. First, the mere use of such hot-button words conjured up entire worlds of association—all of it bad. The most famous passage on the subject in a history was in the widely read (fifth century B.C.E.) Thucydides, *Hist.* 3.82–84, describing the terrible internal strife at Corcyra and its consequences. Tyranny was equally discussed in Greek political discourse, from Herodotus—a tyrant "skews the traditional laws, violates women, and executes the untried" (*Hist.* 3.80)—through Plato and Aristotle, Polybius and Dionysius of Halicarnassus.

Second, against any tendency to demonize the Jews and their elite class as a peculiarly rebellious people, these themes highlight their perfectly ordinary humanness. The Jews' *stasis,* though it had always been a background possibility, broke out only when the pillars of the legitimate ruling class were removed through capture by the Romans or murder by their countrymen. Jerusalem's remaining leaders could not possibly cope with the problem any further, because the rebellious elements had drawn in temporary allies from all parts of the country and beyond.

Finally, and of equal importance, when Josephus arrived in the capital in 71 C.E., Romans were only just beginning to recover from their own fresh and horribly destructive civil war. This had begun several years before Nero's suicide (June 68) with conspiracies and revolts by his generals and close associates. After Nero's death, the city had exploded into open conflict, and Rome received three emperors (Galba, Otho, Vitellius) in the year and half between Nero's death and the city's acceptance of Vespasian's rule at the end of 69. The Roman historian Livy (late first century B.C.E.) refers to tyranny often in his long history, beginning with the Roman king Amulius, who seized power and then tried to rob his brother of heirs, to preclude rivals (1.6.1). The famous Roman senator Catiline, who tried unsuccessfully to seize power in the mid-first century B.C.E., had been described as the embodiment of one lusting after tyranny (Sallust, *Bell. Cat.* 5.4–6). Plutarch features the threat of tyranny in his *Life of Caesar* (e.g., 4.8; 6.3), and Dio Chrysostom devotes an oration to the theme.

Not only does Josephus implicitly play his narrative against this background of recent Roman civil strife, but at crucial points he also explicitly connects the Judean war with Roman parallels. For example, early in the prologue he situates the Judean war's outbreak at a time when "among the Romans domestic affairs were becoming diseased" (1.4, cf. 1.23), disease being the common metaphor for political unrest. We have seen that throughout book 1 he frequently mentions figures from Rome's first-century B.C.E. civil wars as background to Judean history of the same period. For the Jewish-Roman war, too, he briefly recalls the main lines of the Roman civil war in 69 C.E., but then refrains from exploring it because it is already well known to his audience (4.496). He mentions Titus's trip to greet the new emperor Galba, which was aborted because of that ruler's assassination and replacement by Otho—"the Roman empire was reeling" (4.502). A little later he declares pointedly, "Not only in Judea was there *stasis* and civil war, but also in Italy" (4.545–548). This minor theme of *Roman* civil war symbolically concludes at the same moment as the Judean conflict. Vespasian's rise, which was made possible only by his Judean victory, also furnished him with the authority to end the rivalry in Rome itself. Josephus describes the shared triumphal march of Vespasian and Titus, as well as the dedication of the Temple of Peace beside the Roman forum, as marking the end of both internal Roman strife and the foreign war in Judea (*War* 7.157). The point of all this seems clear enough: Josephus implies that if the Judean aristocrats failed to contain tyrants and sedition, their Roman counterparts, who had so many more resources at their disposal, did no better.

(c) On the basis of this fairly sophisticated and nuanced substructure—the Jewish hereditary aristocracy did more than could be expected in managing the popular outrage caused by local Roman provocations, and the civil war that finally overwhelmed the city was of the predictable sort—Josephus develops two other themes that pointedly confront the standard Roman assumptions. First, Titus may have destroyed the temple, but he and his legions (and their gods) really had little to do with the Roman success in this war. Second, the Judeans were not a pushover for the mighty Romans, as everyone jeers, but their barely trained and desperate ranks often proved more than a match for the renowned legions.

In a passage quoted above from *War*'s prologue (1.10), Josephus refers to "the Romans' unwilling hands" as the immediate cause of the fire that burned down the temple. He continues by saying of Titus:

> Toward the populace [of Jerusalem], kept under guard by the insurgents [i.e., the tyrants], he showed mercy throughout the entire war; and often, deliberately postponing the capture of the city, he gave opportunity even during the siege for a change of mind on the part of those responsible. (*War* 1.10)

Josephus's image as a mouthpiece for, or patsy of, the Flavian rulers has been justified by many such passages. Throughout the *War* Josephus consistently displaces Vespasian and especially Titus from their apparent role as Jerusalem's destroyers. Even though Titus and his armies obviously did the deed in the end (*War* 1.10; *Ant.* 20.250), Josephus insists that this was never their intention. Concluding the lengthy story of how the temple was burned, 6.266 states: "So in this way the sanctuary was set on fire *against Caesar's will*" (emphasis added). Although this may sound like praise of Titus, the famous "clemency of Titus" theme presents more problems than readers customarily realize.

The standard argument is that Josephus wished to shield Titus from blame for the temple's destruction by pinning it on the Jewish rebels. The most obvious motive has seemed to be that he hoped to improve his powerful friend's reputation. All the other evidence, however, from the Roman triumph itself and the celebratory measures mentioned above to a passage in the fifth-century Christian chronicler Sulpicius Severus, indicate that Titus had not the slightest hesitation about killing everyone who got in his way and utterly destroying the rebels' temple fortress. The passage from Severus, though written by a Christian author several centuries after the fact, is thought to borrow from the much earlier and more reliable Roman historian Tacitus (in a lost section of his *Histories*), who lived his adult life in the generation after Jerusalem's fall. The passage in question (*Chron.* 2.30.6–7) claims that in the war council convened by Titus to discuss the fate of Jerusalem, it was he who firmly decided for destruction. In Josephus's account (*War* 5.236–243), Titus decides to preserve the sacred temple—though his intention is ultimately confounded by God. The conclusion that Josephus was trying to conceal Titus's violent intent in order to improve the young emperor's image has seemed obvious.

Yet if we think of the concrete situation in Rome, this explanation is insufficient. The Flavian rulers reveled in their violent destruction of Jerusalem and its temple, which they later portrayed as vividly as possible to their people. Such harsh dealing with intransigent rebels was required by Roman elite values. Softness would only encourage the troublemakers. This particular bloody conquest of Jerusalem, this toughness, was the very foundation of the new regime's reputation.

We are faced with a fairly clear choice in reading Josephus. Was he trying *to shield Titus from blame* for the destruction of Jerusalem and its temple, or rather trying in a subtle way *to deny him the credit* for that event? Josephus knew what everyone was saying in Rome, and how the imperial family themselves were portraying the war. They did not need someone to present them in a kinder and gentler way. If Josephus was writing mainly for a Roman audience, did he really hope to persuade Romans of a picture that was contrary to the official and accepted line? Or was he rather trying to undercut the Flavians' self-representation in the least offensive manner, by attributing to them one set of virtues—clemency, mildness, and relentless forgiveness—in order to deny them another—taking mighty Jerusalem by force of arms, brilliant generalship, and the favor of the Roman gods? It seems that the latter reading explains the evidence. Josephus's over-the-top praise of Titus's kindheartedness, far from being obsequious flattery, is in fact spiked with irony.

If we consider Josephus's portrait of Titus's activities as general against the background described above, the point seems clear. Titus's first significant military engagement comes in Galilee, while his father Vespasian is still supreme commander. Vespasian delegates his son, with a thousand-strong professional cavalry force, to take the northern base of local strongman John (*War* 4.84–120), a town called Gischala (modern Gush Halav). This is an opportunity for the younger general (about thirty-one at the time) to achieve glory for himself.

When Titus offers the Gischalan population terms of surrender, rather than devastation by his formidable cavalry, John ("a trickster of extremely wily character"; *War* 4.85) replies that Titus must first allow them to observe the approaching Sabbath (4.101). Unbelievably, Titus is not only persuaded by this rebel leader's gambit (4.104)—Josephus observes that John "bluffed" him (4.103)—but he also fails to take even the elementary safeguard, facetiously recommended by John, of "camping around the city's perimeter" (4.101)! Instead, he removes his force to the secure embrace of Kedasa (4.104), a satellite town of coastal Tyre. Predictably, Titus's withdrawal allows not only John himself but a vast train of combatants and their families to escape during the night, unimpeded by the gullible Roman general (4.106). Even though Josephus graciously credits Titus's failure to divine causes (God was "preserving John to bring final ruin upon the city of the Jerusalemites," 4.104), his portrait of the Roman general certainly differs from the common perception in Rome.

Tellingly, Josephus implies that he himself was considerably more astute than young Titus. In the Roman era, warfare had much to do with stratagems *(stratēgoi)*, the tricks and ruses of generals to outfox their enemies. Josephus's accounts of his own generalship in *War* 3 and the *Life* are filled with such tactics, made famous in Roman tradition by the general Julius Caesar in his *Gallic War*. Whereas Josephus understood the trick from the start, Titus had to learn the hard way that "in hostilities mercy was mischievous" (*War* 5.329). This episode is introduced by a remarkable editorial observation from Josephus. The Jewish combatants, he says, were careless of their own suffering. In true martial spirit they considered their own deaths trivial if they could but kill one of the enemy. "Titus, on the other hand, was taking precautions for the security of his soldiers as much as for their victory" (*War* 5.316).

In the narrative that follows, the innocent Titus is painfully slow to learn from such encounters but continues to show gentle patience while the Jewish fighters cause him and his soldiers extreme anxiety and loss of life by their "daring" (*War* 6.12, 29–32, 78–79, 152–156, 190). Even after Titus hears about the abomination of Mary's cannibalism in Jerusalem (see chapter 1) and determines—again—to move decisively against the rebels, his assaults are repelled by the Jews' clever tactics, resulting in great loss of Roman life (*War* 6.214–227). "Titus, as he observed that sparing these foreign sacred precincts had meant only injury and slaughter for his troops, ordered them to set the gates on fire" (*War* 6.228). Nevertheless, Josephus stresses Titus's helplessness in the face of divine control. He convenes the war council mentioned above, but allegedly decides after all to extinguish the flames around the temple in order to preserve it (*War* 6.236–243). God thwarts his plans (6.250), having ordained that the polluted sanctuary must go. At best Titus, who "happened to be resting in his tent after the fighting," can only be informed that the temple is burning (*War* 6.254). His utter helplessness is unsettling to watch. He shouts and waves to no avail. His own legionaries, famed for their severe discipline, pretend not to hear him. He is unable to restrain the impetuosity of the frenzied soldiers, who go on a rampage. Indeed, only after the temple has been set ablaze, and the long conflict is all but concluded, does Titus decide that "everything from now on would go according to the law of war. To the soldiers he gave the signal to burn and plunder the city" (*War* 6.353), a truly decisive move, but perhaps a little late.

On one level, all of this might have had a certain plausibility for a war-experienced audience, since it was an open secret that although military commanders worked hard to maintain the image of control and discipline, they could not manage their soldiers in such circumstances.[7] But Josephus chooses what and how to narrate. Against the background of that audience's prior knowledge, this whole presentation appears ironic. Josephus plays with the theme of Titus's clemency, using it to portray him as an innocent caught in the wily war-fighting of the Judeans, in which Josephus himself was also fully adept. At the same time, his notice that Titus finally decided to unleash the typical Roman hell on the enemy gives him an exit strategy for explaining the outcome that everyone well knew. While systematically undermining the Flavian representation of the war, he offers Titus the naive clemency of a humanist as consolation prize (cf. *War* 6.356). Contrast Josephus's own clemency as general in the *Life* (99–103, 169, 307, 329, 375, 385, 388), which is always balanced by a matchless ability to see through his enemies' tricks (*Life* 148, 163, 169, 265, 379).

If we return to our question—Is Josephus absolving Titus from blame or denying him the credit?—it seems that we may be fairly confident of the solution. The standard reading goes astray in assuming an opposition between Titus and the Jewish rebel leaders as the cause of Jerusalem's destruction. Instead "it was internal sedition that brought it down, and . . . the Judean tyrants drew both the Romans' unwilling hands and the fire upon the sanctuary" (*War* 1.10). Josephus does not mean that the rebels (rather than the Romans) actually destroyed the temple. He means that the rebels' actions led the God of the Jews to destroy the temple by purging his sanctuary with fire through the agency of Roman hands. God was in control of the whole scene. If Josephus moves responsibility from the Romans to God, then we must conclude that destruction was a formidable achievement for which he is unwilling to allow the Romans credit.

---

[7] Adam Ziolkowski, "*Urbs Direpta,* or How the Romans Sacked Cities," in *War and Society in the Roman World* (ed. John Rich and Graham Shipley; London: Routledge, 1993), 69–91.

Indeed, Josephus says this plainly and often throughout the story. Early in the narrative King Agrippa II speaks of divine support for the Romans and of the inevitability that God would punish the rebels when they violated the laws in prosecuting the war (2.390–395). Josephus attributes to divine agency the fateful withdrawal of Cestius's legion from Jerusalem, which gave the rebels great hope and thus ignited the war (2.539). During the heat of the later conflict, he remarks again and again on God's use of the Romans to purge the temple (5.367–368, 378, 408–412, 442–445; 6.251). If the Romans had not acted according to script, Josephus claims, God would have caused the very earth to swallow up the Jewish rebels (5.566). Most important, Titus is made to concede repeatedly that only with the help of "the Deity" or "God" can his army overcome the Jews and their indomitable fortress (6.39–40, 126–128). At the crucial moment, a nameless Roman soldier, "moved by a certain supernatural impulse" (6.252), ignites the fateful fire against Titus's will. Consider in particular the last major speech of the *War,* which is given to Eleazar at Masada. He makes the point with extreme lucidity: the rebels lost because they were fighting God, not the Romans (7.331–333). And so he admonishes his colleagues:

> Do not affix the blame to yourselves, and *do not credit the Romans,* that this war against them has ruined us all, for it was *not their might* that brought these things about, but a more powerful Agent has intervened and furnished them with *the appearance of victory.* (7.360; emphasis added)

Although we should not simply trust any of the speeches Josephus writes for his characters as journalistic reports, still this one accords with the consistent theme of the *War:* not the Romans, not even Titus, but the Jewish God destroyed the temple.

Now, although Josephus consistently denies the Roman imperial family the credit that they have emphatically claimed, I do not mean to suggest that he is openly critical of his patrons. To have mounted an open challenge might have been suicidal; at the very least it would have cost Josephus an audience and a voice. When a historian such as Tacitus begins to write after Domitian's death, he portrays the preceding period as one of terror for those who wished to speak plainly (*Agr.* 1.1–3). Poets who wrote in the period, such as Martial, Statius, and Valerius Flaccus, have been accused of the most extreme sort of flattery, and the prologue to Josephus's *War* similarly characterizes his contemporaries. Yet Josephus has much to say in the *War* about Titus's personal courage or Vespasian's wisdom. He even claims that the springs near Jerusalem, which had begun to fail, gushed again with Titus's arrival in the region (*War* 5.409–411). What are we to make of such praise?

In imperial Rome—and under tyrannical governments ever since[8]—if writers wished to maintain their self-respect they had to resort to safe criticism, through coded or figured speech. If both the writer and the audience understood that the writer intended more than (or different from) what was actually said, such communication was called "ironic." I am suggesting that much of Josephus's *War* should be read in this light. We know that he had a taste for doubletalk because he credits both himself and his adversaries in Galilee with such deception, more or less constantly (e.g., *Life* 17–22, 40, 85–87, 126–144, 163, 175–178, 217–218). Rhetorical education and its widely disseminated values meant that no one took speech at face value. At any given time there was a good chance that a speaker or writer was dissembling or playing with words in some way.

In Josephus's treatment of the imperial family, a good case in point seems to be his portrait of the eighteen-year-old Domitian (*War* 7.75–88). At the very beginning of Vespasian's reign, while the emperor was still absent from the capital, tribes in Gaul and Germany revolted. Apparently, the teenaged Domitian disobeyed the advice of his father's advisers and joined up with a seasoned general's march to the scene. Before they had come anywhere near the fighting, however, another general put down the revolt. According to common rumors, young Domitian was disdained by the Roman generals and rebuffed when he asked for his own command. His father was furious when he learned of the youth's recklessness and forced him to live under his eye in Rome. In response Domitian withdrew from public life for a long time (so Suetonius, *Dom.* 2; Tacitus, *Hist.* 4.75–85).

Yet in Josephus's hands, this apparently well-known story becomes an absurd hymn to Domitian's prowess: "Enjoying his father's manliness by natural inheritance, and having perfected his training beyond

---

[8] Vasily Rudich, an ancient historian who emigrated from the former Soviet Union, compares the doublespeak he finds in the texts of imperial Rome with his experience under a modern authoritarian regime: *Political Dissidence under Nero: the Price of Dissimulation* (London: Routledge, 1993); *Dissidence and Literature under Nero: The Price of Rhetoricization* (London: Routledge, 1997). See also Shadi Bartsch, *Actors in the Audience: Theatricality and Doublespeak from Nero to Hadrian* (Cambridge, Mass.: Harvard University Press, 1994).

that suited to his age, against the barbarians he immediately marched. They, crumbling at the report of his approach, gave themselves entirely over to him, finding subjection under the same yoke again, without suffering disaster, a great advantage over their fear [of Domitian]" (*War* 7.87). Then, when he had "put all the affairs of Gaul in order," he returned to Rome, to illustrious honor and universal admiration (*War* 7.88). It seems equally unlikely either that the citizens of Rome did not know the story of Domitian's embarrassment and looked to the foreign writer Josephus to inform them, or that they knew other versions but were still willing to be persuaded by Josephus of a story more favorable to Domitian. His extreme language already invites skepticism. Had Domitian really enjoyed a triumphant return to Rome after this episode? People would have known very well that this was not true. If so, then Josephus's story could only be read ironically.

The theme of Titus's extreme clemency and patience is not as obviously ironic. Still, against the common Roman perception of Titus as Jerusalem's fearless conqueror, Josephus's long-suffering and gullible gentleman Titus comes off as quite an alter ego. The great advantage of criticism with excessive praise, however, is that it is much harder for the victim-honoree to deal with than either outright condemnation or too-faint praise. Powerful rulers are unlikely to challenge those who offer praise. Although the story about Domitian's youthful exploits was patent nonsense, and everyone knew it, the emperor was not about to counter with the truth of his embarrassing behavior. In a similar way, since Josephus distances Titus from Jerusalem's fall by praising his long-suffering clemency, Titus could hardly object. That is especially so if Zvi Yavetz is correct in arguing that Titus needed more of a reputation for clemency just when he was approaching accession to imperial power.[9] But such a need for favorable press by itself hardly explains Josephus's account, which at a basic level undercuts the Flavian claim to have conquered Jerusalem by military virtue and the favor of Rome's gods.

(d) The other side of this coin, and the other way we can tell that Josephus is not serving any sort of Roman propaganda, is his determined effort to balance the pro-Roman accounts of the war by insisting upon the valor of his countrymen. Here we return to our original ob-

[9] Zvi Yavetz, "Reflections on Titus and Josephus," *Greek, Roman, and Byzantine Studies* 16 (1975): 411–32.

servations about Josephus as Jewish-Judean aristocrat, whose identity is inextricably bound with that of his people. He will not allow the Roman legions to accept any glory for their defeat of his people. Scholars have seized on his famous digression on the Roman army (*War* 3.70–109)—"perfect discipline"; fortitude of body and soul; never beaten by numbers, by trickery or ruses, by difficulties of ground, or even by fortune—as a primary statement of his views. The problem with this conclusion is that the bulk of his narrative concerning the Roman legions in action against the Jews contradicts it. We are faced again with irony. Josephus establishes the alleged invincibility of the Roman army as a premise from which he may demonstrate the remarkable achievements of the Jews who fought for Jerusalem, even of the rebels with whom he shared no philosophical ground.

He opens the prologue by complaining about the pro-Roman accounts of the war. The issue is so basic to his own reasons for writing that he continues at some length: "I just do not see how those who have conquered insignificant people should seem to be great. . . . I certainly have had no intention of contending with those who heap praise on the Romans' deeds by exalting those of my compatriots. No, I shall go through the actions of *both sides* with precision" (1.8–9; emphasis added). Josephus's promise that he will balance the pro-Roman and anti-Judean accounts is fulfilled with surprising consistency in the narrative. For most engagements he will point out which fighters distinguished themselves on each side.

Examples of Jewish military virtue are anticipated in book 1, where the Hasmonean irregulars overcome impossible odds to create a Judean state (1.36–39, 43–44, 53), and where Herod's armies, too, are the scourge of the region, even when outnumbered, because of their courage (1.380–385). In book 2 the lengthy description of the Essenes includes a passage concerning their courage in war, with specific reference to the recent war with Rome and their contempt for death—when tortured in every possible way by the Romans (2.150–153). The Essenes' cheerful disregard for death and unbreakable spirit are, incidentally, virtues that Josephus will later attribute to all Jews (*Ag. Ap.* 1.42–43).

Predictably, the fullest continuous portrait of Judean courage and cleverness in battle is connected with the general Josephus himself as commander of Galilee. He first trains his soldiers on Roman lines (*War* 2.569–582) and then masterfully puts down the internal opposition to his generalship by one ruse after another (2.585–646). Even when

Vespasian's army of some sixty thousand professional legionaries and auxiliary soldiers arrives outside Josephus's Galilean fortress at Jotapata, he claims that the sight "stimulated the Judeans to acts of daring, for nothing is more conducive to martial valor in war than necessity" (3.149). Josephus himself leads raiding parties into the thick of this overwhelming force (3.153–154). Then, as if he had read Caesar's *Gallic War* and Frontinus's *Stratagems*, he uses every trick in the book, including the pouring of boiling oil and fenugreek down the slopes, to demoralize the enemy—delaying the fateful day as long as possible. Vespasian himself is wounded in this conflict (3.236), Josephus proudly notes, causing temporary Roman despair.

Josephus's habit of singling out Judean soldiers for special mention, as if in dispatches, is not limited to his own campaign at Jotapata (e.g., 3.229–230). It increases when he describes the siege of Jerusalem, where he has no ideological commitment to the defenders. At 6.147–148 he even lists the Judean heroes according to the faction to which they belonged: Simon's, John's, the Idumeans', and so on. When Titus arrives on Mount Scopus and the Mount of Olives with his four imposing legions, the Judeans within the city respond not with mortal terror, but by uniting their forces and rushing out against the Tenth Legion. Josephus emphasizes here the confusion and disorder of the Roman force, which was driven from its new camp until Titus was able to restore temporary order by his courageous example (5.71–84). Immediately after being driven back down the slope, however, the Judeans renew their attack, prompting most of the legion to flee up the hill so that even the men guarding Titus advise him to retreat (5.85–97). A series of ruses gives the Judeans time and temporary advantage in the long war. Josephus comments, for example:

> Often they [the Judeans] would dash out from the gates and fight hand to hand. Though driven back upon the walls and defeated in these close combats, being unskilled in the Romans' know-how, they prevailed in rampart-warfare. Whereas experience combined with strength encouraged the Romans, for the Judeans it was daring fed by fear, as well as *their natural determination in calamities.* (5.305–306; emphasis added).

Soldiers are supposed to take risks, as Josephus makes clear in his praise of both Romans and Judeans who gave up their lives in heroic suicide missions, and as Titus himself affirms in other contexts (cf. 6.33).

In one such passage the Judean factions temporarily overcome their differences to provide a common front against the Roman battering rams, and thus find some success (*War* 5.277–278). The Judeans rush through a concealed gate and, carrying firebrands, determine to reach the Roman trenches. Though the legionnaires turn to face them, Josephus recounts, "the daring of the Judeans overtook the discipline of the Romans, and having routed those whom they first encountered they pressed ahead against the troops who were gathering up" (6.285). In the ensuing chaos, Judean desperation was proving superior and would probably have won the day, Josephus claims, had not an elite Alexandrian force been there to hold the ground ("for the most part") until Titus arrived (5.287–288).

Josephus even claims that when the Romans completed a new set of earthworks after losing previous efforts to Judean counterstrikes, it was the Romans who were the more dejected. Their despondency resulting from these efforts prompts Josephus to include a number of speeches—one for Vespasian and three for Titus—devoted to rallying the desperate legions in the face of apparent Judean invincibility. After suffering a serious setback in Gamala, for example, Vespasian must console his troops with thoughts about fortune's reversal, while also gently reminding them of good Roman military tactics against this "barbarian" enemy (4.39–48). Titus's first such speech, before the battle for Tarichea in Galilee, is filled with references to the Judeans' refusal to accept defeat even in adversity (3.472–484). His best hope is to reassure his troops that reinforcements are on the way (3.481). But even after those massive reinforcements arrive, including two thousand archers, Josephus relates that the Judeans hold out until they are actually pierced by lances and run over by horses (3.487–488). In another speech, following a rout in Jerusalem at Judean hands, Titus must deliver a harsh reprimand to his troops for breaking discipline (5.120–124).

Most interesting is Titus's speech when his troops discover, after exhausting themselves to destroy the wall protecting the fortress Antonia, that the defenders have built another behind it (*War* 6.33–53). Here we encounter deep despondency on the Roman side. Accordingly, the main part of Titus's oration deals with the glory that comes from death on the battlefield. Abandoning his earlier risk-aversion policy, he now lambastes his soldiers for failing to dare—unlike the Judeans, who act without hope of victory, but only to make a raw display of their courage (6.42). Titus offers the consolation that one who dies in battle is instantly released from life's miseries and suffering to come. Near the end, he adds the qualification: "Indeed those who show themselves to be men may be saved from even the most hazardous operations" (6.50). Even after this stirring speech (or because of it), Titus manages to rouse only twelve of his men, one of whom leads the charge in a spirit that Josephus frankly admires (6.46–52), though unfortunately this man slips and is killed; the other eleven die or return to the Roman side wounded.

All this would make a very peculiar kind of Roman propaganda. Gentle but courageous Titus comes off well enough personally, though not as the conqueror celebrated by Rome. As for the famous, awe-inspiring legions, they certainly have their heroes, but the contest between them and the amateur Jewish forces is by no means the walk in the park that was being advertised in Rome. The war begins with the disgraceful loss of the Twelfth Legion to Jewish irregulars in the pass at Beit-Horon (2.540–2.555; cf. 5.41), and the legions' performances do not qualitatively improve thereafter. It is only because the Judean God himself intervenes to purge the sacred temple that the Romans have even a chance of victory, according to Josephus. Thus, he writes as a proud statesman and representative of his own nation, not as a Roman. A thoughtful and humane writer, he can recognize valor and weakness, virtue and vice, on all sides. He can well understand why the war began as it did, though he thinks that if it had been left to the aristocracy, things would no doubt have turned out better. It was those power-crazed tyrants—the very ones held responsible by the Romans (John and Simon)—who prolonged the war beyond all hope and therefore caused such catastrophe. That being said, his people and their leaders are noble, courageous, and dignified, and they adhere to the basic values (e.g., piety, justice, peace, courage, dignity, and autonomy) recognized by civic leaders around the empire.

That Josephus writes in accord with values best known from Greek authors does not imply that he has suppressed his native outlook. He was raised first on traditional Judean-Jewish texts, the (Hebrew) Bible above all. Yet the Bible includes books, notably Jeremiah and Daniel, that express a view of political history quite compatible with the Greek outlook described above. The priest and prophet Jeremiah lived when the first temple was destroyed in 586 B.C.E. Because he counseled submission to the Babylonian superpower, arguing that God was using the Babylonians to punish the Jews for wickedness (including temple sacrilege), he was maligned as a traitor to the national cause. Josephus has Jeremiah in mind throughout all of his works. In the *War* he compares the recent destruction to the ancient one in several places (e.g., 5.391, 411; 6.104, 268, 437, 439). He borrows Jeremiah's theme of "lamentation" as a key term for his work (1.9, 12; 2.400, 455; 3.263, 501; 4.128, 412; 5.20, 418, 515; 6.7, 96–111, 267, 271–274). He even compares himself with the prophet as he too faces possible death at the hands of his compatriots (5.391–393). And one of the mysterious omens preceding the fall of Jerusalem, as he describes it, has a man named Jesus walking around and citing Jeremianic verse—for seven years (6.301; cf. Jer 7:34).

Moreover, the horrible famine and cannibalism story of *War* 6.193–213, discussed in chapter 1, vividly recalls Lam 2:20 (traditionally attributed to Jeremiah): "Should women eat their offspring, the children they have borne?" Similarly, the story of the rebels' assassination of priestly aristocrats evokes the end of that same verse: "Should priest and prophet be killed in the sanctuary of the Lord?" It is probably no coincidence, therefore, that Jeremiah's famous remark about the temple having become a "den of bandits [or robbers]" (Jer 7:11), which is picked up also in the gospels (Mark 11:17 and parallels), corresponds to Josephus's most typical description of the rebel leaders as bandits, who have perversely made the temple their fortress. He uses the same Greek word that the Greek Bible (Septuagint) has in Jeremiah, and charges the "bandits" of his day with much the same crimes as Jeremiah had cited (*War* 5.402; cf. Jer 7:9).

Daniel is not mentioned by name in the *War,* though we have good reason to think that Josephus also had this work in mind. Daniel was an extremely popular text in the first century, as the New Testament and many other Jewish texts from the period confirm, and even though most modern scholars date the book to about 165 B.C.E., in Josephus's day it was thought to have been written during the same period as Jeremiah. Some details in the *War* suggest Josephus's use of Daniel, but the main point is that Josephus appears to have treasured this book's analysis of political history. Daniel makes it clearer than other biblical texts that nations rise and fall under the sovereignty of God (Dan 2:21; 4:14, 22, 29). In all of this political upheaval, God will protect his own people as long as they are faithful, and it is even possible for faithful Jews to prosper in the courts of foreign kings (Dan 1:20; 2:48; 3:30; 6:29). It is entirely misguided, however, to assert oneself to end foreign domination (Dan 8:14), for only God can do that. God will bring a kingdom that is not made with human hands (Dan 2:34, 45; 8:25; compare *War* 5.400). The "wise" are those who understand God's ways (Dan 1:17, 20; 2:30, 47; 5:11–12; 11:33–35), and they should be distinguished from "the many" who are open to persuasion for good or ill (Dan 8:25; 11:33). All of this language is prominent in Josephus.

Although we students of Josephus have entertained ourselves for many decades debating whether elements are more Greek or more Jewish, most scholars recognize today that this is a futile game because it assumes artificial categories and divisions. I would suggest Josephus believed what he did because it seemed right and true, consonant with his tradition and place in the world. A case in point is the concern with temple purity and pollution that Josephus develops so fully in the *War*. The notion of temple purity may seem particularly biblical and Jewish, but we need to realize that such language was also wholly familiar to Greeks and Romans. They held temples to be inviolable, places of "asylum" ("not to be spoiled"), and believed that the deities watching over them would take revenge for any violations.[10] Livy tells the story of a Roman commander who, having regained some territory from Hannibal's army in 205 B.C.E., proceeded to rob the local temples. Those who participated in the crime, however, were driven mad and the Roman senate had to perform special sacrifices in hopes of relieving the entire nation of responsibility (29.8.8–11). This language of temple purity, pollution, and sacrifice was common throughout the ancient Mediterranean.

Before turning to Josephus's other major composition, the *Jewish Antiquities-Life*, we need to consider the question of his audience. For whom did he write, mainly? It makes a difference because the analysis above depends in part on a Roman context; if he was writing chiefly for Jews in Judea or for some other group, perhaps his remarks about Titus and the Jewish rebels might take on a different hue. Evidence, however, leads to the conclusion that he had in view primarily a non-Jewish, Greek-speaking audience in Rome itself, and only secondarily readers around the empire, whether Gentile or Jewish.

We need to bear in mind the general conditions of book publication in ancient Rome. In the first century the writing process itself was very social. Writers were usually either retired aristocrats or younger

---

[10] See Kent J. Rigsby, *Asylia: Territorial Inviolability in the Hellenistic World* (Berkeley: University of California Press, 1996).

men maintained by wealthy patrons. Josephus fell into the latter category. His patrons for the *War* may have included the imperial family, fellow Jew King Agrippa II (often resident in Rome), or even the Epaphroditus who sponsored his later works (see below). Much as he does not mention sources or other conditions of writing, he simply does not refer to his patrons in this first work. In any case, the patron-client relationship brought with it certain social responsibilities. A writer did not usually disappear to a quiet place to compose. The writing process, not the final distribution of a text, was when an author encountered these intended listeners.

As a Roman writer prepared sections of his book in draft, he would normally present it orally in after-dinner speeches or in halls rented for this purpose by his patron. That was where he met his primary audiences, and those were the people he had to persuade. He might make notes on separate sheets of papyrus or create smaller scrolls for parts of the work in preparation. Only after he was fairly confident of his text would he have it bound more securely, though even then he might need to remove a sheet and glue or stitch another one in its place. Josephus gives a hint of this process when he later notes that King Agrippa II had read pieces of the *War* in development, asking for more as it was completed, and offering additional information on certain points (*Life* 365–366). The eventual publication of a work involved only the duplication of a few copies for gift or sale and perhaps the deposit of one definitive copy in a library (*Life* 361–363; *Ag. Ap.* 1.51), where it could be further copied. In Josephus's case, the support of Titus meant that imperial resources might be used for mass hand-copying by slaves. Ancient book production was thus both more social and more personal than it is for us. It was all connected with the status of the author and, where appropriate, of the patron.

This process of production already implies that Josephus had a local audience in mind while writing. Recall what he says in the prologue concerning the other, pro-Roman historians: "[they] are collecting random and incoherent tales through hearsay, and are writing them up sophist-like" (*War* 1.1). This language confirms an atmosphere in which various writers know what their competitors are up to—through oral presentations or recitations. He is entering the fray in Rome itself. He goes on to imply that he has been "abused" by certain critics (1.13), apparently for his shortcomings in composing Greek, which he seems to have remedied by soliciting the help of collaborators in the later phases (*Ag. Ap.* 1.50). This passage assumes that he has already circulated parts of his work to a specific audience, before publication. His prologue also claims that he is "about to speak" to people who know his past misfortunes (1.22), which implies further oral presentation to a group he knows. When the work was completed, he gave and sold copies to Vespasian, Titus, King Agrippa II, and other descendants of Herodian royalty (*Life* 361–362; *Ag. Ap.* 1.50–51). All of these readers seem to have been in Rome with him.

General considerations about publication and his plain statements about his conditions of writing, therefore, indicate that Josephus envisaged a Roman audience. His assumptions about what his audience knows and does not know—what needs explaining—point in the same direction. Essentially, what the audience does not know includes Jewish law, tradition, culture, and national heroes. Josephus not only instructs them about the existence of a Jewish temple in Egypt (1.33), but also portrays at length the one in Jerusalem (5.184–247) as well as the customs and dress of its priests. He must describe in some detail Jerusalem (5.136–183), Galilee (3.35–58), and other parts of Judea (4.451–485). These are presumably the areas least familiar to his audience. Further, he feels the need to explain that: the Jewish law forbids making images (the second commandment; 1.650; 2.170); the high priest must be free of physical defect (1.270); Passover is connected with the feast of Unleavened Bread, a time of "many sacrifices" and pilgrimage (2.10); Jews have a custom of funeral banquets at the end of seven days' mourning (2.2); Jews make vows, including one that requires abstention from wine, shaving the head, and sacrifice after thirty days (i.e., the Nazirite vow; 2.313); and Jewish custom requires immediate burial of the dead (4.317). Presumably, Jews would know these things.

Yet more strikingly, Josephus must introduce to his audience virtually every figure he mentions from Judea. Although they know about earlier struggles between the Seleucids and Ptolemies for control of Syria (1.31), he must explain that the Judean Onias was a high priest (1.31) and that the Hasmoneans (who were famous among Jews) were priests, had a father named Matthias, and came from "a village called Modein" (1.36–37). He famously introduces the Pharisees, Sadducees, and Essenes—groups that anyone with a Judean heritage could be expected to know about already—describing them at a very elementary and not terribly helpful level (2.118–162). Even though Herod was the most famous of the Jewish rulers in the Roman world, his family background also requires explication (1.181).

In sharp contrast to his careful introductions of Judean figures, places, and things, Josephus assumes his audience's knowledge of Roman affairs in general. He omits any descriptions of Rome or Italy, and when he first mentions "[the emperor] Augustus and [Marcus Vipsanius] Agrippa"—that emperor's close colleague and son-in-law (*War* 1.118)—he does not see any need to explain. His first reference to the Roman general Pompey "the Great" (60s B.C.E.) does not explain who the man was, but only serves to date the Judean history to Pompey's war with Armenia (1.127). Though writing in Greek, he does not use the Greek form of Pompey's title *(Megas),* but rather transliterates the Latin *Magnus,* which was more familiar in Rome. In the same sentence he mentions two of Pompey's legates by their short names without elaboration. Quite matter-of-factly he continues, "When Pompey fled with the senate across the Ionian Sea . . ." (1.183). But when was that? The audience, evidently, should know this event from the Roman civil wars well enough to date Judean history against it. Licinius Crassus, notorious to Romans for having lost his legions at the battle of Carrhae in Parthian territory (53 B.C.E.), simply appears in the text as "Crassus" (1.179). Similarly, C. Cassius Longinus, one of Julius Caesar's later assassins, pops up without explanation as "Cassius" (1.180). Again, at 2.246 Josephus will identify Felix, the new governor of Judea, as "the brother of Pallas." This makes sense only if the audience already knows that Pallas was a hated but influential freedman-secretary of the emperor Claudius whom Nero had executed (Suetonius, *Claud.* 28–29; Tacitus, *Ann.* 12.53; Pliny, *Ep.* 7.29; 8.6).

Examples could be multiplied, but this will suffice to show that Josephus assumes his audience's fairly detailed knowledge of Roman, but not Judean, history. He continually returns to Roman affairs throughout the Judean history, as we have seen with the question of civil war. Since he does not make any such regular links with affairs in Greece, Asia Minor, Egypt, Syria, or other locations, we must conclude that the main audience he envisaged was around him, in Rome.

The final and decisive indicator that Josephus expected an educated Roman audience is the prospectus that he offers in the second half of his prologue, outlining what is to come in the following narrative (*War* 1.17–30). Careful comparison of that prospectus with the narrative that follows reveals that Josephus has artfully selected items that will appeal to a Roman audience, while omitting purely Judean-Jewish affairs—no matter how important these will become in the narrative itself. For example, of the nine personal names mentioned, only one is Jewish, the world-famous King Herod ("son of Antipater"). The others are all Roman figures (Pompey, Sossius, Varus, Cestius Gallus, Nero, Vespasian, Titus), even though some of them are not nearly as important to the story as Judah Maccabee, Josephus himself, King Agrippa II, the chief priest Ananus, or the Judean rebels John, Simon, and Eleazar of Masada.

Further, the prospectus omits such important ingredients of the coming story as: the Hasmonean dynasty; Herod's early years and military campaigns; Herod's sons and the Roman governors of Judea; the Jewish philosophical schools; causes of the war; Josephus's activities as general and his surrender (the focus of book 3); the capture of Gamala, Tabor, and Gischala; factional strife in Jerusalem; and the murders of Ananus and Jesus (most of book 4). Rather he focuses on a few paragraphs at the end of book 4 concerning Roman affairs, Jewish successes and demonstrations of unity as well as Roman setbacks and discouragement, and most of the foreign elements of book 7. Since Josephus omits what is arguably most important and distinctive about his history of the war, while emphasizing items and names that are often minor in the story itself, it seems that he is concerned not to put off a Roman audience at the outset, highlighting rather what is familiar and safe to them.

This is not to say that, following the prologue "hook," Josephus will recite only what might suit a Roman audience. To the contrary, he has challenged his audience right from the opening lines and he will do so throughout the entire book. It is a complex narrative, full of twists and turns, buts and howevers. Roman governors of Judea, from the equestrian class, tend to be no good, but everyone in Rome knows this. The masses are always keen for change and susceptible to charismatic leaders who make absurd promises, but everyone knows this, too. Josephus expects broad sympathy from his audience for the plight of the Judean aristocrats, walking the well-traveled tightropes between pleasing the mob and saying unpopular things, between submission to Rome and national self-respect.

Josephus has a group around him in Rome, of which we otherwise know little, that he must consider at least willing to be persuaded of his alternative perspective and sufficiently interested to hear him out through seven dense volumes. Though not everyone in those audiences was sympathetic (see *Life* 357; *Ag. Ap.* 1.53–56 for the *War*'s detractors), and though it is also uncertain how patiently they heard or read his work, in general it was friends and potential friends who gathered in such audiences.

JEWISH ANTIQUITIES

If we have rightly understood the main lines of Josephus's *Jewish War,* then it is well complemented by his twenty-volume *Jewish Antiquities,* which he completed a decade or more later (93 C.E.), and its appendix, the *Life.* This magnum opus was also written for a non-Jewish audience (*Ant.* 1.5, 9; 20.262). Even more obviously with such a complicated composition as this, the audience must have been positively disposed toward Josephus and Judean culture from the start. Because much of what I have said by way of contextualizing the *War* holds also for the *Antiquities,* we do not require proportionate space to discuss the longer work.

The *Antiquities-Life* is so multifaceted that scholars have struggled to find a way to sketch the whole work in one coherent outline. It is clear that the twenty volumes of the *Antiquities* fall into two symmetrical halves. The choice of twenty may have been inspired by Dionysius of Halicarnassus's Greek-language *Roman Antiquities* a century earlier, though that model is not necessary. In any case, volume 10 ends with the fall of the first temple, placing special emphasis on Jeremiah, Daniel, the exile, a list of high priests to that point, and the decisive proof that God superintends human affairs (*Ant.* 10.276–281; cf. 1.14, 20). Volume 20 concludes on the eve of the second temple's fall in Josephus's day, with a comprehensive list of high priests and kings.

The first half is chiefly a paraphrase of the Bible, which extends to *Ant.* 11. Josephus's version, however, is streamlined by his removal of duplications (e.g., Exodus-Leviticus/Deuteronomy and Kings/Chronicles), and reworked in various ways to appeal to sophisticated Gentile readers. The latter half focuses on the Hasmoneans (vols. 13–14), King Herod (vols. 14–17), and his descendants (vols. 18–20), but with considerable attention to Roman affairs as well (vols. 18–19). Thus:

Introduction (1.1–26)

Part I: First Temple (*Ant.* 1–10)

A. The lawgiver's establishment of the constitution (1–4)
B. First phase: senate, kings, and high priests of Eli's descent (5–8)
C. Second phase: decline through corruption of the constitution (9–10)

Part II: Second Temple (*Ant.* 11–20)

A. Reestablishment of the aristocracy through the glorious Hasmonean house; its decline (11–13)
B. Monarchy writ large: Herod (14–17)
C. Worldwide effectiveness of the Jewish constitution (18–20)

Conclusion (20.259–268)

Given the ancient taste for symmetry discussed above, we should consider whether the entire *Antiquities* also has a concentric structure built around volumes 10 and 11 as a fulcrum. Evidence for this kind of symmetry includes many parallels: the stories of Abraham (1.148–346) and of the royal family of Adiabene (20.17–96), both in or near Chaldea; the peerless Jewish constitution in volumes 3–4 and the Roman constitutional crisis in volumes 18–19; the courageous but deeply flawed kings Saul (vol. 6) and Herod (vols. 14–17); King David (7.290–291) and the Hasmonean John Hyrcanus (13.299–300). We should not press such parallels too hard, but in light of Josephus's interest elsewhere in concentric composition, they are worth exploring further.

The most common explanation of the *Antiquities* holds that it is an "apologetic" written for Gentiles. That is, Josephus writes to defend his nation against widespread slanders about Jewish origins and early history.[11] In a more positive vein, Gregory Sterling has charted the development of what he labels "apologetic historiography" among Oriental authors such as Josephus, and he includes the *Antiquities* in that genre (see chapter 6 below). If one reads the earlier *War* as Roman propaganda, however, the *Antiquities* must then be regarded as an abrupt change of direction toward a new nationalist pride. Either Josephus has sincerely repented of his traitorous services to Rome or he is again acting opportunistically, now trying to catch the eyes of the new rabbinic

[11] Thackeray, *Josephus,* 52.

movement in the Judean town of Jamnia/Yavneh. It used to be thought by scholars that the rabbinic movement, which would ultimately produce the Talmuds, was becoming powerful in Yavneh during Josephus's time in Rome. Having read the *War* as a pro-Roman account, they reasoned that by writing so lovingly of Jewish history and tradition in the *Antiquities* he was trying to make amends, whether sincerely—as he aged and realized his errors—or only for some immediate gain.[12] A slightly different view was that Josephus wrote for some unidentified Roman authorities, to present the Yavnean rabbis (implicitly, since they are nowhere mentioned) as the local leadership group whom the Romans should recognize in postwar Judea.[13]

The *Life* is most commonly understood as a quite separate response to Justus of Tiberias's history maligning Josephus. A minority of scholars have argued, however, that the *Life* addresses other special concerns, perhaps a bid to present Josephus as a Pharisee (to make intelligible his alleged backing of the rabbis in *Antiquities*), and that the response to Justus is incidental, confined to particular sections of the book.[14]

Detailed discussion of these proposals is not possible here. Suffice it to say that they do not satisfactorily explain the entire *Antiquities-Life*, or even the *Antiquities* proper. Problems include the following. Defensive apologetic concerning Jewish origins explains *at best* the first half of the *Antiquities*, for it deals with the more remote history. Even there, however, the work is not usually defensive in tone, rebutting slanders, but rather quite confident in presenting its positive, celebratory case for Jewish culture (below). Next, it is implausible to imagine the Jews' enemies sitting patiently through this meandering story on twenty scrolls. Further, scholarship on Yavneh has minimized the significance of the rabbinic movement there before at least the late second century,[15] and in any case the Pharisaic forefunners of the rabbis receive

[12] Laqueur, *Historiker Flavius Josephus*, 258–61; Hans Rasp, "Flavius Josephus und die jüdischen Religionsparteien" *ZNW* 23 (1924): 27–47, esp. 46; Cohen, 145; Seth Schwartz, *Josephus and Judaean Politics* (Ledien: Brill, 1990), 199–201.

[13] M. Smith, "Palestinian Judaism in the First Century," *Israel: Its Role in Civilization* (ed. M. Davis; New York: Harper & Brothers, 1956), 67–81.

[14] Cohen, 144; T. Rajak, "Justus of Tiberias," *Classical Quarterly* 23 (1973): 345–68.

[15] E.g., L. L. Grabbe, *Judaism from Cyrus to Hadrian* (2 vols.; Minneapolis: Fortress, 1992), 2:592–95.

generally harsh treatment in the *Antiquities-Life*.[16] Finally, the *Life* asks to be read as part of the *Antiquities,* not as a separate piece with its own agenda. In a nutshell, scholarship has not yet explained the question that the *Antiquities-Life* or even the *Antiquities* as a whole answers. Who would read this book, and why? Who stands to benefit *(cui bono)?*

As in the case of the *War,* we had best begin with the prologue and major themes of the *Antiquities.* In doing so, we notice first that Josephus celebrates the *War,* describing it as a work of precise eyewitness accuracy; he would already have treated ancient history in that book, he says, if he could have done so with literary proportion (*Ant.* 1.1–6). This opening reprise, taken together with Josephus's repeated references to the *War* in the body of *Antiquities-Life* (e.g., *Ant.* 13.173, 298) and his boast about the two works together in *Against Apion* (1.47–56), precludes the theory that Josephus felt a need to apologize for the *War.* It is impossible to detect the faintest blush in his later works: he is proud of the *War* and seems to imagine that he is writing from a broadly consistent perspective.

Josephus claims to write the *Antiquities* because he has been pursued by those who are curious about Jewish history (*Ant.* 1.8). They would consider such a work useful and beautiful (1.9). He takes as his model the high priest Eleazar of bygone days, who similarly yielded to the request of a prominent Gentile (Ptolemy II) for a translation of the Jewish laws. Eleazar did not "jealously hoard" this great benefit, because Jewish tradition required that its good things not be kept secret (1.11). Josephus, therefore, will imitate this magnanimity by sharing his tradition with those who are eager to learn. The tone of this section is free of the defensiveness that we find even in the *War.* Rather, Josephus claims to write only under pressure from interested outsiders.

Admittedly, the claim that one has been urged to write was a rhetorical commonplace (e.g., Seneca, *Contr.* 1.pref.1; Quintilian 1.pref.1). But commonplaces often have true stories behind them. Politicians may routinely claim that they have been pressed to run for office, but some *are* drafted. Similarly, some ancient writers *were* encouraged, even badgered, by their friends to publish (Pliny, *Ep.* 5.10—addressing Suetonius). We can decide the matter for Josephus only by asking whether there were Gentiles in Rome at the end of the first century who

[16] Steve Mason, *Flavius Josephus on the Pharisees* (Leiden: Brill, 1990).

were eager to learn about Judaism. And we have already answered this question affirmatively. So his account of his reasons for writing is the best that we have so far. Greeks and Romans who were interested in Jewish culture asked him for an introductory history of his people.

The prologue to the *Antiquities* introduces four major themes that color the entire work. These are: (a) the antiquity of the Jews; (b) their constitution; (c) their philosophy; and (d) Josephus's moralizing evaluation of major figures.

(a) First, Josephus wishes to demonstrate the great antiquity of the Jewish people and their institutions. He titles his book "Jewish Ancient Lore" (*archaiologia: Ant.* 1.5; 20.259, 267). When he later decides that it has failed in its purpose, he writes an essay sequel that some early readers knew as *On the Antiquity of the Jews* (Origen, *Cels.* 1.16; Eusebius, *Hist. eccl.* 3.9.4), though we know it by the misnomer *Against Apion.* Beginning his account with the creation of the world (*Ant.* 1.27) allows him to make his case pointedly: Jewish culture extends back to creation in an unbroken line. If Greek and Roman readers of Herodotus's second volume understood the great antiquity of Egyptian civilization and the Greek debt to Egypt, Josephus claims that it was the Jewish patriarch Abraham who *first taught the Egyptians.* He is very concerned, therefore, to establish external proof for Abraham's early date (1.158–160). Indeed, the Jewish sacred texts underlay all of human history, for they foretold in detail the entire plan of world history, including the rise and fall of nations (10.266–281; 11.1–3, 331–339).

To understand Josephus's concern with antiquity, we need to lay aside the "antiquarian" connotations that this word has today. It is a common observation that the ancient world—or at least, its aristocratic leaders—looked backward rather than forward, as we tend to do, for standards of perfection. In the earliest known Greek texts we already see an image of the world in decline, from a long-lost golden age through successive ages of deterioration to the present (Hesiod, *Op.* 105–199). Among the Roman elite this basic worldview became ever more concrete in the face of a perceived rise in corruption, crime, social dislocation, violence, and political upheaval (Sallust, *Bell. Cat.* 5.9–13.5; Cicero, *Div.* 2.2.4; Horace, *Carm.* 3.6; Livy, *Hist. rom.* 1.pref.6–9; Catullus 64 (end); Juvenal, *Sat.* 3.268–314).

Many Roman authors of Josephus's era saw their generation as vastly inferior to the glorious men of old. For aristocrats, character was dependent on blood lines and the illustrious deeds of one's ancestors. No one doubted that the old ways—the *mos maiorum*—were the best; the older, the better. Progress, by contrast, was not an established good. "Innovation" was often a synonym for revolution, which was bad. Even those on the fringes of society who harbored apocalyptic visions of radical change tended to see the utopian future, not as the result of incremental progress in the liberal sense, but as the sudden reappearance of a lost golden age.

Now, the Romans knew that their own history was not all that ancient, since they dated the founding of their city only about eight hundred years before the first century C.E. (to 753 B.C.E.). To provide a nobler, which is to say older, root, they crafted a national protohistory dating back to the Trojan War (Virgil, *Aeneid*) centuries earlier, or indeed to the gods (Cicero, *Rep.* 2.2.4). Dionysius of Halicarnassus was especially sensitive to the Greek assumption that the Romans were of late origin. To counter this claim he traces the Romans' ancestors back even before the Trojan war (*Ant. rom.* 1.4.1–11.4). When Livy, Virgil, or Dionysius argued for the ancient origins of the Romans, they were not engaged in dusty antiquarian pursuits as we might think of them. They considered their researches to be of the greatest utility for the present, since the very antiquity of the Roman constitution proved its virtue.

The Jews had a similar problem with respect to their origins, but they lacked the Romans' present power to offset it. Outside observers typically treated the Jews as the derivative offshoot of an older people. Most commonly they were held to be Egyptians, who had fled or been expelled from Egypt for some ignoble reason (Tacitus, *Hist.* 5.1–4). In a world in which "old" was axiomatically "good," this kind of slander went hand in hand with an ongoing antipathy to Jews presently living. It is no coincidence that most of our evidence for such defamation of the Jews' origins comes from Alexandria, and from such a scholar as Apion, who actively worked—also in Rome—against Jewish rights in his own day (*Ant.* 18.257–259).

Therefore it makes perfect sense that once Josephus had tried his best to deflect the more intense animosity toward Jewish communities as a result of the war (in the *Jewish War*), he would devote his greatest work to the fundamental question of Jewish antiquity. He aims to provide a positive, celebratory statement of the matter and also, as we see from parallels in *Against Apion,* to furnish his receptive audience with material that will preclude anti-Jewish polemic, even though he seldom responds directly to such polemic in this work (e.g., *Ant.* 2.177).

(b) Josephus's prologue declares his subject to be both the ancient lore and political constitution of the Jews (*Ant.* 1.5). What Ptolemy II wanted to learn from the Jews was their "constitution." Josephus notes that the Jewish Scriptures include accounts of revolutions in the political order (1.13). He confirms the importance of the constitutional theme by mentioning it several times in his concluding remarks (*Ant.* 20.229, 251, 261). Near the end of *Against Apion,* Josephus recalls that his purpose in writing the *Antiquities* was to give "an exact account of our laws and constitution" (*Ag. Ap.* 2.287). In his view, then, his major work was essentially about the Jewish constitution. Furthermore, the prologue to *Antiquities* repeatedly refers to Moses as "our lawgiver" and, in a striking reminder of Polybius (below), asks the reader to "assess" the Jewish lawgiver's work (1.15). Josephus is not, therefore, using language with primarily internal Jewish connotations (contrast the Hebrew word *torah,* which has a much more specific meaning in a Jewish context). For Jews, as for other nations in his account, the laws are the expression of the constitution. He engages his Roman readers in a dialogue concerning the best constitution.

The issue of the preferred political constitution, which the Greek historian Herodotus (*Hist.* 3.80–82) had raised and Plato (*Resp.* 8.543–9.576) and Aristotle had introduced into Greek philosophical discourse, was still very much alive in Josephus's Rome. Herodotus and Aristotle describe three forms of government: monarchy, oligarchy or aristocracy, and democracy (Aristotle, *Pol.* 3.5.1–2 [1279a]). In the sixth volume of his *Universal History,* Polybius assesses Rome's constitution against Aristotle's categories, along with their degenerative forms, and contrasts it with other codes. He invites the reader to "assess" (same word as Josephus's above) whether the Roman constitution is not the best (6.1.4–5). He praises Sparta's government as divine in origin (6.48.2), but finds Rome's even better because it balances all three governmental types and therefore provides a safeguard against any extreme fluctuation from one type to another (6.18).

Cicero's dialogues *Republic* and *On Laws* reach the same conclusion as Polybius about the perfection of the Roman constitution. Like Josephus, Cicero grounds Rome's constitution in the universal law of nature and reason (*Leg.* 2.5.13; cf. 1.6.20–12.34); describes what is basically an aristocratic system (*Rep.* 2.22.39); explores the Roman constitution's glories by means of a historical summary, moving from one great founder to the next (*Rep.* 2.1.3); presents the founder, Romulus, as endowed with a divine wisdom (*Rep.* 2.5.10; 2.9.15–16) and has him mysteriously disappear, creating a popular belief that he had been installed among the gods (*Rep.* 2.10.17); insists that Roman law is not derivative from Greek, but native and divine in origin (*Rep.* 2.14.28–29); has the Romans detest kingship (*Rep.* 1.40.62; cf. 2.30.52); and speaks easily the perfect concord or harmony reflected in the nation's code in spite of the obvious fact that his lifetime was dominated by civil war (*Rep.* 2.42.69). Compare Josephus in *Ag. Ap.* 2.145–296.

In Cicero's ideal Roman system, the priests have a fundamental authority. Cicero, like Josephus, was a priest (*Leg.* 2.12.31) and like many Roman authors he stresses the fundamental role played by the priestly king Numa Pompilius in the investment of Roman laws with a basis in piety *(Rep.* 2.13–14; cf. Dionysius, *Ant. rom.* 2.58–66; Plutarch, *Numa).*

The Roman civil wars during Cicero's lifetime and later, which resulted finally in Augustus's settlement with the senate in 27 B.C.E., sent shock waves that would energize the discussion of constitutions for a long time to come. The first century B.C.E. saw several dictators—theoretically a temporary emergency position—with extended terms and the suspension of ordinary law. And the conspiracy of Catiline, a senator who intended to unite the poorer classes against the aristocracy in 63 B.C.E., left its marks in texts that were still well known to Josephus's contemporaries (Cicero, *Catilinarians* I–IV; Sallust, *Catilinarian Conflict*). Catiline was accused of being a demagogue, of appearing to support the masses only to gain their support for his personal political ends. To the senate's aristocrats, the mob and such elite demagogues who tried to mobilize them were a constant threat to the established order.

The much-discussed issue of the most effective constitution was by no means settled in Domitian's day, when Josephus was writing the *Antiquities.* When Josephus arrived in 71, Rome was only beginning to recover from the devastating "year of the four emperors" (69 C.E.). Now, Domitian's overt movement toward a monarchical court (81–96 C.E.), throwing off the polite deference of his predecessors to the senate, created serious tensions with the aristocracy. Whether they dared to speak of it openly or not, every educated person in Rome must have been thinking about issues of political constitution. And that is what Josephus makes the main subject of the *Antiquities,* with his bold claim that the Jews have the oldest and finest constitution in existence.

Like Cicero, Josephus chooses to explore the constitution through a historical summary of its development. After tracing the ancient precursors, he comes to the heart of the matter in volume 3, where Moses receives the Jewish code at Sinai (*Ant.* 3.84, 213). Although he notes that "even our enemies admit that our constitution was established by God" (*Ant.* 3.322), he downplays the purely theological side of the story, emphasizing rather the time-tested wisdom of the lawgiver (cf. 1.18). When Moses is about to die, he entrusts the nation "to the sobriety of the laws, to the order of the constitution, and to the virtues of those governors who will exercise watchful care over your interests" (4.184)—namely, the priests.

Josephus outlines the terms of the constitution in two separate blocks: *Ant.* 3.224–286 deals with sacrifices, priesthood, and purity, whereas 4.199–319 covers criminal, civil, and family law (4.214–222: magistrates and punishments). His account is replete with constitutional language (*Ant.* 4.45, 184, 191, 193–195, 196–198, 302, 310, 312). The terms of the constitution are important in part because they then provide the criterion against which all characters and events will be judged in the balance of the work (e.g., *Ant.* 5.98, 179; 15.254, 281; 18.9). Josephus's summaries of the constitution emphasize its austerity, discipline, justice, and humanity—characteristically Roman virtues (Polybius 6.7.5–8; 48.3; 56.1–5; Sallust, *Bell. Cat.* 11–13; Livy, *Hist. rom.* 1.pref.10–12; Cicero, *Rep.* 1.27–28; Plutarch, *Cat. Maj.* 1.3–4; 2.1, 3).

But what sort of constitution do the Jews enjoy? Polybius and Cicero had required that the optimal constitution must be both theoretically sound and practically effective. They had rejected Plato's ideal Republic, admirable though it was, because it could never be tested in practice (Polybius 6.47.7–10; Cicero, *Rep.* 2.11.21–22). Josephus is aware of this two-sided test, for he refers to it in *Against Apion* (2.171–172).

On the theoretical side, Josephus insists that the authentic form of the Jewish constitution is one of priestly aristocracy *(aristokratia)*. The Judeans are properly led by the high priest (cf. the Roman office of *pontifex maximus*) in concert with his fellow priests. This form is already assumed in the prologue, where the high priest Eleazar is the Jews' authorized leader (*Ant.* 1.10–12). When first describing the laws given by Moses, Josephus devotes a remarkable amount of space to the cosmic significance of high priestly dress and sacrificial apparatus (*Ant.* 3.159–187; 3.214). Most significantly, when Moses finishes receiving his laws, he consigns them to the high priest Aaron and his subordinates for proper administration in perpetuity (4.304). The priests thus form an aristocracy charged with preservation and administration of the laws (cf. *Life* 1).

That this function of preserving the nation's laws intact is critical to the role of the high priest is indicated in part by Josephus's determination to identify the serving high priest in each period down to his own (*Ant.* 4.152; 5.318; 6.122, 242, passim; 10.150–152; 11.73, 90, passim), and again by his synoptic high priestly succession lists (*Ant.* 10.151–153; 20.224–251). This concern also is developed in *Against Apion* (1.29–38). Near the end of that work, explicitly entering the philosophical debate about the best constitution (2.164), Josephus celebrates the priestly aristocratic form as the best (2.185).

That Josephus is in dialogue with other Greek writers on constitutions is clear from his pointed use of the word "aristocracy" *(aristokratia).* He has Moses caution the people that "aristocracy, and the life associated with it, is the noblest. So do not let the desire for any other constitution snare you" (*Ant.* 4.223). This aristocracy places a senate *(gerousia)* alongside the high priest (4.186, 218, 220, 255, 256, 325). Josephus alters the biblical narrative to make Moses' great successor Joshua consult the senate several times (5.15, 43, 55). Reinterpreting the cycles of sin and repentance in Judges, he adopts the deterioration scheme familiar from Roman authors: "the aristocracy was falling into corruption. No longer did they appoint the senates or the leadership formerly legislated." This failure results in civil war (5.135).

Later, when the people implore the prophet Samuel to appoint a king, Samuel is profoundly upset because he is "strongly committed to aristocracy" (*Ant.* 6.36). Sure enough, once the kingship is in place—already by Solomon's time—it proves ruinous, until it is finally taken away with the Babylonian captivity. The virtues and lawless deeds ascribed by Josephus to the Jewish kings are like those ascribed by Roman authors to their former kings.

When the Jews return from captivity, they revert to their ideal constitution and once again live under "an aristocracy, with the rule of the few" (*Ant.* 11.111). A letter to the Jews from Antiochus III identifies the senate as their governing body (12.138, 142). So also the Hasmonean Jonathan writes as high priest on behalf of "the senate and the body of priests" (13.166, 169). The early Hasmoneans up until John Hyrcanus, whom Josephus reveres, continue this form of government. But then with Aristobulus we see both the "transformation of rule into monarchy" and the consequent decline of the great house (13.300–301). The

Jewish people, as Pompey is hearing the arguments of Hyrcanus II and Aristobulus II as to why each should be king, "requested not to be subject to a king, for it was traditional to obey the priests of the God honored among them. But these men . . . sought to lead the nation into another kind of government, to enslave it" (14.41). The notion that allegiance to one man amounts to slavery is common among Roman aristocratic historians (e.g., Tacitus, *Agr.* 2.3).

When the Hasmonean house eventually fell, Josephus asserts, the Roman Gabinius removed monarchical rule and once again aristocracy was restored (*Ant.* 14.91). That proper state of affairs has been the norm until Josephus's own time. The exceptions to it, especially with the long-ruling monarch Herod (37–4 B.C.E.), were on balance regrettable. If the Jews were going to have a king, Moses mandated that it be one of their own people, as Josephus noted earlier (4.223). Herod, Josephus claims, was a "half-Jew" (14.403). Josephus's portraits of Herod, Herod's descendants, and also Gaius in Rome serve as notorious examples of what happens when political constitutions are corrupted.

In his narrative on Gaius Caligula's reign, as noted above, Josephus takes full advantage of the situation to relate Rome's constitutional problems to the Jewish constitution. The Roman senators imagine that power will finally revert to them after their long experiment with emperors (*Ant.* 19.161; cf. Tacitus, *Hist.* 1.4—after Nero's death). The soldiers consider democracy as an option, but reject it in favor of their choosing, and thus controlling, a new individual ruler (*Ant.* 19.162–164). In the long speech given to the senator C. Sentius Saturninus, which is a harangue against tyrants over the whole century since Julius Caesar, Josephus gives voice to his own views (19.167–184): aristocracy "best guarantees both present loyalty and future immunity from hostile intrigue" (19.178). Alas, it is not to be in Rome.

Given Josephus's marked preference for aristocracy, it comes as no surprise that he looks upon the impulsive masses, the mob, as a constant threat to the divinely constituted order. The mob, after all, supported Caligula (*Ant.* 19.202; cf. Tacitus, *Hist.* 1.4, 32 on popular support for any tyrant). Sharing the fears of Roman authors about democracy or "mob rule" (Polybius 6.9.8–9; 44.9; Cicero, *Rep.* 1.42.65), Josephus considers the people properly dependent on their constitutional (aristocratic) leaders, and vulnerable to demagogues who deceive them with promises of quick benefits.

While still describing the establishment of the constitution, therefore, Josephus turns also to this perennial problem of keeping the people acquiescent. He speaks of "the general mass, with its innate delight in decrying those in authority and its opinion swayed by what anyone said" (*Ant.* 4.37). The biblical figure of Korah becomes the archetypal demagogue, who leads an unprecedented sedition (4.12)—the perpetual enemy of the state (cf. Thucydides, *Hist.* 3.82.2–3). Korah is a Catiline-like member of the aristocracy who, jealous of Moses' honor, uses his rhetorical ability to curry favor with the people, denouncing Moses and Aaron as tyrants (4.14–19). His appearance of concern for the people masks his outrageous ambition (4.20). Later in the story, King David's son Absalom plays the demagogue (7.194–196). Still later, the Pharisees don the mantle of the people to wield their influence for ill (*Ant.* 13.288, 401; 18.9–10, 15, 17) and, most recently, various persuasive messianic pretenders have brought the nation to grief (e.g., 18.3–6; 20.160, 167, 172).

In spite of the recent upheavals in Judea, Josephus wants to argue that the ancient Jewish code is not only perfect in theory but also uniquely effective in practice. In the prologue he offers as the main lesson of the *Antiquities* that:

> For those, on the one hand, who follow after the judgment of God and do not dare to violate what has been finely legislated, they prosper in every way beyond belief, and happiness *[eudaimonia]* is presented as a reward from God; on the other hand, to the degree that they should defect from precise observance of these [laws], what is doable becomes not doable, and whatever seemed good that they were eager to accomplish turns into unstoppable disasters. (*Ant.* 1.14)

Again, in *Antiquities* 1.20, when the legislator Moses was framing his laws, he wished to instruct his fellow citizens that "God, being the Father and Lord of all things, oversees all things," granting to those who follow him a life of bliss, while punishing those who step outside the path of virtue. For readers of the Bible, Josephus's language immediately recalls the Deuteronomic view of history: God rewards faithfulness to the covenant and punishes transgression (cf. Deut 28). But Josephus knows no limitation of these laws to Jews. In fact, he will downplay or omit material from his sources dealing with Israel's land-based election and covenant. According to him, Moses treated the constitution of the universe before framing his laws precisely so that his laws would be uniquely based on universal truths (*Ant.* 1.18–25).

All of this—the question of the best form of government, the constant threat of a drift toward monarchy or tyranny, the problems of popular rebellion and demagoguery—should have found a ready reception among a literate audience in Domitian's Rome.

(c) Intertwined with the theme of political constitutions in the *Antiquities* is the portrayal of Judean culture as philosophical. For Josephus's readers, too, there was a close connection between these two subjects. Normally, discussions of the optimal constitution were conducted by philosophers. For Plato, the only suitable king was a philosopher (*Resp.* 5.473b–d). As we have seen, Cicero derived his laws from the laws of nature, which is to say, "from the deepest mysteries of philosophy" (*Leg.* 1.5.17). In Josephus's Rome, the aristocratic-republican opposition to the principate had been nourished by Stoic philosophy. It must have been meaningful to his readers, then, that his work advocating an ancient aristocratic constitution is also replete with philosophical language.

To appreciate the philosophical strains of the *Antiquities*, it is helpful to recall some commonly observed features of ancient philosophy.

First, as Aristotle's vast corpus best illustrates, philosophers investigated every branch of learning in what we would call the arts (e.g., history, political science, religion, philosophy, language) and sciences (e.g., mathematics, physics, astronomy, chemistry, biology, botany, anatomy).

Second, Socrates's focus on ethics biased the future course of philosophy. By Josephus's time, a philosophy was a way of living in the world: of dressing, eating, and behaving. The understood goal of philosophy was to find well-being or happiness *(eudaimonia)* (e.g., Aristotle, *Eth. nic.* 10.6.1; Seneca, *Ep.* 15.1; Epictetus, *Diatr.* 1.4.32). This ethical bias meant also that the distinctive doctrines of each school—e.g., Platonist, Pythagorean, Peripatetic, Stoic, Cynic, Epicurean—became less important. Reading Josephus's near contemporaries Seneca, Epictetus, or Plutarch, one is hard-pressed to place any of them in a single camp, no matter what his school label. They were all *philosophers.* They professed simplicity, virtue at all costs, fearless freedom of speech, and contempt for both ordinary social values and death. Thus far, the moral direction of philosophy dovetailed neatly with aristocratic Roman ideals (cf. Plutarch, *Cat. Maj.* 2.3–4).

Third, however, an emphasis on virtue at all costs led to potential conflicts between philosophical and political life—and public life was the Roman upper class's main reason for being. If philosophers could fearlessly challenge the *princeps* ("emperor") himself, they were not going to support the compromises that defined politics then as now. Even those Romans who had a deep interest in philosophical matters, therefore, insisted that the state must come first. They rejected out of hand the notion of a sequestered life of unimpeded virtue. The philosopher's refuge must be internal only. Any hint of countercultural extremism was completely unsuited to the Roman man of affairs (Cicero, *Rep.* 3.3; Seneca, *Ep.* 5.2; 56; 108.22; Tacitus, *Agr.* 4.3; Quintilian 11.1.35). Herrenius Senecio was executed by Domitian in the year of *Antiquities'* appearance because he had written a biography of Helvidius Priscus, a frank-speaking Stoic executed by Domitian's father, and because he had refused to hold public office beyond a lower magistracy (Dio Cassius 67.13.2). Those who took their precious virtue too far, who spoke too frankly, often ended up dead or banished. The ideal was, apparently, to be philosophically sophisticated without being too committed to any one school or lifestyle—fanatical, we might say.

Fourth, one reason for this resistance to philosophy was that its all-embracing character invited a kind of conversion. Epictetus describes the philosopher as a physician, and his lecture-hall as a hospital for the spiritually or psychically sick (*Diatr.* 3.21.20; 23.37). Diogenes Laertius recounts an evangelical sort of experience of conversion to philosophy (*Vit. phil.* 4.16). It was in philosophical contexts that one most naturally spoke of "conversion" *(metanoia, conversio)*, a change of thinking and direction—language we would reserve for religious contexts.

Many philosophers reportedly gave speeches or wrote tractates designed to encourage the adoption of the philosophical life (Diogenes Laertius, *Vit. phil.* 5.22.12). One of the best surviving examples of such philosophical "protreptic" is Lucian's second-century *Wisdom of Nigrinus.* In this dialogue, a man has just returned from a life-changing encounter with an Athenian philosopher named Nigrinus. The experience has transformed him into a happy and blissful man (*Nigr.* 1). The other character in the dialogue implores him not to jealously hoard (cf. Josephus in *Ant.* 1.11; *Ag. Ap.* 2.209) the source of such bliss. In response, the convert recounts the speech of Nigrinus, which pierced his soul and led him to embrace philosophy (35–37). This conversion to philosophy had many of the characteristics of religious rebirth.

Finally, Jewish culture appeared to some observers as the home of a philosophical way of life (Aristotle in Josephus, *Ag. Ap.* 1.179;

Theophrastus in Porphyry, *Abst.* 2.26; Diodorus Siculus 40.3.4; Strabo 16.2.35). Outside of Jerusalem, Jews did not have the basic tools of religion or cult, namely temples and sacrificing priests. Rather, throughout the eastern Mediterranean they met in plain buildings or open air settings ("prayer houses" or "synagogues") to study, hear lectures, pray, and discuss ethics. They seemed to believe in the God of the philosophers, the ultimate force behind nature, of whom they permitted no image, and who could not be described. They were distinguished by a disciplined way of life, diet, calendar, dress (perhaps), and mode of social interaction. More than most, they embraced a closely communal way of living. Even those who feared or hated the Jews noticed such features. Accordingly, many Jewish authors, including Josephus (cf. also Artapanus, Aristobulus, Aristeas, Philo), chose to present their culture to others in the prestigious language of philosophy.

The voice Josephus assumes as narrator is that of a philosophical sophisticate, who is nonetheless no fanatical philosopher but a statesman. He claims to have trained thoroughly in all of his nation's schools, and even to have become a youthful enthusiast of the purest and most exotic discipline. Yet he fittingly put that obsession behind him when he took his place in public life (*Life* 10–12). For Josephus, as for the Roman aristocrat Agricola (Tacitus, *Agr.* 4.3), "Soon came reason and years to cool his blood. He achieved the rarest of feats: he was a student, yet preserved a sense of proportion" (cf. Cicero, *De or.* 2.156).

Now Josephus is able to speak with detachment but authority about all aspects of knowledge. He laces his narrative with comments or excursuses on geography, ethnography, astronomy, mathematics, plant and animal life, historiography, language, and many other tools of the savant's trade. He directly challenges the Epicureans (*Ant.* 10.277), who were a favorite target for all Stoicizing writers, and he frequently comments on fate and free will, the soul, and the afterlife (1.85; 6.3; 8.146; 12.282, 304; 19.325). In keeping with his claim elsewhere to be thoroughly trained in the "philosophy" of his people's ancient books (*Ag. Ap.* 1.54), he asserts that the Judean law "philosophizes" on the vexed problem of fate and free will (*Ant.* 16.398).

Particularly noteworthy in the context I have described is Josephus's assertion, repeated from the prologue onward, that only following the laws of Moses brings well-being or happiness (*Ant.* 1.14, 20). He introduces this word *eudaimonia* some forty-seven times into his biblical paraphrase, though it does not appear in his main source, the Greek

Bible. Indeed, what Moses received at Sinai promised "a happy life and an orderly constitution" (3.84). Evidently, Josephus means to present Judaism as an option in the philosophical/constitutional marketplace. In his synthesis of the Midianite Balaam's four prophecies concerning Israel (cf. Num 22–24), he pointedly reinforces his theme: the Jewish nation is singularly happy, Balaam says, indeed happier than all other nations, because it alone has been granted God's "watchful care" as an eternal guide (4.114). In the future, Balaam continues, Jews will dominate the entire earth by population and by fame (4.115–116).

This related theme of God's watchful care or providence *(pronoia)* happens also to be a theme of contemporary Stoicism. Stoics had always emphasized the all-encompassing character of nature or reason. By Josephus's day some of them were speaking of this animating, active principle of the cosmos in personal terms, as providence or God (Epictetus, *Diatr.* 1.6, 16; 3.17). Similarly, Josephus often connects God with providence, fate, and fortune (*Ant.* 10.277–280; 16.395–404; cf. *Ag. Ap.* 2.180–181).

Josephus claims that because the constitution of Moses reflects the natural law, anyone wishing to inquire more deeply about the reasons for the laws would find the exercise "highly philosophical" (*Ant.* 1.25). This is not merely a catchy phrase for the prologue, however. He will portray many key figures in Jewish history as philosophers without rival.

Following Seth's descendants, who discovered the orderly array of the heavenly bodies (*Ant.* 1.69), Abraham inferred from the irregularity of these bodies that there was one ultimate God (1.155–156). With the mind of a true philosopher, he visited Egypt intending that, "if he found [what their priests said about the gods] superior, he would subscribe to it, or, if what he himself thought was found preferable, he would reorder their lives according to the more excellent way" (1.161). In the event, anticipating Socrates, he employed a dialectical method to listen carefully to them and then expose the emptiness of their arguments (1.166). So it happened that he taught the elements of mathematics and science to the renowned Egyptians (*Ant.* 1.167–168).

Moses, as we have seen, studied nature in order to achieve the proper foundation for his laws (*Ant.* 1.18–19, 34). Like Plato (*Resp.* 3.386–417), the lawgiver rejected out of hand the unseemly "myths" about the gods (*Ant.* 1.22–24). His greatness of intellect and understanding were apparent even in childhood (2.229–230). He served as a brilliant Egyptian commander, then as a peerless lawgiver. In sum, he "surpassed in understanding all who ever lived, and used his insights in the best possible ways" (4.328). In a striking parallel to Romulus, the founder of Rome, this supremely virtuous man ended his life mysteriously in an enveloping cloud—creating some speculation about his apotheosis (4.326).

King Solomon, for his part, "surpassed all the ancients, and even the Egyptians, who are said to excel all men in understanding" (*Ant.* 8.42). His knowledge covered not only the whole range of natural science—encompassing every creature in existence—but extended even to occult science, the techniques for expelling demons and effecting cures (8.44–49). These powers remain the unique legacy of the Jews in Josephus's day (8.46).

Daniel is yet another kind of philosopher. He and his companions adopt a Pythagorean-like vegetarian diet, by which they keep their minds "pure and fresh for learning" (*Ant.* 10.193). This in turn enables them to master the breadth of both Hebrew and Chaldean learning (10.194).

In the latter half of the *Antiquities*, Josephus introduces the three Jewish philosophical schools. He explains their differences in terms of the perennial issues of fate, the soul, and the afterlife (*Ant.* 13.371–373; 18.12–20). Whereas the *War* (2.162–166) had made Pharisees and Sadducees diameteric opposites, *Antiquities* adjusts this picture to range Essenes and Sadducees on the poles, with Pharisees in the middle (*Ant.* 13.171–173). Once again, as it happens, Cicero offers a close parallel to Josephus's scheme:

> There were among the old philosophers two schools of thought: the one held the view that everything is determined by fate—that this fate entails a necessary force. . . . The others were of the conviction that the soul's promptings are determined by the will, without any influence from fate. Between these contending options, Chrysippus [the Stoic] wanted to arbitrate by finding a middle way. (*Fat.* 39)

Indeed, Josephus explicitly compares the Pharisees with Stoics (*Life* 12) and the Essenes with Pythagoreans (*Ant.* 15.371). It takes little imagination to realize that his Sadducees, who allegedly deny fate's involvement in human affairs and believe that the soul dissolves with the body (*Ant.* 18.16), mirror the pitiable Epicureans.

As for "conversion," the clearest example comes near the end of the *Antiquities*, where the royal family of Adiabene in Parthia adopts the philosophy and constitution of the Judeans. In Josephus's words: "Helena, queen of Adiabene, and her son Izates changed their way of life to accord with the customs of the Jews" (*Ant.* 20.17). If we have rightly understood the bulk of the *Antiquities*, the royal family's action would be the logical consequence of having discovered the noblest laws and philosophy in existence.

The obvious problem faced by anyone in Rome who might be interested in adopting the Jewish laws was the risk of rejection by their compatriots for having embraced foreign customs. This is precisely the charge Tacitus brings against his contemporaries who adopt Judaism (*Hist.* 5.5). In Domitian's Rome it was a serious problem, especially for a member of the elite, to be found sympathizing with Judaism. Informants had much to gain by reporting such high-level defectors. Josephus anticipates the problem in his story of Abraham in Chaldea, and now tackles it at length. He poses the question whether Izates should be circumcised because of the risk he would run. In the end, Izates opts for circumcision, and his risk is more than rewarded. Josephus illustrates with many examples that:

> God was the one who prevented their fears from coming to fruition, for although both Izates and his children fell into many dangers, he preserved them, having provided a route to safety from impossible circumstances. [God] demonstrated that for those who look away to him, and trust him alone, the fruit of this piety is not lost. (*Ant.* 20.48)

(d) The last major theme to be discussed in the *Antiquities* is Josephus's ongoing moral assessment. He tells the story of Jewish history primarily in terms of great individuals. In other words, history shades into biography. Volume 7 deals, not with a certain period of Israel's history, but with *David.* His account of the Jews in Babylonia is actually focused on the brothers Anilaeus and Asinaeus (*Ant.* 18.310–379). This personal perspective allows him to employ the full range of novelistic techniques. He can more easily build suspense, analyze a character's psychological state or motives, evoke such powerful emotions as fear, jealousy, and hatred, and introduce erotic situations to keep the reader's interest (*Ant.* 14.2). One of the most versatile devices for introducing these elements, and also changing the tempo of the piece, is the crafted speech. A biographical arrangement invites Josephus to create speeches everywhere.

Most important, the biographical approach permits him to draw moral lessons, of virtue and vice, from each life he sketches (e.g., *Ant.*

1.53, 60–61, 66, 72). Typically, these moralizing assessments come in the form of obituaries (*Ant.* 1.256, 346; 2.198–204; 4.327–331; 5.117–118, 253; 6.292–294; 7.37–38, 390–391), though not always (6.343–350). The Bible's own Deuteronomic history provides something of a lead with its notices of righteous and wicked rulers, but Josephus's technique is far more elaborate and has closer models in Roman historiography. He wishes to hold up his virtuous characters as examples for all city-states, peoples, and nations to follow (6.343).

Particularly noteworthy is his effort to achieve balance in his moral assessments. Even when the character is an egregious villain, or someone whom the Bible itself dismisses as wicked, Josephus struggles to find positive qualities. Samson is praised for his valor and strength, and Solomon for his wisdom, though both are criticized for being vulnerable to women's temptations (5.317; 8.211). Saul, who disobeyed God's command and lost divine favor (6.166, 378), serves nonetheless as a paradigm of manliness (6.344–350). It is disconcerting to read Josephus's treatment of Aristobulus, who murdered his brother. There is no question of his pride and guilt, yet Josephus finds a way to praise his temperament (13.318–319). Alexander Janneus, a brutal dictator, is rendered at least human, a victim in part (13.380–383). Alexandra Salome, to whom Josephus most directly attributes the fall of the Hasmonean house, nevertheless "kept the nation at peace" (13.430–432). Even the despicable emperor Gaius Caligula, after his crimes against the Jews and others have been described at length, is credited with being a good orator (19.208–209)! Josephus assesses these lives for the moral instruction of his readers to prove his thesis about the effectiveness of the Jewish God (19.15–16).

Older scholarship frequently commented on the apparent disproportion of *Ant.* 11–20, with its excessive focus on Herod's reign. Often, this was attributed to the constraints of Josephus's sources. He needed material, and he happened to possess it in abundance for Herod (thanks to Nicolaus of Damascus's *Universal History*), so he exploited that treasure to fill in his story. Although there is a measure of truth in this claim, for Josephus did have access to excellent material on Herod, we should not so readily discount his intelligence as an author. In the *War,* where he also had this material concerning Herod on hand, he used it much more sparingly and to a different purpose.

A better solution is suggested by the personal and moralizing focus of his history. Herod's was probably the most famous Jewish name in the Roman world. As we have seen, he had become the friend of several

Roman leaders in succession (Julius Caesar, Marc Antony, Octavian) at a critical period of Roman history. It was he who had put Judea on the map, so to speak, and secured important protections for Jews living throughout the Mediterranean. Indeed, one of Josephus's purposes in dwelling on Herod's reign is to cite dozens of the decrees in favor of the Jews that were passed at that time, reminding the reader of these historic privileges (*Ant.* 14.185–267; 16.160–178). He stresses the friendly relations between Jews and Romans from Herod's time (14.265–267).

Moreover, Herod's descendants would grow up in Rome, among the aristocratic elite. Agrippa I, for example, became the friend of Gaius and then played a role in Claudius's accession. Agrippa II and Berenike were even now close to the Flavian family. Therefore, devoting most of *Antiquities* 14–20 to the fortunes of Herod and his descendants would have made perfect sense in writing for a Roman audience.

The uses to which Josephus puts the Herodian family differ from *War* to *Antiquities,* however. In the *War,* where he was preeminently concerned to portray the Jews as exemplary world citizens against charges of national misanthropy, he painted the famous king as the archetypal friend and ally of the Roman people. In the *Antiquities,* where his goal is to show the effectiveness of the Jewish constitution, he presents a more balanced picture in keeping with the tendency we have observed (cf. *Ant.* 15.165–182, 375–376; 16.150–159; 17.191–192). Herod is still brave and capable of both piety and virtue (14.430, 442–444, 462–463, 482–483; 15.121–154, 305). Yet his kingship is constitutionally illegitimate (14.403), and his overweening pride leads him into serious violations of the laws (15.267–276; 16.1–4, 179–187; 17.151, 180–181), which inevitably bring a disastrous end to his career (16.188–189, 395–404; 17.168–171).

Since Josephus takes every opportunity to moralize on Herod, we should view his preoccupation with the king as deliberate, and not as a mere accident of available source material. Josephus makes all the great kings serve double duty. On the one hand, they are entertaining larger-than-life ancient heroes. On the other hand, Saul and Herod, founders of the first and last royal dynasties respectively, gave kingship a bad name among the Judeans as Tarquin had among the Romans—fulfilling the warnings of the lawgiver and first prophets about the perils of monarchy.

It remains to be noted that this relentless concern with moral assessment was a typical feature of Roman authors. Cicero, as we have seen, fashioned his short history of the constitution from a series of individual lives, morally assessed. Sallust chose to build his histories around the figures associated with Catiline and Jugurtha, and in so doing enshrined a kind of moralizing assessment, both individual and comparative (*Bell. Cat.* 5.1–8; 14.1–6; *Bell. Jug.* 95.3–4). Suetonius told the story of the Caesars through biographies. Tacitus initiated his career as historian with an essay on his father-in-law Agricola, which included much standard historical material. In his later works, he can scarcely mention a person's name without offering a psychological profile and/or a moralizing assessment (e.g., *Hist.* 1.6, 7, 8, 9, 10, 13, 14, 22, 23). Josephus's other contemporary, Plutarch, is most famous for the moralizing assessments and comparisons that accompany nineteen of his twenty-three pairs of *Lives.* Josephus and Plutarch, Greek-speaking contemporaries writing for Romans, apparently assumed similar tastes in their audiences.

As in the case of the *War,* Josephus's efforts to reach his immediate Roman audience should not lead us to the simplistic conclusion that he has perverted his own national history to do so. In the *Antiquities* much more clearly than in the *War,* we can see the traditional, biblical, and Jewish underpinnings of his perspective on world affairs.

It is obvious and well known by scholars that Josephus adds and omits a great deal, also dramatically changing and rearranging in some places what he takes from the Bible despite his promises to set forth the precise details of the Jewish texts, adding and omitting nothing (*Ant.* 1.17; cf. 4.196). However, with both Josephus and the NT authors, we are still quite uncertain which version(s) of the Bible (OT) they used: a Hebrew version closely resembling the traditional one (the Masoretic text); a Hebrew version closer to the ancient Septuagint (or Old Greek) translation or to variant readings represented in the Dead Sea Scrolls and other ancient Jewish texts, which differ from our Hebrew Bible in significant ways; Aramaic translations and paraphrases of the Bible; existing Greek translations of the Bible (recall: Josephus and the NT authors are writing in Greek themselves); and/or oral traditions. But whatever texts and traditions they used, it is clear that each writer felt free—remarkably so from modern perspectives—to alter and reinterpret the Bible as required by current needs.

A good example of Josephus's embellishment is his handling of the story concerning Joseph and Potiphar's wife, which turns the concise account of Gen 39:6–20 into a much more erotically charged, but also more obviously moralizing, tale of temptation and self-control (*Ant.*

1.41–59). In his hands the story is all about passion and lust in opposition to reason, character, and virtue—all terms absent from the Bible but added generously by Josephus in his effort to reach his contemporaries, who understood such matters. Outright additions to the Bible are also numerous, such as Moses' heroic Ethiopian campaign (*Ant.* 4.238–253)—a legend known also to other Jewish writers of the period. Most of Josephus's additions, omissions (e.g., avoiding doublets), rearrangements, and alterations can be explained easily enough in view of his purposes and Roman-Gentile audience, but the fact that he is happy to make such changes *while* insisting that he is presenting the texts as they are tells us a great deal about ancient thinking with respect to sacred texts. Although Josephus does not display the taste for subtle word-interpretation that we find in Philo of Alexandria, the Dead Sea Scrolls (e.g., 4QpNahum), Paul (e.g., Gal 3:10–14; 4:21–31), or Matthew (1:23; 2:23), all of these writers lived in a world where rhetorical assumptions prevailed. Truth had to do with the points that needed making now, not with some dusty pursuit of past meanings—a pursuit that was unknown to them.

In particular, Josephus makes conspicuous the affinities with Jeremiah and Daniel that we uncovered beneath the surface of the *War.* As we have seen, he arranges his work so as to feature Jeremiah and Daniel at the end of the pivotal book; the latter he considers "one of the greatest prophets" (*Ant.* 10.266). Scholars have often been preoccupied with the dissonance between Josephus's claim here and the later rabbinic tradition, which excludes Daniel from the prophets altogether. But surely the really interesting thing is the implication for our understanding of Josephus. He considers Daniel one of the greatest because that prophet alone gave a detailed schedule of future events, to the time of Antiochus Epiphanes, which has been fulfilled with stunning and easily verifiable accuracy. Whereas modern scholarship has adopted the insight of the fourth-century philosopher Porphyry that Daniel must actually have been written at the time of Antiochus (165 B.C.E.), with the result that his apparent predictions are actually recollections, Josephus was innocent of this viewpoint. So he must have been as deeply impressed as he appears to have been with the notion that the Jewish God controls all of history. No wonder he uses Daniel's fulfilled predictions as irrefutable evidence of his main thesis against the Epicureans (*Ant.* 10.277–281). He says that Jeremiah also wrote a book (perhaps he means Lamentations) about the recent capture of Jerusalem by the Romans (10.79).

Josephus's detailed consideration of Jeremiah and Daniel in the *Antiquities* allows him to suggest numerous parallels with his own life. Jeremiah he introduces as a priest-prophet from Jerusalem (10.79–80). The prophet warned the people incessantly that they should abandon hope of alliances (compare the hopes of the Jews for possible alliances with Parthia; *War* 2.398–399) because they were destined to be overthrown by the Babylonians (10.89). Refusing to listen to Jeremiah, however, the people and their leaders accused him of treason and even desertion (10.90, 114, esp. 119). Surrender to the Babylonians, God had shown him, was the only way to avoid having the city and temple burned to the ground (10.126). Josephus even notes that Jeremiah and King Zedekiah colluded in a barefaced lie to cover the real nature of their discussion (10.129–130)—just as Josephus freely admits in the *War* to having lied to others about his intentions (e.g., *War* 2.595–607; 3.136–137, 193–202, 389). God was clearly "on the Babylonian side" (10.139), just as he is now on the Roman side (*War* 5.2).

Parallels with Daniel are equally compelling: this impressive young Jewish nobleman finds himself in the court of the foreign king, where he lives with extreme piety on a carefully selected diet (10.186, 189–190, 194; cf. *Life* 8–10, 20). As a result of his piety he is given the ability to interpret dreams (10.194), and he consequently prospers in the foreign courts.

The size and different aim of *Antiquities-Life* allow Josephus to drop much broader hints than he had in *War* about the future success of the Jewish people, which is in any case a natural consequence of his thesis about their vastly superior constitution. We have noted Balaam's predictions of singular prosperity and growth. In his discussion of Daniel, moreover, Josephus develops rather boldly the image of the final kingdom of Daniel, the stone that will smash to pieces the last worldly kingdom, which must be Rome (10.207). He says quite enough here to disturb any sensitive Roman reader, even though he refrains from elaborating on the stone (10.210). Evidently, he expects a sympathetic audience.

LIFE

The master stroke in Josephus's biographical mode of history-writing is his own *Life,* which concludes the project as a tightly connected appendix (cf. *Ant.* 20.266; *Life* 430). Elated by the completion of his oeuvre on the character of the Jews and their constitution, he moves immediately to show that he himself best exemplifies this character (*Ant.* 20.259–266):

> Perhaps it will not prove an occasion for jealousy or strike ordinary folk as gauche if I review briefly both my own ancestry and the events of my life while there are still those living who can offer refutation or corroboration. (*Ant.* 20.266)

He has the purest aristocratic ancestry, and he is fully trained in the national philosophies even though he has long since given up his youthful fanaticism in favor of public life. An episodic tour of his career of public service illustrates, one by one, the virtues most prized in Rome: gravity, dignity, courage, restraint, moderation, justice, and clemency.

As we have seen, the *Life* has usually been understood as an independent work responding to Justus of Tiberias. Justus wrote a competing account of the Jewish war (*Life* 40, 338), and especially of Josephus's role within the Galilean campaign. He accuses Josephus of having incited Tiberias to revolt (340). Scholars (including myself) have usually supposed that Josephus wrote to deal with this challenge to his standing as a friend of Rome.

The main problems with that view are three. First, it would be strange that Josephus did not follow the usual rhetorical practice, with which he shows himself perfectly familiar in his other writings, of stating his purpose (to refute Justus) clearly at the outset. On the contrary, his direct rebuttal of Justus comes only in a brief digression near the end of the work (*Life* 336–367), after the main story is over. His few statements about the *Life*'s purpose (*Ant.* 20.266; *Life* 430) point in another direction. Second, in the context of ancient patronage and especially in view of the necessity of shifting alliances under various Roman rulers, it is far from clear why Josephus—an obviously favored man—should have been troubled by the accusations of Justus—an obvious loser—twenty-five years after the war. Finally, Josephus tightly connects the *Antiquities* and the *Life.* Not only does he introduce the autobiography at the end of the *Antiquities,* but he also closes the *Life* by asserting that it concludes the *Antiquities* (*archaiologia; Life* 430). Later, he refers to "both my works"—*War* and *Antiquities-Life* (*Ag. Ap.* 1.54). Most manuscripts of Josephus include the *Life* as part of the *Antiquities,* and early readers of Josephus saw it the same way (Eusebius, *Hist. eccl.* 3.10.). If possible, therefore, we should try to come up with an explanation of the *Life* that integrates the two works very closely.

That is what I have proposed above. At the end of the *Life* (430), Josephus claims that he has presented a case for his character: "These are the deeds I have accomplished through an entire lifetime; from them, let others *judge my character* as they might wish" (emphasis added). Demonstration of character, whether of a defendant in court or of his prominent advocate/patron, was a critical feature of persuasion in ancient rhetoric (Isocrates, *Antid.* 278). One typically made such a demonstration with reference to the person's public activities (Aristotle, *Rhet.* 1.2; cf. *Life* 344). It stands to reason that the author of such a work as the *Antiquities* might want to celebrate his own character if he considered himself an unusually impressive spokesman for his nation, even if this seems rather vain to us. Tacitus remarks on the virtuous good old days: "Indeed, many men counted it not presumption, but self-respect, to narrate their own lives. A Rutilius, a Scaurus, could do so without being disbelieved or provoking a sneer" (*Agr.* 1.3).

Reading the *Life* as an essay on Josephus's character also explains other puzzling features of the book. For example, it is written in a rather sloppy style and with obvious disregard for historical precision. The reader who is curious about the actual unfolding of events in Galilee finds here a thick soup of unexplained references to people and places, doublets, and apparent self-contradictions, all written in a fairly crude and repetitive Greek. Oddities begin in the opening lines with the glaring problems of arithmetic in Josephus's lineage and education (*Life* 1–11) discussed in chapter 2. Then he fails to explain where Varus is located (*Life* 48–49), and mistakenly thinks that he has already introduced Jesus, son of Sapphias (66), Silas (89), and others (168). It is impossible to construct a clear picture of people and places from this story. With his disregard even for chronology (179), Josephus appears almost deliberately to frustrate historical analysis.

Every single episode that has a parallel in *War* 2–3 is retold differently here, from the details to the order to the persons involved. At the beginning we find him not as a solitary general dispatched from Jerusalem (*War* 2.562–568), but as one of three (*Life* 28–29)—a triumvirate, familiar to Roman audiences—who is sometimes outvoted by his two priestly colleagues (70–73). While he is in Galilee, sole commander after the departure of his colleagues, some Dabarittan youths rob a royal official's wife, seizing five hundred gold pieces and uncoined silver (*Life* 126–127), whereas in the *War* (2.595–596) they had robbed the royal official himself (no wife mentioned), taking six hundred gold pieces and silver goblets. In the *Life* (189–205), John of Gischala appeals to close friends among the Jerusalem elite, whom he convinces to send a four-man delegation to oust Josephus from Galilee. The delegation is escorted by six hundred troops. When Josephus hears about it, he intends to leave until he is persuaded otherwise by a dream. The four men are Jonathan the Pharisee (leader), the Pharisee Ananias, the Pharisaic priest Jozar, and the chief priest Simon. In the *War* parallel (2.626–629), the ne'er-do-well John appeals to unnamed leaders in Jerusalem, who also send four distinguished men. But these men are Yoesdrus, Ananias, and the *brothers* Simon and Judas, both *sons* of a Jonathan who does not appear. (The Simon of the *Life* cannot have been brother to another delegate in that scheme, or he too would have been called a chief priest, since that status comes from the family.)

These are only a few of the obvious differences between the *War* and the *Life*. They indicate plainly that historical precision was not among Josephus's main concerns, and they finally remove any suspicion that he was terribly worried by the criticisms of another author, and was trying to set the record straight. While referring the reader to the *War* for more details (*Life* 27, 412), he blithely contradicts the earlier account at every turn. This almost aggressive carelessness may in fact be a deliberate clue to his purposes. Notice that within the *Life* itself, he makes a theme of his deception and duplicity, constantly alerting the audience to the games he is playing. This begins when he first tries to dissuade the masses from revolt against Rome but then, fearing for his life because of their passion, begins to tell them what they wanted to hear: "Given the clear and present danger to ourselves, we said that we concurred with their opinions" (22). Although we might ridicule this approach as cowardly, the fates of King Abdullah of Jordan, Anwar Sadat of Egypt, Bashir Gemayel of Lebanon, and Yitzhak Rabin of Israel in modern history remind us that public figures have every right to be afraid of popular emotion, and they normally accommodate their speech accordingly. In the *Life*, indeed, Josephus undertakes a *program* of deception—just as his opponents also do (see 37–40, 70–72, 85–87, 130–131, 138–144, 175–178). Indeed, a good part of the story is taken up with elaborate descriptions of the way in which Josephus's deceptions triumphed over the intended deceptions of his enemies. In some respects the *Life* is a meditation on successful rhetoric.

Thus, although historical precision is cavalierly disregarded in the *Life*, what we find in its place is a consistent attention to the moral lessons of Josephus's career, and also characteristic sensitivity to the Roman reader (e.g., *Life* 1, 12, 16). Virtually every episode in the *Life* serves to illustrate one or another of the author's virtues. According to the accepted standards of Roman rhetoric, to demonstrate character one must ideally prove a brilliant ancestry and education, as well as a public career—preferably with military connections—illustrating all of the appropriate virtues (cf. Cicero, *Inv.* 75–82; *Leg. man.* 36–48). These include: courage, gravity, dignity, practical wisdom, ingenuity, humanity, clemency, piety (toward family as well as the gods) and consequent divine protection, moderation and the avoidance of greed or luxury, justice and avoidance of bribery, faithfulness or loyalty, patience in adversity, liberal treatment of and by friends, and success in one's affairs.

At the same time, one should ideally prove that one's opponents have dubious ancestries, and are base, greedy, faithless, disloyal, violent, impious, corrupt, cowardly, and therefore unsuccessful and subject to punishment by the deity. It was always useful to throw one's positive case *(probatio)* into sharper relief with the counterexamples of one's enemies *(refutatio)*. This is the model that Josephus follows.

Here is an overview of the book's contents:

I. Ancestry, education, and juvenile honors (1–12)

  A. Ancestry (1–6)
  B. Education (7–12a)

II. Josephus's public life (12b–413)

  A. Beginnings of public life (12b–29)
    1. Qualification for public life: embassy to Rome (13–16)
    2. Basis of mission to Galilee (17–29)
  B. Basic fulfillment of his mission, but personal opposition (30–188)
    1. Survey of Galilean situation (30–63)
    2. Confidence-building measures with the populace, fortifications, resistance to Josephus's command, and revolt in various regions; opposition led by John of Gischala (64–188)
  C. The delegation sent from Jerusalem to replace Josephus (189–335)
    1. The delegation's basis and mandate (189–203)
    2. Josephus's quandary and dream (204–212)
    3. First negotiations with the delegates (213–241)
    4. Confrontation at Gabara (242–265)

5. Josephus's counterembassy to Jerusalem (266–270)
6. Confrontation at Tiberias (271–304)
7. Josephus confounds, captures, and expels the delegation (305–335)

D. The unhappy sequel for Josephus's enemies; his own successes (336–413)

1. Digression: Justus of Tiberias, lying historian (335–367)
2. John of Gischala neutralized (368–372)
3. Sepphoris humiliated (373–380)
4. Tiberias threatened (381–389)
5. Justus of Tiberias, frustrated, flees (390–393)
6. Sepphoris narrowly escapes as Romans arrive (394–397)
7. Royal troops held in check by Josephus's army (398–406)
8. Philip son of Jacimus rescued from unjust punishment (407–409)
9. Justus of Tiberias condemned by Vespasian (410)
10. Summary remarks (411–413)

III. Domestic life (414–429)

A. In Alexandria and Jerusalem area (414–422)
B. In Rome (423–429)

Epilogue (430)

If we search for a plan within the *Life,* we find that Josephus moves from his personal and family life (1–11) to the brief (five- or six-month) period of his war leadership in Jerusalem and mainly Galilee, until Vespasian's arrival in the area (17–412)—by way of a deliberate transitional episode (13–16)—and after the story of his command, he pointedly reverts to personal and familial issues (413–430). This movement from personal life to public leadership to personal life prompts us to consider whether the *Life,* like Josephus's other works, has a concentric structure. Not surprisingly, it does.

To begin with, the parallels between the opening and closing sections are impressive. Not only do they deal with Josephus's family and children, in marked contrast to the body of the story, they also have him traveling to Rome (13–16, 422). He not only goes to Rome, but also moves in the circles of the imperial court: Nero's (13–16) and the Flavians' (423). Remarkably, in both cases he singles out an emperor's wife—Nero's Poppaea (16) and Domitian's Domitia Longina (429)—and uses the same language of both women: they gave him many "benefits." In both places Josephus refers to his accusers (6, 424–425). Only twice in the *Life* does Josephus say that he has been rescued by divine providence: in these opening (15) and closing (425) sections.

The clearest evidence of an artful structure to this work comes, however, at the one-quarter and three-quarter points in the main narrative. In each case we find a fairly lengthy story of the Galilean city of Tiberias's revolt from Josephus's leadership (84–103, 271–308 [–335]). The degree of similarity between these stories is remarkable. The first begins with John of Gischala's arrival in Tiberias for "the care of the body," ostensibly, at the nearby hot springs (85). The only other occurrence of this phrase comes at the end of the second revolt, when Josephus turns to the same diversion (329). Both revolts depend on John (85–87, 292, 304). In both, Josephus is warned by one Silas, concerning whom he claims to have spoken earlier—even when he first mentions him (89, 272)! There are only two references to a stadium facility in the *Life,* one in the first Tiberian revolt (92) and one in the second (331). In both stories, Josephus addresses the people of Tiberias (93–94, 297) and then flees Tiberias by boat, via a secret passage to the lake, retreating north to Tarichea (96, 304). At the conclusion of both stories, Josephus emphasizes that he had to dissuade the enraged Galileans from attacking John (97–100, 305–308; cf. 368–389), who had retired to Gischala, he notes (101, 308).

Most important, comparison with *War* 2.614–625 shows that in composing the *Life* Josephus has actually divided into two or three distinct episodes what the *War* had presented as a single set of events in Tiberias. The first part of *War*'s story (2.614–619) provides a fairly close match to the first Tiberian revolt in the *Life* (85–103). But in the conclusion of that story, Josephus deals with John's threat by gathering the names of his followers and threatening their families and property if they do not yield to him (*War* 2.624–625). This produces thousands of defections from John and leads directly to the delegation being sent from Jerusalem (*War* 2.626). Deprived of his following, John turns to Jerusalem for support against Josephus. The parallel story in the *Life* concerning the rounding up of John's followers, however, occurs only near the end (369–372), *after* the delegation from Jerusalem has come and failed, and long after the first Tiberian revolt (85–103). There is an obvious reason for the change: Josephus could not have dispensed with John's followers as early as *Life* 103, after the first Tiberian revolt in this account, because he has much more to say about John in the *Life.* So he has apparently split *War*'s one episode into two. This bifurcation of a single conflict suggests that Josephus has deliberately created a concentric pattern.

The final test of a proposed concentric pattern must lie in the central panel itself. If we search around the middle section of the *Life*'s 430 paragraphs for a fulcrum, we find in 208–209 the divine revelation to Josephus, through a dream, that keeps him in Galilee—in spite of his desire to return to Jerusalem after the delegation has been sent. This is the only such revelation in the *Life:*

> During that night I observed a wonderful sort of dream. For when I retired to bed, sorrowful and disturbed because of what had been written, a certain one standing over me appeared to say: "Look, you who are hurting, calm your mind! Let go of all fear! For the matters about which you are now sorrowful will produce greatness and the highest fortune in every respect. You will set right not only these matters, but many others as well. Do not exhaust yourself, but remember that you must also make war against the Romans."

It can hardly be a coincidence that this revelatory dream is so similar to the one at the end of *War* 3, in which God prevents Josephus from taking his own life on the ground that he still has a grand mission remaining in his future. Since Josephus has a great investment in his ability to interpret revelatory dreams, this episode in the *Life* must be significant indeed.

That this panel serves as a pivot for the narrative seems clear from the paragraphs immediately preceding (204–207) and following (210–211) the dream. They are somewhat repetitive, both dealing with Josephus's intention to leave Galilee (even after the revelation he wants to leave at first) and the hysterical reaction of the Galilean populace to this news. These paragraphs also use four key terms that run in one order in the section preceding the dream and then in reverse order in the section following the dream. Working out from the center, the terms are: "women and children" (207, 210); "they were begging" (206, 210); "leave them in the lurch" (205, 210); and "their territory" (205, 210).

Although we should not necessarily demand that a literary "center" in such a pattern also be the dramatic high point or even the most important feature of the story (in the gospels the dramatic climax and patterned structures often do not coincide), it certainly fits with what we know of Josephus elsewhere that he should feature this dream in his autobiography. His alleged divine mission here recalls the crucially important revelations he claims to have received before his surrender at

Jotapata (*War* 3.351–352), and we also remember the major role that he has given to dreams in the *Antiquities*—those of Joseph, Daniel, and Archelaus among others. In this case, the divine revelation puts beyond doubt both his authority for the position and his justice. He was quite willing to leave on orders from Jerusalem, had it not been for this mission. This declaration of God's favor provides an anchor for his stories of divine protection—the ultimate sign of virtuous character for Roman moralists also—at the beginning (in shipwreck, 13–16) and the end (from enemies, 424) of the story.

Once we have identified those major structural features of the *Life*, several other symmetrical pairs fall into place. For example, the major digression on Josephus's literary adversary Justus of Tiberias (336–376) is matched by a shorter one near the beginning (36–42). Although less formal, the first counts as a digression because it is disproportionately long in the otherwise crisp summary of factions at Tiberias. There are also several parallels of language and theme between the two: Justus's bent toward "revolutionary activities" (36, 391); Justus's bid to manufacture power for himself (6, 391–393); the Tiberians "proceed toward weapons" (31, 391—only); Justus's conflict with King Agrippa II (39, 355–356); and sarcasm concerning Justus's education and literary talent (40, 336, 340). When Josephus first approaches Tiberias in the narrative, he stops at a village "four stadia from Tiberias" called Bethmaus (64); in his last conflict with the city he again sets up at a village four stadia away (322). Early in the Galilean narrative he writes to Jerusalem for confirmation of his mandate (62–63); near the end, he writes again and receives confirmation (309; cf. 266–268). An important episode in the early narrative involves the plundering of Herod Antipas's palace in Tiberias, after which Josephus entrusts the stolen furnishings to Capella's group (64–69). The incident is recalled in the second half, when Josephus is interrogated as to the whereabouts of the plunder, and Capella's group acknowledges its possession of the furnishings (296). Josephus offers moralistic summaries of his virtuous command at 80 and at 259, in both cases noting that he left women "unmolested."

Related to the technique of mirroring episodes in this way is Josephus's habit of creating dramatic tension by beginning a story and bringing it to a critical point, but then leaving it for resolution at some later point. This technique operates at microlevels as well as the macrostructure we have considered. Some of the more impressive examples are as follows. The life-threatening plight of Philip son of

Jacimus is introduced at 46–61, though his superior King Agrippa will not learn whether he is dead or alive until 179–181. Furthermore, a nasty rumor about him created by Varus early on is resolved only at the end of the story (407–409). The fate of certain refugee dignitaries from King Agrippa's territory, who are introduced at 112–113 when Josephus must defend them against popular demands for their circumcision, is disclosed only in 149–153. This is sometimes called a "sandwich" technique: moving from bread to filling and back to bread. It is also used by some NT writers, notably Paul in 1 Cor 8–10 (idol meat, apostolic authority, idol meat) and most famously by the author of Mark. In Mark 5:22–43 the author has Jesus going to cure a synagogue leader's daughter who is "on the point of death" when he is interrupted by a woman with a hemorrhage, which heightens tension considerably. Indeed, the delay causes the little girl to die, so that Jesus' intervention must now be not merely a cure but a raising of the dead.

Space does not permit analysis of individual episodes in the *Life,* but a couple of representative examples will illustrate my point about the moral lessons Josephus wishes to provide. First, the short story about his transition from youth to public service, when he was sent on a mission to Rome at age twenty-six to secure the release of some priestly friends awaiting trial (*Life* 13–16), makes numerous points. Most obviously, he was willing to undertake heroic measures for his friends. These friends are described as noble gentlemen *(kaloi kagathoi),* a traditional phrase that reinforces Josephus's own eminent status. He develops the themes of piety and discipline when he notes that the prisoners were subsisting on figs and nuts, so as not to violate Jewish dietary prescriptions, and that he was especially moved by this (*Life* 14). Then he claims to have been dramatically rescued by divine providence from the stereotypical shipwreck in the Adriatic (*Life* 15). Finally, he describes his remarkable reception in Rome. Nero's wife Poppea, not only arranged for the priest's release, but also gave him large gifts. Readers should understand that this man is the perfect aristocrat, favored by mortals and the deity alike.

Another paradigmatic example of Josephus's public career comes in *Life* 80–86, where he pauses the narrative to dwell on his virtues. These include: his mastery of his passions, though of an age and rank in which temptations abounded; his utter avoidance of greed, to the point of refusing all gifts and even his legal due as a priest; his pious care for his family members; his determined clemency, even though he repeatedly had his most troublesome enemies at his mercy; his consequent divine protection; the affection and loyalty of those under his care; the envy and scheming of his opponents, whom he had so often treated mercifully; and his determined innocence in the face of such evil.

Other episodes of the *Life* may not be as full of obvious moralizing as these examples, but almost every one carries some moral lesson.

With this general picture of the *Life* in view, we are in a position to answer perhaps the most obvious question about the work, namely: if this is a book about Josephus's whole life, as he says, why does it focus with such an obvious lack of proportion on the five or six months of his time in Galilee? He gives short shrift to his personal life before (1–12) and after those months (414–430). This consideration was a major support for the older hypothesis that Josephus wrote in order to refute Justus. He dealt with this period because this was the one that Justus had challenged so thoroughly. But now we have another answer ready. Josephus dwelt on his time in Galilee because in Rome one should prove one's character through public (including military) service, and his Galilean command was the only period that offered him this material. After his capture at age thirty, his functioning public life as a Judean aristocrat was over. Before the revolt, we may presume, he had no such position of leadership. This was simply the most obvious theater in which he could illustrate his personal qualities, using convenient two-dimensional opponents to throw his virtues into even greater relief.

Further, the interpretation of the *Life* that I have proposed here integrates it fully with the *Antiquities*, to which it is attached. The *Life* also becomes broadly consistent with the *War*. When Josephus now changes the details, it is not because, having shifted political allegiances, he wishes to make subtle new points, as scholars have often thought. Such motives would not explain the general sloppiness of detail in this book. Rather, Josephus exploits his brief period of command in Galilee to make some claims about his aristocratic virtue in support of his magnum opus. In the spirit of his age, which we find also among the gospel writers, he shows not the slightest hesitation in changing details or disregarding precision altogether in the interest of making his present rhetorical points.

AGAINST APION

Thus far we have seen Josephus writing refutation of postwar slander *(War)* and then a celebratory manual of Judean history, law, and culture with an appendix on the author's character *(Antiquities-Life).* In spite of the different aims of his two major works, they both presuppose a well-disposed Gentile audience: a group in Rome who are *a priori* sympathetic to things Jewish and to Josephus himself. These interested Gentiles, Josephus expects, will help to mediate the truth (as he presents it) about the Jewish revolt and also find encouragement from his exploration of Jewish culture. When we turn to Josephus's last known composition, the so-called *Against Apion,* we must ask how this work fits in with his established Roman audience and literary aims.

Josephus did not call the work "Against Apion," as we have seen, but probably something like "On the Antiquity of the Jews," which better reflects its contents. Refutation of anti-Jewish slander accounts for only about half the book, the middle section 1.219–2.144, which again raises the prospect of a concentric or symmetrical structure. Certainly, the parts that precede and follow the systematic refutation (author by author) are both devoted to more positive declarations about the Jews. And one might note such parallels as Josephus's use of other nations to support Judean antiquity in the first part (1.69–218), and the appeal of Judean customs in the latter (2.282–283); some of the ridiculed customs in the first part (e.g., Sabbath) are the very ones emulated in the second. Still, the themes, tone, and literary forms of those first and final parts are quite different in many respects. Though the *Apion* is in one respect the most obviously concentric, because of the middle section's difference and internal coherence, it does not seem that Josephus has bothered to fully develop a symmetrical focus on refutation here. Instead, in his brief prologue (*Ag. Ap.* 1.1–5), Josephus says that he will consider the antiquity of the Jews for three reasons: to refute slanderers (who should have realized their errors after he wrote the *Antiquities*), to inform the ignorant, and to instruct those who desire to know the truth (1.3). The final group in this list matches Josephus's closing address to his friend Epaphroditus and, through his efforts, "those who likewise are determined to know [the truth] concerning our ancestry" (2.196). Since both Epaphroditus and the determined inquirers appear already in the prologue to *Antiquities* (1.12; "lovers of learning"), we seem to have more or less the same audience of Judeophiles in Rome. Indeed, Josephus assumes that readers of this last work know his earlier writings (e.g., *Ag. Ap.* 1.1, 47–56).

After a lengthy digression on the superiority of Oriental and especially Jewish record-keeping to its Greek counterparts (1.6–56),

Josephus restates his aim as essentially proving the antiquity of the Jews and refuting the calumnies of those who defame the nation and its origins. The former point requires his attention to the preliminary question as to why—or indeed, whether—the ancient Greeks were silent about the Jews (*Ag. Ap.* 1.58–59). So the book is at its heart a positive case for Jewish antiquity, since we have seen that for a Roman audience antiquity implies also virtue. This argument will be strengthened, in standard rhetorical fashion, by the refutation of contrary claims.

We may envision the content of the work thus:

Prologue (1.1–5)

Digression: Greek and Oriental history-writing (1.6–56)

Second introduction (1.57–59)

I. Greek silence concerning the Judeans (1.60–68)

II. Other (Oriental) witnesses to Judean antiquity—and the Greeks after all! (1.69–218)

III. Refutation of insults concerning Judean origins (1.219–2.144)

Peroration: The glory of the Jewish constitution (2.145–286)

Conclusion (2.287–296)

Josephus's witnesses for Jewish antiquity are drawn from all over the Orient—from Phoenicia, Ephesus, Babylonia—and even from enemies of the Jews such as the Egyptian Manetho. He also finds unnoticed evidence of the Jews in Pythagoras, Herodotus, Aristotle, and others. By contrast, he pointedly isolates the malicious attacks on Jewish origins in Egypt, which gives him an opportunity to speculate on the base motives—envy, feelings of inferiority, hatred—the Egyptians had for slandering the Jews (1.223–226). Then he takes up the statements of Manetho, Egyptian high priest of the early third century B.C.E., and the later Alexandrian scholars Chaeremon, Lysimachus, Apollonius Molon, and Apion. The grammarian and Homeric scholar Apion receives the greatest attention, perhaps because he had taught in Rome under Tiberius and Claudius, and so his portrait of the Jews might still have been the most influential.

Following his refutation of the Egyptians' false claims about Jewish origins, Josephus turns to a final presentation of the Jewish constitution, which marks the climax of his literary legacy. He will show that this constitution promotes piety *(eusebeia),* friendly relations with one another *(koinōnia),* and humanity *(philanthrōpia)* toward the world—responding forthrightly once again to charges of impiety and misanthropy (2.146–147). The ancient priestly aristocracy that guarantees the preservation of this constitution, under divine mandate, is so special that Josephus ventures to coin the term "theocracy" for it (2.165):

> Could there even be a more excellent or just [constitution] than that which, having established God as ruler of all things, having assigned to the priests as a body the administration of the greatest issues, has entrusted the rule of the other priests to the high priest? (2.185)

According to Josephus, this constitution produces a social harmony that is unmatched elsewhere (2.179–181). Though humane, it absolutely controls vice (2.211–217, 276–278). It promotes such a high level of virtue that it instills contempt for death—the sure sign of an effective philosophy (2.232–233, 271–275). Recall the Jews' contempt for death in the *War.* For these reasons and more, it is the envy of the entire world, and the major Greek philosophers borrowed extensively from it (2.168; cf. 1.162, 166–167, 175, 182, 190), though they could not actually implement their ideals on a large scale (2.220–231). A big difference between Moses and these other philosophers—and here Josephus articulates fully what he has often implied—is that Moses welcomed all those from other nations who wished to come to live under his constitution (2.209–210, 257–261). This is much more than the famous Spartans or Athenians offered, though somewhat like the Roman extension of citizenship to others.

This minor parallel with Roman society is matched by a number of elements in the *Apion* that establish connections between Jewish and Roman cultures. When he is speaking of the Judean priests' concern to maintain their genealogies even after major upheavals in the land, he mentions three invasions of Judea as examples. Of the many invasions in Jewish history, however, he names only those that would be familiar to Romans: by Antiochus Epiphanes (enemy of Rome who had grown up in the capital), by Pompey the Great ("great" is the transliterated Latin *magnus* rather than the Greek translation), and by Quintilius Varus—a general infamous in Rome and featured by Josephus in his *War* (*Ag. Ap.* 1.34–35). When Josephus tries to explain the silence of early Greek authors about the Judeans, he claims that this resulted in part from the maritime situation of their cities in contrast to others, such as Jerusalem and Rome, which have no seacoast; hence the silence of early Greek writers about Rome, too (1.66).

Indeed, Josephus's treatment of Greek writers in the *Apion* is often very sarcastic. They were late learning the alphabet and found the lesson hard (1.10); their writings are not that old (1.12); Greek historians disagree with each other at every turn, basing their accounts on mere conjecture and hearsay (1.15–16); Greek cities neglected to keep records (1.20–21); Greek authors are preeminently concerned with language, rhetoric, appearances, and flattery—not with historical truth (1.23–27); and consequently, Greeks have no great respect for their own writings and would not risk anything for them (in stark contrast to the Jews; 1.44–46). If we ask why Josephus treats the Greeks with such disdain, the answer can only partly be that this is necessary for his argument, since he goes much further than is necessary. Moreover, he has always had a tendency to speak of Greeks with similar ridicule, from his first writing (*War* 1.13–16; *Ant.* 1.121, 20.262–263; *Life* 40). The easiest explanation of this enduring attitude on Josephus's part toward the Greeks appears to be that it matches traditional Roman attitudes. Although by Josephus's time the Roman upper class had thoroughly adapted Greek culture, as had Josephus's Judean peers, the Romans had a long history (still continuing) of nasty remarks about the Greeks: as lightweights, concerned with image and rhetoric (rather than gravity and moral truth), money-grubbers, effeminate, and so on. Although Romans might have considered Josephus a "Greek" in the broad sense, since he came from the eastern Mediterranean and communicated in Greek, his ridicule of the Greeks appears to be an effort to move closer to his Roman audience through shared prejudices.

To understand Josephus's aims in this work, and the impact he might have expected it to have, we cannot treat it as a text without historical context. Determining his likely audience is critical for imagining the extratextual resources shared by him and his readers, and thus his purpose, for the same words have different meanings in different social contexts. A politician who stands before an audience to declare, "It is time to cut taxes and reduce social programs!" will be understood very differently by a group of businessmen than by a nurses' union. Writers and speakers, to be effective, must work from certain assumptions about what their audiences already know and feel. It would be easy to suppose that because Josephus targets the Jews' detractors rhetorically, his intended audience comprised enemies of the Jews. Or scholars sometimes argue that he addressed some "neutral" Gentiles who innocently wondered about the truth concerning the Jews.

The problem with these abstract images lies in the realities of ancient book production, which we have already discussed. Authors needed first of all a real circle of readers/hearers, people who would willingly gather in homes and lecture halls to listen to the author recite, or at least to read drafts of the manuscript. The *War,* though it is at its root a refutation of false claims (*War* 1.3, 6), assumes such a group of supporters, and so does the *Antiquities-Life.* Neither work could plausibly have been aimed directly at the Judeans' hard-core enemies, and in fact the accounts of such hostile writers as Tacitus (*Hist.* 5.1–4) show no knowledge of Josephus's claims concerning Jewish antiquity.[17] Fair-minded but neutral Romans would have had no obvious motive to seek out a rare copy of the *Against Apion,* or to spend an evening listening to Josephus. Self-satisfied aristocratic enemies of the Jews would have had even less motive.

We have already seen that Josephus's first audience for *Apion* appears to have included the interested Gentiles of Epaphroditus's circle carried over from *Antiquties-Life,* and perhaps others. But why would he address his refutation of slander to them? Had they been convinced by such lies?

Perhaps our best clues come from Josephus's tone and method of argument, in addition to the work's contents. It has been widely observed that his arguments, clever though they are, would not have persuaded a determined critic.[18] He demonstrates a great deal of wit, but wit is appreciated more by a kindred spirit than by a genuine antagonist or a skeptic. His logic leaves something to be desired. In his zeal to prove that Manetho of Egypt inadvertently attests to the antiquity of

---

[17] Tacitus, *Hist.* 5.13, does refer to three omens also mentioned by Josephus (*War* 6.294–300). But these might have gone into wide circulation as omens of the Flavians' rise, wrenched from their context in Josephus—if he was the first to mention them.

[18] For what follows, see S. J. D. Cohen, "History and Historiography in the *Contra Apionem* of Josephus," *History and Theory* 27: *Essays in Jewish Historiography* (1988), 1–11; Arthur J. Droge, "Josephus Between Greeks and Barbarians," in *Josephus' Contra Apionem: Studies in its Character & Context with a Latin Concordance to the Portion Missing in Greek* (ed. L. H. Feldman and J. R. Levison; Leiden: Brill, 1996), 115–42; John M. G. Barclay, "Josephus v. Apion: Analysis of an Argument," in *Understanding Josephus: Seven Perspectives* (ed. Steve Mason; Sheffield: Sheffield Academic Press, 1998), 194–221.

the Jews, he identifies the Jews with the mysterious Hyksos people mentioned by Manetho (*Ag. Ap.* 1.91), even though this association would otherwise undermine his portrayal (since the Hyksos ruled by terror), and even though he will later accuse the same Manetho of insisting on the Egyptian origin of the Jews (1.229). He also implies that Manetho made the identification of Hyksos and Jews, though he did not (1.228). He uses several quotations from other authors who he claims support his conclusions, although they do not clearly do so if read by themselves (e.g., 1.135–141, 146–153). When he cites the Greek authors who allegedly confirm the antiquity of the Jews, it appears that he invents at least some of this evidence. In spite of the energy and sarcasm that Josephus applies to his investigation, his arguments could not withstand—and so presumably were not intended for—truly critical analysis. In this respect, *Apion* is no different from Josephus's earlier works. In the same way, his excursus devoted to refuting Justus of Tiberias in *Life* 336–367 is highly sarcastic and extremely loose with logic. It might convince Josephus's friends, but not Justus or his supporters.

That Josephus expected an audience that would not analyze his logic too closely is indicated also by the tone of his language. For example, he plans to expose the "utterly absurd slanders of the slanderers of our nation" (1.59) and "to deprive our jealous enemies" of a pretext for controversy (1.72). Such harsh language reveals that the reader is assumed to be on his side; he is preaching to the choir, so to speak. Again, when he traces the defamation to envious Egyptians, he remarks: "These frivolous and utterly senseless specimens of humanity, accustomed from the first to erroneous ideas about the gods, were incapable of imitating the solemnity of our theology, and the sight of our numerous admirers filled them with envy" (1.225). Although it is true that aristocratic Roman authors disdained Egyptian influences in Rome, the same people disdained the Jews at least as much. Such a bold dismissal of the Egyptians, coming from a Judean, would not carry a self-evident force with skeptics.

Yet again, Josephus sarcastically describes Apion's suffering from ulceration of the genitals and eventual submission to circumcision, after Apion had mercilessly ridiculed circumcision, with great delight (2.144). But presumably these barbs could be appreciated only by an audience that already accepted circumcision presumably (cf. also 2.115, 318). Although the anti-Jewish stories obviously disturb him, the posture he assumes with his readers is one of trust and familiarity, not of hostility or even dispassionate reasoning.

Reading the content of the *Against Apion* in light of its literary and social contexts—as a sequel to the *War* and *Antiquities-Life,* prepared for a group of amenable Gentiles in Rome—it is difficult to avoid understanding its purpose somewhat as follows. Those inhabitants of Rome who were keenly interested in Jewish culture had to encounter widespread antipathy toward the Jews following the failed revolt. We know from Tacitus (*Hist.* 5.1–13) and others (above) that characterization of the Jews as misanthropic and bellicose went hand in hand with depictions of their origins as base and derivative of greater cultures. Josephus appears to target all his works at a group of friends who are aware of the slanders, but still enough on side to be heartened by his spirited attacks and defenses. Being "lovers of the truth," as Josephus calls them, they are eager to be armed with the intellectual ammunition that will allow *them* to dismiss the false accounts.

Although it is not a significant theme of *Against Apion,* one continues to detect the substructure provided by Jeremiah and Daniel in Josephus's outlook, particularly in his critique of Apion. There he confronts the claim that the Jews have typically found themselves in servitude to others with this observation: "For although it has been the lot of a few [nations] to become an imperial power by watching for the right moment, the reversals of fortune have once again yoked even these nations in slavery to others. Most every tribe has often had to submit to others" (2.127). His mention of Athenians and Spartans as examples recalls the words that the *War* had put in the mouth of Agrippa II (*War* 2.358–359). Josephus continues to hold that nations rise and fall under God's sovereignty.

In reading *Apion,* it is important for modern scholars to keep this agenda for referring to the prophets in mind. Tempting though it is to use Josephus to answer our more specific questions, reading his work in context often shows that he has something else entirely in view. *Against Apion* 1.37–41 offers a good example of the perils of reading Josephus without regard for his own contexts. Having stressed the great antiquity and faithful preservation of the Jews' historic writings, Josephus continues:

> The *prophets alone* learned the highest and oldest matters by the inspiration of the God, and by themselves plainly recorded events as they oc-

curred, so among us there are not myriads of discordant and competing volumes, but only twenty-two volumes containing the record of all time, which are rightly trusted. Now of these, five are those of Moses, which comprise both the laws and the tradition from human origins until his passing; this period falls little short of three thousand years. From Moses' passing until the Artaxerxes who was king of the Persians after Xerxes, the prophets after Moses wrote up what happened in their times [or, as they saw things] in thirteen volumes. The remaining four [volumes] comprise hymns toward God and advice for living among humanity. From Artaxerxes until our own time all sorts of things have been written, but they have not been considered of the same trustworthiness as those before them, because the exact succession of the prophets failed. (emphasis added)

New Testament scholars have used this passage in two main ways. First, they have taken the final sentence about the failure of "the exact succession of prophets" in support of a claim that Josephus and many other Jews were somehow frustrated by the absence of prophets in their time, that they saw their period as one of *waiting* for the arrival of a true prophet. Although this view is common, it runs directly counter to Josephus's main points and values. As we have seen, for him "old is good," and in this context it is a great advantage that the Judean records, which were written exclusively by prophets, were finished way back in the time of Artaxerxes—unlike the more famous texts, of the Greeks, who were "born yesterday" (*Ag. Ap.* 1.17). There is no feeling of prophet-deprivation here; it is a good thing that the Jewish prophets are in the far distant past. In the *War* Josephus has vehemently rejected any claims by his contemporaries to be latter-day prophets. For Josephus, if anyone could be a prophet now it would surely be him, since his Jeremiah-like self can predict the future at times. Yet he denies the title even to himself. Prophets are part of the golden age in Josephus's view, and he has no time for people who desire upheaval in the present. This is not to deny that perhaps some *other* Jews were hoping for a new prophet, but Josephus was not among them.

Second, this passage is used by those who want to construct a picture of what the Bible (OT) looked like in the time of the first Christians. Some of the NT evidence indicates a three-part structure (Luke 24:44), such as the rabbis would later adopt (Torah, Prophets, Writings), although much NT evidence mentions only Law and Prophets (Matt 5:17; 7:12; John 1:45; Acts 13:15; 24:14; 28:23), leaving the third category unmentioned or limited to Psalms (e.g., Luke 24:44). Was the overall form of the Bible, then, still unformed in the first century C.E., or was it already thought of as in three sections (by some groups or generally)? At first glance, Josephus's remarks appear—to both sides—to settle the question. He appears to divide Jewish Scripture into three groups (Moses, prophets after him, and a third group), and yet the third division is rather skimpy in contrast to the Writings section of the rabbinic Bible.

In fact, however, a careful reading of Josephus's passage in context shows that it simply has no bearing on this modern question and cannot resolve it. Most important, his reference to "prophets after Moses" creates a false parallel with the Prophets section of the rabbinic Bible. In Josephus's thinking *all* of those who wrote these texts were inspired prophets, including Moses and also the last writers; after them the prophetic "succession" ended, so that the nation's texts have been completed for a very long time (unlike those of the Greeks). "Prophets" is not a division. He is rather describing the various kinds of material found in these twenty-two books: law and history in the books by Moses, a large amount of history by others, and then some hymns and advice for living (possibly Psalms, Proverbs, Song of Songs, Ecclesiastes). It is clear that Josephus considered all of Jewish Scripture finished long before his time. (His twenty-two books can be reconciled with the thirty-seven of the OT by counting some multivolume or shared-scroll texts together as one.) But he says nothing about divisions within this body of ancient writing. The apparent link between his language and our questions is illusory.

Whereas the *War* had left only the vaguest hint of future Jewish supremacy, and the *Antiquities* had been somewhat more forthright, Josephus now seems to believe that he is actually witnessing the rise of Jewish influence. At the end of *Against Apion,* he dwells on the vitality and spread of Jewish customs throughout the entire world (2.279–286). All of this inclines us to classify the *Against Apion* as his last and best effort for sympathetic Gentiles.

CONCLUSION: JOSEPHUS, THE MAN AND THE WRITER

Josephus has usually been either loved or hated. The hatred has stemmed from his personal biography, which, even on the most charitable reading, smacks of opportunism and routine deception. In Jewish circles he has been reviled as an arch traitor. Christians have tended to value him for what they thought he said about the destruction of the temple and about Jesus as Messiah. This traditional bifurcation of opinion lives on among scholars in a milder form. Those who are concerned with his biography usually regard him with deep skepticism; those who focus on his writings as literary productions tend to admire his dedication to a theme.

It is natural that we should want to choose between these options. We want to know whether Josephus was one of the "good guys" in history or one of the "bad guys." Our assessment depends on our starting point. On the one hand, if he could behave like *that,* then his writings must be dismissed as self-serving rhetoric. On the other hand, if he could write so passionately in defense of his people, in a time of crisis, then we should give his behavior the benefit of the doubt.

I propose that we resist our natural inclination to make such neat assessments. Our own experience of the world teaches us that people who are capable of inspiring speech or writing (the two were closely linked in antiquity) often lead less than exemplary lives. This does not mean that their speech is worthless or even deliberately deceitful; it may reflect their deepest yearnings, and it may be powerfully effective. People are more complex than the labels "good" and "bad" suggest. We could all be accused of hypocrisy by someone or other, if we were in positions that attracted such attention.

In Josephus's case, we ought to bear in mind three further considerations: (a) his biography is not something that we *know,* but it must be hypothetically reconstructed from his own highly stylized accounts; (b) his writings, which *are* immediately accessible, show him to have labored tirelessly and persuasively in defense of his people; and (c) in many cases, his duplicity is quite deliberately recounted by *him* in an effort to demonstrate his resourcefulness or other virtues as a public figure. We can hardly use these rhetorical ploys as evidence against him. I, for one, take his real personality to be unknown and unknowable. At the same time, I have deep respect and gratitude for the writings that he has left us.

FOR FURTHER READING

On the place of Jews in the Greco-Roman world, see:

- Molly Whittaker, *Jews and Christians: Graeco-Roman Views* (Cambridge: Cambridge University Press, 1984), 1–130, which contains the most important texts in translation, with notes and introductions.
- Menahem Stern, *Greek and Latin Authors on Jews and Judaism* (3 vols.; Jerusalem: Israel Academy of Sciences, 1976), which provides the complete texts of relevant passages, in the original language and in translation, with commentary.
- Louis H. Feldman, *Jew and Gentile in the Ancient World: Attitudes and Interactions from Alexander to Justinian* (Princeton, N.J.: Princeton University Press, 1993).
- Peter Schäfer, *Judeophobia: Attitudes toward the Jews in the Ancient World* (Cambridge, Mass.: Harvard University Press, 1997).
- J. P. V. D. Balsdon, *Romans and Aliens* (Chapel Hill, N.C.: University of North Carolina Press, 1979), which provides a larger view of the Romans' treatment of foreign groups.

On Roman attitudes to war and rebellion, the first two books offer much insight. The third and fourth are large collections of essays on aspects of Rome in the period of the Flavian emperors, when Josephus lived there:

- John Rich and Graham Shipley, eds., *War and Society in the Roman World* (London: Routledge, 1993).
- Susan P. Mattern, *Rome and the Enemy: Imperial Strategy in the Principate* (Berkeley: University of California Press, 1999).
- A. J. Boyle and W. J. Dominik, eds., *Flavian Rome: Culture, Image, Text* (Leiden: Brill, 2002).
- Jonathan Edmondson, Steve Mason, and James Rives, eds., *Flavius Josephus and Flavian Rome* (Oxford: Oxford University Press, forthcoming).

For some fundamental aspects of Roman religion, education, literary culture, book production, and rhetoric see:

- David S. Potter, "Roman Religion: Ideas and Actions," in D. S. Potter and D. J. Mattingly, *Life, Death, and Entertainment in the Roman Empire* (Ann Arbor, Mich.: University of Michigan Press, 1999), 113–67.
- Mary Beard, John North, and Simon Price, *Religions of Rome* (2 vols.; Cambridge: Cambridge University Press, 1998).

- H. I. Marrou, *A History of Education in Antiquity* (trans. G. Lamb; Madison, Wis.: University of Wisconsin Press, 1956).
- Catherine Salles, *Lire à Rome* (Paris: Les Belles Lettres, 1992).
- William V. Harris, *Ancient Literacy* (Cambridge, Mass.: Harvard University Press, 1989).
- George A. Kennedy, *A New History of Classical Rhetoric* (Princeton, N.J.: Princeton University Press, 1994).
- Elaine Fantham, *Roman Literary Culture: From Cicero to Apuleius* (Baltimore, Md.: Johns Hopkins University Press, 1996).
- William J. Dominik, ed., *Roman Eloquence: Rhetoric in Society and Literature* (London: Routledge, 1997).

For Josephus's historiography in general see:

- Klaus-Stefan Krieger, *Geschichtsschreibung als Apologetik bei Flavius Josephus* (Tübingen: Francke Verlag, 1994).

Balanced and readable introductions to each of Josephus's writings are offered by:

- Harold W. Attridge, "Josephus and His Works," in *Jewish Writings of the Second-Temple Period* (Compendia Rerum Iudaicarum ad Novum Testamentum 2.2; ed. Michael Stone; Assen: Van Gorcum/ Philadelphia: Fortress, 1984), 185–232.
- Per Bilde, *Flavius Josephus between Jerusalem and Rome* (Sheffield: Sheffield Academic Press, 1988), 61–122.

Of the older general introductions, the following, by two great Josephus scholars, are still worth reading:

- Benedictus Niese, "Der jüdische Historiker Josephus," *Historische Zeitschrift*, n.f. 40 (1896): 193–237.
- Henry St. John Thackeray, *Josephus: The Man and the Historian* (New York: Ktav, 1929; repr. 1967).

For various interpretations of the *Jewish War* see:

- Wilhelm Weber, *Josephus und Vespasian: Untersuchungen zu dem Jüdischen Krieg des Flavius Josephus* (Hildesheim: Georg Olms, 1921; repr. 1973).
- Helgo Lindner, *Die Geschichtsauffassung des Flavius Josephus im* Bellum Iudaicum (Leiden: Brill, 1972).
- Tessa Rajak, *Josephus: The Man and His Society* (London: Duckworth, 1983).

- Per Bilde, "The Causes of the *Jewish War* According to Josephus," *Journal for the Study of Judaism* 10 (1979): 179–202.
- Menahem Stern, "Josephus and the Roman Empire as Reflected in the *Jewish War*," in *Josephus, Judaism, and Christianity* (ed. Louis H. Feldman and Gohei Hata; Detroit: Wayne State Univeristy Press, 1987), 71–80.
- Martin Goodman, *The Ruling Class of Judaea: The Origins of the Jewish Revolt against Rome AD 66–70* (Cambridge: Cambridge University Press, 1987).
- Jonathan J. Price, *Jerusalem under Siege: The Collapse of the Jewish State, 66–70 C.E.* (Leiden: Brill, 1992).
- Gottfried Mader, *Josephus and the Politics of Historiography: Apologetic and Impression Management in the Bellum Judaicum* (Leiden: Brill, 2000).

For the *Jewish Antiquities* see:

- Harold W. Attridge, *The Interpretation of Biblical History in the Antiquitates Judaicae of Flavius Josephus* (Missoula, Mont.: Scholars Press, 1976).
- Louis H. Feldman, *Josephus's Interpretation of the Bible* (Berkeley: University of California Press, 1998).
- Louis H. Feldman, *Studies in Josephus' Rewritten Bible* (Leiden/New York: Brill, 1998).

For the *Life* see:

- Richard Laqueur, *Der jüdische Historiker Flavius Josephus: Ein biographischer Versuch auf neuer quellenkritischer Grundlage* (Darmstadt: Wissenschaftliche Buchgesellschaft, 1920; repr. 1970).
- Shaye J. D. Cohen, *Josephus in Galilee and Rome: His Vita and His Development as a Historian* (Leiden: Brill, 1979).
- Jerome H. Neyrey, "Josephus' *Vita* and the Encomium: A Native Model of Personality," *Journal for the Study of Judaism* 25 (1994): 177–206.
- Folker Siegert and Jürgen U. Kalms, eds., *Internationales Josephus-Kolloquium Münster 1997: Vorträge aus dem Institutum Judaicum Delitzschianum* (Münster: LIT, 1998), a collection of essays on the *Life.*
- Steve Mason, *Life of Josephus* (vol. 9 of *Flavius Josephus: Translation and Commentary;* ed. Steve Mason; Leiden: Brill, 2001).

For the *Against Apion* see:

- Louis H. Feldman and John R. Levison, eds., *Josephus'* Contra Apionem: *Studies in Its Character and Context with a Latin Concordance to the Portion Missing in Greek* (Leiden: Brill, 1996).
- Christine Gerber, *Ein Bild des Judentums für Nichtjuden von Flavius Josephus: Untersuchungen zu seiner Schrift Contra Apionem* (Leiden: Brill, 1997).

Chapter 4

Who's Who in the New Testament World?

The three preceding chapters have dealt with Josephus on his own terms; the next three will deal with New Testament questions. That is, we shall now take issues that arise for us as readers of the NT and present them to Josephus for clarification. Because we now have some familiarity with his world of thought, we should be better positioned to understand his replies. The illumination to be gained from Josephus is potentially infinite, however, so we shall need to restrict our inquiries in some way. I propose in this chapter to consider selected groups of people in the NT world who are discussed by Josephus. Chapter 5 will narrow the focus to figures from the early Christian tradition who are mentioned by Josephus. Then, in chapter 6, we shall look at parallels between Josephus and Luke-Acts. A concluding chapter will summarize the results of our study and suggest some wider aspects of Josephus's significance.

If we want to study the background of the NT—historical, political, social, geographical—everything that Josephus wrote is relevant to some degree. All we can do in this chapter is ask him about some obvious, representative features of the NT world. I have selected the following groups of people: Herod the Great and his family; the Roman governors of Judea; the Jewish high priesthood; and the Jewish "philosophical schools" (especially Pharisees and Sadducees). My goal in discussing these groups is to provide examples of how one can read Josephus's evidence about any given topic within the context of his own thought. The point is not, in the first instance, to discover the *truth*

THE ROMAN EMPIRE
• City
THRACE Roman province
Boundary of Roman Empire 65 C.E.
Roman road
0 100 200 Miles
0 100 200 Kilometers
©2003 CHK AMERICA WWW.MAPSUSA.COM
NORICUM
PANNONIA
DACIA
ILLYRICUM (DALMATIA)
ITALIA
THE ADRIATIC SEA
MOESIA
MACEDONIA
THRACE
THE TYRRHENIAN SEA
Corsica
Sardinia
SICILIA
Melita (Malta)
EPIRUS
THESSALY
ACHAIA
THE AEGEAN SEA
Lesbos
Chios
Samos
Patmos
MYSIA
LYDIA
Propontis
Hellespont
Crete
Rhodos
Cauda
THE MEDITERRANEAN SEA
AFRICA
SYRTIS
TRIPOLITANIA
CYRENAICA
Danube R.
Tiber R.
Appian Way
Egnatian Way
Genua
Portus Veneris
Luca
Florentia
Arretium
Perusia
Pola
Ravenna
Ariminum
Ancona
Siscia
Sirmium
Singidunum
Viminacium
Solonae
Naissis
Oescus
Novae
Istros
Tomi
Odessus
Mesembria
Debeltum
Sardica
Scupi
Scodra
Philippopolis
Rome
Ostia
Antium
Three Taverns
Forum of Appius
Capua
Tarracina
Beneventum
Puteoli
Canusium
Pompeii
Paestum
Apollonia
Brundisium
Tarentum
Sybaris
Croton
Carales
Dyrrhachium
Amphipolis
Philippi
Neapolis
Thessalonica
Byzantium
Beroea
Apollonia
Cyzicus
Troas (Alexandria)
Larissa
Assos
Prusa
Adramyttium
Pergamum
Thyatira
Mitylene
Nicopolis
Actium
Panormus
Messana
Rhegium
Utica
Carthage
Agrigentum
Catana
Syracuse
Madaurus
Delphi
Thebes
Corinth
Cenchreae
Athens
Smyrna
Sardis
Philadelph
Ephesus
Laodicea
Colossae
Piraeus
Same
Olympia
Miletus
Sparta (Lacedaemon)
Cnidus
Rhodos
Patara
Hadrumetum
Thapsus
Salmone
Phoenix
Lasea
Fair Havens
Sabratha
Oea
Lepcis Magna
Cyrene
Alexandria
Oxyrhyn

F
G
H
I
J
1
2
3
4
5
6
BOSPORUS
Chersonesus
THE BLACK SEA
SARMATIA ASIATICA
COLCHIS
THE CASPIAN SEA
Cyrus R.
Ionopolis
Sinope
Amastris
BITHYNIA & PONTUS
Amisus
Side
Trapezus
KINGDOM OF ARMENIA
Lake Seyan
Artaxata
Araxes R.
Gangra
Amasea
Comana
GALATIA
Ancyra
Tavium
Dorylaeum
Gordium
Pessinus
Halys R.
Lake Tuz
LYCAONIA
Antioch in Pisidia
CAPPADOCIA
Caesarea (Mazaca)
Archelais
Malatya
Lake Van
Tigranocerta
MEDIA
ATROPATENE
Lake Urmia
GORDYENE
Samsat
COMMAGENE
Iconium
Derbe
Lystra
PAMPHYLIA
Perga
Tarsus
Issus
CILICIA
Seleucia
Zeugma
Europus (Carchemish)
OSROENE
Edessa
Carrhae (Harran)
Nisibis
ADIABENE
Ninus
Arbela
MEDIA
Antioch
Seleucia Pieria
Euphrates R.
PARTHIAN EMPIRE
Tigris R.
Apamea
Epiphania
SYRIA
Emesa
Palmyra
Dura-Europos
CYPRUS
Salamis
Paphos
Tripolis
Berytus
Sidon
PHOENICIA
ABILENE
Damascus
MESOPOTAMIA
Ctesiphon
Seleucia
Babylon
ELAM
Tyre
Ptolemais
Caesarea Philipi
Tiberias
Scythopolis
Caesarea
Sebaste
Jordan R.
JUDEA
Joppa
Jerusalem
Gaza
Dead Sea
Canopus
Sais
Pelusium
NABATEAN KINGDOM
Petra
Dumah
Heliopolis
Babylon
Aila (Aelana)
THE PERSIAN SEA
EGYPT
Nile R.
ARABIA
Tema
THE RED SEA
N

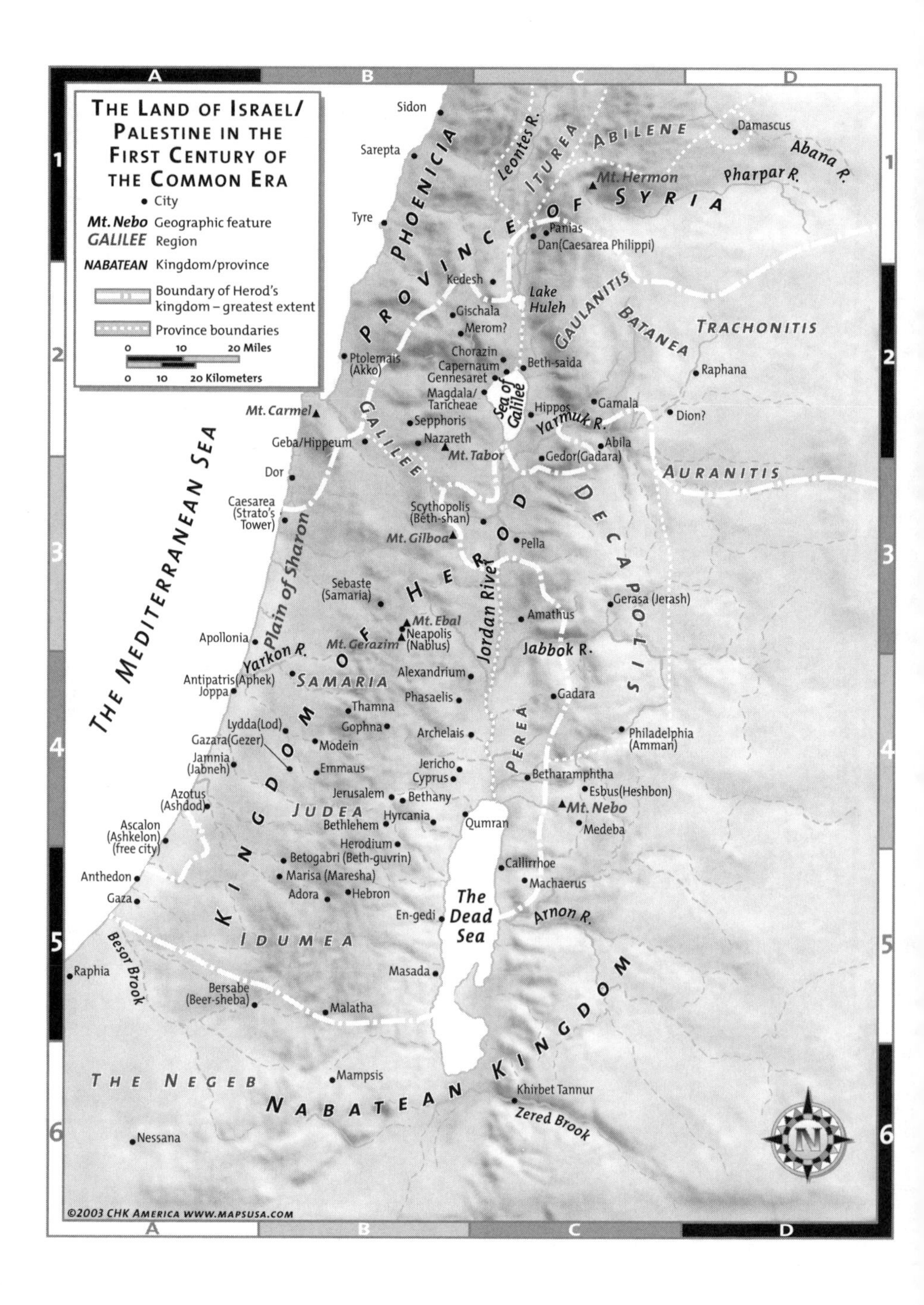
THE LAND OF ISRAEL/ PALESTINE IN THE FIRST CENTURY OF THE COMMON ERA
• City
Mt. Nebo Geographic feature
GALILEE Region
NABATEAN Kingdom/province
Boundary of Herod's kingdom – greatest extent
Province boundaries
0 10 20 Miles
0 10 20 Kilometers
Sidon
Sarepta
Tyre
PHOENICIA
PROVINCE OF SYRIA
Leontes R.
ITUREA
ABILENE
Damascus
Abana R.
Pharpar R.
Mt. Hermon
Panias
Dan(Caesarea Philippi)
Kedesh
Lake Huleh
GAULANITIS
BATANEA
TRACHONITIS
Gischala
Merom?
Ptolemais (Akko)
Chorazin
Capernaum
Gennesaret
Beth-saida
Magdala/ Taricheae
Sea of Galilee
Raphana
Gamala
Hippos
Dion?
Yarmuk R.
Mt. Carmel
Sepphoris
GALILEE
Nazareth
Geba/Hippeum
Mt. Tabor
Abila
Gedor(Gadara)
Dor
AURANITIS
Caesarea (Strato's Tower)
Scythopolis (Beth-shan)
Mt. Gilboa
Pella
DECAPOLIS
THE MEDITERRANEAN SEA
Plain of Sharon
KINGDOM OF HEROD
Jordan River
Sebaste (Samaria)
Gerasa (Jerash)
Mt. Ebal
Amathus
Neapolis (Nablus)
Apollonia
Mt. Gerazim
Jabbok R.
Yarkon R.
Antipatris(Aphek)
SAMARIA
Alexandrium
Joppa
Phasaelis
Gadara
Thamna
Lydda(Lod)
Gophna
Archelais
Philadelphia (Amman)
Gazara(Gezer)
Modein
PEREA
Jamnia (Jabneh)
Emmaus
Jericho
Cyprus
Betharamphtha
Azotus (Ashdod)
Jerusalem
Bethany
Esbus(Heshbon)
JUDEA
Mt. Nebo
Ascalon (Ashkelon) (free city)
Bethlehem
Hyrcania
Qumran
Medeba
Herodium
Betogabri (Beth-guvrin)
Callirrhoe
Anthedon
Marisa (Maresha)
Machaerus
Gaza
Adora
Hebron
The Dead Sea
En-gedi
Arnon R.
IDUMEA
Besor Brook
Raphia
Masada
Bersabe (Beer-sheba)
Malatha
NABATEAN KINGDOM
THE NEGEB
Mampsis
Khirbet Tannur
Zered Brook
Nessana
N
©2003 CHK AMERICA WWW.MAPSUSA.COM

Major Figures in the Herodian Family

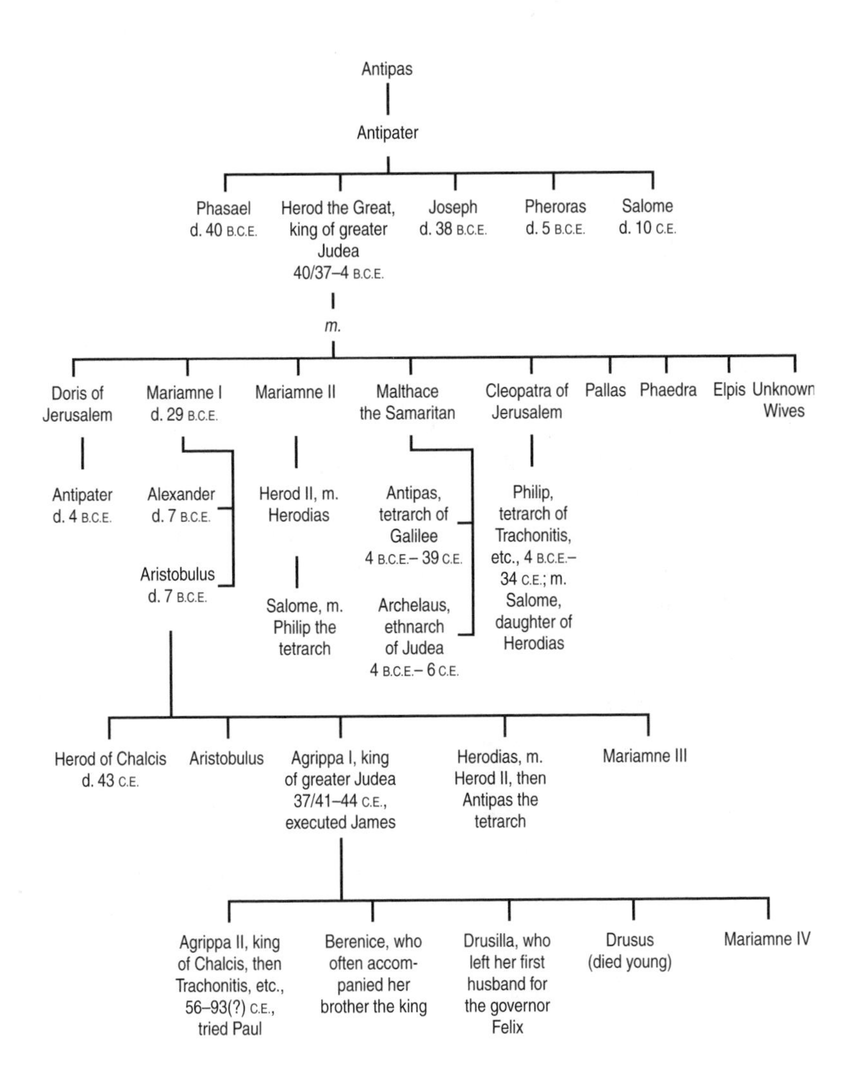

about these people, which would require the massive investigation of all relevant sources that typifies the large manuals of Jewish history. Our purpose is rather to understand how these groups function in Josephus's narratives, and what *he* wants to say about them. With such experience, I hope, the reader will then be able to consult the text of Josephus itself on any number of other questions that might be of further interest. So this is not a comprehensive treatment of the NT background; it is rather a primer for further study.

HEROD THE GREAT AND FAMILY

Of the various political figures who provide the setting for the gospels and Acts, Herod the Great and his descendants are the most prominent. Four generations of the Herodian family are mentioned in the NT.

(a) The infamous King Herod himself (reigned 37–4 B.C.E.) ruled all of Palestine[1] at the time of Jesus' birth (Matt 2:1–19; Luke 1:5).

(b) At Herod's death, his kingdom was partitioned by the Roman emperor Augustus and given to three of Herod's sons, but none of them was granted the title of king, which Herod had enjoyed.[2] Archelaus became ethnarch, or "national ruler," and was given the heartland of Judea, Samaria, and the coastal plain. He was hated by his subjects and, proving hopelessly incompetent, was removed by the Romans in 6 C.E. Herod's son Antipas, by contrast, governed Jesus' home region of Galilee for more than forty years (4 B.C.E.–39 C.E.), throughout Jesus' entire life, along with the region of Perea across the Jordan River. It was this tetrarch, or "ruler of a quarter," who executed John the Baptist (Matt 14:1; Luke 3:19), and according to Luke he also played a role in Jesus' death (Luke 13:31; 23:6–12). Still a third son, Philip, was made tetrarch of the more remote northern and eastern parts of Herod's kingdom (4 B.C.E.–34 C.E.). His only claim to fame in the NT is the notice that his wife Herodias had been taken by his brother Herod Antipas (Matt 14:3–4; Mark 6:17–18; cf. Luke 3:1).

(c) Herod Agrippa I, a grandson of Herod the Great, was king over his grandfather's entire territory for a critical two- to three-year period

[1] That is, Judea, Samaria, Galilee, Trans-Jordan, Idumea, and the coastal plain. This would later be called Palaestina by the Romans.

[2] For the division of Herod's kingdom, see Josephus, *War* 2.94–98.

in the young church's history (41–43/44 C.E.).[3] He executed the apostle James, brother of John, and imprisoned Peter, who then miraculously escaped (Acts 12:2–19).

(d) Finally, Agrippa II, son of Agrippa I and great-grandson of Herod the Great, served as king, first of Chalcis in Lebanon (48/49–53 C.E.) and then of the former territories of Philip in the northeastern region of Palestine (53–93/95 C.E.).[4] This is the King Agrippa who, while visiting the new Roman governor in Caesarea (about 59 C.E.), allegedly interviewed Paul and found him innocent of any serious charge (Acts 25:13–26:32).

It is a compelling example of Josephus's importance for NT studies that the above sketch, basic though it is, could not have been written without his help. Obviously, the family of Herod played a major role in the lives of Jesus and the first Christians. But remarkably, the gospel writers refer to this dynasty in the vaguest of terms. Only the author of Luke-Acts displays any interest in clarifying the relations among various rulers, and even he is often unclear. Acts refers to Agrippa I as simply "Herod the king" (12:1) and to his son (Agrippa II) as "Agrippa the king" (25:13) without any further explanation. Mark, for his part, says that it was a "King Herod" who executed John the Baptist, after offering his stepdaughter as much as half of his "kingdom" (Mark 6:14–29). But the Baptist worked under Herod's son Antipas, the tetrarch of Galilee and Perea, and Josephus insists that none of Herod's sons was permitted to be called king or to have a kingdom (*War* 2.20–38, 93–100). Matthew and Luke, significantly, both call the Herod who executed John the Baptist a *tetrarch* (Matt 14:1; Luke 3:19), in agreement with Josephus. They seem to be correcting Mark. We should be in a sorry state indeed if we did not have the accounts of Josephus for clarification.

I have argued, however, that it is insufficient for us merely to rip out from Josephus's accounts those bits of information that help us, while discarding the rest like old rags. Josephus has both a sustained interest in and outstanding sources for his accounts of the Herodian dynasty. He uses these rulers to illustrate major themes of his various works. If we are to understand his "evidence" about

---

[3] On Agrippa I, see Josephus, *War* 2.214–222; *Ant.* 19.292–352.

[4] On Agrippa II, see Josephus, *War* 2.223–284; 3.56–57; *Ant.* 20.104, 138–140.

the family of Herod, we must first examine the roles these figures play in his stories.

In the *Jewish War*

In general, as we saw in the last chapter, the entire family of Herod appears rather differently in the *War* and the *Antiquities.* In the *War,* we first meet Herod's father, Antipater, the clever governor of Idumea. Through courage and shrewd diplomacy, Antipater manages to win successive favors from various Roman leaders, culminating in the governorship of Judea, which Julius Caesar grants him in about 47 B.C.E. He appears as a staunch ally of the Romans and a vigorous opponent of all rebellion (1.201–203). His son Herod is first appointed by his father as governor of Galilee, where he too rids the country of rebels and is thus greatly admired by the people. Some people oppose Herod, to be sure, but these are "malicious" advisers of the high priest and "wretches" (*War* 1.208, 212). Herod appears throughout as brave (1.369–385, 429–430), virtuous, compassionate (1.295), pious (1.354–357), aided by providence (1.331, 341), and especially devoted to his family (1.263–267). This might seem difficult to maintain in view of the fact that he would ultimately murder his own wife and several sons, but Josephus explains these acts as the result of vicious intrigues against the king: he was largely the innocent victim of his own devotion to his wife Mariamne I, who was his undoing (1.431–440). For Josephus as for his Roman audience, it was easy to blame women for a man's failings (*Ant.* 2.43, 53; 4.219; 8.318; 15.98; 13.430–431; 15.219; 17.351–353; *Ag. Ap.* 2.201; Plutarch, *Cat. Maj.* 8.2).

The *War* says little about the tenure of Herod's sons in their respective jurisdictions but focuses rather on the turbulence that arose in Judea while they were away in Rome bidding for the right to succeed Herod. In describing the rebellion at home, Josephus takes the opportunity to illustrate his major themes: that the problem of legitimate succession is a basic weakness of monarchy (2.1–110); that only a few of the Jews had rebellious instincts, even though the masses had real grievances (2.73, 84–89); that the rebel leaders were truly tyrants, out for personal power, who squabbled among themselves and terrorized other Jews (2.56–65); and that the Roman authorities, by contrast, were readily able to distinguish the few belligerents from the innocent or misled populace. Significantly, right where we might expect Josephus's account of the Herodian princes' governments, he inserts his lengthy account of the Essenes' politically docile mode of life, in contrast to that of the rebel faction (2.118–166). This interlude avoids the messy details of Judean politics during this period while drawing the reader's attention to the philosophical heart of Judaism. The Essenes' discipline, gravity, mastery of their passions, contempt for death, imperviousness to the wiles of women, and many other qualities should resonate quite precisely with characteristically Roman virtues.

Herod's grandson, King Agrippa I, appears in the *War* mainly as a central figure in Roman political circles, for he served as intermediary between the new emperor Claudius and the Roman senate, which initially opposed Claudius (2.204–213). And Herod's great-grandson, Agrippa II, makes a long speech to those rebelling against Rome in 66 C.E., in which he argues that God is now with the Romans; he castigates the rebels for their belligerent, non-Jewish behavior (2.345–404). As a Roman ally and client, he also provides auxiliary troops for the Roman campaign in Jerusalem (3.68).

Obviously, Josephus's description of the Herodian dynasty in the *War* has been tailored to fit that work's larger aims. These important figures illustrate his claims that the the Jews and their traditional leaders have always understood the need to cooperate with world powers, who rule by God's permission, and that rebellion is alien to Jewish ancestral custom. He even offers the Romans an implicit paradigm for their treatment of the Jews after the recent rebellion of 66–74 C.E.: just as the Romans had not allowed earlier rebellions in Judea to weaken their support for the Herodian family and its supporters, so also now they should not harass all Jews for the troubles caused by a few renegades.

In the *Jewish Antiquities*

Because the purpose of the *Antiquities* is somewhat different from that of the *War,* Josephus uses the family of Herod to different effect in this narrative. To begin with, the larger scope of the *Antiquities* allows him to devote much more space to the Herodian dynasty; King Herod alone receives the greater part of four volumes (14–17). Much of the new coverage serves to point out the shortcomings of Herod's family. This new theme is plainly geared to illustrate one of *Antiquities'* theses—that, according to the ancient and noble constitution of the Jews, those who stray from the laws come to a disastrous end. Since Herod and many of his successors came to disastrous ends, and since Josephus has available excellent accounts of Herod's reign (see below), he elects to use this first-rate material to illustrate his argument.

The new angle is already apparent in Josephus's discussion of Herod's father, Antipater, who is now introduced to the reader as a "rabble-rouser" or troublemaker: he gains influence in Judea as a result of his scheming, lies, and secret intrigues (14.8–18). Likewise, Herod himself appears as a violator of the nation's laws. Whereas the *War* had attributed such charges to some "malicious" members of the high priest's entourage (1.208), the *Antiquities* makes it clear that Herod really was a violator who literally got away with murder. He is opposed in court by one Samaias, "an upright [or righteous] man and for that reason superior to fear" (14.172). When Herod is appointed king by the Romans, the legitimacy of his rule is openly questioned (14.403). Indeed, the Jewish nation as a whole seems to oppose his rule (15.8–10). Josephus elaborates considerably on Herod's execution of the high priest Hyrcanus II: in the *War,* this had been merely an unfortunate incident that was part of Herod's domestic trouble (1.433–434); now he concludes firmly against Herod, that it was an act contrary to both justice and piety (15.182). Josephus goes on to assert that Herod's introduction of Greek-style games and institutions into Jerusalem was a perversion of Jewish ancestral custom and a cause of the city's later destruction (15.267; cf. 328), and the king's impious act of opening David's tomb brought God's wrath on his family (16.179–188).

In several revealing passages, Josephus reflects on Herod's character. He takes issue with those who find Herod's combination of generosity and cruelty paradoxical. Josephus himself believes that these apparently conflicting tendencies arise from a single motive, namely unbridled greed and ambition. Herod was generous only when it served his ends; otherwise he was harsh, immoderate, bestial, and evil. Josephus hastens to add that Herod's character stood in opposition to the values of Jewish law and tradition (16.150–159). In another place, he recognizes the role of "fate" in Herod's career and also assigns some blame to his sons. But he is strongest in his denunciation of the king himself, who had an "irreligious spirit" and a "mind that could not be turned from evil" (16.395–404). While narrating Herod's death, Josephus describes him as "cruel to all alike and one who easily gave in to anger and was contemptuous of justice" (17.191). The *Antiquities* dwells at length on the horror of Herod's worsening illness and declares that his unparalleled suffering was the result of his sacrilege (17.150–152). While elaborating on *War*'s treatment of Herod's succession woes in the latter half of book 17, Josephus now liberally portrays Herod and his sons as a tyrannical dynasty. And all of this has the important new purpose of exposing Roman monarchy-tyranny in books 18 and 19 (see chapter 3). This new moralizing in the *Antiquities* is calculated to demonstrate the work's thesis that the wicked suffer divine retribution.

The same thesis explains the significant new information about Herod's son Antipas, who governed Galilee from 4 B.C.E. to 39 C.E. The tetrarch, we are now told, built the city of Tiberias over a former graveyard, in violation of Jewish law (Num 19:11–16). He had to bribe and force the poor into living there, for he knew that he had built it in contravention of religious law (18:36–38). Especially interesting is the complex of events associated with Antipas's marital affairs. Married for some time to the daughter of a neighboring Arab king, the tetrarch became infatuated with his stepbrother's wife Herodias while on a trip to Rome. (This brother was an otherwise unknown son of Herod the Great by his wife Mariamne II, daughter of the high priest Simon.) These two conspired to elope, but Herodias would marry him only if he dismissed his Arab wife, and thus they plotted. Their proposed marriage, of course, flatly violated Jewish law, which prohibited a man from marrying the wife of a brother who was still alive (Lev 18:16).

But Antipas's first wife got wind of the plot and escaped to her father, the Arabian king, who took the opportunity to settle by war an old boundary dispute with Antipas. In the ensuing conflict, Antipas was soundly thrashed and his army would have been destroyed, says Josephus, had the Romans not intervened (18.109–124). It is within this story of Antipas's affairs that Josephus includes an account of John the Baptist (18.116–119). The tetrarch's execution of this good and righteous man, says Josephus, was held by many Jews to be the cause of his military defeat (18.116).[5] Josephus pointedly concludes that his whole narrative of Herod's family is germane to his account because it demonstrates that no degree of worldly power will succeed if it is not matched by piety toward God. This lesson contributes to the "moral instruction of mankind" (18.128).

---

[5]We shall consider Josephus's discussion of the Baptist more closely in chapter 5.

The brief career of King Agrippa I is described in much greater detail in the *Antiquities* than in the *War.* It is shaped to illustrate both sides of Josephus's thesis: the Jewish God and his constitution ensure that the righteous prosper and the wicked suffer. On the one hand, the king successfully intercedes with the emperor Gaius Caligula, who temporarily stays the order that would have put his statue in the Jewish temple (18.297–301). Later, Agrippa persuades the emperor Claudius to speak in favor of Jewish rights in Alexandria and around the empire (19.279, 288). Thus Agrippa is a key figure in Josephus's larger claim that Roman emperors have consistently recognized the legitimacy of Jewish traditions. Further, Agrippa champions the "laws of his fathers" by demanding the punishment of some men who had erected a statue of the emperor in a Jewish synagogue (19.299–311). Indeed, Josephus claims that he "scrupulously observed the traditions of his people" and neglected nothing in the way of proper observance and sacrifice (19.331).

On the other hand, Josephus relates that the young Agrippa had been a hopeless profligate who had recklessly depleted his funds and managed to offend many Roman aristocrats who had initially befriended him (18.143–204). He was at one point imprisoned by the emperor Tiberius for his impudent hope that this emperor would soon die and be replaced by Agrippa's friend Gaius. It seems to have been Agrippa's early exercise of improper ambition that came back to haunt him at the end. Josephus relates that when Agrippa attended games in Caesarea, the sun reflected off his clothing in such a way that he appeared superhuman. Some of the nobility hailed him as divine, and, since he did not correct them, he was immediately felled with a heart attack, which five days later proved fatal (19.343–352). Once again, Josephus's thesis is illustrated: those who violate the laws are punished.

Agrippa II is not a major figure in the *Antiquities,* though he does play an important role in the appended *Life.* Significantly, Josephus mentions widespread rumors of an incestuous relationship between Agrippa II and his widowed sister Berenice (20.145) and also Agrippa's unprecedented violation of Jewish custom by building an addition to his palace that enabled him to watch sacrifices in the temple (20.191). Nevertheless, Josephus continues to speak of Agrippa II with respect. He appeals to the king's endorsement of his own work in the *Jewish War,* even citing letters from him, against Justus of Tiberias (*Life* 364). He consistently portrays himself as a friend of the king's, and as having worked for his interests during the war (*Life* 68, 128). His portrayal of

Agrippa II therefore matches his presentation of other major figures, especially the Herodians, in the *Antiquities-Life*. As we saw in chapter 3, he seems to aim at a balanced assessment, but this allows the introduction of considerable criticism.

The differences between the *War* and the *Antiquities-Life* in their portrayals of the Herodian dynasty have usually been explained on the bases of (a) Josephus's new sources in the later works, and (b) some shift in his own thinking and/or political allegiances that made him either less charitable or more honest concerning this powerful family. It certainly seems likely that he has, or has now chosen to use, new sources on the Herods. His generally positive portrayal of Herod in the *War* accords with what he later dismisses as the flattering whitewash written by Herod's aide Nicolaus of Damascus, who "wrote to please him and be of service to him, dwelling only on those things that redounded to his glory" (*Ant.* 16.184). Nicolaus had written a universal history in 144 books, perhaps the largest of its kind, and had included several books on Herod's reign. It seems that Josephus relied heavily on this work when writing *War,* for which it served his purposes adequately: it showed the Judean king's great favor and prestige in Roman circles. By the time he writes the latter part of the *Antiquities,* having lived and studied in Rome an additional fifteen years, he is aware of several other sources on Herod and uses them to expand and qualify the earlier account (*Ant.* 15.174).

Conceding that Josephus had new sources at his disposal, however, does not mean that he used them slavishly. Obviously he does not, since as we have seen he freely criticizes Nicolaus. Rather, his literary aims and rhetorical constraints, which change somewhat from *War* to *Antiquities,* provide the main reason for the changes in presentation. Even in the *War* Josephus lets slip some indirect religious criticisms of Herod (*War* 1.649–650; 2.84–86), but to dwell on them there would not have helped his argument. In the *Antiquities,* by contrast, his purpose is to show that divine judgment inexorably follows departure from the laws of Moses, so his treatment of Herod's career is replete with illustrations of this point. It is this change of purpose in the *Antiquities* that explains his willingness to employ the new material and the critical language.

In the New Testament

We may now ask how the NT references to the Herodian family might be better understood against the background of Josephus's portrayals. The only actions of Herod the Great described by a NT writer come in Matthew's infancy narrative (Matt 1–2). This is the story of the Persian astrologers, the magi, who follow a star to Jerusalem in search of the newborn "king of the Jews." When Herod hears of this birth, he orders that all male children in the vicinity of Bethlehem two years of age or younger (in accordance with the time of Jesus' birth) be killed (Matt 2:16). Joseph and Mary flee to Egypt, however, and while they are there Herod dies. Joseph intends to return home to Judea but, finding that Herod's son Archelaus has come to power, settles instead in Nazareth of Galilee (2:19–23).

The atmosphere of this story fits well with Josephus's descriptions of Judean life under Herod and Archelaus: many Jews at the time lived in great fear, and any rival claimant to the title "King of the Jews" would have been ruthlessly exterminated. Such a story would have resonated with people living in the region who knew the Herodian legacy. It is strange, though, that Josephus does not mention any slaughter of male children near Bethlehem, right at the end of Herod's reign where his account is most detailed. Such a monstrous action could hardly have escaped public notice. Josephus would arguably not have mentioned it in the *War* even if he had known about it because that work holds Herod up as a fine example of good Jewish-Roman relations. But in the *Antiquities,* as we have seen, the gloves come off and Josephus goes into all sorts of grisly details about the king's rule, in order to explain the unparalleled suffering that eventually killed him. In this context, in which he dwells on even less dramatic infractions of the law, it would plainly have served his purpose to mention a massacre of infants; that would have been Herod's basest action. Killing one's own family members, monstrous though that was, was a common enough practice in royal families as also in the Roman imperial courts; it was understood as a political fact. A massacre of innocent infants was of another order entirely. The probability, therefore, is that Josephus did not know the story of the massacre, although he had not only Nicolaus's history but also several other accounts of Herod's reign at his disposal. Further, it seems clear that Luke did not know the story, for in his account Joseph and Mary come from Nazareth to Bethlehem for a census and then return home after Jesus' birth (Luke 2:1–39); there is no room here for Matthew's two years in Bethlehem followed by a sojourn in Egypt.

In the case of Herod Antipas too, much of the gospel material is well complemented by Josephus's account. In particular, the gospels' notice that the Baptist was imprisoned for criticizing the tetrarch's marriage to his sister-in-law Herodias (Mark 6:17) makes abundant sense. Josephus says only that John was imprisoned because he had a large following and therefore was suspected of revolutionary motives; however, in view of what was going on at the time of John's arrest, it would not contradict Josephus's point if the preacher had also said of Herodias "It is not lawful for you to have her" (Matt 14:4). Also compatible with Josephus's portrayal is Luke's account of Antipas as "that fox" who was seeking to kill Jesus (Luke 13:31) and participated in his trial (23:6–12).

Significant problems arise, however, when we compare Mark's and Josephus's accounts of John the Baptist's death. Chief among these are Mark's claims: that the tetrarch Antipas was "King Herod" (6:14); that Herodias had been Philip's wife (6:17), whereas Josephus claims that she had been the wife of Herod the Great's son by Mariamne II; that Antipas was involuntarily trapped by his own oath into executing John, for he knew him to be righteous, heard him gladly, and wanted to keep him safe (6:20), whereas Josephus had Antipas arrest and execute John out of sheer self-interest (agreeing with Matt 14:5; Luke 3:19); and that Herodias's daughter, a noblewoman who *was* married to the tetrarch Philip, according to Josephus, was brought in to dance for the viewing pleasure of Herod and his friends (Mark 6:21–29). Such erotic dancing was in the job description of slaves, not of elite women, for whom it would be scandalous.

In making historical determinations about this episode, one ought to note: (a) that Matthew, by radically abbreviating the story, removes or mitigates many of these problems; (b) that Luke, who also used Mark as a source and seems to have known a good deal about Herod Antipas, omits the story of the party altogether; (c) that later manuscripts of both Matthew and Luke omit the name "Philip" from the designation of Herodias's former husband (presumably since Josephus's writings were becoming known when the texts were copied); and (d) that one cannot easily challenge Josephus's account of the Herodian family tree because it is a tightly woven and intricate whole, based on excellent sources; the gospel of Mark, for its part, has no sustained interest in Antipas but mentions only this single episode. Like Matthew and Luke, the gospel that we call "Mark" is really an anonymous document; we do not know who wrote it or where his information came from.

The Political World of Josephus and the New Testament

Emperors	**High Priests**	**Governors in Judea/Samaria**	**Rulers in Galilee/Perea**
Augustus (27 B.C.E.–14 C.E.)	Simon b. Boethus (5 B.C.E.)	Herod the Great (40/37–4 B.C.E.)	Herod the Great (40/37–4 B.C.E.)
	Mattaiah / Joseph / Joezer / Eleazar / Jesus b. See (5 B.C.E.–6 C.E.)	Archelaus (4 B.C.E.–6 C.E.) Coponius (6–9)	Herod Antipas (4 B.C.E.–39 C.E.)
Tiberius (14–37)	Ananus (6–15)	Ambivulus (9–12) Rufus (12–15)	
	Ishmael b. Phabi / Eleazar / Simon (15–18)	Valerius (15–26)	
	Joseph Caiaphas (18–37)	Pontius Pilate (26–36)	
Gaius Caligula (37–41)	Jonathan and Theophilus b. Ananus (37–41)	Marcellus (37) Marullus (37–41)	
Claudius (41–54)	Simon Cantheras / Matthias / Elionaeus / and Joseph b. Camei (41–47)	King Agrippa I (41–44) Fadus (44–46)	King Agrippa I (41–44) Fadus (44–46)
Nero (54–68)	Ananias b. Nebedaeus (47–59)	T. J. Alexander (46–48) Cumanus (48–52) Felix (52–59/60)	T. J. Alexander (46–48) Cumanus (48–52) Felix (52–56)
	Ishmael b. Phabi II (59–61)	Festus (59/60–62)	King Agrippa II (56–95)
	Joseph and Ananus II (62)		
	Jesus b. Damnaeus (62–64?)	Albinus (62–64)	
	Jesus b. Gamaliel (64–65?)		
Galba / Otho / Vitellius (68/69)	Matthias b. Theophilus (65–67) Phanni b. Samuel (67–70)	Florus (66–70)	
Vespasian (69–79)		Bassus (70–72) Silva (72–75)	
Titus (79–81)		Commodus (75–80)	
Domitian (81–96)		Salvidenus (80–86) Longinus (86–95)	

Within the NT corpus, King Agrippa I and his son Agrippa II appear only in Acts. The story of Agrippa I, in Acts 12, corresponds well to the general tone of Josephus's account in the *Antiquities*. The comment that because Agrippa's execution of James "pleased the Jews" he also arrested Peter (Acts 12:3) fits with Josephus's observation that the king, unlike his grandfather, devoted himself to Jewish life and causes. Since Josephus presents Agrippa's care for the tradition as a shift from his earlier prodigality, he may be suggesting that it was a strategy for ruling and maintaining popular support, more than a heartfelt commitment. The claim in Acts that Agrippa was trying to maintain the favor of the Jewish people presupposes the kind of political motivation that Josephus asserts. Moreover, Josephus and Acts (12:22) agree that the king died because he accepted praise as a god.

As we have come to expect, however, the details in Acts do not correspond exactly to those offered by Josephus. Whereas Josephus had claimed that Agrippa I was stricken with a heart attack in the theater at Caesarea, after failing to correct those who hailed him as a god, and died five days later, Acts has him seated on his throne in the palace at Caesarea. A delegation from Tyre and Sidon had come to appease the king's anger, and when he had finished a speech to them, these Gentiles hailed him as a god. Then "immediately an angel of the Lord struck him, because he did not give the glory to God; he was eaten up with worms and expired" (Acts 12:23). Interestingly, Acts mentions that Agrippa had first put on his royal robes (12:21), but it does not say with Josephus that the glimmer of the robes inspired the worship. Why, then, are the robes mentioned? It almost seems as if the author (we do not know who wrote Luke and Acts) has Josephus's story in mind—that he has adapted Josephus's story for his own narrative purposes (see chapter 6). Once again, Josephus's evidence cannot be easily dismissed, since he was in close contact with the king's son (Agrippa II), from whom he even cites personal letters (*Life* 363–366); he had detailed information about both father and son.

As for Agrippa II, the account in Acts of his interview with Paul (25:13–26:32) dovetails nicely with Josephus's portrayal. Josephus nowhere mentions Paul, and that is probably evidence of the limited impact that Christianity had on the turbulent life of first-century Judea. Josephus does mention several other persecuted leaders of small groups, and according to Acts 21:38 Paul is mistaken for one of these men. (More about that in chapter 6.)

But the story of Paul's hearing before Agrippa II matches Josephus's account in its repeated reference to his companion Berenice (Acts 25:13, 23; 26:30). Acts does not explain that she is Agrippa's sister, nor does it divulge why she is there, since she does not figure in the exchanges with Paul. The modern reader might easily suppose that she is his wife. But once we know Josephus's account, the episode takes on a sharply sarcastic tone. Here is the great king in all his pomp (25:23), brought in by the Roman governor Festus because of his purported expertise in things Jewish (25:26), which the governor lacked. Indeed, Paul repeatedly appeals to the king's familiarity with Jewish teaching: "With all that I am being accused of by the Jews, King Agrippa, I consider myself fortunate that I am to defend myself before you today, above all because you are expert in Jewish customs and issues" (26:2–3, 26–27). But if the reader knows that this august Jewish leader, who presumes to try Paul, is all the while sitting next to the sister with whom he is reportedly having an incestuous affair, in violation of the most basic Jewish laws, then the whole trial becomes a comedy. Paul's appeals to Agrippa's Jewish knowledge are, in that case, devastating barbs.

None of this requires that either the author of Acts or his first readers knew Josephus's writings, since the rumors about Agrippa II and Berenice circulated widely (cf. Juvenal, *Sat.* 6.158). But the fact that, in its stories of both Agrippa I and Agrippa II, Acts seems almost to ride "piggyback" on Josephus's accounts, forces us to examine more closely the relationship between these two works. We shall do so in chapter 6. For now, we simply note that although the NT accounts of the Herodian family fit with the general portrayal of their character and motives drawn in Josephus's *Antiquities,* the details sometimes differ.

THE ROMAN GOVERNORS OF JUDEA

Closely related to the family of Herod were the Roman governors of Judea. The whole of Palestine had fallen under Roman control in 63 B.C.E., with the arrival of the general Pompey. But the Romans were disinclined to invest their own administrative and military resources into the rule of a faraway territory unless it were absolutely necessary. So for a couple of decades (63–40 B.C.E.), they was content to let the native Jewish Hasmonean dynasty, which had been in power for about seventy-five years, continue to serve as high priests with some political control over internal Jewish affairs. But the last representatives of the Hasmonean dynasty proved politically weak, and that is why Herod's father, an Idumean, could insinuate himself into Judean affairs. Ultimately, Herod himself achieved the remarkable privilege of ruling as "king" under Roman patronage (appointed in 40, ruled 37–4 B.C.E.). But when Herod's son Archelaus was banished for incompetence (6 C.E.), the Romans finally decided that it was time to make Judea an imperial province, bringing it under the direct control of Roman governors and armies.

Of the fourteen governors who served between 6 C.E. and the outbreak of the Jewish revolt in 66 C.E., only three are mentioned in the NT. Most famous is Pontius Pilate, who executed Jesus. Antonius Felix and Porcius Festus appear in Acts' account of Paul's arrest and imprisonment. We shall examine Josephus's descriptions of these men in the context of his larger portrayals of the Roman governors.

In the *Jewish War*

In the *War*, Josephus uses the Roman governors to introduce at least two nuances into his general thesis about the Jewish revolt. First, he wants to show that, although the vast majority of Jews were peace-loving and did not desire rebellion, they had to contend with numerous provocations from the later governors. The rebels were grossly misguided, to be sure, but one can see the reasons for their hostility. Those who opposed rebellion were not themselves enamored of the Romans but rather exercised the Jewish virtues of patience and self-control. So Agrippa II is made to say: "Granted that the Roman ministers are intolerably harsh, it does not follow that all the Romans are unjust to you" (*War* 2.352, LCL). The rebels, by contrast, displayed an un-Jewish zeal for confrontation from the beginning.

Second, Josephus has to explain the conspicuous fact that, in spite of his own peace-loving inclinations, he himself ended up as a "general" in the rebel cause. Today, we can understand such a paradox in view of the many current examples of Eastern and Middle Eastern leaders who are thoroughly Westernized culturally, perhaps by education, but find themselves in conflict with Western governments because of social-political constraint. But Josephus does not explore this paradox. Describing his appointment as general, he simply remarks that the Jewish rebels in 66 C.E. "won over those who still favored Rome—both by force and by persuasion" (2.562), leaving open the possibility that he was persuaded or coerced into fighting. Thus he was appointed a general, as was John the Essene (2.567), even though the Essenes have already been portrayed as peaceful and politically docile (2.140–142). His point seems to be that by the end of 66, with the initial success of the rebels and the atrocities of the last Roman governors, even the most moderate aristocrats, including himself and the high priestly family, were caught up in the swirl of events. But to make this case plausible, he must recount the misdeeds of the last governors.

The first governor, Coponius (6–9 C.E.), is mentioned only in passing (2.117–118). With his arrival in 6 C.E., Judea fell under direct Roman administration and so was subject to tribute payments. Josephus takes this opportunity to introduce Judas the Galilean, the archetypal rebel, who immediately called for revolt on the ground that Jews should have no lord but God (2.118). This notice permits him, in turn, to discuss at length the three legitimate "schools of Jewish philosophy," which hold no such views (2.119–166). Of Coponius himself, Josephus remarks only that he held "equestrian" rank (i.e., of the Roman lower nobility)—this may be an intended slur coming from Josephus, who postures as an elite aristocrat; the sending of equestrians to govern the provinces was also a source of complaint from the Roman senatorial class—and that Coponius came with full powers, including that of capital punishment (2.117). This last point has stimulated much scholarly discussion because of its possible bearing on the thorny question whether the *Jewish* court was also permitted to execute criminals (e.g., in the case of Jesus). We cannot discuss that question here because Josephus does not pose it. We may note, however, that Josephus seems to mention Coponius's power here in order to set the stage for the subsequent actions of the governors, who will indeed execute Judean provincials at their discretion. So the notice helps to build a sense of tension that steadily increases throughout the remainder of the book. His point is not that the Jewish leaders were deprived of the power to execute, but only that Coponius *had* it.

Interestingly enough, for the NT reader, in the *War* Josephus omits any mention of the next three governors but chooses to discuss Pontius Pilate's career (26–36 C.E.) at some length (2.169–177). He relates two episodes that illustrate this man's insensitivity and cruel capriciousness. First, upon his arrival in Judea, Pilate arranged to have standards of the emperor Tiberius, with sculpted images attached, brought into

Inscription bearing the name of the Roman governor Pilate.
Photo courtesy of Southwest Missouri State University.

Jerusalem during the night. The Jews saw this as a violation of the second commandment (Exod 20:4), which prohibited the making of images.[6] Jewish refusal to tolerate images of God was known to at least some Greek and Roman observers, and Josephus portrays Pilate's action, "by night, under cover," as a deliberate offense. But the Jews responded with overwhelming zeal. Masses of them visited Pilate's residence in coastal Caesarea (where governors preferred to stay) and lay motionless on his lawns for five days. Finally, he summoned them to a hearing in the outdoor theater, surrounded them with troops, and threatened to kill them if they remained obstinate. But they offered their necks to his soldiers' swords, preferring to die than to violate their laws. Impressed by their "superstition" (from his perspective), Pilate ordered the standards removed from Jerusalem (2.174).

In the second episode, Pilate was not so pliable. He had appropriated funds from the temple treasury to pay for the construction of an aqueduct, to carry water to Jerusalem. Josephus does not say that this action violated Jewish law, but he does say that the indignant

[6] Josephus says that the laws forbade erection of images "in the city," but there is no such specific law.

Jerusalemites surrounded Pilate as he heard cases, and protested angrily. Pilate, however, had taken the precaution of planting "plain-clothes" soldiers among the crowd. At the appropriate moment he signalled for them to draw their clubs and beat the protesters. Josephus says that many Jews perished, either from the blows or from being trampled in the escape. Thus, according to Josephus's sketch, the Jews under Pilate were reduced to fearful silence (though these two incidents by no means account for Pilate's ten-year term).

It is noteworthy that Josephus begins his account of the governors' escalating offenses with the tenure of Pilate. This man was removed from office in the year before Josephus's birth, and Josephus doubtless grew up hearing tales of Pilate's behavior. A Jewish contemporary of Pilate, Philo of Alexandria, heard a good deal about Pilate and listed his crimes: "the briberies, the insults, the robberies, the outrages and wanton injuries, the executions without trial constantly repeated, the ceaseless and supremely grievous cruelty" (*Embassy* 302). Philo is no doubt exaggerating here for his own literary purposes: he wants to use the wicked Pilate as a foil for the virtuous Emperor Tiberius, who opposed Pilate's misdeeds. Nevertheless, where there is smoke there may be fire. Philo's depiction would explain why Josephus chose to begin his account of governors' offenses with Pilate. Also noteworthy is Josephus's admission that "the Jews," without distinction, were upset by these provocations. It was not the rebels alone who opposed such insensitive acts.

In the *War* Josephus does not mention Pilate's replacement, for the period after Pilate (37–40 C.E.) was overshadowed by one of the greatest provocations in Jewish history to that point. The emperor Gaius Caligula, motivated by a desire to be worshiped, ordered that a statue of himself be installed in the Jewish temple. He sent the general Petronius with three legions to execute the order (2.184–187). The Jewish populace was so horrified that its leaders met the general in the coastal city of Ptolemais and followed him to Galilean Tiberias for an audience. The general spoke about his duty to enforce the order, the Jews about their duty toward their laws. Once again, they declared themselves ready to die rather than violate the law. Petronius, amazed at their persistence, ultimately decided that it would be better for him to risk death in failing to implement the order than to drive the nation to rebellion (2.201–202). In the end, Gaius was assassinated in Rome and Petronius was relieved of the order. But once again, Josephus makes it clear that this provocation, following soon after Pilate's odious tenure, was indeed an affront to Jewish laws and was thus opposed by all Jews alike.

Significantly, Josephus passes over the next two governors (Cuspius Fadus, 44–46, and Tiberius Julius Alexander, 46–48), after the reign of King Agrippa I (41–44 C.E.), with the simple notice that they, "by not violating the local customs, preserved the nation in peace" (2.220). Once again, whereas the rebels were consistently and philosophically opposed to Roman rule, most Jews were quite willing to cooperate as long as they were not asked to disregard their laws.

With the arrival of Cumanus (48–52 C.E.), relations between Jews and Romans deteriorated quickly. Josephus narrates three episodes representative of his misconduct, which was so egregious that the emperor Claudius finally tried and banished him. First, at a Passover feast early in his tenure, a Roman soldier standing on the roof of the temple portico turned his back to the crowd, raised his robe, and "mooned" the pilgrims in the temple courtyard, while making noises to match the gesture. Some of the outraged worshipers, the "hotheaded youths and those rebellious by nature," began to pelt the soldiers with stones. A riot ensued, and Josephus claims that more than 30,000 Jews were killed in the conflict (2.224–227). The number seems implausibly high, though Josephus later claims that at least 2.5 million persons normally gathered in Jerusalem for Passover (*War* 6.423–425), several times the normal population of the city.

In the second episode under Cumanus, some Jewish terrorists attacked and robbed one of the emperor's slaves. In the aftermath, a Roman soldier who was searching for the culprits found a Torah scroll and threw it into a fire (2.228–231). Once again the local Jews protested en masse to the governor. In this case, Cumanus thought the wiser course was to execute the guilty soldier. But tensions had been raised.

The events that brought Cumanus's governorship to a close began when a Galilean Jew was murdered by some Samaritans while traveling to Jerusalem for Passover (2.232). Some Galileans immediately set out for Samaria to retaliate, and the Jewish authorities implored Cumanus to intervene and punish the guilty Samaritans before the Galileans did. But Cumanus, occupied with other matters, brushed them aside. At that point many Jerusalemites, especially the terrorists and rebels, hurried off to Samaria for revenge; they massacred the villagers of one region. Now Cumanus was forced to act, and his troops killed many of the Jews who had attacked the Samaritans (2.236). Some of the Jews escaped, however, and continued to foment strife around the country (2.238). Finally, the governor of Syria, a superior to the governor of Judea, intervened. He crucified the Jewish prisoners taken by Cumanus, but also sent the Jewish and Samaritan leaders as well as Cumanus himself to Rome to explain their actions. With King Agrippa II's support in Rome, the Jewish case persuaded the emperor Claudius and he banished Cumanus (2.245–246).

These stories provide clear examples of Josephus's thesis: the Jews were pressed beyond all reason by several of the Roman governors, and yet most of them, certainly their aristocratic leaders, had the wisdom to seek peace with the Romans. They had no intention of bringing Roman wrath on Jerusalem and the temple (2.237). What distinguished the rebels from the Jewish mainstream was their obstinate and shortsighted commitment to the path of war for their own satisfaction rather than for the good of the state.

Josephus's accounts of Antonius Felix (52–59? C.E.) and Porcius Festus (59?–62) in the *Jewish War* are ambivalent. On the one hand, they dealt severely with both terrorists and the many religious impostors ("pseudo-prophets") who appeared at the time (2.253–265, 271). Since Josephus detests both groups, he seems to be grateful for the governors' efforts. As an example, he describes the "Egyptian pseudo-prophet" as a "charlatan" who had attracted some 30,000 "dupes" as followers; this deceiver intended to take Jerusalem from the Romans and install himself as tyrant (2.262). Josephus claims that when Felix sent the infantry against him, "the whole [Jewish] population" joined the soldiers, for they too were scandalized by such behavior. (According to Acts 21:38, right about this time Paul was mistaken for the Egyptian. See chapter 6.) On the other hand, Josephus points out the partiality of the governor and his troops toward the Greek-speaking citizens of Caesarea in their disputes with the Jewish residents; on one occasion Felix confronted the Jews and killed many of them (2.270). Josephus says nothing about Paul's appearances before Felix or Festus.

With Albinus (62–64 C.E.), who succeeded Festus, Josephus says that provincial affairs reached a new low. This governor, he claims, used his authority to steal private property and to exact extraordinary taxes. Moreover, he encouraged bribery from all sides, and emptied the prisons of all the terrorists who had formerly been put away: only those who were unable to bribe the governor remained in confinement. So the country exploded in factional strife, with numerous rebel groups intimidating the peaceful folk into submission, plundering at will, and killing those who demurred (2.275). Josephus flatly states that Albinus acquiesced in all of this, abetting the rebel cause, because his cooperation had been bought (2.274).

Finally, the *War* asserts that Albinus's successor, Gessius Florus (64–66 C.E.), made his predecessor look like the "best of men" (2.277). The detailed account of Florus's government (2.277–343) inevitably draws the reader into sympathy with the rebel cause, in spite of Josephus's denunciation of the rebels. This is part of his literary art. While evoking understanding for the plight of the Jews, he simultaneously castigates the rebels for not displaying the (heroic) endurance and political wisdom that Jewish tradition taught (cf. 2.343–357, 393, 410, 412–414). As for Florus, he was violent, shameless, cruel, and crafty (2.278). He not only sided with the Greeks against the Jews and accepted bribes, but also pilfered funds from the temple in Jerusalem (2.293). When some young Jews made fun of this by passing around a basket for the needy governor, he became enraged and turned his soldiers loose in the market square, to kill and plunder at will (2.293–306). He even crucified upper-class Jews who held Roman citizenship and equestrian status—an unprecedented travesty (2.308). Josephus claims that Florus actually plotted to stir up rebellion: he told his soldiers not to return a greeting from the people, so that when the people complained, the soldiers would have reason to cut them down (2.318–329).

War's portrayal of Florus's term climaxes its general point about the Roman governors' administration. In effect, Josephus concludes: if anyone had reason for rebellion, we did, though the rebel leaders were *still* wrong. It is easy to understand the predicament of the aristocracy.

In the *Jewish Antiquities*

In its treatment of the Roman governors, *Antiquities* does not differ substantially from *War*. It agrees that they oppressed the Jews beyond reason, and that they reached their nadir in Gessius Florus (64–66 C.E.). This governor "constrained us to take up war with the Romans, for we preferred to perish together rather than by degrees" (*Ant.* 20.257). As in *War*, Josephus allows that the whole nation, himself included, was by necessity caught up in the final catastrophic war. But *Antiquities* also sustains, and even intensifies, *War*'s disparagement of those who were rebellious by disposition. In keeping with its thesis, it devotes more space to the theme of the Jews' collective sins as the cause of their catastrophe. In addition to these emphases, the longer account in *Antiquities* adds a significant amount of detail and makes a few minor changes.

Although the *Antiquities* mentions the names of the governors between Coponius and Pontius Pilate, this is mainly to provide a framework for Josephus's chronicle of the high priests, in whom he has a greater interest (18.30–35). The early governors themselves are dispensed with quickly. A significant addition is his notice that the occasion of Judas's rebellion in 6 C.E. was not merely the incorporation of Judea into a Roman province but the attendant census of property for taxation purposes, administered by Quirinius the governor of Syria (18.2). This census is mentioned in Luke 2:2 as the occasion for Jesus' birth; it will be discussed in chapter 6.

Like the *War*, the *Antiquities* presents Pontius Pilate (26–36 C.E.) as the first example of the governors' abusive behavior toward the Jews. Josephus now stresses Pilate's guilt in the episode of the military standards by noting that previous governors had taken care to remove the standards when entering Jerusalem (18.56). He also adds the story of how Pilate dealt with a Samaritan messianic figure who led his followers to Mount Gerizim in Samaria; Pilate killed many of them (18.85–87). Most significant for us, Josephus introduces into this account of Pilate's tenure his trial and execution of Jesus (18.63–64). This passage has almost certainly been retouched by Christian copyists of Josephus's text. We shall consider it in chapter 5.

Concerning Cuspius Fadus (44–46 C.E.), who followed King Agrippa I, Josephus adds significant details to the brief mention in the *War*. First, he notes that Fadus permitted the auxiliary troops made up of locals (Gentiles) from Caesarea and Sebaste to stay in Judea, contrary to the emperor Claudius's orders, and that these men contributed to the final revolt by their aggravation of the Jews (19.366). Second, however, Josephus credits Fadus with prudence in his dealings with the Jewish terrorists who were removed from Judea (20.5). Likewise, Fadus is praised for his handling of "a certain impostor" named Theudas. This man, who is also mentioned in Acts 5:36 (see chapter 6), rallied a huge popular following. Claiming to be a prophet, he promised to part the Jordan river. But Fadus's men fell on the crowd, killed many, and cut off Theudas's head (20.99). Here is another example of Josephus's supporting what he considered to be the legitimate role of the governors—to maintain order and to prosecute troublemakers.

Tiberius Julius Alexander (46–48 C.E.) is an interesting case. In the *War* he appeared as a strong supporter of Vespasian and Titus during the Judean campaign (*War* 4.616–617; 5.45–56), but little was said about his term as governor. The *Antiquities* continues this restraint. It adds that Alexander crucified the rebel sons of the arch rebel Judas the Galilean, which seems to be meant as a compliment (20.102). But Josephus also blurts out the quick notice that "this man did not remain within the traditional customs" (20.100)—apparently, that he was a Jew who had given up the distinctive practices of Judaism. This unelaborated assertion reflects the tendency of the *Antiquities* to point out who was or was not faithful to the Jewish laws, though it might have been more compelling if Josephus had related some awful consequence of Alexander's nonobservance. Josephus's tentativeness may well be attributable to Alexander's high status in Rome. The son of an Alexandrian Jewish official and nephew of the philosopher Philo, he belonged to a family that was closely connected with both Jewish royalty (through Agrippa's sister Berenice) and the ruling family in Rome. His heirs apparently went on to senatorial careers in Rome. In this case, discretion may have required Josephus not to dwell for too long on Alexander's departure from tradition, though perhaps to his credit he does raise the problem.

In general, the *Antiquities* is milder on Cumanus (48–52 C.E.) than the *War* had been. Josephus now says that the Roman soldier at Passover exhibited his "genitals," not his backside, to pilgrims in the temple courtyard (20.108). Perhaps this act intended ridicule of Jewish circumcision. In any case, we are now told that Cumanus first pleaded with the offended Jews not to riot, but to set aside their "lust for revolution" (20.110). Only when this failed did he send troops to confront the Jews; even then, most of the casualties died while trying to flee the soldiers (20.111). Surprisingly, the *Antiquities* devotes less space than the *War* to the Jews' outrage at the soldier who destroyed a copy of the Torah (20.116); Cumanus handles the affair prudently. Yet the *Antiquities* gives much more attention than the *War* to the conflict between the Galileans and Samaritans (20.118–136). It now claims: (a) that many Galileans were murdered (not just one); (b) that Cumanus was bribed by the Samaritans not to punish the offenders; and (c) that Quadratus, governor of Syria, quickly determined that "the Samaritans had been responsible for the disorder" (20.129). This elaboration seems intended to support Josephus's general position, common to the *War* and the *Antiquities*, that the Jews were not troublemakers by nature.

New material about Felix (52–59?) in the *Antiquities* includes the information that he contracted an unlawful marriage with Drusilla, sister of King Agrippa II, who was already married to Azizus, the king of Emesa; Azizus had converted to Judaism and undergone circumcision in order to be her husband (20.143). It is probably no coincidence that Josephus immediately reports the tragic death of the son who was born of the illicit relationship between Felix and Drusilla (20.144). He goes on to say that the death of the high priest Jonathan, incidentally mentioned in the *War,* was actually plotted by Felix: the governor was fed up with the high priest's constant admonitions to improve the government (20.162). In the *Life,* Josephus reports with obvious displeasure that Felix sent some priests, "excellent men" and friends of Josephus, to face trial in Rome on a "minor and insignificant charge" (13).

Josephus is clear about the misdeeds of Felix, and claims that the governor would have been punished by the emperor had not Felix's brother Pallas been influential with Nero (20.182). Indeed, it seems that Felix's misconduct was notorious. The Roman historian Tacitus, who had no interest in siding with the Jews and opposed the promotion of freedmen to equestrian status and governing posts, singles out Felix among the Judean governors as one who "practiced every kind of cruelty and lust, wielding the power of a king with all the instincts of a slave" (*Hist.* 5.9).

Whereas the *War* had said that Porcius Festus captured and killed large numbers of terrorists (2.271), the *Antiquities* says only that there were large numbers of *sicarii* (see chapter 6) in Judea during his governorship, not that Festus did anything about them (20.185–187). Yet Josephus goes on to say that Festus "also" sent troops against "a certain impostor," who promised salvation and respite to those who would follow him into the wilderness (20.188). It is noteworthy: (a) that Josephus seems to have had the *War* passage in his mind while writing this part of the *Antiquities,* and so understood (but forgot to say) that Festus put down the rebels; (b) that the unnamed deceiver sounds very much like Theudas, under Fadus's tenure, who was also called "a certain impostor"; and (c) that the *War* had spoken of several such deceivers, who wanted to lead people out into the wilderness, under Felix's government (2.259). Josephus has apparently reintroduced discussion of this general problem here in order to fill out his account of Festus's term in office.

New to the *Antiquities* is the notice that Festus died in office (20.197). This sets the stage for Josephus's account of the death of

James, Jesus' brother, who is stoned along with other Christians while there is no governor in Judea. Josephus castigates the high priest who was responsible for this action (20.200–201). We shall discuss the episode in chapter 5.

The *Antiquities* is milder than the *War* toward Albinus (62–64 C.E.). It says only that he began his government by taking every possible precaution to ensure peace in Judea; to that end, he "exterminated most" of the *sicarii* (20.204). Those prisoners who were obviously guilty of serious crimes he executed; those who were guilty of minor infractions he released. Josephus presents this as a fair policy, even though it had the unwanted effect of filling the country with terrorists (20.215)—quite a different emphasis from the *War.*

With his account of the evil Gessius Florus (64–66 C.E.), Josephus brings to a close the narrative of the *Antiquities.* As in the *War,* this governor marks the ultimate deterioration of Roman government in Judea. Strangely, Josephus compares him to Albinus (20.253) as he had done in the *War,* but this makes little sense in the *Antiquities* because this work has not treated Albinus harshly. Once again, it seems that Josephus has the *War* in mind as he writes the *Antiquities;* he even takes over the exact language of the earlier work (*War* 2.277//*Ant.* 20.254). And, having stated that Gessius's actions compelled the Jews to revolt, he refers the reader to his precise account in the *War.* This reference indicates that Josephus does not see himself as presenting radically new material in the *Antiquities.*

Indeed, there is no simple way to categorize *Antiquities'* changes to *War*'s portrayal of the Roman governors. In general, Josephus maintains his position that (a) the governors from Pilate onward behaved intolerably, yet (b) the Jewish rebel-terrorists had the wrong attitude and were even more to blame for the catastrophe that befell the city (cf. 20.166, 180–181). The larger scope of the *Antiquities* allows for the introduction of significant new material on the governors. Some of this has the effect of moderating their atrocities or emphasizing the misdeeds of some Jews at the time; this tendency supports the *Antiquities'* thesis that departure from the traditional Jewish laws brings catastrophe. Occasionally, as with Felix and Pilate, the new material exacerbates the governors' misconduct. Josephus could assume that his readers understood Roman officials sent to govern the provinces would typically behave in a greedy and violent manner, being chiefly concerned to make their own fortunes with impunity while abroad. This problem was so well known that in the second century B.C.E. the Romans had established a permanent court to handle accusations against former governors, and we know of quite a few individuals who faced extortion charges. Josephus even claims that the emperor Tiberius allowed governors like Pilate to remain for long periods because he assumed their avarice. Better to let them remain and govern moderately, after satisfying their greed, than to replace them quickly with others who would bleed the country, for "It is in the nature of all government to practice extortion" (*Ant.* 18.172).

In the New Testament

How does Josephus's portrayal of the Roman governors throw light on the various NT presentations? If we read Acts with Josephus's accounts in mind, we find the same sort of irony as we did in Acts' portrait of King Agrippa II. On the surface, these governors are praised for their great beneficence toward the Jews. The Jewish spokesman who accuses Paul before Felix declares: "Being favored with abundant peace through you, and in view of the reforms that have come to this nation through your concern, most excellent Felix, in every way and everywhere we receive [this] with all gratitude" (Acts 24:2–3). Paul sustains the congeniality: "Since you have been a judge to this people for many years, I readily speak in defense of my case" (24:10). Acts presents the governors as defenders of Roman justice: they agree with Paul that they cannot condemn a man unless his accusers are present to make a cogent case (24:19; 25:16). As in the case of Jesus, these model magistrates find in Paul "nothing deserving of death" (25:25; cf. Luke 23:15, 22). It is a consistent theme of Luke-Acts that, whereas the Jews relentlessly persecuted Jesus and his followers, the Roman officials in Judea consistently found the Christians innocent. This theme arises from obvious social constraints on Christians at the time of Acts, which we shall discuss in chapter 6.

But knowing Josephus's account allows us to penetrate beneath the surface. Thus when we read that Felix came with his wife Drusilla to visit Paul while the latter was in chains (24:24), we recall that Drusilla, the object of Felix's overwhelming passion (according to Josephus) had abandoned both her lawful husband and Jewish custom when she succumbed to Felix's enticement. And Felix was notorious for his cruelty toward the Jews. Now, when this couple came to visit Paul, according to Acts, the preacher discussed with them "justice, self-control, and coming judgment" (24:25). Why these themes in particular, and not the resurrection of Jesus or faith in Christ, which provide the main apostolic message in Acts? Their significance would not be lost on the reader who knew Josephus's accounts. Whether the reader was expected to know this background or not, the author of Acts plainly has some such information in mind, for he describes Felix's reaction to this exhortation as follows: "Felix became afraid and answered, 'Go away for now; when I have opportunity I shall send for you' " (24:25). Paul's discussion of justice, self-control, and coming judgment seems to have been carefully tailored to the governor's situation. The writer even notes that Felix expected to receive a bribe from Paul (24:26).

What is peculiar here is that the narrative of Acts almost *assumes* knowledge of an account such as Josephus's. That is, Acts itself only praises the conduct of the governors; it is not clear on internal grounds why Felix (with Drusilla present) should have been upset by a discourse on self-control and coming judgment, or why this great "reformer" should have expected a bribe. These details make sense only if we have another perspective, like that offered by Josephus. An intriguing question, then, is: what did the author of Acts expect his readers to know in advance? This question, in turn, depends on the identification of his readers (Jews? Gentiles? Roman elites? urban provincials? of which province?). Without resolving that thorny issue here, we may at least conclude that the author of Acts has "encoded" his story with irony. If some of his readers knew other perspectives, as the author did, then they would have been party to the irony. Otherwise, the book's regular appeal to Roman decency over against Jewish malice would provide the key motif.

Much more difficult to understand in the light of Josephus are the gospels' presentations of Pontius Pilate. Whereas Josephus (like Philo) treats him as the prototype of the cruel, capricious, and insensitive Roman governor, slaughtering Jewish provincials on a whim, the gospels all show him insisting on Jesus' innocence, and deeply concerned that he receive a fair trial. Even here, Luke-Acts is the most intelligible of the gospels against Josephus's background. When Jesus first plans to come to Jerusalem, he sends some people ahead to make sure he can pass through Samaria, which lay between Galilee and Judea (Luke 9:51–56). But his delegation is rebuffed, for the Samaritans will not let him pass if he is headed for the Passover in Jerusalem. This episode accords perfectly with Josephus's story about the Galileans who were killed en route to a Passover feast in Jerusalem—twenty years later, under Cumanus. The author seems to know a lot about the tensions that Josephus reports. Even the disciples' hostile response to this rejection (9:54) is typical of the Galilean response described by Josephus.

As for Pilate, some of Luke's characters allude to certain Galileans "whose blood Pilate mingled with their sacrifices" (13:1). Josephus does not mention Pilate's attack on any Galileans, though he does describe: (a) Cumanus's later confrontation of Galileans and Judeans who took vengeance on the Samaritans for the murder(s) mentioned above, and (b) Pilate's attack on a Samaritan leader and his followers. At least we can say that this notice in Luke matches the atmosphere of Pilate's tenure evoked by Josephus; it may even be that the author of Luke has imperfectly remembered some specific story in Josephus. Also matching Josephus's portrait is Luke's claim that Herod Antipas of Galilee and Pilate "became friends" on the day of Jesus' trial (23:5). We have seen that Luke does not like Antipas; this connection with Pilate implies that the two were partners in mischief.

The most serious difficulties come with the other gospels. In Mark, the Jewish plot against Jesus that was hatched early in the gospel (3:6) comes to a climax with his arrest by a delegation from the "chief priests and scribes" (14:43). Bent on killing him (14:1), the Jewish leaders have no qualms about sentencing him to death on trumped-up charges (14:59–65). They have no concern for justice or due process; the distinguished judges even beat him and spit on him (14:65). But then Jesus appears before Pilate, who marvels at Jesus (15:5). This judge of character knows that the Jews oppose Jesus out of envy (15:10) and tries to release him by the clever ploy of offering them either Jesus or the convicted murderer Barabbas (15:9). But these Jews are so opposed to Jesus, the story says, that they prefer the murderer and thus foil Pilate's plan. Even so, he pleads with them: "Why, what did he do wrong?" (15:14). In the end, in spite of his own feelings, Pilate feels compelled by the Jewish crowd to condemn Jesus to death (15:15).

This unusual presentation of Pilate as a sensitive and just man, as a pawn in the hands of the Jewish leaders, is intensified in Matthew. This gospel says that Pilate's wife, having suffered in a dream because of this "righteous man," told her husband not to harm Jesus (27:19). The dutiful and conscientious governor even declares his innocence in Jesus' death with the *Jewish* symbol of washing his hands (27:24; cf. Deut 21:6–9). Who then is responsible? The author leaves no doubt that it is "all the Jewish people" and their descendants (27:25), who deliberately assume the blame. Once again, Pilate appears here as the instrument of the Jewish leaders who had long since plotted against Jesus. Though committed to justice, he was compelled to carry out the people's wishes.

The author of John seems to be aware of the problem of reconciling Pilate's reputation with the claim that he was innocent in Jesus' death. So he begins his relatively lengthy exchange between Jesus and Pilate by having the governor act in a suitably cavalier and distracted manner. He says to the Jewish leaders, "You take him and judge him by your own law" (18:31). In response to Jesus, he scoffs "Am I a Jew?" (18:35). And this jaded bureaucrat rhetorically poses the famous question, "What is truth?" (18:38). His soldiers, in character with Josephus's portrayal, beat and mock Jesus even before the trial (18:2–3). Still, Pilate quickly becomes afraid when he hears that Jesus calls himself the son of God (19:8—not mentioned in the other accounts) and wants to release him in response to Jesus' wise answers (19:12). He protests on behalf of Jesus' innocence, and John seems to say that he even handed Jesus over to the Jewish leaders so that *they* would conduct the execution (19:16). Only John answers the question why, if Pilate was innocent in Jesus' death, he was involved at all. John has the Jewish leaders helpfully remind the Roman governor that he alone has the power of capital punishment (18:31).

A particular problem in the gospel accounts is their claim that Pilate used to release a criminal chosen by the Jews every year at Passover (Mark 15:6; Matt 27:15; John 18:39). The story is difficult for several reasons: (a) it violates both Jewish and Roman law, according to which the guilty, especially murderers, must be punished—they cannot simply be freed by public vote; (b) it is not attested anywhere else in Jewish or Roman history and literature; (c) according to Josephus, feasts such as Passover were precisely the occasions when the Romans were most concerned about maintaining order, and so were most severe in their punishments (*War* 2.10–11, 42, 224, 232–234); (d) if Pilate could release one man to the crowds, he could presumably also have released Jesus; (e) Luke, who seems most familiar with Roman law, transforms the story so that Pilate simply yields to popular demand for Barabbas as a one-time concession, not as an annual custom (23:18); and (f) Barabbas is a peculiar name because it means "son of a father," which is hardly a distinction. None of this means that the episode is impossible, only that it is difficult to understand. On the other hand, the story does fit well with the gospels' attempts to demonstrate the depth of Jewish opposition to Jesus: given the opportunity to choose him over a convicted terrorist, they chose the terrorist.

The gospels' attempts to relieve Pilate of any guilt and to place it squarely on Jewish heads are understandable in light of the Christians' social-political situation after 70 C.E.: the Jews were already considered troublemakers as a result of their failed revolt, and the Christians were in desperate need of a claim to legitimacy. Christians had to explain to the Roman world (and to themselves) how it happened that their Lord had been crucified by a Roman governor. It was natural that in such circumstances, the Jewish role in Jesus' death would be exaggerated and the Roman role minimized. And it was inevitable that Christian portrayals written in these circumstances would conflict with the writings of the Jewish author Josephus. The Roman governors' misdeeds were so predictably notorious that Josephus could cite them as causes of the revolt while still maintaining that Jews were on the whole committed to peace with the central, divinely supported Roman government.

THE JEWISH HIGH PRIESTS

A third important group in the background of the NT that also looms large in Josephus's writing is the Jewish priesthood. In the gospels' accounts of Jesus' death, the "chief priests" appear regularly as his opponents (Matt 16:21; 20:18; Mark 8:31; Luke 9:22; 19:47; John 7:32; 11:47–53; 12:10). The high priest hosts Jesus' trial and passes judgment on him (e.g., Mark 14:53–64). And the book of Hebrews presents the risen Jesus as the heavenly high priest (Heb 5:10; 7:26). Josephus, for his part, is proud of his priestly heritage. We have already seen that he presents the high priests as the "successors" of Aaron in Moses' time, the guardians of the constitution that was given to Israel. Under the direction of the high priest, the priests serve as teachers and administrators of the divinely revealed laws.

But Josephus cannot simply praise the high priesthood as the authorized vehicle for transmitting Moses' teaching, for recent Jewish history, up to the revolt against Rome, involved individual high priests in various ways. Especially in the *Antiquities,* therefore, where he wants to expose Jewish sins as a cause of the calamity, he must also recount in detail the lawless actions of priests and high priests. In other words, he must at the same time maintain his ideal portrait of Judaism as an ancient and established tradition and explain how it was that such a noble tradition recently fell to such ignominious depths. The high priests figure on both sides of the ledger.

To understand Josephus's remarks, it is helpful to have some background knowledge of the high priesthood. In the biblical story, God designates Moses' brother, Aaron, as the first high priest. Once the sacred tent (or "tabernacle") is in place, God takes up residence above the box called the ark of the covenant in the "most holy place"—the innermost cube-shaped room (Exod 25:22). The high priest performs the critical role of mediator between God and the people, for he is the only one who may enter the holiest place, and that but once a year (Exod 29:44; Lev 16:2–5). This chief of all the priests is charged with representing the people to God by supervising the whole sacrificial system, and with representing God to the people by ensuring that the divine teachings are propagated and observed (Lev 10:8–11). Under King Solomon (tenth century B.C.E.), the temple of Jerusalem was built as a permanent replacement for the tent, where God met Israel. All descendants of Aaron were priests by birth, though only those without physical defects could serve in the temple. The high priesthood, however, became customarily associated with a small group of priestly families—first, the sons of Zadok, who was high priest under David and Solomon, then a progressively restricted group of clans.

The book of Deuteronomy reflects what we might call a separation of powers among the priesthood, the Israelite king, and authorized prophets: the man with executive political power must learn and observe the laws taught by the priests (Deut 17:14–20), and everyone must listen to the prophet who declares God's will (18:15–22). But after the Babylonian exile (586–538 B.C.E.), there were no longer kings or regular prophets in Israel, so the high priest inevitably assumed such political functions as the Jews retained under foreign domination. By about 300 B.C.E., perhaps much earlier, he had become head of a senate or "council of elders" *(gerousia),* the precursor of the council mentioned in the gospels. After the exile, the high priest's power was determined by the degree to which the foreign master (Persian, Macedonian, Egyptian, Syrian, Roman) wished to interfere directly. At two points in particular, we see the political rulers breaking with Jewish tradition by deposing legitimate high priests early in their tenure (they had originally served for life) and replacing them with others who would serve the king's interests better. Such aggressive rulers were the Seleucid King Antiochus IV (175–164 B.C.E.) and Herod the Great (37–4 B.C.E.).

In the *Jewish War*

In the *War,* Josephus effectively uses the case of the high priesthood to isolate the rebel "tyrants" as untypical of mainstream Jews, in keeping with his literary aims: the priesthood in general represents traditional, established Judaism, opposed to the "innovations" of the terrorists. In the very first paragraph, therefore, he introduces himself as a priest from Jerusalem (1.3). There were priests and high priests throughout the Greco-Roman world, in every significant town, for they ran the temples of the various regional gods. In those other cultures, priestly families often handed down the sacred craft from one generation to another. But at the same time, the role of chief officiator or "high priest" was usually a civic honor, to which noted citizens were elected on an annual basis. In Rome, a very close connection had developed between the priesthood and the aristocracy, as we have seen; by the first century, only prominent aristocrats could hold seats in the principal priestly colleges. Augustus had tried hard to tighten this connection between priests and aristocrats. For the Jews, however, this ideal was already a fact of life, a long-standing tradition. They had a rigidly maintained caste system in which priesthood was determined by lineage. The hereditary priesthood was also the native aristocracy, by definition. As in some other Oriental countries, one could not choose either priesthood or high priesthood as a vocation. Many Roman readers were fascinated by the exotic ways of the East, with their mysterious and powerful priests, and Josephus plays to this audience by identifying himself as a priest-nobleman.

In describing his surrender to Vespasian, which we have discussed in another context, Josephus exploits his priesthood at a key moment—to explain how it was that he came to know of Vespasian's future. Having appealed to some "nightly dreams" in which God revealed the future to him, he continues: "He [Josephus] was not unfamiliar with the prophecies of the sacred books, being himself a priest and a descendant of priests" (3.352). This association of the Jewish priesthood with both traditional wisdom and mysterious power is a consistent theme in Josephus's writings. He goes on to claim that he had regularly predicted the future (3.406). Moreover, he has already said that his favorite Hasmonean ruler, John Hyrcanus, uniquely combined the rule of the people with high priesthood and a prophetic gift: "For so closely was he in touch with the Deity that he was never ignorant of the future" (1.69, LCL). Josephus's Hasmonean ancestry and priestly descent are prominent features of his self-understanding.

In accord with its priestly bias, Josephus's *War* presents the rebels as violators of both the sacred temple precincts and the priestly traditions. When the governor Gessius Florus pillages the temple and is mocked by some young upstarts, it is the chief priests and eminent citizens who appeal to him (in vain) for clemency, wishing to maintain peace (2.301). While the governor plots to further aggravate the populace, the chief priests earnestly assemble the people and plead with them, against the rebels' policies, to show courtesy to the Roman soldiers, so as to avoid irreversible damage to the holy place (2.318–324). Even when Florus ridicules this policy by attacking the Jews, and though a rash young priest persuades other priests to stop offering sacrifices on behalf of the Romans, Josephus claims that "the chief priests and the notables strenuously admonished them not to give up the traditional offering for the rulers" (2.410). The chief priests and other leaders accuse the rebels of "introducing a strange kind of worship" that did not admit sacrifices for rulers (2.414). They then produce "priestly experts in the traditions, who reported that all of their forebears had welcomed the sacrifices of foreigners" (2.417). Finally, when Jerusalem is under siege, it is the chief priests who take up the Romans' offer of surrender and quit the city (6.114). In spite of the actions of some younger priests who were deceived by the rebels, therefore, Josephus aligns himself with the priestly establishment in solid opposition to the revolt.

Most revealing of the *War*'s perspective is a lengthy passage in which Josephus fumes against the rebels for their unprecedented violation of priestly tradition (4.147–325). He has already told us that, once they had gained control of Jerusalem, the rebels first burned down the house of the former high priest Ananias, then murdered him along with his brother (2.426, 441). But now, most outrageous of all, they dare to elect their own high priest: "Abrogating the claims of those families from which in turn the high priests had always been drawn, they appointed to that office ignoble and low born individuals, in order to gain accomplices in their impious crimes" (4.148, LCL). Josephus says that they convened one of the twenty-four priestly clans and cast lots for a high priest. As it happened, the lot fell to a simpleton who lived in the countryside and did not even understand what the high priesthood was. But the rebels used this turn of events to their advantage, dragged the reluctant man out of his home, and dressed him up as high priest. They recklessly made their new "high priest" the object of much sport and laughter (4.155–157).

We must remember that this is entirely Josephus's perspective. Historically speaking, the legitimacy of the high priesthood had often been ignored: the Seleucid kings and later Herod the Great appointed whomever they wished to the office. And an insistence on choice by lot quite possibly reflected the rebels' protest against the corruption of the office under the wealthy, traditional high priestly families. But this historical perspective only serves to highlight Josephus's literary aim, which is to remove the rebels completely beyond the pale of normal Judaism.

In response to the rebels' actions, Josephus continues, the eminent former high priests Ananus and Jesus severely chastised the people for not preventing this outrage against the sacred office (4.160). The *War* devotes a good deal of space to the speeches of these two leaders, in which they complain that murderers have now polluted God's sanctuary (4.163, 242). Ananus even leads the people against the rebels, but the Zealots receive support from Idumeans. Together, as we have seen, the Jewish rebels and Idumeans defeat the chief priests. Finally, the Idumeans murder Ananus and Jesus; they further violate Jewish custom by casting the corpses out of the city without burial (4.316–317).

The aristocratic priest Josephus claims that these outrages against temple and priestly tradition were the causes of God's punishment (see chapter 3). The high priests serve to establish the *War*'s thesis concerning the nontraditional, un-Jewish character of the rebels.

In the *Jewish Antiquities*

In the *Antiquities, the Life,* and its sequel, *Against Apion,* the high priests are even more prominent than in the *War.* On the one hand, the high priesthood is the cornerstone of Josephus's argument that Jewish traditions have been handed down intact from the time of Moses. On the other hand, and in some tension with this theme, individual high priests are exposed as sinners whose transgressions brought God's punishment on Jerusalem.

We have seen that one of Josephus's techniques in the *Antiquities* is to present Judaism as an ancient *philosophy*—a school of virtue, founded by Moses, which offers *eudaimonia,* or happiness, to those who follow its precepts. Within this scheme, the high priests have a critical function as Moses' "successors," who transmit the founder's teachings unchanged from generation to generation. So Aaron, the first high priest, is introduced with considerable fanfare. Josephus describes his special clothing in detail and then attributes to Moses a speech in praise of Aaron that has no parallel in the Bible (3.151–192). Among Aaron's virtues, significantly, is the gift of prophecy (3.192). In his subsequent narrative of Israel's history, Josephus regularly introduces the high priest where he is not mentioned at all in the Bible: a striking example is Josephus's paraphrase of Joshua, which has the great commander routinely turning to the high priest and his "council of elders" for advice (*Ant.* 5.15, 43, 55–57). These embellishments offer a fascinating insight into how Josephus assumed that things should work, based on conditions of his own day, even though the Bible said nothing about them. For him, the high priest is the authorized head of Jewish public life. In accordance with this view, Josephus regularly identifies the current high priest as his narrative progresses. Most significantly, in his conclusion to the lengthy *Antiquities,* he thinks it important to recap the whole "succession" of high priests from Aaron to the end of the recent war (20.224–251, 261)—a span of two thousand years.

The centrality of the high priesthood to Josephus's understanding of Judaism is spelled out in his apologetic work *Against Apion.* Contrasting the Jewish historical records with the untrustworthy Greek accounts, he argues that the Jews entrusted their writings to "chief priests and prophets" who preserved them through the ages with scrupulous accuracy (*Ag. Ap.* 1.29). Notice again his connection of the priesthood with prophecy. And the high priests have been the guarantors of this tradition (1.36). Josephus wants to present Judaism as a beautiful and harmonious system, working in accord with the laws of nature:

> Could there be a [constitution] more splendid and just than that which makes God the master of everything, assigns the greatest matters to the administration of the priests as a unit, and then entrusts to the supreme high priest the direction of the other priests? . . . This [responsibility] included scrupulous care for the law and for the various pursuits of life. (*Ag. Ap.* 2.184–187)

Picking up on the biblical notice that Moses entrusted the laws to the priests (Deut 31:9, 25; cf. *Ant.* 4.304), Josephus presents the high priest as conductor of an orchestrated effort to preserve and disseminate the divine teachings.

But the *Antiquities* must also demonstrate its thesis that violation of the Jewish laws leads to disaster. Within this scheme, Josephus does not hesitate to point out the shortcomings of individual high priests who departed from the traditions and consequently suffered for it. These included the greedy and mean-spirited Onias II, who brought the Jews to the brink of disaster (12.158), and the later Hasmonean high priests, who brought about the end of Jewish independence through their internecine strife and murder (cf. 13.300–319, 431–432).

Most revealing are the *Antiquities*' revisions of the *War*'s portraits of the high priests in the years before the revolt. Ananus, whom *War* had praised as a moderate and virtuous man, over against the violent rebels, is introduced in *Antiquities* 20.199 as "rash and conspicuously bold in manner." This Sadducean high priest took advantage of the governor's absence in Judea after the death of Festus by convening the Sanhedrin and passing a death sentence on James, the brother of Jesus, and some others (see chapter 5). Ananus's mischievous behavior earned him the opposition of the law-abiding Jews, the new Roman governor, and King Agrippa II, who removed him from the high priesthood (20.200–203). This is the same high priest who later, along with a chief priest named Jesus, accepted bribes in order to oust Josephus from his command in Galilee (*Life* 193, 196). Then the distinguished former high priest Ananias is described as one who freely engaged in bribery; his servants were "utter rascals" who would rob the tithes from the poorer priests, leaving them to starve to death (20.206–207, 213). It was this sort of lawlessness among the aristocracy that brought destruction on Jerusalem (20.214, 218).

What are we to make of these changes between the *War* and the *Antiquities* concerning the prewar high priests? No one can deny that Josephus frequently contradicts himself in small matters, even within his own chronicles of the high priests. But the obvious shifts here are not mistakes. They are better explained as resulting from a change of literary aim and rhetorical need. We have seen that Josephus takes his theses very seriously, and so spells them out in elaborate prefaces. Since *War* is a tightly written attempt to isolate the rebels from the Jewish mainstream, it is not the place for him to expatiate on the high priests' shortcomings; he wants rather to make the sole point that the high priests represented the normal establishment over against the rebels. The *Antiquities* assumes the same general thesis but also intends to demonstrate the efficacy of Jewish laws by proving that transgressors are invariably punished. In this context it is important to point out Jewish sins, even those of the high priests, that contributed to the recent divine punishment. Josephus's careful selection of "what to include" was perfectly in keeping with a rhetorical tradition that taught one to make different cases from the same body of evidence.

In the New Testament

Josephus's portrayals of the high priests throw considerable light on the NT. First, they explain how it is that the high priest appears in the NT as the head of a council, composed of the eminent citizens, leading Pharisees, and Sadducees (Mark 11:27; 14:1, 53; Acts 5:21–39; 22:30–23:10). This constellation is apt to seem strange, both because the OT does not put the high priest at the head of a council and also because Pharisees and Sadducees are not supposed to get along (see below). Even a modern scholar expresses his bafflement at the NT accounts:

> Anyone with knowledge of the religious and political scene at this time in Judaea feels the presence of an important problem here: the High Priest was not a Pharisee, but a Sadducee, and the Sadducees were bitterly opposed to the Pharisees.[7]

But Josephus everywhere assumes that the high priest is the head of the Jewish council, and that this council comprises eminent citizens of all parties (e.g., *War* 2.411; *Life* 21); indeed, it is the chief priests, including the Sadducee Ananus, who send a delegation composed mainly of Pharisees to replace him as Galilean commander (*Life* 193–197). In Josephus's mind at least, the various parties could work together in government, in spite of their real and deep differences.

Second, Josephus describes a coincidence of interest between Jewish chief-priestly circles and the Roman government. He presents the chief priests by and large as favoring cooperation with Rome, even in the face of severe provocation. Not only do these eminent citizens support the governors' harsh treatment of political terrorists and

---

[7] Hyam Maccoby, *The Myth-Maker: Paul and the Invention of Christianity* (San Francisco: Harper, 1986), 8.

religious fanatics, they also cooperate in removing such troublesome individuals. A particularly interesting case concerns one Jesus son of Ananias, a common peasant who predicted the fall of the temple four years before the outbreak of the revolt. For more than seven years, especially at festivals, this Jesus would reportedly cry, "Woe to Jerusalem!" and "A voice against Jerusalem and the sanctuary, a voice against the bridegroom and the bride, a voice against all the people." The exasperated temple leaders punished him without success, and eventually passed him over to the Roman governor. As he would not answer any questions, he was flayed to the bone and released on grounds of insanity (*War* 6.300–309). This cooperation of the leading citizens with the Romans, when it came to a person who had disrupted the already tense festival periods in Jerusalem, fits with the general picture of political relations painted by Josephus. This picture in turn helps one to imagine some cooperation between the Jewish leadership and the Roman governor in the trial of Jesus.

Third, Josephus often confuses the reader by speaking of various individuals as "high priest" at the same time, or by calling someone high priest when he was no longer in office (e.g., *War* 2.441; *Ant.* 20.205; *Life* 193). Yet the Bible and Josephus both insist that only one person may serve as high priest at one time. On closer examination, we realize that Josephus allows former high priests to retain the title and prestige of the office as long as they live. Perhaps this usage reflects his assumption that high priests *ought* to serve for life. In any case, we have a similar confusion in the gospels and Acts. Luke 3:2 and Acts 4:6 mention several high priests (especially Annas and Caiaphas) as though they were current. More baffling yet, John 18:12–28 has Jesus interrogated by Annas (=Ananus I), who is first called "the father-in-law of the high priest" (18:13) but is then addressed as "high priest" (18:15, 19, 22). And when Jesus' interview with the high priest is finished, he is sent in chains to "Caiaphas the high priest" (18:24). If the authors of Luke and John made the same assumptions as Josephus, and expected their readers to do so, then their accounts become somewhat less puzzling. Ananus I was an extremely distinguished high priest in Josephus's view, for five of his sons followed him in office (*Ant.* 20.197–198). So it makes sense that the gospel authors would remember his name in conjunction with Caiaphas, the serving high priest at the time of Jesus' trial.

Fourth, on a more theological level, Josephus plainly regards the high priesthood and the temple service as the heart and soul of Judaism.

JEWISH HIGH PRIESTS 6 TO 70 C.E.

Jesus son of See (to 6 C.E.)	*Ant.* 17.341
*Ananus (=Annas) I (6–15 C.E.)	*War* 2.240; *Ant.* 18.26, 34
Ishmael son of Phabi I (15–16 C.E.)	*Ant.* 18.34
Eleazar son of Ananus (16–17 C.E.)	*Ant.* 18.34
Simon son of Camith (17–18 C.E.)	*Ant.* 18.34
*Joseph Caiaphas (18–37 C.E.)	*Ant.* 18.35, 95
Jonathan son of Ananus (37 C.E.)	*Ant.* 18.95, 123
Theophilus son of Ananus (37–41 C.E.)	*Ant.* 18.123; 19.297
Simon Cantheras son of Boethus (from 41 C.E.)	*Ant.* 19.297, 313
Matthias son of Ananus	*Ant.* 19.316, 342
Elionaeus son of Cantheras (44 C.E.)	*Ant.* 19.342; 20.16
Joseph son of Camei	*Ant.* 20.16, 103
*Ananias son of Nebedaeus (47–59 C.E.)	*War* 2.243, 409–442; *Ant.* 20.103, 131
Ishmael son of Phabi II (59–61 C.E.)	*Ant.* 20.179, 194
Joseph Kabi son of Simon (to 62 C.E.)	*Ant.* 20.196
Ananus (=Annas) II son of Ananus (62 C.E.)	*War* 2.563, 648–653; *Ant.* 20.197, 203
Jesus son of Damnaeus (62–64 C.E.)	*Ant.* 20.203, 213
Jesus son of Gamaliel (64–65? C.E.)	*Ant.* 20.213, 223
Matthias son of Theophilus (65–67 C.E.)	*Ant.* 20.223
Phanasus (=Phanni) son of Samuel (67–70 C.E.)	*War* 4.155; *Ant.* 20.227

* Appears in NT

This is important because several modern scholars have argued that the whole priesthood was reduced to the status of mere "functionaries" by the rise of the Pharisees and/or scribes in the two centuries before Jesus.[8] Although some Pharisees may have had such a perspective, however, Josephus the priest enthuses about the vitality of the priesthood. Josephus's perspective helps to make sense of Hebrews, which presents Jesus as a new and ideal high priest. If the priesthood were no longer a vital force, this author would merely be dredging up tired old images.

Yet Josephus presents the NT reader, once again, with difficulties as well as assistance. A notable difficulty is the question of who was the serving high priest at the time of Jesus' trial. This problem is only partly solved by the custom of allowing former high priests to retain the title. Josephus presents a fairly clear chronicle of the first-century high priests, and even where his dates are not precise, we can usually figure them out within a year or two on the basis of current events mentioned in the surrounding narrative.

[8] See S. N. Mason, "Priesthood in Josephus and the Theory of a 'Pharisaic Revolution,'" *JBL* 107/4 (1988): 657–61.

As the table above indicates, Caiaphas was high priest throughout Jesus' adult life, and throughout the governorship of Pilate (26–36), who ordered that Jesus be executed.

But the gospel writers as a group do not seem to have a clear idea of who the high priest was at Jesus' trial. The earliest of them, Mark, simply says that Jesus was interrogated and sentenced to death by "the high priest" and council (14:53–15:1). It is peculiar that Mark, like all of the gospel writers, knows the name of Pilate (15:1), whom he presents as innocent in Jesus' death, but that he does not disclose the name of the one he holds truly responsible, the high priest. Matthew makes up for this deficiency. Following Mark's narrative closely, when he comes to the mention of the high priest he identifies this villain as Caiaphas.

Mark 14:48–54	**Matthew 26:55–58**
48 "*Have you come out to arrest me with swords and clubs, as if against a robber?* 49 *Day after day* I was with you *in the temple teaching, and you did not arrest me!* But *in order that the scriptures might be fulfilled.*" 50 *And leaving him,* they *all fled.* 51 And a certain young man was following him, wearing only a linen cloth over his naked body. And they seize him, 52 but, abandoning the linen cloth, he fled naked.	55 "*Have you come out to arrest me with swords and clubs, as if against a robber? Day after day I* sat *in the temple teaching, and you did not arrest me!* 56 Now this all happened *in order that the scriptures* of the prophets *might be fulfilled.*" Then *all* the disciples, *leaving him, fled.*
53 And they *led Jesus off to the high priest,* and all the chief priests, and *the elders,* and *the scribes* assembled. 54 And *Peter, from a distance,* followed *him.*	57 Now those who had seized him *led Jesus off to* Caiaphas *the high priest,* where *the scribes* and *the elders* had gathered. 58 But *Peter* was following *him from a distance.*

This passage illustrates the standard view that the author of Matthew used Mark as a source. On the one hand, we see extensive verbal agreements between the two texts, to a degree that one does not find in independent accounts of the same event. Greek (the original language of the gospels) offers countless possibilities for expressing similar ideas, but these two authors basically agree in their choice of sentence structure, vocabulary ("as if against a robber," "day after day," "led Jesus off"), word order, and in their manner of weaving together different plots (Jesus with the high priest, Peter in the courtyard). Such differences as remain are usually explained as Matthew's attempt to improve the story, thus: (a) he substitutes other conjunctions and sentence structures to replace Mark's monotonous "and"; (b) he completes and clarifies Mark's sentence about the fulfillment of Scripture; (c) he omits the story about the naked young man, which might have seemed both irrelevant to the story line (since he does not appear again) and not entirely in good taste. Most important for us: Matthew seems to think it necessary to identify the high priest, since he plays such a crucial role in the story of Jesus' trial. His insertion of the name Caiaphas agrees with Josephus.

Luke's gospel also seems to follow Mark as a source, and, like Mark, Luke declines to name the high priest *within the trial narrative itself* (cf. Luke 22:54). Yet the omission is understandable in Luke's case because he has already identified the various rulers at the beginning of his gospel. There, he says that John the Baptist began preaching "under the high priest [singular] Annas and Caiaphas" (Luke 3:2). This is a peculiar construction because the singular "high priest" does not match the pair of names that follows. If we suppose that Annas, as a *former* high priest of distinction, offered the serving high priest his ongoing counsel, we are still left with the problem that Caiaphas's name should have appeared first; having been in office for a decade or more, he was no novice. In this awkward construction, however, the name of Caiaphas is left dangling, and it seems that Luke thinks of Annas as the high priest. The problem is compounded by Acts 4:6. Describing the situation shortly after Jesus' death, that passage says that the Jerusalem council met "with Annas the high priest, and Caiaphas, John, and Alexander, and whoever was of the high priestly family." This text plainly sets Caiaphas on a level with several other members of "the family"; the author implies that Annas was the serving high priest.

In other words, if we had only Luke-Acts, we would not have guessed that Caiaphas was high priest during Jesus' trial (according to Josephus and Matthew), for this author implies that Annas held the office. Josephus is also confusing at times in his use of the title "high priest," but the difference is that he clarifies the situation, if we but read on for a few paragraphs. Luke does not, so it remains a question whether he knew who was high priest at the time of Jesus' death. Nevertheless, Luke's later identification of Ananias as serving high priest at the time of Paul's arrest, under the governorship of Felix (Acts 23:2; 24:1), agrees with Josephus.

We have already noted the problem in John's gospel, which has Jesus first appear before the "high priest" Annas, father-in-law of the high priest Caiaphas, and then sent to the (serving) high priest (John 18:13–24). Much of this apparent confusion, we saw, could be explained by Josephus's use of "high priest" to designate also former high priests. Josephus does not say that Annas was Caiaphas's father-in-law, and the omission seems odd in view of his claim about Annas's great influence through his five sons, but the relationship is nonetheless plausible. Yet two problems remain. First, John repeatedly identifies Caiaphas as "high priest that year" (11:51; 18:13). A non-Jewish reader would presumably infer that the Jewish high priest, like many others in the Greco-Roman world, was annually elected as a civic official. Even though the high priesthood had lost its lifelong tenure by Jesus' time, however, it was by no means an annual position. According to Josephus, Caiaphas held it for about eighteen years. The other problem is that John makes the trial before Annas the main one and omits any mention of what happened before Caiaphas, the serving high priest. Moreover, Peter's denial is set within the framework of the trial before Annas rather than Caiaphas as in the synoptics (18:13–24; cf. Mark 14:67 on Peter's warming himself by the fire). So, in spite of the partial help that we get from Josephus's liberal use of the title "high priest," John's narrative remains a problem.

In sum: on the one hand, it is remarkable that the gospel authors unanimously and without equivocation know that the Roman governor at the time of Jesus' death was Pontius Pilate, and yet he is said by all of them to have been a mere pawn in the hands of the Jewish leaders. On the other hand, Mark does not even name the chief Jewish official; Matthew seems to have researched or recalled that his name was Caiaphas; Luke implies that he was Annas; and John makes Caiaphas an annually appointed high priest but places Jesus' significant trial before Annas.

The most obvious conflict between Josephus and the NT authors concerns the general character of the "chief priests." Josephus regards the high priestly class as the vital center of Judaism and its typical leaders as deeply pious, cultured, moderate men like himself. This broad perspective makes his isolation of unworthy high priests that much more significant. The NT authors usually portray the whole Jewish leadership as ignorant of God's designs and opposed to Jesus' mission. Notice their tendency to implicate "all" or "the whole" of the "chief priests, elders, and scribes." It is a high priest who declares the fateful sentence against Jesus, and a high priest who leads the attack against Paul.

Who is right? Were the chief priests sincerely committed to their faith, or were they self-satisfied enemies of the truth? I would suggest that the question cannot be resolved in such terms. But Josephus's portrayal forces us to realize that the gospels represent only one perspective on the Jewish leadership. The gospels' accusations, made in the heat of controversy, should not be taken as objective facts: it is not as if the chief priests arose every morning wondering what kinds of evil they could perpetrate in the world. They were public figures with a high profile. We do not have access to their private thoughts and goals. All we have are images left from one of their members (Josephus) and several of their opponents (the NT writers). Inevitably, such figures attract admiration and hostility, depending on whom one asks.

PHARISEES AND SADDUCEES

We come finally to the Jewish groups most frequently mentioned in the gospels and Acts, the Pharisees and Sadducees. Once again, Josephus is our only contemporary source of information about these groups outside the NT. Like the high priests, the Sadducees and Pharisees appear in two quite different contexts in Josephus's writings. On the one hand, he wants to work them into his immense tapestry of idealized Jewish culture, with which he is trying to impress his readers—an awe-inspiring tradition that deserves respect. On the other hand, he must also relate Jewish history in a plausible way, to explain how the Jews have fallen on such dreadful times. Within this story, some Sadducees, but especially the Pharisees, play a critical, destructive role.

Unlike the family of Herod and the high priests, the Pharisees and Sadducees do not perform significantly different functions in the *War* and the *Antiquities.* Indeed, they are not major figures in the *War,* and the two sides of the portrayal appear throughout Josephus's works. Instead of examining the *War* and the *Antiquities* in isolation, therefore, we shall first consider how the Pharisees and Sadducees support Josephus's idealizing presentation of Judaism, and then we shall examine how these groups functioned in his account of Jewish history.

In Josephus's Ideal Portrait of Judaism

It is intriguing that no NT author mentions the Essenes, for Josephus always includes them with the Pharisees and Sadducees in his idealizing portraits of Judaism. Of the three groups, in fact, it is the Essenes who elicit his highest praise. Characteristic of these idealizing portrayals is Josephus's claim that the three groups represent "philosophical schools" within the larger national philosophy of Judaism (see chapter 3). Judaism represents a high philosophical culture, comparable to that of the Greeks, with its parallel spectrum of philosophical opinion.

In *War* 2.162–166, having lavishly praised the Essenes as a class by themselves, he simply places the Pharisees and Sadducees on opposite ends of the philosophical spectrum: the Pharisees affirm the activity of fate and the immortality of the soul (2.163); the Sadducees deny both positions, insisting on absolute freedom of will and rejecting afterlife with its rewards and punishments (2.164–165). It was customary for those who wrote summaries of Greco-Roman philosophy to align the various schools on two poles, according to their affirmation or denial of such principles (cf. Diogenes Laertius, *Vit. phil.* 1.16; Cicero, *Fat.* 39): Josephus does the same for the Pharisees and Sadducees, after distinguishing the Essenes as a unique group.

Josephus compares the three schools again in *Antiquities* 13.171–173. Here, instead of polarizing Pharisees and Sadducees, he creates a spectrum to include all three schools, in which the Essenes take up the fatalist wing, the Sadducees take their place on the opposite end, but now the Pharisees assume the middle ground, for they assign some matters to fate and others to free will.

In his third passage on the Jewish philosophical schools (*Ant.* 18.11–23), Josephus again uses them to represent normal Judaism, over against the rebels, who introduced a bizarre "fourth philosophy" (*Ant.* 18.9, 24). Once again he mainly sketches different views of fate and immortality among the three "ancient" schools. But he also mentions a dispute between Pharisees and Sadducees over authority: the Pharisees have their own special tradition in addition to the Scriptures, whereas the Sadducees accept only the biblical laws (18.12, 16). Josephus had not originally mentioned this issue, probably because it would detract from his depiction of a cosmopolitan Jewish culture engaged with the issues common to all humanity. Nevertheless, this dispute over authority came up unavoidably in one of his stories (*Ant.* 13.288–298); now that he has explained the point anyway, he is willing to restate it in this summary.

A final passage in *Life* (10–12) merely recalls that the Jews have three "philosophical schools" in order to explain Josephus's training in each. The audience is referred to earlier discussions.

It should be noted that Josephus's idealizing portrayal of the three traditional schools does not by itself imply that he is personally committed to any of them. On the contrary, his autobiography claims that he did not find any of them satisfying, so he became a student of the desert monk Bannus (*Life* 10–11; see chapter 2). He groups the schools together because: (a) he wants to impress his readers with the depth and variety of Judaism and (b) he wants to expose the rebels as antisocial renegades from the traditions. Whereas the other three schools deal with common human issues, only the rebels separate themselves and therefore deserve the charge (often leveled against all Jews) of misanthropy. In his narrative Josephus occasionally mentions, incidentally, that some noted Pharisees were among the moderate leaders who opposed the revolt (*War* 2.411; *Life* 21); like the school passages, these notices serve to isolate the rebels from the mainstream population.

Within this ideal presentation, however, one can easily detect that Josephus is less than enthusiastic about the Sadducees and Pharisees. Only the Essenes receive unqualified praise. Josephus consistently offers them to the reader as exemplary Jews. They lead an admirably simple, philosophical life, according to a strict regimen. Holding all their possessions in common, they renounce both marriage[9] and slave ownership. They are masters of their emotions and impervious to pain. They possess secret knowledge, by which they can perform cures and predict the future. Their virtue is unmatched, whether by Greeks or barbarians (*Ant.* 18.20). Josephus even declares that those who once sample their doctrines are irresistibly attracted (*War* 2.158), which has led more than one scholar to suggest that Josephus wanted to pass himself off as one of them. Indeed, he describes Bannus, the only one who could satisfy his philosophical quest, in language that recalls the Essene lifestyle (*Life* 11).

Although Josephus concedes that the Sadducees count some of the worthiest citizens among their members, their denial of fate and the afterlife seem to him quite wrong. His attack on Epicurean philosophy for its rejection of divine providence (*Ant.* 10.277–281) applies equally well

[9] It should be noted that Josephus alludes to "another order of Essenes" (LCL) that allows marriage (*War* 2.160). This is an odd exception and stands over against evidence elsewhere in Josephus and Philo (e.g., *Hypoth.* 11.14–17). It is generally held that the Essenes repudiated marriage.

to the Sadducean position (*War* 2.164). And his firm belief that Moses promised a blissful future existence to those who obey the laws (*Ag. Ap.* 2.218; cf. *War* 2.157) flatly contradicts the Sadducean view as he presents it (*War* 2.165; *Ant.* 18.16). Of course, it would hurt his case to denounce the Sadducees when he is appealing to their legitimate status, over against the rebels' innovations. So the school passages omit any forthright attack on the group. Nevertheless, the attentive reader knows that Josephus's recognition of the Sadducees' historic legitimacy does not entail his own allegiance. Even within the school passages, he cannot resist noting that the Sadducees, perhaps like the Cynics in this regard, behave in a rude and disputatious manner (*War* 2.166; *Ant.* 18.16).

Josephus likewise has no quarrel with the philosophical views of the Pharisees: he agrees with their belief in an afterlife, rewards and punishments, and also with their acceptance of both providence and free will. He thinks that these principles are taught in the Jewish laws (cf. *Ant.* 16.396–399). Indeed, most people hold such views, Josephus says, and that is why the Pharisees are the most influential school: their beliefs resonate with the mainstream of the populace (*Ant.* 18.15). But notice how he phrases this point. His Greek says that the Pharisees "as chance would have it" *(tynchanousin)* are the most persuasive of the schools (*Ant.* 18.15). This phrase (which he repeats in the same sentence) is clarified by his subsequent remark that even the most eminent Sadducees must defer to "what the Pharisee says" (18.17) and by his further claim that the Essenes excel all others in virtue (18.20). That the Pharisees enjoy the greatest popular support is not something over which Josephus exults. Similarly in the *War* he presents the Pharisees as "the foremost" or "first"of the schools in popular influence (*War* 2.162; cf. 2.411), but his summary presentation of them, after his lengthy disquisition on the Essenes, is hardly flattery.

Still another subtle jibe is his notice that the hated rebel faction, which "sowed the seeds of every kind of misery" with its murderous behavior (*Ant.* 18.6–8), was cofounded by Judas the Golanite *and* Saddok, a Pharisee (18.4). To be sure, he explains that the Pharisees were not as a group inclined to revolt (18.23); otherwise his attempt to isolate the rebels would be ineffective. But then, why raise the Pharisaic connection at all? Like the Sadducees, they are coopted to show that the Jews have old and established philosophical schools. But even in this context Josephus is less than enthusiastic about either party.

In Josephus's Historical Narrative

Outside of these idealizing passages, Josephus's narrative of Jewish history consistently sets the Essenes in a radiant light, but deprecates both Sadducees and Pharisees. He speaks glowingly of Judas the Essene, who never once erred in his predictions (*War* 1.78–80); he praises John the Essene (or possibly, "man of Essa"), who was appointed like him as a commander in the revolt, as a man of "first-rate prowess and ability" (*War* 3.11); and he asserts that many Essenes had been granted a knowledge of the future because of their virtue (*Ant.* 15.371–379). Essenes reliably predicted the rise and fall of both Herod the Great and his son Archelaus (*Ant.* 15.371–379; 17.346). These narrative accounts support the prominence given to the Essenes in the school passages: they appear as the spiritual heroes of the Jewish world.

The Sadducees per se do not play a regular part in Josephus's narratives. This is noteworthy because he claims that Sadducees are "men of the highest standing" (*Ant.* 18.17), a wealthy elite with no following among the masses (13.298). It seems probable, therefore, that many of the "eminent citizens" who shared Josephus's moderate outlook on the revolt, and whom he praises for their wisdom, were in fact Sadducees. But then it is striking that he never mentions their Sadducean links in any positive context. The only time he raises the issue is when he criticizes the high priest Ananus for unlawfully convening the Sanhedrin in order to try James. He explains there that Ananus "followed the school of the Sadducees, who are, when it comes to judgments, savage beyond all other Jews" (*Ant.* 20.199). Interestingly, Ananus's Sadducean affiliation had not come up in *War,* where Josephus had praised his *virtues.*

That this group has negative associations in Josephus's mind is confirmed by the only other story he tells about them. When his favorite ancestor, the Hasmonean ruler John Hyrcanus, was accused by a dinner guest of holding the high priesthood unlawfully (more below), a Sadducean at court persuaded Hyrcanus that the Pharisees agreed with this insult. The Sadducee inflamed his anger and "worked on him" until he abandoned the Pharisees in favor of the Sadducees (*Ant.* 13.293, 296). These unflattering references to the Sadducees complement Josephus's distaste for their philosophical teachings. They may also explain why he does not usually disclose the party affiliation of the leading Jewish moderates: he likes their politics in spite of their religious-philosophical views.

Of the three recognized schools, only the Pharisees play an ongoing role in Josephus's narratives. He presents them throughout as the dominant party in Jewish society, but also as troublemakers for those in power—from Josephus's beloved Hasmonean ancestors to Herod the Great to Josephus himself.

In *War* 1.110–114, he describes the actions of the Pharisees under the Hasmonean Queen Alexandra Salome. He has already said that the Hasmonean dynasty reached its greatest moment under John Hyrcanus and steadily declined thereafter (1.69). The downward spiral began with a disastrous one-year reign of Hyrcanus's son Aristobulus, who imprisoned his entire family out of suspicion and ultimately killed his most loved brother (*War* 1.77, 81). It continued with Alexander Janneus, who at first seemed to be a moderate ruler (1.85) but ended up in a brutal civil war with his unhappy subjects (1.91, 97). Queen Alexandra, Janneus's widow, is introduced as a ray of promise: a frail, pious woman, who was indeed gentle and scrupulous in observing the sacred laws (1.108). She wisely gave the high priesthood to her elder, docile son, and confined her younger son, a "hothead," to private life (1.109). But her downfall, and so the continuing decline of the Hasmonean dynasty, was the result of the Pharisees' activity: this powerful group took advantage of her religiosity to insinuate themselves into power (1.110–111). They quickly took de facto control of domestic affairs and launched a reign of terror (1.113–114) that left the country in disarray (1.117).

Significantly, Josephus retells the story in the *Antiquities* in a way that changes the roles of several key characters. He now claims that the queen actually contrived with her dying husband to grant the Pharisees full domestic power as a way of conciliating the masses (*Ant.* 13.399–400). This is not the frail old woman of the *War*, but a strident and determined ruler who "showed none of the weakness of her sex" (*Ant.* 13.430). She was not duped by the Pharisees, but deliberately gave them their desired power as part of a strategic alliance. Josephus also changes his view of her sons, for he now thinks that the younger Aristobulus, a man of action and character, should have been given the high priesthood (13.407, 417, 423). But in the midst of this revision, the Pharisees maintain their consistent role as villains: Josephus presents them as troublemakers who disrupted the peace that would otherwise have prevailed under Alexandra (13.410); he expands greatly on their victims' plight (13.411–417); he claims that they "played drunken games" with the Hasmonean house (13.426). He concludes at length that Alexandra's experimental alliance with them was an unqualified disaster, which sealed the dynasty's fate (13.430–432). Since he is himself a proud descendant of the Hasmoneans, his bitterness is palpable.

The *Antiquities* also includes a story about the Pharisees in its account of John Hyrcanus's peerless government (13.288–298). Whereas the *War* had simply noted that Hyrcanus faced opposition from some of his "envious countrymen," whose rebellion was quashed (1.67), the *Antiquities* clearly identifies the leaders of this agitation as Pharisees. This school has such great influence with the masses that they are easily able to stir up trouble even for a king and a high priest (13.288). Given Josephus's attitude toward all forms of sedition and his fondness for John Hyrcanus, we cannot interpret this description of the Pharisees as anything but hostile. To document his charge, Josephus recounts a traditional story about a dispute between Hyrcanus and the Pharisees (13.289–296). It occurred at a banquet, at which a guest named Eleazar boldly demanded that Hyrcanus give up the high priesthood because the circumstances of his birth disqualified him for that office. Notice that the traditional story itself is not anti-Pharisaic. It does not clearly identify Eleazar as a Pharisee, and it insists that "all the Pharisees" were indignant over the charge (13.292). The banquet story seems to have come from circles in which both the Pharisees and the Hasmoneans were well thought of. It was the Sadducee Jonathan, as we saw before, who used the issue to create a rift between Hyrcanus and the Pharisees. But Josephus takes over this legend and furnishes it with an introduction that is plainly hostile to the Pharisees.[10]

At the end of the story of John Hyrcanus's break with the Pharisees, Josephus appends an important footnote (ancient writing offered no opportunity for footnotes in our sense) on the differences between

---

[10] In their belief that Josephus was himself a Pharisee, many scholars have suggested that he did not write the introduction to the story, that it comes from one of his sources and does not reflect his views. This view is untenable, however, since: (a) the author refers to his earlier remarks on the schools (cf. 13.171–173); (b) his language about their influence with the masses establishes a theme that continues throughout the *Antiquities* (cf. 13.298; 14.400; 18.15); and (c) the language about success producing envy is quite characteristic of Josephus, even in his autobiography (*Life* 80, 85, 122, 204, 423), where reliance on sources is unlikely. For a full discussion, see Steve Mason, *Flavius Josephus on the Pharisees* (Studia Post-Biblica 39; Leiden: Brill, 1991), 213–45.

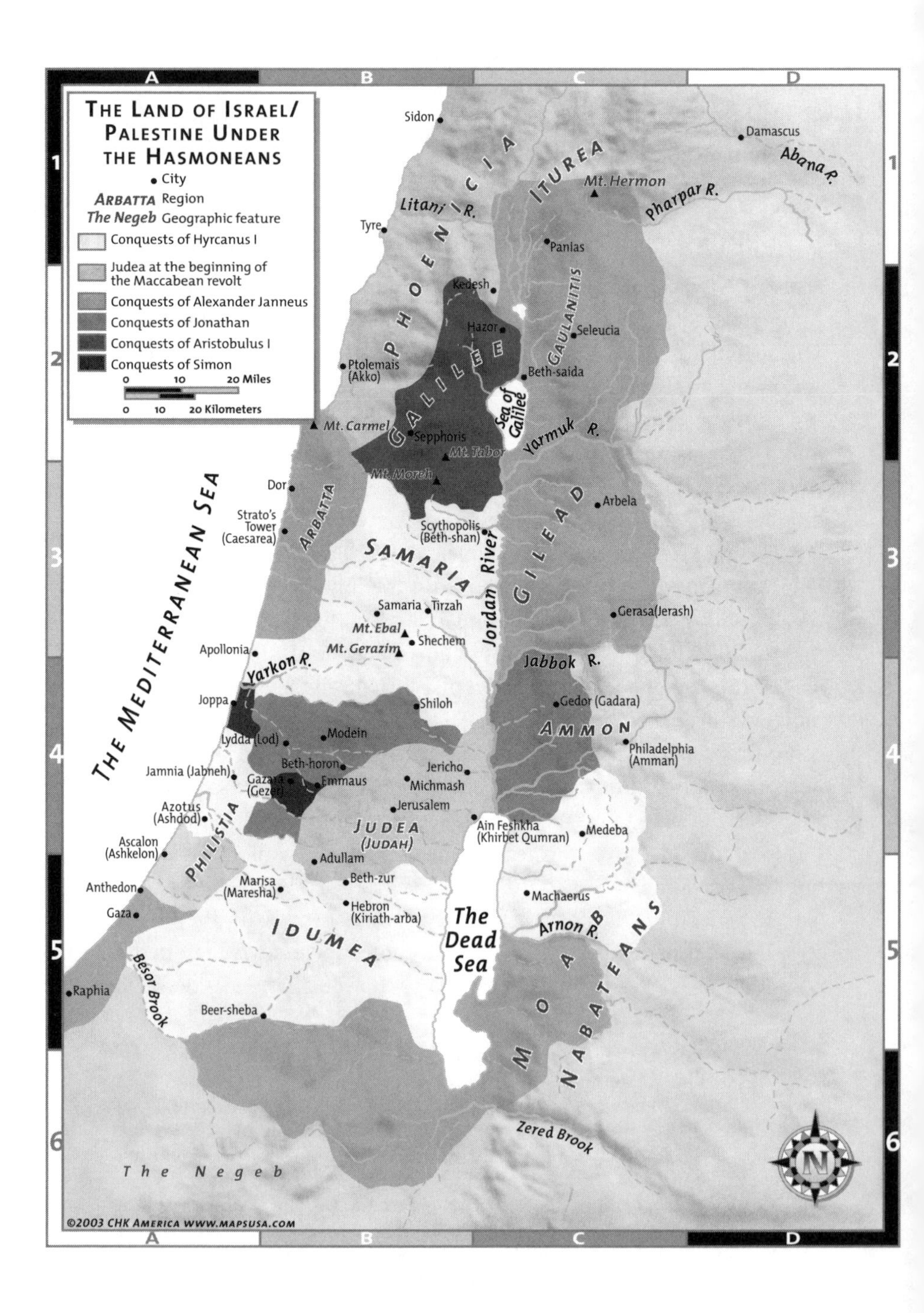
THE LAND OF ISRAEL/ PALESTINE UNDER THE HASMONEANS
City
ARBATTA Region
The Negeb Geographic feature
Conquests of Hyrcanus I
Judea at the beginning of the Maccabean revolt
Conquests of Alexander Janneus
Conquests of Jonathan
Conquests of Aristobulus I
Conquests of Simon
0 10 20 Miles
0 10 20 Kilometers
Sidon
Damascus
Abana R.
PHOENICIA
ITUREA
Mt. Hermon
Pharpar R.
Litani R.
Tyre
Panias
Kedesh
GAULANITIS
Hazor
Seleucia
GALILEE
Ptolemais (Akko)
Beth-saida
Sea of Galilee
Mt. Carmel
Sepphoris
Yarmuk R.
Mt. Tabor
Mt. Moreh
Dor
ARBATTA
Arbela
Strato's Tower (Caesarea)
Scythopolis (Beth-shan)
SAMARIA
Jordan River
GILEAD
THE MEDITERRANEAN SEA
Samaria
Tirzah
Gerasa(Jerash)
Mt. Ebal
Shechem
Mt. Gerazim
Apollonia
Yarkon R.
Jabbok R.
Joppa
Shiloh
Gedor (Gadara)
Modein
AMMON
Lydda (Lod)
Philadelphia (Amman)
Jamnia (Jabneh)
Beth-horon
Jericho
Gazara (Gezer)
Emmaus
Michmash
Azotus (Ashdod)
Jerusalem
JUDEA (JUDAH)
Ain Feshkha (Khirbet Qumran)
Medeba
Ascalon (Ashkelon)
PHILISTIA
Adullam
Beth-zur
Anthedon
Marisa (Maresha)
Machaerus
Gaza
Hebron (Kiriath-arba)
The Dead Sea
IDUMEA
Arnon R.
MOAB
NABATEANS
Besor Brook
Raphia
Beer-sheba
Zered Brook
The Negeb
N
©2003 CHK AMERICA WWW.MAPSUSA.COM

The Hasmonean Dynasty (B.C.E.)

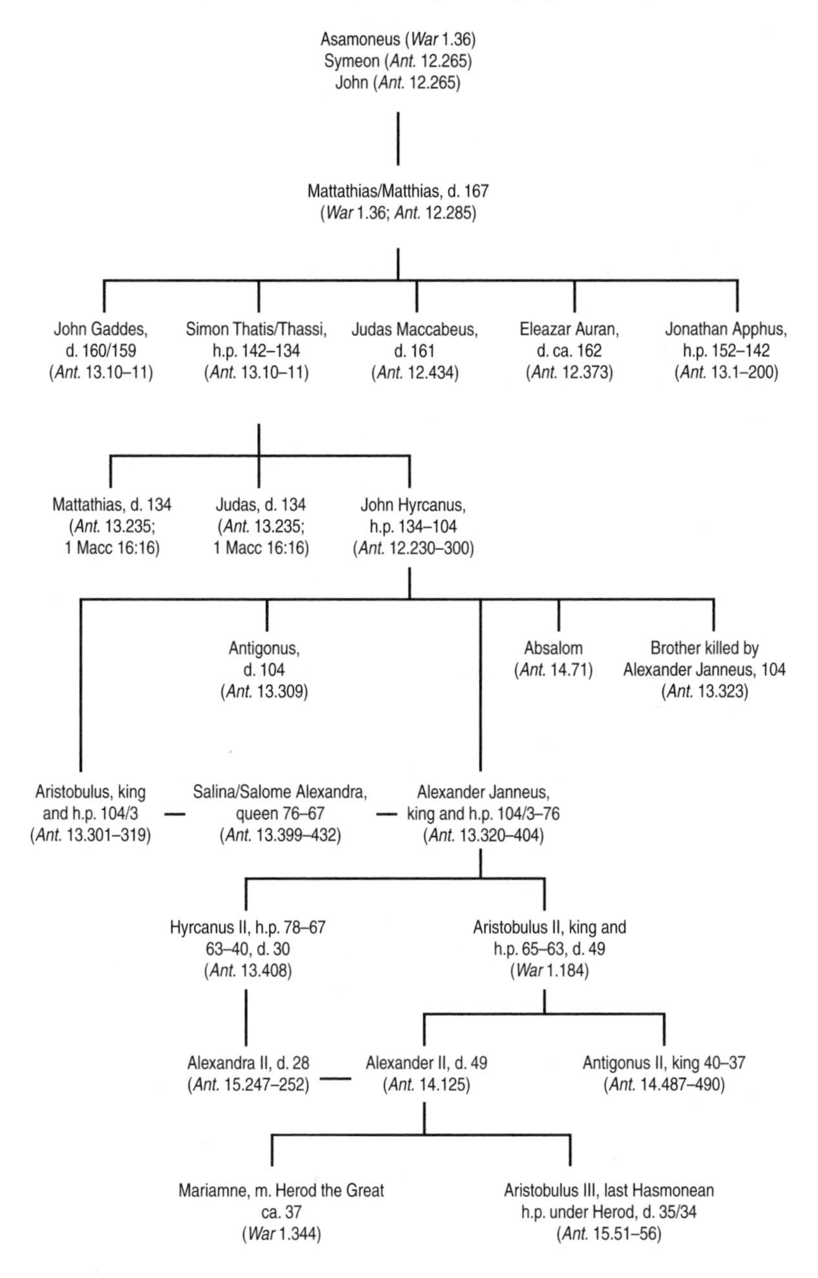

Pharisees and Sadducees, in order to explain what it was that Hyrcanus abrogated when he annulled Pharisaic law (13.297–298). The essential point is that the Pharisees accept certain ordinances that are not among the laws of Moses but issue from a "tradition of fathers"—the Pharisees' name for their living tradition. But the Sadducees claim to accept only what is written in Moses' laws. This difference represents a major source of controversy, though the conflict is alleviated by the fact that the Pharisees have massive popular support whereas the Sadducees persuade only a wealthy few. We may note here that although Josephus is plainly not a Sadducee, his own view of Moses' constitution, as a comprehensive written code not to be tampered with, seems to correspond to that of the Sadducees. At least, he nowhere else mentions, much less endorses, such an extrabiblical tradition. He speaks of the laws as revealed entirely to Moses, in writing, and inviolable for all time.

During the reign of Herod the Great, the Pharisees appear in a similar light, as powerful yet baneful influences. As with Queen Alexandra, this is all the more noteworthy because Josephus's portrait of Herod changes significantly between the *War* and the *Antiquities.* In the *War,* where Herod appears as a victim of domestic plots, the Pharisees are simply part of the intrigue, bribed for their services by Herod's scheming sister-in-law (*War* 1.571). Although Josephus is eager in the *Antiquities* to illustrate Herod's lawlessness, it does not follow that Herod's opponents automatically become virtuous. On the contrary, he maintains his stern portrayal of the "female clique" that plotted the king's demise (*Ant.* 17.32–40). He now elaborates on the involvement of the Pharisees, whom he numbers at more than six thousand: this was a group that "thought very highly of its precision with respect to ancestral custom, and pretended [to observance] of such laws as the Deity approves" (17.41). These men, who dominated the female clique, used their religious authority to "combat and injure" the king (17.42). They did this by manufacturing false predictions, in which they promised Herod's brother and sister-in-law (who had paid the Pharisees' fine for not swearing an oath of allegiance) that they would become rulers after Herod's removal (17.43). The Pharisees also secured the support of a eunuch named Bagoas by promising the poor fellow that he would sire a future (messianic?) king of Israel (17.45). Josephus leaves no doubt, in spite of his animosity toward Herod, that this sort of behavior was scandalous.

The only Pharisee who receives unqualified praise from Josephus is one Samaias, "an upright man and for that reason superior to fear" (*Ant.* 14.176). He was the only member of the Jewish court who was willing to stand up and confront the young Herod when the latter was charged with executing bandits in Galilee without due process. But significantly, Josephus neglects to mention, while praising the man's virtues, that he was a Pharisee. This piece of information turns up only incidentally in the following volume (15.3). As with the Sadducean high priest Ananus, Josephus does not connect Samaias's admirable qualities with his party allegiance.

Finally, Josephus's account of his command of Galilee during the revolt includes considerable attention to the actions of some high-ranking Pharisees. They become involved in the story, he says, because of his opponent John of Gischala, who competed with him for influence in the region. John was able to win the support of his friend Simon, son of Gamaliel, a very prominent Pharisee (*Life* 190). Josephus has no choice but to concede Simon's credentials (191), but he immediately goes on to say that Simon tried to persuade the Jerusalem authorities to remove him from his position (193). When Simon's first bid was unsuccessful, this renowned Pharisee resorted to underhanded bribery (195)—a tactic that was successful (196). Moreover, once the council had decided to remove Josephus, they sent a delegation of four dignitaries, accompanied by sufficient troops, to do the job. Three of the four delegates were also Pharisees. Predictably, Josephus accuses his adversaries of all sorts of crimes: they were deceitful, slanderous, and violent (*Life* 216, 233, 237, 245, 261, 274, 281, 301–303); one of the Pharisees was "a wicked man and an evildoer" (290).

All of this vitriol is to be expected where Josephus is promoting himself. In this case, it happens to be Pharisees who run afoul of his self-aggrandizement. But this episode in his own career makes his overall portrayal of the Pharisees' activities in Jewish history consistent: they use their great reputation for religious scrupulosity, and their consequent influence with the masses, to effect their own political goals. They typically resort to bribery, intrigue, and even violence to accomplish their ends. So their actions belie their popular reputation for piety. It is *not* one of Josephus's major literary goals, let me emphasize, to denigrate the Pharisees. But if *we* ask what he says about the group, it is that they have exercised a detrimental influence on Jewish history, from their destructive actions under the independent Hasmonean state to their plots against Josephus.

In spite of this consistent presentation, it has usually been thought that Josephus either was a devoted Pharisee or wanted to present himself as one. How could such a view have arisen? In describing his adolescent philosophical quest (considered in chapter 3), Josephus claims that, having studied with the Pharisees, Sadducees, and Essenes and found them unsatisfying, and having then studied with Bannus for three years, he returned to the city (Greek *polis; Life* 10–12a). The following line has usually been translated: "and began to conduct myself according to the rules of the sect of the Pharisees" (Whiston, 1737) or "I began to govern my life by the rules of the Pharisees" (Thackeray, 1926). Thereafter, virtually every commentator has taken the statement to be Josephus's claim that he became a Pharisee or joined the Pharisaic school. In a book devoted to Josephus's Pharisees, however, I have argued that such a translation overlooks the context: Josephus has already said that he studied with the Pharisees, but he dismisses that conventional experience as unsatisfactory.[11] So it makes no sense for him to say, without explanation, "Then I became a Pharisee." That statement would be especially puzzling in view of his descriptions of the Pharisees, which do not endear them to the reader, and given that elsewhere he shows no attachment to the Pharisees' distinctive "tradition of the fathers" (*Ant.* 13.297–298). He seems to preclude such attachment by his consistent promotion of Moses' laws as complete and final.

Further, as German translations of the work have usually noted, the Greek sentence actually has two parts. The main verb *(politeuesthai)*, which has usually been taken to mean "behave" or "conduct my life," is better translated as "take part in public affairs." That is how Josephus normally uses the word elsewhere. Furthermore, that fits the context, in which he is about to describe his public career (*Life* 13ff.). So, he returned from the desert to the city *(polis)* and began to engage in public affairs *(politeuesthai)*. The second part of the sentence is a dependent clause, "following the lead of the school of the Pharisees." Thus, Josephus's *public* career entailed following, or deference toward, the school of the Pharisees. What does this mean? As we have seen, he consistently presents the Pharisees as the dominant school in Jewish

---

[11] Mason, *Flavius Josephus on the Pharisees*, 213–45.

political life: all the religious aspects of life follow their plan (*Ant.* 18.15), and even the most eminent Sadducees must defer to the Pharisees *when they assume public office* (*Ant.* 18.17). Whether any of this is historically true[12] is not germane to understanding Josephus's point. He claims that the Pharisees controlled public life, and so it makes sense within his presentation that his own beginning in civic affairs would also entail deference to the Pharisees. This does not mean that he became a Pharisee, just as it does not mean that office-holding Sadducees became Pharisees.

In the New Testament

How do Josephus's portrayals of the three main Jewish schools assist the reader of the NT? As we have come to expect, they are both supportive and problematic.

On the supportive side, Josephus agrees with the gospels' general assumption that the Pharisees were the most prominent group in Palestinian Jewish life. They seem to represent the popularly recognized religious authority. Moreover, they appear in the gospels as scrupulous in their observance of the Jewish law, especially concerning Sabbath observance, tithing, and religious purity laws. Thus Matthew's Jesus uses them as illustrations of scrupulosity: when laying down an extreme standard for his own followers, he can do no better than admonish them to be even more righteous than the scribes and Pharisees (5:20); that is understood to be a tall order. Josephus does not mention tithing and Jewish purity laws, perhaps because they would not be easily understood by his readers, but he does often say that the Pharisees are reputed to be the most precise interpreters of the laws.

---

[12] Many scholars in the last few decades have come to doubt the old view, based largely on Josephus, that the Pharisees were the dominant group in Jewish society before the temple fell in A.D. 70. So Rudolf Meyer and H. F. Weiss, *TDNT* 9, 31; Morton Smith, "Palestinian Judaism in the First Century," in *Israel: Its Role in Civilization* (ed. Moshe Davis; New York: Harper & Brothers, 1956), 67–81; Jacob Neusner, *From Politics to Piety: The Emergence of Pharisaic Judaism* (Englewood Cliffs, N.J.: Prentice-Hall, 1973); Anthony J. Saldarini, *Pharisees, Scribes and Sadducees* (Wilmington, Del.: Michael Glazier, 1988), 157, 211, 214, 229. E. P. Sanders, *Judaism: Practice and Belief, 63 B.C.E.–66 C.E.* (London: SCM/Philadelphia: TPI, 1992), 380–490, credits the Pharisees with popularity but not political control in pre-70 Judea. This is a helpful distinction, though it is not made by Josephus.

Paul's claim that he had been a Pharisee or held to a Pharisaic view of the law before his conversion to Christianity (Phil 3:5) also illustrates that the Pharisees were a prominent, well-known school in the first century. Interestingly, Paul elsewhere says that he had been zealous, while still in Judaism, for the "traditions of my fathers" (Gal 1:14). This phrase is very close to the one that Josephus uses for the Pharisees' special tradition in *Antiquities* 13.297. It is also paralleled by Mark, who explains that the Pharisees wash their hands before eating, "observing the tradition of the elders" (Mark 7:3).

Some scholars have labeled both Jesus and Josephus as Pharisees because they agree in various ways with Pharisaic positions. We have seen that there is no good reason to think that Josephus was or wanted to be seen as a Pharisee, for he was highly critical of the group. There is a superficial similarity here with Jesus, who charges the Pharisees with hypocrisy. But there is an important difference. Josephus writes as a member of the aristocratic elite; he looks down his nose at the Pharisees for being mere pretenders. He is convinced that priests like him are the real adepts in the law; they are the traditional heart and soul of Judaism. So he feels qualified to dismiss the Pharisees' reputation among the naive masses as unfounded. And his criticisms of the Pharisees are at the highly political level, which would interest only a politico like himself. He is convinced that they contributed to the downfall of his Hasmonean ancestors, and he accuses some of them of trying to subvert his own career. Josephus's critique of the Pharisees shows that, although he portrays them as the dominant party, they did have literate opponents, and not exclusively among the Sadducees. It was quite possible to dislike the Pharisees and still stand wholly within Judaism.

Jesus, for his part, is portrayed as moving about the peasant population of Galilee and criticizing the Pharisees mainly for their hypocrisy. Hypocrisy is the characteristic charge of the disaffected and the injured, those who are hurt by the failure of those in power to live up to their stated principles. (It is still probably the most common charge leveled against Western governments.) Jesus' classic statement is given in Matthew 23:2–3:

> The scribes and the Pharisees sit upon the seat of Moses. Whatever they might say, therefore, do and observe; but do not act according to their behavior, for they say and do not perform!

We see here what is plainly an in-house criticism. The Pharisees' legitimacy as scriptural interpreters is assumed and is not an issue. The only issue is their behavior: like all preachers and politicians, they inevitably draw the charge of "Hypocrite!" from some of their compatriots. So Josephus and Jesus both castigate the Pharisees, but from quite different perspectives and for different reasons.

In confining the Sadducees' appearance to Jesus' last days in Jerusalem (Mark 12:18–27), the gospels and especially Luke agree with Josephus's limitation of their influence. Like Josephus, the gospel authors also know that this group denies resurrection and afterlife (Mark 12:18; Acts 23:8). According to Acts 23:8, the Sadducees also deny the existence of angels and spirits. Although Josephus does not mention this point, it fits well with his claim that the Sadducees accept only what is written in the law. The Torah (Genesis–Deuteronomy) assumes that death is the end of life, and it does not present a developed picture of angels (though a few divine "messengers" appear) or demons. The fairly elaborate scheme of angels and demons led by archangels and arch demons, which would become traditional in both Judaism and Christianity, begins to appear in Jewish writings only with the very latest biblical books, from about 200 B.C.E. So the Sadducees' rejection of heavenly beings would fit with their dismissal of afterlife, since neither is clearly developed in the laws of Moses. Josephus's notice that the disagreement between Pharisees and Sadducees led to serious conflicts also fits well with the presentation of Paul's trial before the Sanhedrin in Acts 23. All he had to do was mention resurrection and "a great clamor arose" between the Sadducees and Pharisees (23:9).

Conspicuously absent from the NT are the Essenes, of whom Josephus speaks most fondly. There seems to be a good reason for this absence: since Josephus claims that the Essenes lead quiet lives, removed from public affairs, they would have little occasion to run into conflict with Jesus and his followers. If the Essenes were to be found in "each town" of Palestine (*War* 2.124), they must have been known to Jesus. Given their simple and virtuous lifestyle, however, it may well be that Jesus' followers too admired them. Indeed, in the book of Acts, as we shall see, the role that should belong to the Essenes (according to Josephus's presentation) is taken by the early Christian movement. We must reserve that discussion for chapter 6.

Some of the apparent problems created by Josephus's accounts of the schools may be solved with relative ease. For example, his focus on the issue of fate and free will as the central issue distinguishing the schools does not appear at all in the NT. Nevertheless, from his own writings we can tell that he dwells on that issue mainly in order to dignify the Jewish schools by making their subjects of discourse sound like those of the Greco-Roman schools. That he deliberately refrains from mentioning more exotic "Jewish" themes, which might have reinforced his readers' prejudices about the strangeness of Jewish culture, is clear from his later admission that the main controversy between Pharisees and Sadducees was over the question of authoritative traditions. Once this issue is on the table, he leaves it there, for it is in fact the central issue from which the others flow (cf. *Ant.* 18.12). But his original effort to conceal this question suggests that he consciously omitted other matters as well, perhaps matters relating to ritual purity, tithing, and the like, that appear in the NT but would be of little interest to his readers.

Still, some tensions remain. For example, Matthew tends to group the "Pharisees and Sadducees" together as Jesus' opponents; the Pharisees and Sadducees who come to John for baptism are rebuffed (Matt 3:7). This tandem also tests Jesus by requesting a sign from heaven (Matt 16:1). Jesus, in turn, tells his disciples to beware of the "leaven" of the Pharisees and Sadducees, by which he means their teaching (Matt 16:12). This pairing is strange in view of Josephus's account, because recognizing their quite different social constituencies and outlooks on religion, one would not expect the Pharisees and Sadducees to spend a lot of time together—outside of the governing council where their cooperation was necessary. Moreover, none of the other gospels cites the Pharisees and Sadducees working together like that. Luke simply has "the crowds" coming out for baptism and being rebuffed by John (Luke 3:7). In Mark 8:11, it is the Pharisees alone who seek a sign from him. In Mark 8:15, it is the leaven of the Pharisees and of *Herod* that the disciples are warned against. From all of this it appears that the pairing of "Pharisees and Sadducees" in Matthew is intended by the author to signify all of Israel, and that it makes more sense in this symbolic use than as a historical portrait.

Again, Luke's claim that "the Pharisees were lovers of money" (Luke 16:14) is hard to square with Josephus. Although he dislikes the group, he does concede that they lead a simple lifestyle, not yielding to luxury (*Ant.* 18.12). To be sure, he does accuse them of both offering and accepting bribes, but these are isolated incidents and do not imply a luxurious lifestyle. The charge of being a lover of money was a standard polemical tactic in antiquity, and it still shows up today. It gained currency with Plato's attack on the "sophists"—philosophers who made a living by traveling around and teaching philosophy to upper-class youth. It was repeated endlessly by philosophers who attacked their competition as unworthy practitioners, and it appears to have been used against Paul as well (1 Thess 2:5, 9). It seems safest to take the charge in Luke as this kind of stock polemic rather than as a telling statement about the Pharisees' general behavior.

In examining Josephus's portrayals of the family of Herod, the Roman governors, the high priests, and the Jewish religious parties, we have learned a lot about the background of the NT. This does not mean that we have taken Josephus as some sort of repository of facts. Rather, we have tried to understand his presentations of these groups within the context of his own literary aims. Only when we have completed that task have we asked about *his* significance for NT interpretation, and it turns out that his significance is multifaceted. In some cases, he confirms points made in the gospels. In others, his information almost seems necessary to a proper interpretation of the NT, especially of some passages in Acts. In still other cases, such as his portrait of Pontius Pilate or his dating of the high priests, Josephus's perspective helps us to appreciate that the NT documents too are products of a given time and place, and so have their own limited perspectives. His accounts help us to sharpen our awareness of the NT authors' literary aims, and to realize that they too do not represent objective facts but rather interpretations of facts.

FOR FURTHER READING

General treatments of Josephus and the NT world have fallen out of fashion in recent decades. As we have noted, however, all handbooks on the historical environment of the NT depend heavily on Josephus. Of these, the most essential are:

- Emil Schürer, *The History of the Jewish People in the Age of Jesus Christ* (3 vols. in 4; rev. and ed. Geza Vermes, Fergus Millar, Martin Goodman, and Matthew Black; Edinburgh: T&T Clark, 1986–1987).

- S. Safrai and M. Stern, eds., *The Jewish People in the First Century* (2 vols.; Compendia Rerum Iudaicarum ad Novum Testamentum, Section 1; Assen: Van Gorcum/Philadelphia: Fortress, 1987).

These handbooks include some assessment of Josephus's literary aims, whereas most others are concerned with a larger historical construction. Beyond these, one might look at books and essays on Josephus's treatments of the various groups in question, such as:

- Arnold H. M. Jones, *The Herods of Judaea* (Oxford: Clarendon, 1967).
- Stewart Perowne, *The Life and Times of Herod the Great* (London: Hodder and Stoughton, 1956).
- Samuel Sandmel, "Herod (Family)," *Interpreter's Dictionary of the Bible* (4 vols.; ed. G. A. Buttrick; Nashville: Abingdon, 1962), 2:584–94.
- Abraham Schalit, *König Herodes: Der Mann und sein Werk* (Berlin: de Gruyter, 1969).
- Peter Richardson, *Herod: King of the Jews, Friend of the Romans* (Columbia, S.C.: University of South Carolina Press, 1996).
- Nikos Kokkinos, *The Herodian Dynasty: Origins, Role in Society and Eclipse* (Sheffield: Sheffield Academic Press, 1998).

A contemporary effort to distinguish Josephus's sources concerning Agrippa I is:

- Daniel R. Schwartz, *Agrippa I: The Last King of Judaea* (Tübingen: Mohr Siebeck, 1989).

On the other groups and issues raised in this chapter, see:

- Paul Winter, "Pilate in History and in Christian Tradition," in his *On the Trial of Jesus* (rev. and ed. T. A. Burkill and Geza Vermes; Berlin/New York: de Gruyter, 1974), 70–89.
- Helen Bond, *Pontius Pilate in History and Interpretation* (Cambridge: Cambridge University Press, 1998).
- Clemens Thoma, "The High Priesthood in the Judgment of Josephus," *Josephus, the Bible, and History* (ed. Louis H. Feldman and Gohei Hata; Leiden: Brill, 1989), 196–215.
- Steve Mason, "Priesthood in Josephus and the 'Pharisaic Revolution,' " *Journal of Biblical Literature* 107 (1988): 657–61.
- Jacob Neusner, *From Politics to Piety: the Emergence of Pharisaic Judaism* (Englewood Cliffs, N.J.: Prentice-Hall, 1973), 45–66

(for a famous but no longer tenable treatment of Josephus's Pharisees).

- Anthony J. Saldarini, *Pharisees, Scribes and Sadducees in Palestinian Society* (Wilmington, Del.: Michael Glazier, 1988), 79–198 (on the Pharisees, Sadducees, and others in Josephus and the NT, with special attention to social history).
- Steve Mason, *Flavius Josephus on the Pharisees* (Leiden: Brill, 1991).
- Günter Stemberger, *Pharisäer, Sadduzäer, Essener* (Stuttgart: Katholisches Bibelwerk, 1991).
- Albert I. Baumgarten, *The Flourishing of Jewish Sects in the Maccabean Era: An Interpretation* (Leiden: Brill, 1997).

Chapter 5

Early Christian Figures Mentioned by Josephus

The most obvious reason for Christian interest in Josephus is that he mentions three prominent NT personalities: John the Baptist, Jesus, and Jesus' brother James. I have delayed considering those figures until now because the passages in which they appear are not central to Josephus's literary aims. All three occur only in the closing volumes of the *Antiquities* (18–20), which are not the first place one should look to understand Josephus. In my view, his significance for the NT reader would remain almost as great if he had said nothing about John, Jesus, and James.

Nevertheless, he does mention them, and his unique perspective is helpful for NT interpretation. Of the three passages, the one concerning John the Baptist is the most revealing. Josephus's description of Jesus is full of problems, but most of those seem capable of resolution. His reference to James, though very brief, is also useful. Even as we turn to consider his discussions of these figures, we need to keep in mind everything that we have observed so far about his literary aims.

JOHN THE BAPTIST

It is a mark of Josephus's complete isolation from the early Christian world of thought that he devotes significantly more space to John the Baptist than to Jesus—even if we admit his account of Jesus as it stands (but see below). He mentions the Baptist while discussing the marital indiscretions of Herod Antipas, which we considered in chapter 4. Recall that the tetrarch's passion for his brother's wife led him to abandon his own, who happened to be the daughter of the neighboring king, Aretas IV. That king was already upset with Antipas over a border dispute. When he heard his daughter's story, he engaged Antipas in battle and routed his army. Josephus comments:

> But to some of the Jews the destruction of Herod's army seemed to be divine vengeance, and certainly a just vengeance, for his treatment of John, surnamed the Baptist. For Herod had put him to death, though he was a good man and had exhorted the Jews to lead righteous lives, to practise justice *[dikaiosynē]* towards their fellows and piety *[eusebeia]* towards God, and so doing to join in baptism. In his view this was a necessary preliminary if baptism was to be acceptable to God. They must not employ it to gain pardon for whatever sins they had committed, but as a consecration of the body implying that the soul was already cleansed by right behaviour. When others too joined the crowds about him, because they were aroused to the highest degree by his sermons, Herod became alarmed. Eloquence that had so great an effect on mankind might lead to some form of sedition, for it looked as if they would be guided by John in everything that they did. Herod decided therefore that it would be much better to strike first and be rid of him before his work led to an uprising, than to wait for an upheaval, get involved in a difficult situation and see his mistake. Though John, because of Herod's suspicions, was brought in chains to Machaerus, the stronghold that we have previously mentioned, and there put to death, yet the verdict of the Jews was that the destruction visited upon Herod's army was a vindication of John, since God saw fit to inflict such a blow on Herod (*Ant.* 18.116–119, LCL)

So in Josephus's view, John was a good and virtuous teacher, well respected among the Jews. His unjust death once again exposed the lawlessness of the Herodian family. In keeping with the thesis of the *Antiquities,* Antipas was quickly punished by God for his misdeeds.

Since John died before Josephus's birth, the historian must be recounting a tradition, either oral or written. Perhaps the legend of the Baptist was so famous that Josephus knew it from childhood and simply chose to insert it here in his account of Antipas's rule. Or perhaps his written source for the political history of the period referred to John's death. In any case, Josephus tells the story in his own way, to make his own points. Most obviously, he welds the episode into his ongoing demonstration that violation of the divine laws brings inevitable punishment.

Notice also that Josephus reduces the content of John's preaching to the maxim "piety toward God and justice toward one's fellows." This is Josephus's usual way of describing Jewish ethical responsibility.[1] Against the charges that Jews were atheists and haters of humanity, he says that all Jewish customs *(ethē)* are concerned with "piety [toward God] and justice [toward humanity]" (*Ant.* 16.42). He ascribes this pair of virtues to the great kings of Israel (*Ant.* 7.338, 342, 356, 374; 9.236) and paraphrases David's deathbed speech to Solomon so as to include them (*Ant.* 7.384). He even claims that the first two oaths sworn by Essene novices were "to behave with piety toward God and with justice toward their fellows" (*War* 2.139). This terminology, which summarizes the popular morality of the Greco-Roman world, is part of Josephus's apologetic arsenal: he wants to present Judaism as a philosophical tradition that embraces the world's highest values.[2] John the Baptist appears as another Jewish philosopher, a modern heir of Abraham, Moses, and Solomon. But he is a persecuted philosopher of the sort familiar to Josephus's readers, condemned by an unjust ruler for his fearless virtue (see chapter 6).

How does Josephus's account of John relate to the gospels' portrayals? On the one hand, it offers striking independent confirmation of John's demand that people coming for immersion first repent and resolve to behave righteously. In Josephus's words, "They must not employ it [baptism] to gain pardon for whatever sins they had committed, but as a consecration of the body implying that the soul was *already* cleansed by right behaviour" (*Ant.* 18.117). In the language of the gospels:

Matthew 3:7–10	**Luke 3:7–9**
But when he saw many of the Pharisees and Sadducees coming for immersion, he said to them:	He used to say to the crowds that came out to be immersed by him:
"Brood of vipers! Who warned you to flee from the coming wrath? Produce, therefore, fruit worthy of repentance, and do not consider saying among yourselves 'We have Abraham for a father.' For I am telling you that	"Brood of vipers! Who warned you to flee from the coming wrath? Produce, therefore, fruits worthy of repentance, and do not begin to say among yourselves 'We have Abraham for a father.' For I am telling you that

[1] Cf. Steve Mason, *Flavius Josephus on the Pharisees* (Leiden: Brill, 1991), 85–89.

[2] Cf. Mason, *Josephus,* 184–86.

God is able to raise up children for Abraham from these stones. But the axe is already being set at the root of the trees; so every tree that does not produce good fruit is being rooted out and thrown into the fire."	God is able to raise up children for Abraham from these stones. But the axe is already being set at the root of the trees; so every tree that does not produce good fruit is being rooted out and thrown into the fire."

The gospel of Luke elaborates on the kind of behavior that was required:

> Now the crowds used to ask him, "What, then, should we do?" And he would answer, "A person who has two coats should give to someone who has none, and a person who has food should do the same." Tax collectors would come to be immersed and would say to him, "Teacher, what should we do?" He said to them, "Do not make a surplus, beyond what is scheduled for you." And soldiers would ask him, "What about us? What should we do?" He said to them, "Do not extort or blackmail, but be content with your wages." (Luke 3:10–14)

There is, to be sure, a difference of tone between Josephus's and the gospels' accounts. His discussion of soul and the body and of "right action" is a translation of John's preaching into the philosophical language that he typically uses to describe Judaism. There is also a difference of content, to which we shall return below. Nevertheless, Josephus and the gospels agree that John typically demanded repentance as a prior condition of immersion.

Some scholars have found a problem in the different reasons given for John's arrest. Josephus says that it was because of the preacher's great eloquence; in a period marked by successive popular movements that made the authorities very nervous, his popularity seemed sure to lead to disturbances. Just as the Roman governors of Judea did not hesitate to destroy such movements in Judea proper, so the tetrarch of Galilee and Perea thought it best to nip this group in the bud by destroying its leader. (Notice, however, that whereas Josephus usually detests such popular leaders, he only speaks well of John.) The gospels, for their part, claim that Antipas killed John because the preacher had denounced the tetrarch's unlawful marriage to his sister-in-law: "For John was saying to Herod, 'It is not lawful for you to have your brother's wife' " (Mark 6:18; Matt 14:4; Luke 3:19).

On examination, the two explanations are not mutually exclusive, but actually fit together quite well. The gospels do not explain any details of the marital affair, and Josephus's account provides helpful background. Luke, at least, allows that the Baptist made many other criticisms of the ruler (Luke 3:19). Conversely, although Josephus does not mention John's criticism of the tetrarch's marriage, we have seen that he greatly simplifies John's preaching in schematic form. Such popular movements were inherently antiestablishment, and it would make sense if John or his followers had spoken against Antipas's lawlessness. Moreover, if John did chastise the tetrarch on this score, that would lend a kind of poetic justice to the story, for he receives his punishment at the hand of the abandoned wife's father. That connection may even explain why this particular military defeat was traditionally seen as punishment for Antipas's treatment of John.

Yet we see an obvious and major difference between Josephus and the gospels in their respective portraits of the Baptist. To put it bluntly, Josephus does not see John as a "figure in the Christian tradition." The Baptist is not connected with early Christianity in any way. On the contrary, Josephus presents him as a famous Jewish teacher with a message and a following of his own, neither of which is related to Jesus. This is a problem for the reader of the NT because the gospels unanimously declare him to be essentially the *forerunner* of Jesus the Messiah.

Mark, the earliest gospel, sets the tone. He opens his narrative with a composite quotation from the prophets that interprets John as one who prepares for the Lord's coming (1:2–3):

> Just as it is written in Isaiah the prophet, "Look, I am sending my messenger before your face, who will prepare your way, the voice of one who cries in the desert, 'Prepare the Lord's way; make his paths straight!' "

Although Mark attributes the quoted words to Isaiah, the first two lines are a paraphrase of Malachi 3:1; Matthew (3:3) and Luke (3:4) correct the oversight. For Mark, as for the early Christians generally, the title "Lord" refers to Jesus and not God as in the OT.[3] So John plays a key role in the story of salvation: he comes as a herald to prepare the way for Jesus. Mark's description of his preaching stresses its preparatory role: what he said to the people when he immersed them was that someone mightier was coming, someone who would immerse them in "holy spirit," and that he was totally unworthy of the coming one's company (1:7–8).

---

[3] Cf. 1 Thess 1:1, 3; 1 Cor 1:2–3, 7–8, passim; 1 Pet 1:3; Jas 1:1; Acts 2:36; 4:26, 33; 7:59. In Isa 40:3 itself, the LXX expression "Lord" stands in obvious synonymous parallelism with "God" *(theos/elohim).*

> The more powerful one is coming after me, the thong of whose sandals I am unworthy to stoop down and untie. I immersed you in water, but he will immerse you in holy spirit.

Thus John's preaching is basically forward-looking, pointing ahead to Jesus. He predicts the arrival of the Spirit in the church. Significantly, Jesus' career does not begin (in the synoptic gospels) until the forerunner is in prison, having completed his role (Mark 1:14).

Matthew and Luke continue to develop this portrayal of John as herald. They agree that he played the role of Elijah, who, according to Mal 4:5, would come before the "day of the Lord," to reconcile families so that the day of judgment would not be too catastrophic (Matt 11:14; Luke 1:12–17). He is a close ally of Jesus, drawing his power from the same source (Matt 11:16–19; 21:23–27); Luke even says he is a cousin (1:36). Nevertheless, when John is still in the womb he and his mother recognize the priority of Jesus and Mary (Luke 1:41–42). Matthew and Luke strictly relegate John to the old order, before Jesus' coming: "Among those born of women, none greater than John the Baptist has arisen; yet he who is least in the reign of heaven is greater than he" (Matt 11:11; Luke 7:28). He represents the highest point of the "law and prophets," before the coming of the gospel (Matt 11:13; Luke 16:17). Because the author of Luke also writes Acts, he has considerable opportunity to emphasize John's preparatory function: he repeatedly notes that John's immersion in water anticipated the outpouring of the Spirit, the characteristic mark of the young church (Acts 1:5; 11:16).

The independence of the Fourth Gospel from the first three is indicated by its claim that Jesus and John worked side by side before John was arrested (John 3:22–23) and by its pointed denial of the Elijah role to the Baptist (1:21). But otherwise it maintains the synoptics' tendency both to claim John as a herald for Jesus and to subordinate him to Jesus. While introducing Jesus to the reader as the light of the world, the author takes the trouble to note that the Baptist was *not* the light of the world, but only bore witness to it (John 1:6–8). The Baptist says that his whole reason for immersing people was that he might reveal Jesus to Israel (1:31). Once he has fulfilled this mission, he releases his own disciples to follow Jesus (1:37). Then he utters the classic statement of Christian self-negation: "He must increase, but I must decrease" (3:30).

From beginning to end, therefore, the gospels incorporate John wholly into the Christian story of salvation. His basic mission was to prepare the way for Jesus, to identify and "anoint" the Messiah. So too his preaching was entirely contingent on the future: what he preached about was Jesus' coming.

We have seen, however, that Josephus mentions nothing of John's association with Jesus. In Josephus's account, John has a large following and a self-contained message with its own logic. He does not encourage his students to follow Jesus. On the contrary, Antipas can disperse his many followers only by getting rid of him. This difference of portrayal forces us to ask whether it is more likely that Josephus has taken a figure who was a herald for Jesus and, erasing his Christian connection, made him into a famous Jewish preacher, or whether the early Christian tradition has coopted a famous Jewish preacher as an ally and subordinate of Jesus.

The answer seems clear. On the one hand, Josephus had no discernible reason to create a famous Jewish teacher out of one of Jesus' associates. He has no sustained interest in John, but mentions him quite incidentally in his description of Antipas's government. He has already mentioned Jesus and will mention James, so he is not dedicated to removing all traces of Christianity from his writings. On the other hand, we can easily see in the gospels themselves, in spite of their overall tendency to make John into a subordinate herald, traces of another story—one that left the Baptist with his integrity, his own message, and his own following.

John's independence from Jesus appears, for example, in the passages cited above, in which he plainly tells his audience what is required of them—*not* to believe in Jesus, but to behave generously toward one another, especially to the poor. We see it also in passages that reflect differences of practice between John's and Jesus' followers on the matter of fasting and diet (Mark 2:18; Matt 11:18–19). Most impressive, however, is the account in Acts 19:1–5. At Ephesus, some years after the deaths of both Jesus and John, Paul comes upon a group of "students" or disciples:[4]

> Paul passed through the upper district and came to Ephesus. When he found some students there, he said to them, "Did you receive the Holy Spirit with your faith?" They said to him, "But we did not hear that there was a 'holy spirit.' " So he said, "With what, then, were you immersed?" And they said, "With the immersion of John." But Paul said, "John immersed

[4] To the original readers of Acts, the Greek word *mathētēs* did not have the aura that we have come to associate with "disciple." So I prefer to translate with the more neutral "student."

> with an immersion of repentance, saying to the people that they should trust in the one coming after him; this one is Jesus." When they heard that, they were immersed in the name of the Lord Jesus.

The students report that they have never heard of a "holy spirit," and the author connects this with the fact that they are disciples of the Baptist, having experienced only his immersion. Interestingly enough, Paul also has to explain to them that the coming one announced by John was in fact Jesus. The function of the story in Acts seems clear enough: Luke wants to show that the outpouring of the Spirit is the hallmark of the young church; he takes over this tradition about John's disciples as one example of the many groups, Jewish and Gentile, that joined the church and received the Spirit. But the story seems to be at odds with his earlier presentations of the Baptist (in Luke), according to which John's primary concern, indeed his mission from birth, was precisely to declare the arrival of Jesus and to announce the coming baptism in the Spirit. This unassimilated tradition suggests, therefore: (a) that John's followers survived his death, were still known as an independent group, and had spread to Asia by the middle of the first century, and (b) that John's teaching was not predicated upon either the arrival of Jesus or a future Spirit-immersion.

Another NT passage that points in the same direction tells of an inquiry about Jesus' identity by John. It comes as something of a surprise to the reader of Matthew and Luke that, after John has recognized Jesus while still in the womb (Luke), after he has immersed Jesus, witnessed the descent of the dove, heard the heavenly voice, and knowingly declared his unworthiness to baptize Jesus—all of which are presented as the climax of his career—he should later hear about Jesus' wonderful deeds and innocently send messengers to ask, "Are you the coming one or should we wait for another?" Thus:

Matthew 11:2–6	**Luke 7:18–23**
Now when John, in prison, heard about the accomplishments of the Christ, he sent word via his students and said to him,	John's students reported to him concerning all of these things. And John, calling in two of his students, sent them to the Lord saying,
"Are you the coming one, or should we expect another?"	"Are you the coming one or should we expect another?" When they had come to him, the men said, "John

	the Baptist sent us to you saying, 'Are you the coming one, or should we expect another?' " In that hour, he cured many of diseases and torments and evil spirits and he granted sight to many who were blind.
And Jesus answered and said to them, "Go and report to John what you hear and see: the blind see again and the lame walk, lepers are cleansed and the deaf hear, the dead are raised and the poor receive good news. Happy is the one who takes no offense at me."	And he answered and said to them, "Go and report to John what you saw and heard: the blind see again, the lame walk, the lepers are cleansed and the deaf hear, the dead are raised, the poor receive good news. Happy is the one who takes no offense at me."

The standard solution to the problem is to suppose that John was beginning to have some doubt about Jesus' messiahship. Thus the force of his question would be, "I thought that you were the Messiah. If you are, when are you going to do something Messiah-like (take political control, expel the Romans, etc.)?" It has sometimes been thought that Jesus' miracles disturbed John, for he wanted a political leader, not a healer. So the story would present the beginning of John's doubt about Jesus. Indeed, the closing line suggests that this is how Matthew and Luke understood it.

The problem with this interpretation is the internal logic of the story. Read by itself, it clearly implies the beginning of John's *interest* in Jesus as Messiah. He hears about Jesus' wonders and so is encouraged to ask whether Jesus is the coming one. In quiet response, Jesus performs more wonders in the presence of John's messengers, thus evidently confirming that he *is* the coming one. The sense is one of discovery and excitement. John's students return to him and report that what they had heard about Jesus is true! They have seen it with their own eyes. Although it is conceivable that the story has to do with John's doubt, it seems more adequately explained as an incident remembered by Jesus' followers in which the great Jewish preacher expressed an initial interest in Jesus' work. That explanation would fit with both Josephus's presentation of John as an independent figure and the NT passages (above) that assume the ongoing vitality of the "Baptist movement."

In sum, then, Josephus's account of John the Baptist, independent as it is from the tendencies of the Christian tradition, forces us to ask whether the wilderness preacher has not been posthumously adopted by the church in a way that he did not anticipate. It seems clear enough that he did immerse Jesus, among many others, and that this event marked a watershed in Jesus' life. Jesus' immersion by John caused problems for early Christians, for they then had to explain why Jesus was immersed "for the forgiveness of sins."[5] It is unlikely, therefore, that Christians created the story of Jesus' baptism. But since the renowned Jewish preacher had immersed him, the early Christian retelling of the story increasingly coopted John into the Christian story, gradually diminishing his own message and making him a prophet for the church. This kind of process seems inevitable with famous and well-liked people: notice how Jesus himself has been adopted by Marxists and Capitalists, Enlightenment thinkers and fundamentalists, not to mention virtually every world religion. Josephus's account of John helps us to see another side of him, independent of the young church's perspective.

Yet we have seen that Josephus has his own biases. He too has schematized John's preaching to fit his overall story. John is made to speak, in Josephus's language, of "justice toward one's fellows and piety toward God." In this case, the gospels can help us to interpret Josephus, for they provide more information about the Baptist's language. If we strip away the obvious Christian themes overlaid on John's preaching in the gospels, we find an underlying core of Jewish "apocalyptic" thought—that is, a declaration that the fiery judgment of God was about to fall on the world, bringing an end to this present evil age. Thus:

Matthew 3:12	**Luke 3:17**
His winnowing fork is in his hand, and he will clear his threshing floor and gather his wheat into the	His winnowing fork is in his hand, to clear his threshing floor, and to gather the wheat into his storehouse,

[5] Matthew already deals with this problem by having John protest that he ought not to be immersing Jesus (Matt 3:14–15). The second-century *Gospel of the Nazaraeans* tells the story of Jesus' family's trip to be baptized: "Behold, the mother of the Lord and his brethren said to him: John the Baptist baptizes unto the remission of sins, let us go and be baptized by him. But he said to them: Wherein have I sinned that I should go and be baptized by him? Unless what I have said is a (sin of ignorance)." In Edgar Hennecke, *New Testament Apocrypha* (2 vols.; ed. Wilhelm Schneemelcher; trans. R. McL. Wilson; Philadelphia: Westminster, 1963), 1:146–47. Cf. also the *Gospel of the Ebionites* as reconstructed by Hennecke, 1:157–58. Ultimately, the church had to understand Jesus' immersion as a unique event, indicating some special moment in his mission, not as an immersion for repentance.

storehouse, but the chaff he will burn up with inextinguishable fire.	but the chaff he will burn up with inextinguishable fire.

Or again:

> But the axe has already been set to the root of the trees; so every tree that does not produce good fruit is being rooted out and thrown into the fire (Matt 3:10//Luke 3:9).

The idea of coming fiery judgment was quite common in ancient Jewish imagination. In that hot and dry region, the image of precious bodies of water (lakes and rivers) turned to *fire* was an especially terrifying symbol of punishment. So we find many references to lakes or rivers of fire in apocalyptic writings from the time. Daniel already envisaged a river of fire streaming from God's throne, into which the evil fourth beast would be thrown (Dan 7:9–11). Another famous apocalyptic text draws this picture of the judgment:

> In the meantime I saw how another abyss like it, full of fire, was opened wide in the middle of the ground; and they brought those blinded sheep, all of which were judged, found guilty, and cast into this fiery abyss and they were burned. (1 En. 90.26)[6]

The Dead Sea Scrolls (1QH[a] 3.27–32) and the book of Revelation (20:10) use the same imagery. What distinguished John's preaching, and may have suggested his nickname "the Baptist," was that he offered a symbolic immersion in water *now* instead of the coming immersion in fire, to those who would repent and behave righteously.

If this apocalyptic message was the core of John's teaching, then both Josephus and the NT writers have obscured it to some degree. The NT writers did so, perhaps unconsciously, as they reinterpreted John's role within their view of history. Josephus, as we have seen, presented a distinctly nonapocalyptic portrait of Judean culture. He seems to have found in John the Baptist a figure who appealed on some levels—his simplicity of life, freedom from corruption, and fearless honesty in the face of great personal danger from the politically powerful—and who could impress his Roman readers. Either he did not know about John's apocalyptic tendencies or he chose not to raise them because they were incidental to his main point, and he found them uncongenial in any

---

[6] Trans. E. Isaac, in James H. Charlesworth, ed., *The Old Testament Pseudepigrapha: Apocalyptic Literature and Testaments* (2 vols.; Garden City, N.Y.: Doubleday, 1983), 1:71.

case. The recently failed revolt in Judea, which had brought the Jews such bad press, had been partly fueled by apocalyptic hopes—the anticipation that God would choose that moment to intervene in world affairs and restore Israel's glory (cf. *War* 2.390–394). As we saw in chapter 3, Josephus wants no part of this "deliverance" mentality. It has often been argued that he privately embraced some apocalyptic hopes of his own, but suppressed them in his writing out of concern for his readers. This view draws its principal support from *Ant.* 10.210, where Josephus declines further comment on the stone of Nebuchadnezzar's dream in Daniel 2 thus: "I have not thought it proper to relate this, since I am expected to write of what is past and done and not of what is to be." Some scholars see here a reluctance to discuss the future destruction of Rome. It seems to me, however, that this statement does not really conceal any information from the reader, since Josephus has already indicated that another kingdom will ultimately replace the Roman. And educated Romans expected that anyway. Rather, Josephus's thirty volumes present another view of the world—nations rise and fall under God's direction—that appears so basic to his thought, it can hardly be a mere pretense for his readers' sake. Nevertheless, it seems clear that Josephus has accommodated John the Baptist to his portrayal of Jewish virtue by removing—whether deliberately or without knowing—his apocalyptic overtones. So in this case it is the gospels that provide important background for understanding Josephus. From their fuller account of John's preaching, we are able to distill a plausible apocalyptic core:

> Whereas I am immersing you in water for repentance, the coming one will immerse you in fire. His winnowing fork is in his hand, to clear his threshing floor and to gather the wheat into his storehouse, but the chaff he will burn up with inextinguishable fire. (Matt 3:11–12)

If we have correctly recreated the original flavor of John's preaching, it corresponds well to another text from first-century Jewish baptist circles:

> Ah, wretched mortals, change these things, and do not lead the great God to all sorts of anger, but abandon daggers and groanings, murders and outrages, and wash your whole bodies in perennial rivers. Stretch out your hands to heaven and ask forgiveness. . . .
> God will grant repentance
> and will not destroy. He will stop his wrath again if you all practice honorable piety in your hearts. But if you do not obey me, evil-minded

> ones, but love impiety, and receive all these things with evil ears, there will be fire throughout the whole world. . . . He will burn the whole earth, and will destroy
> the whole race of men
> and all cities and rivers at once, and the sea. He will destroy everything by fire, and it will be smoking dust. (*Syb. Or.* 4.162–178)[7]

The case of John the Baptist underscores the point that we ought not to treat Josephus as a kind of "fact book" for the background of the NT. He too has a perspective, with its own limitations. His elaborate work often stimulates us to ask new questions of the NT, but, in turn, the NT can shed light on his narratives.

JESUS, A WISE MAN

We come now to Josephus's much-debated paragraph on Jesus, the so-called *testimonium flavianum* or "witness of Flavius [Josephus, to Jesus]." That this short paragraph has come to have its own Latin title reflects its vast and unique importance in the Christian tradition. Because Josephus talks about John the Baptist's death only in a flashback, while discussing the defeat of Antipas, his passage on John (*Ant.* 18.116–119) comes after his description of Jesus (*Ant.* 18.63–64). It seems clear from various independent statements within the NT, however, that John's arrest and execution preceded Jesus' trial.

Josephus mentions Jesus while relating some events during the governorship of Pontius Pilate (26–36/37 C.E.).[8] We have discussed most of these events in the previous chapter and may now summarize them as follows:

- Pilate arrives in Judea — 18.35
- First incident: Pilate's introduction of imperial images into Jerusalem by night — 18.55–59
- Second incident: Pilate's expropriation of temple funds for aqueduct — 18.60–62

---

[7] Trans. J. J. Collins, in Charlesworth, *Pseudepigrapha* 1:388–89.

[8] The dates of Pilate's governorship have been debated. One can reach probable hypotheses only after carefully considering all of the relevant literary sources, coins, inscriptions, and other factors. I give here the dates commonly accepted by those who know the evidence.

- *Third incident: Jesus and his followers* 18.63–64
- Fourth incident (contemporary, in Rome): seduction of a chaste, aristocratic follower of Isis in Rome, resulting in the crucifixion of Egyptian priests and destruction of the temple of Isis 18.65–80
- Fifth incident (contemporary, in Rome): four Jewish scoundrels conspire to defraud an aristocratic convert to Judaism of money sent to the Jewish temple, resulting in the expulsion of Jews from Rome 18.81–84
- Sixth incident (back in Palestine): Pilate quashes popular Samaritan movement 18.85–87
- Pilate's removal from office 18.88–89

This overview highlights several key points. (a) To fill out his narrative of Pilate's governorship, Josephus has strung together an assortment of episodes, probably from different sources. The fourth and fifth incidents occur in Rome and have nothing to do with Pilate directly. It seems that they are out of order chronologically, for the expulsion of Jews and Egyptians (the cult of Isis) from Rome probably occurred in 19 C.E., before Pilate's arrival in Judea. (b) All of the episodes, except perhaps the Jesus affair, are described as "outrages" or "uprisings" or "tumults." Josephus is trying to paint a picture of escalating tension for Jews around the world. (c) These episodes also serve Josephus's larger literary aims in the *Antiquities,* for example: the first, second, and sixth incidents illustrate the cruelty and insensitivity of the Roman governors; the sixth incident reflects the gullibility of the masses (here Samaritan) toward false prophets; and the parallel Egyptian and Jewish incidents at Rome show both that the Jews are no worse than other national groups and, more important, that Jews share the morals of the Romans. Josephus plainly expresses his own abhorrence of the scoundrels' activities; they were led by a man who only "pretended to interpret the wisdom of the laws of Moses" (18.81). The entire Jewish community suffered then (as also now, after the war) for the actions of a few reprobates (18.84).

In the midst of these stories of outrage and tumult, Josephus mentions Jesus and his followers. As we have it, the text in Josephus reads:

> About this time comes Jesus, a wise man, if indeed it is proper to call him a man. For he was a worker of incredible deeds, a teacher of those who ac-

> cept the truth with pleasure, and he attracted many Jews as well as many of the Greek [way]. This man was the Christ. And when, in view of [his] denunciation by the leading men among us, Pilate had sentenced him to a cross, those who had loved him at the beginning did not cease [to do so]. He appeared to them on the third day alive again, for the divine prophets had announced these and countless other marvels concerning him. And even now the tribe of the "Christians"—named after him—has not yet disappeared. (*Ant.* 18.63–64)

I say "the text as we have it" because this brief passage is brimming with problems. Scholars first noticed them in the sixteenth century. By 1863, when a German scholar wrote an entire book on this paragraph, he had to begin by justifying his study, since the question had already been so thoroughly debated.[9] That was 1863! His own analysis was by no means the final word. During the period 1937–1980, one bibliographer counts eighty-seven more studies of the subject.[10] The passage continues to attract scholarly interest in journal articles (see "For Further Reading").

So, what is the problem? (a) To begin with, the most obvious point: the passage does not fit well with its context in *Ant.* 18. Like the tourist negotiating a bustling, raucous Middle-Eastern market who accidently walks through the door of a monastery, suffused with light and peace, the reader of Josephus is struck by this sublime portrait. Josephus is speaking of upheavals, but there is no upheaval here. He is pointing out the folly of Jewish rebels, governors, and troublemakers in general, but this passage is completely supportive of both Jesus and his followers. Logically, what should appear in this context ought to imply some criticism of the Jewish leaders and/or Pilate, but Josephus does not make any such criticism explicit. He says only that those who denounced Jesus were "the leading men among us." So, unlike the other episodes, this one has no moral, no lesson. Although Josephus begins the next paragraph by speaking of "another outrage" that caused an uproar among the Jews at the same time (18.65), there is nothing in this paragraph that depicts any sort of outrage.

(b) Most problematic of all is the terse sentence concerning Jesus: "This man was Christ." This affirmation is difficult for several reasons. First, the word "Christ" (Greek *christos*) would have special meaning

[9] E. Gerlach, *Die Weissagungen des Alten Testaments in den Schriften des Flavius Josephus* (Berlin: Hertz, 1863), 5.

[10] Louis H. Feldman, *Josephus and Modern Scholarship: 1937–1980* (Berlin: de Gruyter, 1984), 679–91.

only for a Jewish audience. In Greek it means simply "wetted" or "anointed." Within the Jewish world, this was an extremely significant term because anointing was the means by which the kings and high priests of Israel had been installed. The pouring of oil over their heads represented their assumption of God-given authority (Exod 29:9; 1 Sam 10:1). The Hebrew word for "anointed" was *mashiach*, which we know usually as the noun Messiah, "the anointed [one]." Although used in the OT of reigning kings and high priests, many Jews of Jesus' day looked forward to an end-time prophet, priest, king, or someone else who would be duly anointed.

But for someone who did not know Jewish tradition or Christian preaching, the rather deliberate statement that this Jesus was "the wetted" or perhaps "the greased" would sound most peculiar. There was a fairly common Greek slave name, *Chrēstos* (cf. Suetonius, *Claud.* 25.4), but this word *christos*, which was not known as a personal name, would have been entirely puzzling.

Since Josephus is usually sensitive to his audience and pauses to explain unfamiliar terms or aspects of Jewish life, it is very strange that he would make the bald assertion, without explanation, that Jesus was "Christ." He has not used this term before and will use it again only when he calls James the "brother of Jesus, the one called Christ" (*Ant.* 20.200). That formulation, "the one called Christ," makes much better sense because it sounds like a nickname. Nicknames were necessary among first-century Jews because there was a relatively small number of proper names in circulation. We have already met several people with the name Jesus (= Joshua), and the index to Josephus's writings lists some twenty-one individuals with this name. So it would make sense for Josephus to say, "This man had the nickname Christos," and he could do so without further explanation. But simply to say that Jesus *was* Christ, or Messiah, is a peculiar formulation. It is doubly suspicious, of course, because we know that Josephus's writings were preserved and recopied by Christians, for whom Jesus was indeed the Christ.

A second issue with the statement "This man was Christ" is that its solemn phrasing makes it seem to represent Josephus's own confession of faith: he believed Jesus to be Messiah. In addition to that direct statement, the passage says things that only a Christian could have written, it seems, about Jesus' appearances after death, his being more than just a man, and the many ancient prophecies concerning him. Indeed, William Whiston, who translated Josephus's writings in 1737, thought on the basis of this passage that Josephus must have been a Christian. But that seems impossible. As we have seen, he writes as a passionate advocate of Judaism. Everywhere he praises the excellent constitution of the Jews, codified by Moses, and declares its peerless, comprehensive quality. (Yet even Moses, who was as close as possible to God, is never credited with being more than a man.) Josephus rejoices over converts to Judaism. In all of this there is not the slightest hint of any belief in Jesus. Whiston thought that this omission was because Josephus was a *Jewish* Christian. But from everything we know of Jewish Christians in the first century (James, Peter, those mentioned in Acts), the figure of Jesus was still central to their faith. That is obviously not the case with Josephus. His total commitment to the sufficiency of the Jewish constitution seems to preclude any Christian affiliation.

The strongest evidence that Josephus did not declare Jesus' messiahship is that the passage under discussion does not seem to have been present in the texts of the *Antiquities* known before the fourth century. Recall that we do not possess the original Greek text that Josephus wrote; we have only copies, the earliest of which (known as P and A) date from the ninth and tenth centuries. These relatively late copies provide the basis for our current Greek editions and English translations of Josephus. But we know of about a dozen Christian authors from the second and third centuries who were familiar with Josephus's writings. Since many of them were writing to help legitimize the young church, drawing on every available means of support, it is noteworthy that *none* of them mentions Josephus's belief in Jesus. If the famous, imperially sponsored Jewish historian had declared Jesus to be Messiah, it would presumably have helped their cause to mention the fact, but they do not.

Most significantly, the renowned Christian teacher Origen (185–254 C.E.) flatly states, in two different contexts, that Josephus did not believe in Jesus' messiahship. Commenting on Josephus's (allegedly favorable) description of James, the "brother of the one called Christ," Origen expresses his wonder that the Jewish historian "did not accept that our Jesus is Christ" (*Comm. Matt.* 10.17). Similarly, in his apologetic work, *Against Celsus,* he directs the reader to Josephus's own defense of Judaism, but then laments that he "did not believe in Jesus as Christ" (1.47). Origen knew Josephus's writings quite well: he cites accurately from *War, Antiquities,* and *Against Apion.* So it is hard to see how he could have made these statements about Josephus's unbelief if he had known of the *testimonium* that we find in our copies of Josephus. Evidently, his copy of *Antiquities*, like those of his predecessors, did not contain it.

The first author to mention the *testimonium* is Eusebius, the church historian who wrote in the early 300s. In the opening volume of his *Ecclesiastical History*, Eusebius cites Josephus extensively as an independent witness to the Gospels' statements about Jesus, John the Baptist, and the political events of the period. Following his quotation of the passage on John, he cites the *testimonium* just as it appears in our Greek manuscripts of Josephus (*Hist. eccl.* 1.11; quoted above). Another of his works, the *Theophany*, which exists only in Syriac, also includes Josephus's "witness to Jesus." Interestingly, a third work includes it, but with several variations of language (*Dem. ev.* 3.5). These minor variants seem to indicate that even at Eusebius's time the form of the *testimonium* was not yet fixed. Furthermore, Eusebius erroneously places it *after* Josephus's discussion of John the Baptist.

Long after Eusebius, in fact, the text of the *testimonium* remained fluid. Jerome (342–420), the great scholar who translated the Bible and some of Eusebius into Latin, gives a version that agrees closely with the standard text, except that the crucial phrase says of Jesus, "he was *believed to be* the Messiah."[11] In the tenth century, the Christian author Agapius wrote a history of the world in Arabic, in which he reproduced Josephus's statement about Jesus as follows:

> At this time there was a wise man who was called Jesus. His conduct was good, and [he] was known to be virtuous. And many people from among the Jews and the other nations became his disciples. Pilate condemned him to be crucified and to die. But those who had become his disciples did not abandon his discipleship. They reported that he had appeared to them three days after his crucifixion, and that he was alive; accordingly he was perhaps the Messiah, concerning whom the prophets have recounted wonders.[12]

And at the end of the twelfth century, Michael, the Patriarch of Antioch, quotes Josephus as saying that Jesus "was thought to be

---

[11] Jerome, *Lives of Illustrious Men* 13 in *NPNF*^{2} (repr. Peabody, Mass.: Hendrickson, 1994), 3:366.

[12] This passage was brought to light by Shlomo Pines in his book *An Arabic Version of the Testimonium Flavianum and Its Implications* (Jerusalem: Israel Academy of Sciences and Humanities, 1971). His translation of the Arabic passage is on pp. 9–10. He compares it to the standard text of Josephus on p. 16.

the Messiah. But not according to the principal [men] of [our] nation. . . ."[13]

Where did such equivocal versions of Josephus's account come from? Who had an interest in altering Josephus's enthusiastic statement so as to introduce doubt about Jesus' messiahship? The Christian dignitaries who innocently report these versions as if they came from Josephus had no motive, it seems, to weaken their testimony to Jesus. On the one hand, everything that we know of Christian scribal tendencies (for example, in the transmission of the NT texts) points the other way: they tend to heighten Jesus' grandeur and status. On the other hand, these accounts are not obviously *anti*-Christian, and so do not seem to have arisen from Jewish or pagan polemical corruptions of Josephus. Anti-Christian writers would presumably have left some trace of their disdain for Jesus in such corruptions. It seems probable, therefore, that the versions of Josephus's statement given by Jerome, Agapius, and Michael reflect alternative textual traditions of Josephus, which did not contain the emphatic statements that we find in the standard (medieval) manuscripts of Josephus's *Antiquities* or in Eusebius.

(c) A third kind of problem with the *testimonium* as it stands in Josephus concerns its vocabulary and style. It uses some words in ways that are not characteristic of Josephus. For example, the word translated "worker" in the phrase "worker of incredible deeds" is *poiētēs* in Greek, from which we get "poet." Etymologically, it means "one who does" and so it can refer to any sort of "doer." But in Josephus's day it had already come to have a special reference to literary poets, and that is how he consistently uses it elsewhere (nine times)—to speak of Greek poets such as Homer.

Notice further that the phrase "they did not cease" has to be completed by the translator, for it is left incomplete in the text; the action from which his followers ceased must be inferred from the preceding phrase. This is as peculiar in Greek as it is in English, and such a construction is not found elsewhere in Josephus's writing.

---

[13]The relevant portion of the text is given by Pines, *Arabic Version,* 26. Mention should also be made here of the "Slavonic Josephus," an old Russian translation of the *War* (not the *Antiquities*) that contains a good deal of extra material on both John the Baptist and Jesus, not found in the standard text. Although this version has contributed to much of the scholarly debate this century, it is generally viewed as a late Christian embellishment of Josephus's text. One can read the "Slavonic additions" in the appendix to vol. 3 of the LCL edition of Josephus, edited by H. St. J. Thackeray.

Again, the phrase "the tribe of the Christians" is peculiar. Josephus uses the word "tribe" *(phylē)* eleven other times. Once it denotes "gender," and once a "swarm" of locusts, but it usually signifies distinct peoples, races, or nationalities: the Jews are a "tribe" (*War* 3.354; 7.327) as are the Taurians (*War* 2.366) and Parthians (*War* 2.379). It is very strange that Josephus should speak of the Christians as a distinct racial group, since he has just said that Jesus was a Jew condemned by the Jewish leaders. (Notice, however, that some *Christian* authors of a later period came to speak of Christianity as a "third race.")

These examples, along with the use of "Christ" and other peculiarities, illustrate the stylistic difficulties of the *testimonium.* Stylistic arguments are notoriously dicey, because writers are quite capable of using words in unusual ways, on a whim. If a writer uses a high concentration of peculiar words within a short space, however, and if other factors cast doubt on the authenticity of a passage, the stylistic features may become significant.

Taking all of these problems into consideration, a few scholars have argued that the entire passage as it stands in Josephus is a Christian forgery. The Christian scribes who copied the Jewish historian's writings thought it intolerable that he should have said nothing about Jesus and spliced the paragraph in where it might logically have stood, in Josephus's account of Pilate's tenure. Some scholars have suggested that Eusebius himself was the forger, since he was the first to produce the passage.

Most critics, however, have been reluctant to go so far. First, they have noted that, in general, Christian copyists were quite conservative in transmitting texts. Nowhere else in all of Josephus's voluminous writings is there strong suspicion of scribal tampering. Christian copyists also transmitted the works of Philo, who said many things that might be elaborated in a Christian direction, but there is no evidence that in hundreds of years of transmission the scribes inserted their own remarks into Philo's text. To be sure, many of the "pseudepigrapha" that exist now only in Christian form are thought to stem from Jewish originals, but in this instance it may reflect the thorough Christian rewriting of Jewish models, rather than scribal insertions. That discussion is ongoing among scholars. But in the cases of Philo and Josephus, whose writings are preserved in their original language and form, one is hard pressed to find a single example of serious scribal alteration. To have created the *testimonium* out of whole cloth would be an act of unparalleled scribal audacity.

Second, if Christians had written the paragraph from scratch, they might have been expected to give Jesus a little more space than John, and to use language that was more emphatically Christian. Rather than merely doubting that Jesus could adequately be called a man, for example, they might have said something more positive, unless they were very clever in creating a plausible forgery. As it stands, the reticence to call Jesus a man seems like a rejoinder to the previous, already flattering statement that he *was* a wise man. It seems more like a qualification of an existing statement than part of a free creation.

Third, if some of the vocabulary and phrasing sound peculiar for Josephus, much of the rest is perfectly normal. The opening phrase "about this time" is characteristic of his language in this part of the *Antiquities,* where he is weaving together distinct episodes into a coherent narrative (cf. *Ant.* 17.19; 18.39, 65, 80; 19.278). He uses the designation "wise man" sparingly, but as a term of considerable praise. King Solomon was such a wise man (*Ant.* 8.53), and so was Daniel (10.237). Interestingly, both men had what we might call occult powers—abilities to perform cures and interpret dreams—of the sort that Jesus is credited with in the *testimonium.* So to call Jesus a "wise man" here presents no special difficulties. If Josephus said it, it was a term of high praise. Moreover, Josephus often speaks of "marvels" and "incredible" things in the same breath, as the *testimonium* does. He even uses the phrase rendered "incredible deeds" in two other places, once of the prophet Elisha (*Ant.* 9.182; cf. 12.63). Josephus often speaks of the "leading men" among the Jews with the phrase used in the *testimonium,* especially in book 18 of the *Antiquities* (17.81; 18.7, 99, 121, 376). Although the phrase "divine prophets" sounds peculiar at first, there is a close parallel in Josephus's description of Isaiah (*Ant.* 10.35). Even the word used for what the prophets "announced" is commonly used by Josephus in conjunction with prophecy. Consequently, although some of the language in the *testimonium* is odd, we have no basis in his language for dismissing the whole paragraph.

These lexical considerations have led many scholars to think that Josephus must have said something about Jesus, even if it is not what we currently have. Moreover, his later reference to James (*Ant.* 20.200) seems to presuppose some earlier reference to Jesus. James is introduced, rather oddly, as "the brother of Jesus who is called Christ, James by name." Josephus's primary identification of James as Jesus' brother, and his inclusion of James's own name as an incidental detail, suggests that this "Jesus who is called Christ" is already known to his readers. That expectation is easiest to explain if Josephus had mentioned Jesus in the foregoing narrative.

Finally, the existence of alternative versions of the *testimonium* has encouraged many scholars to think that Josephus must have written something close to what we find in them, which was later edited by Christian hands. If the laudatory version in Eusebius and our text of Josephus were the free creation of Christian scribes, who then created the more restrained versions found in Jerome, Agapius, and Michael? The version of Agapius is especially noteworthy because it eliminates, though perhaps too neatly, all of the major difficulties in the standard text of Josephus: (a) it is not reluctant to call Jesus a man; (b) it contains no reference to Jesus' miracles; (c) it has Pilate execute Jesus at his own discretion; (d) it presents Jesus' appearance after death as merely reported by the disciples, not as fact; (e) it has Josephus wonder about Jesus' messiahship, without explicit affirmation; and (f) it claims only that the prophets spoke about "the Messiah," whoever he might be, not that they spoke about Jesus. That shift also explains sufficiently the otherwise puzzling term "Christ/Messiah" for Josephus's readers. In short, Agapius's version of the *testimonium* sounds like something that a Jewish observer of the late first century could have written about Jesus and his followers.

We cannot resolve the problem of Josephus's "testimony" about Jesus here. Among the hundreds of books and articles on the subject, every conceivable position has been taken between two opposite poles. On the one side, as we have seen, some scholars are convinced that Josephus said nothing whatsoever about Jesus, and that is why no one before Eusebius mentions the *testimonium*. On the other extreme, a few influential scholars have held the passage to be entirely authentic. Some reconcile it with the rest of Josephus's writings by suggesting that Josephus saw Jesus' death as the end of messianic hope: Jesus did indeed fulfill Israel's hope, but his horrible execution shows the futility of persisting in such belief. Others propose that Josephus included the passage so as to curry favor with the Christians, because he was in trouble with his own Jewish compatriots. Still others interpret the passage as intended sarcasm, though the argument for that view is too convoluted to summarize here. Note: even those who accept the authenticity of the *testimonium* do not share Whiston's belief that Josephus was a Christian. That theory seems highly improbable.

The vast majority of commentators hold a middle position between authenticity and inauthenticity, claiming that Josephus wrote *something* about Jesus that was subsequently edited by Christian copyists. Such a view has the best of both worlds, for it recognizes all of the problems with the passage as well as the factors that support its authenticity. Of the many scholars who take this position, a significant number have tried their hand at reconstructing the hypothetical original by removing Christian glosses. Their assessments of Christian influence vary greatly. The copyist might merely have changed the sentence "This man was believed to be Christ" to "This man was Christ." Or he might have practically rewritten the piece, inserting and omitting freely. The following two examples will give the reader an idea of the possibilities. Robert Eisler (1929), relying heavily on hypothetical alterations suggested by the Slavonic version of Josephus (see note 14) and on consistently unfavorable translations of the Greek, proposed:

> Now about this time arose (an occasion for new disturbances) a certain Jesus, a wizard of a man, if indeed he may be called a man (who was the most monstrous of all men, whom his disciples called a son of God, as having done wonders such as no man hath ever done). . . . He was in fact a teacher of astonishing tricks to such men as accept the abnormal with delight. . . . And he seduced many Jews and many also of the Greek nation, and (was regarded by them as) the Messiah. . . . And when, on the indictment of the principal men among us, Pilate had sentenced him to the cross, still those who before had admired him did not cease (to rave). For it seemed to them that having been dead for three days, he had appeared to them alive again, as the divinely-inspired prophets had foretold—these and ten thousand other wonderful things—concerning him. And even now the race of those who are called "Messianists" after him is not extinct.[14]

An article by John P. Meier (1991) offers a somewhat milder restoration. In Meier's view, the three most obvious Christian insertions can be easily removed to leave a perfectly acceptable sense:

> At this time there appeared Jesus, a wise man. For he was a doer of startling deeds, a teacher of people who receive the truth with pleasure. And he gained a following both among many Jews and among many of Greek origin. And when Pilate, because of an accusation made by the leading men among us, condemned him to the cross, those who loved him

[14] So Robert Eisler, *The Messiah Jesus and John the Baptist* (trans. A. H. Krappe; London: Methuen & Co., 1931), 62.

> previously did not cease to do so. And up until this very day the tribe of Christians, named after him, has not died out.[15]

The problem with any such restoration, of course, is that we simply have no copies of Josephus dating from the time before Eusebius. Once it is granted that the standard text is corrupt, a wide variety of hypothetical reconstructions must remain equally plausible.

What, then, is the value of the *testimonium flavianum* for the reader of the NT? Limited. Paradoxically, the intense effort to reconstruct the "original" reading, in order to make it historically useful, itself diminishes the value of the passage, for each new reading has to share plausibility, so to speak, with all other proposals on the table. No matter how convincing a restoration may seem to any given interpreter, he or she will not be able to put much weight on it in the course of scholarly argumentation, in the knowledge that few others will accept it. Unless one of the many proposals manages to win the allegiance of a significant majority, this situation will continue indefinitely. But consensus is likely to come only with a major new insight into the state of Josephus's text before the fourth century, likely as the result of some new discovery.

It would be unwise, therefore, to lean heavily on Josephus's statements about Jesus' healing and teaching activity, or the circumstances of his trial. Nevertheless, since most of those who know the evidence agree that he said something about Jesus, one is probably entitled to cite him as independent evidence that Jesus actually lived, if such evidence were needed. But that much is already given in Josephus's reference to James (*Ant.* 20.200) and most historians agree that Jesus' existence is the only adequate explanation of the many independent traditions among the NT writings.

JAMES, THE BROTHER OF JESUS

The only other figure from within the early Christian tradition mentioned by Josephus is James, the brother of Jesus. He says very little about this man, but the fact that he mentions him incidentally is strong support for the authenticity of the passage. No copyist has tried to turn

---

[15] From John P. Meier, "The Testimonium: Evidence for Jesus Outside the Bible," *Bible Review* 7/3 (June, 1991): 23. This restoration agrees almost exactly (independently, it seems), with that offered by Paul Winter in the revised E. Schürer, *A History of the Jewish People,* 1:437.

this passage into a religious confession of any sort. In fact, the passage is not about James; it is about some other issues that Josephus is developing in *Ant.* 20.

Josephus mentions James near the end of the *Antiquities,* while discussing political events in Judea of the mid-60s C.E. We have already examined some of the major themes of the *Antiquities.* Let us now focus on *Ant.* 20 and the place of this passage that mentions James within this book. It is the shortest book in Josephus's repertoire, comprising more than two hundred paragraphs before the summary list of high priests (20.224–251) and epilogue (20.259–268), in contrast to the usual standard of four hundred to seven hundred paragraphs per book. Josephus brings us to the eve of the revolt against Rome that was the main subject of the *Jewish War* and, though he has already retold much of *War* 1–2.275 at considerably greater length (=*Ant.* 12–20), he "fades out" the story with the arrival of the despicable Gessius Florus as governor, the crucial figure in the *War.* He refers the reader to his earlier history for the sequel (20.252–258). That Josephus ends his account just before Florus's enormities indicates that his purposes in this long history are somewhat different from the *War*'s, though related.

If we look for a thematic unity within *Ant.* 20, in light of the work's overall concerns, two issues stand out. The longer section, *Ant.* 20.1–159, is occupied with the fortunes of the Judean constitution in foreign circles. This is mainly a story of stunning success, anticipating the claims at the end of *Against Apion* about the growing influence of the Jewish laws. First, through the intervention of Agrippa II in Rome, the Jewish chief priests win permission from the emperor Claudius to retain custody of the high priest's robes. This is an important symbolic statement of autonomy (20.1–14). Claudius also intervenes at Agrippa's behest to punish the Samaritan leaders for their people's attacks on Jews traveling to Jerusalem (20.118–136). Dominating the first half of book 20, however, is the detailed and moving story of the royal family of Adiabene, a client kingdom in the Parthian empire to the east who adopt the Judean constitution as their own—converting to Judaism. Josephus waxes eloquent on the courage displayed by Queen Helena of Adiabene, who would become a famous patron and resident of Jerusalem, and especially on the courage of her son Izates in adopting "foreign customs" over the violent objections of the Adiabenian nobility. God was to ensure their protection and great prosperity in reward for their piety (20.17–96).

At *Ant.* 20.160 Josephus marks an abrupt turn to internal Judean affairs, in contrast with the foreign success of the Judean constitution, by observing: "But in Judea, matters were constantly going from bad to worse." Causes of this unrest include the rise of bandits and religious charlatans, the Roman governors' incompetence, and relations between Jews and Greeks in the neighboring cities (20.160–178)—all covered more fully in the *War.* But a new emphasis in this section of *Ant.* 20, in keeping with the longer work's sustained interest in the office of high priest, is the infighting that broke out once again among candidates for and former occupants of this highest position.

Beginning in 20.179, a few paragraphs before the passage that mentions James, Josephus claims that the appointment of Ishmael son of Phabi as high priest kindled fighting *among* various high-priestly factions as well as *between* the group of high priests and the group of lower priests and popular leaders. Each of the factions enlisted fighters or "heavies," and when they came in conflict matters quickly turned violent (20.180). The factions were so pervasive that more or less everyone was involved, with no one to take the initiative in settling matters. Josephus tells some lurid stories by way of illustration, including accounts of robbery, stone-fights, and starvation. The passage that mentions James is only one further illustration of this ongoing theme.

In addition, in *Ant.* 20 the chief priests run into conflict with King Agrippa himself. Because he has built an extension to his palace that overlooks the temple proceedings, they build a wall to block his view (20.189–193). Resolution of this dispute requires the high priest himself and several associates to travel to Rome. This is a major undertaking and, because that delegation is detained in Rome, King Agrippa must appoint a new high priest, Joseph Kabi (20.194–197). Our story begins right at this point, with the death of the Roman governor Festus and, to coincide, Joseph Kabi's apparently rapid replacement with another new high priest Ananus.

> Now when he learned about the death of Festus, Caesar [Nero] sent Albinus to Judea as governor. And the king [Agrippa II] took the priesthood away from Joseph [Kabi] and gave the succession in government to the son of Ananus, who was also named Ananus. (They say that this Ananus Senior was extremely fortunate, for he had five sons and it happened that they all served as high priest to God, after he himself had enjoyed the honor for a long period; this had never happened with the high priests among us.)

> Now the younger Ananus, who received the high priesthood, as we stated, was arrogant in manner and an extremely brash man; he was also involved with the school of the Sadducees, who are savage when it comes to legal judgments in comparison with all the [other] Judeans, as we have already explained [i.e., *Ant.* 13.293–296]. Being a person of such qualities, and figuring that he had a convenient opportunity with Festus having died and Albinus [his replacement] yet en route, Ananus convened a council of judges and hauled before it the brother of Jesus the so-called Christ (a man by the name of Yakob [=James]) and some others. He brought the charge that they had broken the law and then handed them over to be stoned.
>
> Now those in the city [Jerusalem] who were reputed to be most fair-minded, and precise in relation to the laws, found this intolerable. They secretly sent word to the king [Agrippa], requesting him to write to Ananus not to act in such ways any longer, for he had not done even the first thing [in office] correctly. Some of them also went to greet Albinus, making his way from Alexandria, and instructed him that it was not appropriate for Ananus to convene a council without his consent. Persuaded by what was said, Albinus wrote to Ananus in anger, threatening to exact vengeance from him. And for this reason King Agrippa took the high priesthood away from him—he had governed for three months!—and appointed Jesus [son] of Damnaeus. (*Ant.* 20.197–203)

A quick glance shows how well this account fits into both the larger and smaller contexts of *Ant.* 20. It begins with the appointment of the new high priest (Ananus II) and the announcement of a new Roman governor to replace the one who has died in office (20.197). It ends with the leading citizens achieving a remarkable feat: they cleverly get rid of a high priest they cannot stand, after he has served only three months, so that a new one is in place by the time the new governor arrives (20.201–203).

Notice, too, that much of the language is typically Josephan, and some of it fits with word-choices that appear only in *Ant.* 20 and the following *Life,* but not before. The phrase "convened a council," for example, occurs only here and at *Ant.* 20.216; *Life* 236, 368. "Without [his] consent," similarly, occurs here and at *Ant.* 20.2; *Life* 309. The word for en route is here and at *Ant.* 20.113; *Life* 157, though also *Ant.* 14.226. It has been widely observed that Josephus's writing style changes in the last book of the *Antiquities* and continues in the *Life.* This passage reflects some of the new language he prefers—language that seems to be more his own, in contrast to his imitations of great authors, such as Thucydides in *Ant.* 17–19. Although some scholars have doubted the authenticity of this passage that mentions James in Josephus, there is no reason to question it on the basis of language and style.

Now to the story. When one governor (Porcius Festus) dies in office (62 C.E.), Caesar sends a new man named Albinus. At the same time, Agrippa decides to appoint a new high priest, Ananus. We do not know why he makes this apparently abrupt change, perhaps to match personalities of governor and high priest, perhaps only to reward as many as possible with the high-priestly honor.

In any case, Josephus uses one of his favorite techniques to introduce this new high priest. Namely, he contrasts the father, a man of great virtue, honor, and fortune as evidenced by his five sons who all held the high priesthood as he had done, with this bad seed of a son (20.198–199). At the same time, he portrays the son in terms familiar from Aristotle *(Nicomachean Ethics),* Thucydides, and Polybius as a "youthful hothead" (20.199). As we saw in chapter 3, wherever Josephus mentions "youth," there is a good chance that he will append adjectives such as "arrogant, reckless, violent, and impetuous." And so it is here. As soon as Josephus has contrasted the son Ananus with his father, and called him "the younger," he lets loose his arsenal of typically youthful character traits. This little episode is about the ongoing struggles between the high priests and the other eminent citizens, brought to a head because this particular high priest had, in part, the defects of youthful aristocrats.

Now, one might object that Ananus Junior cannot have been a very young man. His father was high priest from 6–15 C.E. alongside the first Roman governor of Judea (*Ant.* 18.26), whereas the story time is now 62 C.E. To hold the office, Ananus I should have been at least a mature man of thirty and was probably older. Even if we suppose that Ananus Junior was born by about 20 C.E. (when his father was at least 45), then he was well into his forties by the time he received the office from King Agrippa. This is not the only time he squeezes a middle-aged man into the category of youth in order to wield the "youth" stereotype against him. In *War* 2.409 he called Eleazar son of Ananias (a high priest), administrator of the temple, a "daring youth" in the year 66, though the man seems already to have had long involvement at high levels of the Jerusalem elite. He cannot have been that young (*Ant.* 20.208, 211). Such language highlights again Josephus's willingness to bend his material for his immediate rhetorical purposes.

Another obvious clue to this tendency is that in the *War,* this same Ananus appears as a brilliantly wise and moderate leader in the revolt (see chapter 3). Recall that for Josephus he is a model of aristocratic virtue and wisdom, whose death at the hands of Idumeans and Zealots

Josephus chose as the turning point for his whole narrative. There, he was a *victim* of the youthful hotheads who wanted to prosecute the war at all costs, whereas his goal was to bring his people to safety. The Ananus of this passage, which occurs only four years earlier, could not be more different. Evidently, consistency does not matter to Josephus; everything serves his present rhetorical needs.

Added to his generally repulsive youthful character, Josephus explains, was his involvement with the Sadducees, a group he has earlier described as harsh in their administration of the law and lacking in popular support (see *Ant.* 13.293–298; 18.17). As Josephus presents it, this particular instance of elite infighting is caused by the outstandingly unpleasant character of the new high priest and the influence of the Sadducean company he kept.

Purely as an example of that harsh and reckless character, Josephus mentions that one of the first things the new high priest did was to convene a court of judges in order to remove some of his enemies. The story implies that this was all his doing: *he* convened a council; *he* laid the charges; and *he* (singular) handed his enemies over to be stoned. Josephus does not need to use the word "tyrant" for his audience to understand that this, too, is tyrannical behavior, a theme that he developed at great length in the *War* and the *Antiquities* (see chapter 3). Whereas the proper form of Judean government is by aristocratic council, with the "senate" of leading citizens (based in the priesthood) collaborating in judgment, this episode shows one man acting rashly, on a vendetta. Accusation, trial, and execution of sentence follow swiftly and at his sole instigation.

Notice incidentally that the court he convenes is not—or is not said to be—the main Jewish council, the famed "Sanhedrin." The fair-minded citizens and those reputed to be most careful about the laws, who oppose Ananus, would no doubt have been part of that proper council of elders. Rather, Ananus convenes *a* "council of judges." This language of "convening a council (or simply a meeting [Greek *synedrion*])" is new to *Ant.* 20 and the *Life*, and in each case it has to do with more informal arrangements than the meeting of the Jerusalem council. In the *Life*, both Josephus (368) and his opponent Jonathan (236) "hold a meeting of friends" to decide what to do. In *Ant.* 20.216, King Agrippa is persuaded to convene a meeting, presumably also of his advisers, as a consequence of which he permits the Levites to wear linen robes like the priests, a decision Josephus deplores, and hardly likely to have come from an essentially priestly council. Political leaders, both Eastern kings and Roman generals and emperors, were assisted informally by personally arranged committees of friends. Augustus (recall from chapter 3) summons a council—ad hoc, not a standing body—to determine the fate of Herod's kingdom (*War* 2.25), though the final decision is entirely his and not a matter for collective (2.37–38). Herod summoned similar groups.

This is the kind of personal court that Ananus creates to do his bidding, and that is precisely the problem for the fair-minded. He behaves as a tyrant, acting imperiously and consumed with his new power. Josephus has mentioned other "kangaroo courts," as perversions of proper government. Compare in particular the "ironic" mock court established by the rebels, discussed in chapter 3 (*War* 4.334–344).

So the story is not really about James, but about the decline of the high priesthood before the fall of Jerusalem and about this allegedly nasty specimen named Ananus. There is no trial worth mentioning, but the high priest "brings the charge," a phrase used about a dozen times in Josephus from *Ant.* 15 through the *Life* and *Apion,* and the defendants are as good as dead. Notice, too, that the charge Ananus brings is not described. The verb Josephus uses *(paranomeō)* simply means "be a criminal," or a "lawbreaker." It is the vaguest and most general sort of word, which tells us nothing about the specific charges laid by Ananus. This is frustrating for us, since we would like to know what James was charged with, but Josephus emphasizes precisely the shakiness of Ananus's legal basis. In effect, he "brought some sort of criminal charges" and quickly got rid of these men.

When we come to the sentence that actually mentions James, two things stand out. First, the identities of the people involved do not matter that much to Josephus, because it is not really about James. It is characteristic of Josephus, however, when he is talking about groups of people or periods of time, to single out one individual as an example of the whole. As we have seen, his entire *Antiquities* is written this way, not in chronological periods, but as a kind of serial biography, which invites the reader to ponder and assess the character of individuals. But even when he is dealing with lower-class and disreputable individuals, he likes to give one or two examples of the many. For instance, at the outbreak of revolt in 4 B.C.E. Josephus claims that many men suddenly tried to make themselves rulers (*War* 2.55), but he then gives three examples (2.56–60). The "young" priest Eleazar son of Ananias, who halted the catastrophe in Jerusalem, he introduces notes of devilishly clever —this time at the expense of a vain and gullible Roman governor. his reading has merit, it illustrates once again the difficulty in sephus to answer questions that arise from NT studies. Scholars amined this passage very carefully for evidence about James and ne powers of the Jewish court (Sanhedrin) to try cases involving punishment. For example, it is commonly understood (as the anslation) that the court convened by the high priest was the rusalem court, which encourages debate concerning the legal o which the fair-minded citizens might have been objecting. hat the Sanhedrin executed people, or that it met without per- of the governor? What was the "first step" that Ananus did not in this process? If James was executed for "breaking the law"— violating the Law of Moses—on what grounds might he have arged? The reading I have offered here undercuts all of these ns. The Sanhedrin is not in question, but only an ad hoc group st do as the tyrant demands. James and the others are charged he most general way (with being criminals, somehow) as far as s wishes to tell us. The "first step" apparently refers to Ananus's ions in office. Most importantly, the fair-minded appear—ad- in Josephus's view—as pulling a fast one in order to get Ananus l, not as worrying over any particular point of law.

at is extremely interesting here for the NT reader, it seems to he very hostility of a Sadducean high priest to James and his By contrast, Mark (2:16, 24; 3:6; 7:1; 12:13), Matthew (9:11, 14, 15:1, 12; 16:6; 22:15; 23:13–36), and to some extent John (1:24; , 45; 9:16; 12:42) put the Pharisees forward as Jesus' principal nts in Galilee. The two-volume work Luke–Acts takes quite a tack, insisting that although Jesus and the Pharisees were mu- itical of each other—he was rather harsher on them—they still d him as a teacher and even kept inviting him to dinner (7:36; 3:31; 14:1). In Luke–Acts it is the Sadducean temple-based lead- not the Pharisees who are the truly lethal opponents of Jesus' followers (Acts 4:1–2; 5:17–18, 34–39; 23:6–10). The Pharisees newhat closer to both Jesus and his followers. Josephus has no d interest in this question, but his story does tend to confirm re in Luke–Acts.

also noteworthy that Jesus' brother James, of all people, should rrested and executed on some presumed illegality, since in the

temple sacrifice for foreigners (*War* 2.409–410), was at the head of a much larger, nameless, group of troublemakers. Again, Josephus mentions many deceivers and impostors who led the people into the desert in hopes of salvation (*Ant.* 20.167) but gives one example (20.169). Other rebel leaders such as Korah or Eleazar ben Ananias are named even as Josephus asserts that there were hundreds of other unnamed men behind them. Everything is personalized. So the mention of James along with a few nameless others is only his usual technique of giving a human face to groups of people.

Second, if we ask "Why James?" the answer seems to lie in the construction of the passage. Josephus does not name him as *James* in the first instance, but rather as *the brother of Jesus, the so-called Christ.* The easiest explanation of this construction is that he has recently mentioned "Jesus the so-called Christ," so that it is now economical to mention his brother as a quick example of those Ananus killed. Since our text of the *Antiquities* does have a passage on Jesus in 18.63–64 (above), and that passage appears to have been altered in our texts, that is the most likely place for Josephus to have mentioned Jesus. And we have a clue as to what he actually said about Jesus there: not simply "the Christ," as our manuscripts read, but rather "the so-called Christ." That would make much better sense coming from Josephus.

It is highly likely that Josephus knows a great deal more about this episode than he bothers to mention, quite possibly including the names of Ananus's other victims. Josephus was an adult in Jerusalem at the time of the incident and a member of the upper class. Since it was a major event, resulting in the change of high priest, he must have known some details. But neither he nor his envisaged audience in Rome has any particular interest in the fate of the victims. He wants rather to demonstrate Ananus's character. He offers James's name only because he has a link in the preceding narrative with Jesus, and so he can easily refer to him as an example.

So much for Ananus. Now comes the really interesting part in Josephus's construction: the way in which the high priest's enemies react to his outrageous behavior. Josephus's description of these adversaries as those regarded as most fair-minded or reasonable, and precise in relation to the laws, does not alas contain any hidden codes that might reveal their identities more precisely. These phrases roughly match the many descriptions of the Jerusalem elite throughout this volume (the powerful, the leaders, the prominent, the more fair-minded), and they seem deliberately vague. We might be inclined to speculate, in historical terms, that such an opposition must have included at least some leading Pharisees, given that Josephus often places Pharisees and Sadducees in opposition (see chapter 4) and that they are found together in Jerusalem's leadership (*War* 2.411; *Life* 21, 189–198). But he foregoes the opportunity to mention Pharisees, which might distract the audience from his purpose. This is not a Pharisee-Sadducee conflict, but one between a reckless new high priest who is out of control and the main body of more reasonable leaders: one troublesome high-priestly faction against the main body of the aristocracy.

What these other popular leaders do in response to Ananus is fascinating. They do not confront him directly, perhaps because that would only exacerbate the dangerous infighting, which it is their primary and collective task to avoid. Similarly, Josephus himself does not usually confront his opponents directly, at least not for long once he decides that opposition is implacable. He typically takes back roads and detours in order to neutralize them. Similarly, these aristocrats decide on a two-pronged strategy, targeted at the two external authorities mentioned in the opening sentence: King Agrippa in the north, who had appointed Ananus, and Albinus, the new governor en route to Judea. First they complain to Agrippa, alerting him to their indignation that the new appointee has not made a promising start ("he had not done even the first thing [in office] correctly"), but is already behaving as a tyrant.

Simultaneously, they send a delegation to greet the new governor and "instruct" him about something he apparently has never heard before, just as we, Josephus's audience, have never heard it before. Namely, the high priest is not supposed to convene a council without the governor's agreement. Whether this claim has any historical merit, Josephus does not clarify. In terms of general probability, we might have assumed that the situation would be much as in the Greek cities (Pliny, *Ep.* 10.79.3).[16] Although the Roman governor *could* intervene in local councils whenever he felt it was necessary, both he and the local councils preferred the local government to handle its own affairs in normal circumstances.

[16] See Giovanni Salmeri, "Dio, Rome, and the Civic Life of Asia Minor," in *Dio Chrysostom: Politics, Letters, and Philosophy* (ed. Simon Swain; Oxford: Oxford University Press, 2000), 53–92.

earliest Christian writings we possess, Paul's letters, he appears to be deeply concerned with avoiding violation of Jewish law. Paul first mentions the brothers of Jesus ("the Lord"), without naming individuals, as among those who travel, in their propagation of the Jesus movement, with wives (1 Cor 9:5)—unlike him. In Galatians, Paul mentions James as one of the leaders ("pillars") of the Jerusalem church whom he had met three years after he began proclaiming Christ (Gal 1:18–19). Then on a subsequent visit after fourteen years, James was one of those who had, Paul insists, acknowledged the legitimacy of the "special announcement" (*euangelion* or "gospel") that Paul was taking to Gentiles (Gal 2:6–10), which did not entail any observance of Jewish law. But when Paul and Cephas (Peter) were at Antioch, he notes, it was the arrival of "men from James" who persuaded Peter to give up his eating with Gentiles (unkosher food?) and to withdraw; indeed, Paul calls these men from James "the circumcision [faction]," apparently indicating that they required circumcision and conversion to Judaism of those who would follow Jesus (Gal 2:11–14).

So it is peculiar that Jesus' brother James, who was apparently scrupulous about legal observance, should be the one accused of breaking laws. Josephus's passage certainly leaves open the possibility that the charges against him were thoroughly contrived by Ananus to get rid of an influential leader in the Jesus movement whom he simply could not tolerate for the sorts of reasons suggested in Acts. Also worth noting, however, is Paul's claim that those who insist in Jewish legal observance do so only to avoid persecution themselves (Gal 6:13). If this is more than merely rhetorical license on Paul's part, he may have seen that leaders such as James in Jerusalem were facing real problems with Sadducean elements in the aristocracy, not because of their own lack of observance but because, as leaders of the Jesus movement, they were being held responsible for the actions of others. It is possible that James paid the penalty for this kind of responsibility. Yet we should probably not press such purely "legal" issues too far. The impression given in both Acts 4 and Josephus is that James's death had much more to do with political issues and old animosities and that the charge of "criminal behavior" was merely a pretext.

Finally, Josephus's passage indirectly confirms the paradox that Jesus' brother had indeed risen to a position of prominence in earliest Christianity. This is paradoxical because the NT is strangely reticent or ambiguous about James. He was not one of Jesus' followers, but in both

Mark (3:19–31; 6:1–6) and John (7:2–5) he is among the *unbelieving* family of Jesus. Without explanation, however, he suddenly appears in Paul's letters (above) and in Acts (12:17; 15:13–22; 21:18) as apparently the most important figure in the Jerusalem church. The failure of the NT authors to explain how James came to such prominence is more than compensated for by later Christian authors, to be sure. They tell of his miraculous conversion in response to a special appearance of the risen Jesus (Eusebius, *Hist. eccl.* 2.1.4; *Gos. Heb.; Acts Jas.* 1). Paul had mentioned an appearance of Jesus to James (1 Cor 15:7), but without any elaboration, and the NT itself is otherwise silent about such a "conversion." Josephus's incidental notice at least offers a perspective outside the Christian sphere that confirms James's central role in first-generation Christianity. He also confirms, in case there was any doubt, that James was distinguished by being Jesus' actual brother—a significant point in view of later Christian thinking about Mary's status as "perpetual virgin" and speculation as to whether Jesus' "brothers and sisters" were really only spiritual relatives or more distant physical relations.

CONCLUSION

In this chapter, we have looked at Josephus's discussions of three people who played prominent roles in the origins of Christianity: John the Baptist, Jesus, and Jesus' brother James. Our analysis of these passages has produced a wide variety of results. In the case of John, Josephus and the NT authors are mutually illuminating. Incidental clues in the gospels help us to reconstruct John's original preaching, which Josephus has adapted for his own ends, and Josephus's independent perspective allows us to trace the gospel writers' adoption of John as one of their own. Josephus's account of Jesus provides little direct help because the version that we find in our manuscripts is almost certainly corrupt. Nevertheless, the exercise of analyzing that passage is useful for making us aware of the many stages through which all ancient texts have passed before reaching us. Finally, Josephus's reference to James, brief though it is, throws valuable light from outside the Christian tradition on one of the early church's most significant but little-known figures.

FOR FURTHER READING

On apocalypticism in ancient Jewish circles, see (among many fine studies):

- John J. Collins, *The Apocalyptic Imagination: An Introduction to the Jewish Matrix of Christianity* (New York: Crossroad, 1987).

See also the introduction with selected Jewish and Christian texts in:

- Mitchell G. Reddish, ed., *Apocalyptic Literature: A Reader* (Nashville: Abingdon, 1990).

A comprehensive collection of available texts in English translation is:

- James H. Charlesworth, ed., *Apocalyptic Literature and Testaments* (vol. 1 of *The Old Testament Pseudepigrapha;* Garden City, N.Y.: Doubleday, 1983).

The intriguing figure of John the Baptist has stimulated much research. The most important works are:

- C. H. Kraeling, *John the Baptist* (New York: Charles Scribner's Sons, 1951).
- Charles H. H. Scobie, *John the Baptist* (London: SCM, 1964).
- Walter Wink, *John the Baptist in the Gospel Tradition* (Cambridge: Cambridge University Press, 1968).
- Robert L. Webb, *John the Baptizer and Prophet: A Socio-Historical Study* (Sheffield: Sheffield Academic Press, 1991).
- Joan E. Taylor, *The Immerser: John the Baptist within Second Temple Judaism* (Grand Rapids: Eerdmans, 1997).

There is a huge bibliography on Josephus's paragraph on Jesus. Of the numerous recent discussions, some of the most accessible and/or comprehensive are:

- Shlomo Pines, *An Arabic Version of the Testimonium Flavianum and Its Implications* (Jerusalem: Israel Academy of Sciences and Humanities, 1971).
- Emil Schürer, *The History of the Jewish People in the Age of Jesus Christ (175 B.C.–A.D. 135)* (3 vols.; trans. T. A. Burkill; rev. and ed. Geza Vermes and Fergus Millar; Edinburgh: T&T Clark, 1973), 1:428–41.

- J. Neville Birdsall, "The Continuing Enigma of Josephus' Testimony about Jesus," *Bulletin of the John Rylands University Library of Manchester* 67 (1985): 609–22.
- John P. Meier, "The Testimonium: Evidence for Jesus Outside the Bible," *Bible Review* 7/3 (June 1991): 20–25, 45.
- John P. Meier, "Jesus in Josephus: A Modest Proposal," *Catholic Biblical Quarterly* 52 (1990): 76–103.

Works that explore the importance of Jesus' brother James in early Christianity, from rather different perspectives, include:

- Gerd Lüdemann, *Antipaulinismus im frühen Christentum* (vol. 2 of *Paulus, der Heidenapostel;* Göttingen: Vandenhoeck & Ruprecht, 1983).
- Ray A. Pritz, *Nazarene Jewish Christianity* (Jerusalem: Magnes/ Leiden: Brill, 1988).
- Richard Bauckham, *Jude and the Relatives of Jesus in the Early Church* (Edinburgh: T&T Clark, 1990).
- John Painter, *Just James: The Brother of Jesus in History and Tradition* (Minneapolis: Fortress, 1999).

Most of the interest in Josephus's reference to James's death has focused on the implications of that episode for our assessment of the Sanhedrin's powers and, consequently, of the trial of Jesus. The section in Schürer mentioned above includes a discussion of Josephus and James, as well as some bibliography. Independently, my reading of Josephus on James comes to many of the same conclusions as:

- James S. McLaren, "Ananus, James, and Earliest Christianity: Josephus' Account of the Death of James," *Journal of Theological Studies* 52 (2001): 1–25.

Chapter 6

Josephus and Luke-Acts

At various points in this study, we have noticed especially close parallels between Josephus's narratives and the two NT volumes known as Luke and Acts. For example: Luke omits Mark's story of John the Baptist's death, which is rather kind to Herod Antipas, in agreement with Josephus's hostile portrayal of the tetrarch; the story of King Agrippa's death in Acts 12:20–23 is quite similar to Josephus's account; Josephus's characterizations of Agrippa II and the governor Felix throw valuable light on Acts' presentation of these men; and Acts agrees with Josephus that it was the Sadducees, the harshest judges on the Jewish court, who most violently opposed the early Christians.

We cannot conclude our analysis of Josephus and the NT without discussing as a separate issue the many affinities between Josephus and Luke-Acts. They have been the subject of much debate. In 1894, one German scholar published a detailed study arguing that the author of Luke-Acts used Josephus as a main source. In the following year, another argued that Josephus used Luke-Acts.[1] Neither position has much of a following today, because of the significant differences between the two works in their accounts of the same events. A third position, that the two writers shared common oral and written sources, has more adherents, because it allows some flexibility. Josephus and the author of Luke could merely have heard similar stories.[2]

---

[1] Max Krenkel, *Josephus und Lukas* (Leipzig: Haessel, 1894); J. E. Belser, "Lukas und Josephus," *ThQ* 77 (1895): 634–62; see the full discussion by H. Schreckenberg, "Flavius Josephus und die lukanischen Schriften," 179–209.

[2] Instead of saying "the author of Luke-Acts," in the remainder of this chapter I shall refer to the author as Luke. The reader should be aware, however, that we do not know who wrote the work traditionally known as Luke-

However the question of the Josephus/Luke parallels is resolved, it is illuminating to review them in their own right. Usually, scholars investigating the question have isolated and compared the common episodes in the two accounts. Some have also looked at shared vocabulary. For our purposes, however, it will be useful to place those particular affinities within a larger context. We shall begin by looking at the general similarities between Josephus and Luke-Acts in literary type, or "generic" parallels; we shall then consider the incidents recounted by both authors; finally, we shall examine specific agreements in aim, themes, and vocabulary. As to whether one author used the other as a source, the generic parallels can say nothing, for many other works of the period shared similar features. Nor can the commonly reported incidents prove dependence, in the absence of extended verbal agreement. The third kind of coincidence, however—of aim, themes, and vocabulary—*seems* to suggest that Luke-Acts builds its case with knowledge of Josephus's advocacy of Judaism.

GENERIC PARALLELS

Josephus's work is of the same broad literary type or genre as Luke-Acts: they are both histories, written in Greek according to the conventions of their period, which we may loosely call Hellenistic.[3] Although we usually lump the four gospels together in the NT, Luke is really quite different from the others on this point. It is the only one that self-consciously presents itself as a volume of history, along with Acts. In addition to being historians, both Josephus and Luke write from the margins of society, using their accounts to convey essential features of their communities' values. Both of them also come from the Jewish world—in the broadest sense: whether or not the author of Luke-Acts was a Jew, he and Josephus were both heavily influenced by Jewish Scripture (OT) and tradition.

Acts. The text is anonymous, and the author indicates that he only knows the story of Jesus' life at second or third hand (Luke 1:2). He is not among the "eyewitnesses." When I use the name Luke for convenience, it does not imply that I accept the second-century speculation that identified the author by this name.

[3] As a historical era the "Hellenistic period" ended in 31/30 B.C.E., with the end of Egyptian autonomy under Cleopatra, and thus the collapse of the last kingdom remaining from Alexander the Great's conquest. In literary terms, however, the "Hellenistic" style of writing continued for centuries thereafter.

By the time of Josephus and Luke-Acts, the writing of history had become a lively and refined art. Herodotus (ca. 484–420 B.C.E.) is often called "the father of history" for his pioneering research into the war between the Greeks and Persians. He was the first to conceive of the study of the past as scientific research (the original meaning of "history"), not as the mere repetition of old stories. He made a conscious distinction between the accounts of various interested parties and historical truth, identifying the latter with what he could personally verify. But it was Thucydides (ca. 460–400 B.C.E.), author of a *History of the Peloponnesian War,* who formulated the principles and standards of evidence for the accurate portrayal of the past. He insisted that the historian seek out living witnesses, where possible, and rigorously compare differing accounts to get at the truth. Centuries later, Polybius (ca. 200–115 B.C.E.) wrote a so-called *Universal History* (actually a recent history of Roman power) in which he reflected at length on the principles enunciated by Herodotus and Thucydides. These three Greek-speaking historians were acknowledged masters by Josephus's time. Meanwhile, the study of rhetoric had progressed steadily for hundreds of years and had helped to formalize conventions for writing history. By the first century C.E., therefore, anyone who took up the task could draw on a vast reservoir of familiar devices.

As we saw in chapter 3, an indispensable feature of any Hellenistic history book was the prologue. The Greek sense of order required that written treatises have a clear beginning, middle, and end. In contrast to the Hebrew Scriptures, which tend to jump right into the narration of events, Greek historians were required to begin with an introductory prospectus. This opening statement had to accomplish several things at once. It had to state clearly the aim, scope, and thesis of the work. Even more crucial to the writer's success, it had to convince the reader that the subject was of the utmost significance, and that the writer was singularly qualified to deal with it.

To achieve all of this tactfully and within a short space was a tall order. Inevitably, the more that historians tried to outdo each other, the more they began to sound the same. If we compare a large number of prefaces from the period, we see numerous commonplaces or *topoi.* Typically, a preface included remarks on: (a) the subject and its importance; (b) the inadequacy of previous histories of this period; (c) the author's circumstances and reasons for writing; (d) the author's complete impartiality and concern for the truth; (e) the author's strenuous research efforts and access to eyewitness testimony (the original meaning of "aut-opsy"); (f) the author's thesis, including a view of the causes of the events in question; and occasionally (g) a brief outline of the work's contents.

Because every author ended up making much the same kind of appeal, the trick for the successful historian was to use the conventions in an original way. The historian had to make a convincing case that his history really was superior to all of the others. Josephus's preface to the *War* is an admirable example. Although all of the conventions are conspicuously present, the reader hardly recognizes them as conventions because Josephus weaves them into an original, compelling statement. The Jewish war was the most important ever, he says, because the eastern part of the empire was in danger (1.1, 4–6). Previous accounts of it are defective because they were written either to flatter the Romans or denigrate the Jews, and many of the authors were not even eyewitnesses (1.2). Josephus is in a unique position to tell the truth, however, because he is intimately acquainted with both the Jewish and the Roman sides of the campaign: he is an extremely rare kind of eyewitness (1.3). So he is determined to give the world, at last, a perfectly accurate account of the revolt (1.6–8). His thesis is that the revolt was driven by an aberrant, untypical handful of power-seeking tyrants (1.10). Josephus makes the conventions come alive in a plausible way: he tells readers what to expect and also entices them to read on.

Although the preface to Luke-Acts is much briefer than *War*'s, in keeping with the work's brevity, the author manages to work in all of the crucial points:

> Since many have taken it upon themselves to write up an account of the deeds that have been accomplished among us, just as they were passed down to us by those who from the beginning were eyewitnesses and servants of the word, it seemed right that I, who have followed everything from the beginning with precision, should write a sequential account for you, noblest Theophilus, so that you might know the secure basis of the things about which you have been instructed. (Luke 1:1–4)

The very familiarity of this prologue to the reader of the NT makes it difficult to appreciate the force of its language. Nevertheless, the key ingredients of the historical preface are all here. The author begins by referring to previous treatments of his subject. Admittedly, he does not openly trash those earlier accounts in the way that many historians did, but it is not difficult to see that he finds them seriously defective. If he considered them reliable, then the logic of the prologue would make no sense. We expect him to say: "Since many have already written about this, there is *no need* for me to do so." Originality was and is the most basic justification for any writer; if it has already been done, one does not need to do it again. But the author bases his eagerness to write on the fact that "many"—often a slightly pejorative term in Greek—have already done so. This can only mean that he sees much room for improvement.

Such a reading is confirmed by what follows. First, the verb he uses to describe those other efforts by Christian authors is that they have "taken it upon themselves" to write. In its other occurrences, this verb has the sense of presumptuous or misguided effort, as when the hapless Jewish exorcists "take it upon themselves" to cast out devils in Jesus' name (Acts 19:13), or when some Jews try ineffectively to kill Paul (Acts 9:29). In Josephus this word has the same sense of "vain effort." Second, in verses 3 and 4 the author makes it clear that he will offer something that the others have not provided, namely, he has researched everything "with precision" from the beginning (a standard term in historical prologues), and he is going to provide the "secure basis." The word rendered "secure basis" is *asphaleia,* from which we get "asphalt," and it more literally means "nonslipping" or "not stumbling." Notice that the three occurrences of the related adjective in Acts (21:34; 22:30; 25:26) all concern the problem of sorting out *reliable ground in the midst of conflicting claims.* That is also the sense here in the prologue. The author says, in effect: "you have read many competing accounts; now I shall set the record straight." Although his criticism is restrained, he clearly means to present a story that is superior to the others.

How will it be superior? Verses 1 and 2 describe the work of the previous authors. They and the present writer share the same basic task: to "write up an account of the events fulfilled among us" on the basis of evidence handed down by eyewitnesses and by people who have been active in this teaching ("the word"). What this writer hopes will distinguish his account from the others comes in verses 3 and 4. Only he has researched everything from the start and so he alone is in a position to write "precisely" and "in order" (or "sequence"). Although claims to precision were standard among history writers, the adverb "in an orderly manner" (Greek *kathexēs*) is distinctive and important for this author.

A careful reading of Luke-Acts shows that we could hardly have come up with a better term to describe these books. First, the mere fact that only this author includes a history of the church after Jesus' resurrection means that he alone can reserve many of his major points for the second volume. For example, Mark (3:6) and John (5:18) place Jesus in dire conflict with the Jewish authorities almost from the beginning and, in their different ways, make Jesus' own Jewish identity more or less irrelevant to his role as savior. In Luke-Acts, however, Jesus operates comfortably within the Jewish world throughout the entire gospel, attending temple and synagogue (2:21, 41, 49; 4:16), consorting in a friendly manner with popular Jewish teachers (7:36; 11:37; 14:1), and debating with other teachers the correct interpretation of Sabbath law. In the end, it is only a small group of Jerusalem leaders who have him killed. For Luke, the serious conflict with Judaism begins only with the events immediately before Jesus' death. It then builds in stages in the book of Acts. At first, Christian leaders are told simply to refrain from teaching in the name of their recently crucified leader (Acts 4:18). Over time, it is the successive revelations from God (Acts 8, 10–11) and the momentous decisions taken on the basis of them (Acts 15), which further lead to Christian criticism of the Jerusalem temple, of dietary and other laws, and of the Jewish people, and to the Christians' open dealings with Gentiles. These bring the conflict with Judaism to a climax only at the end of the second book (Acts 28:23–28).

It may be, then, that the author found other gospels inadequate in part because they read too much of the church's own situation back into Jesus' lifetime, and thus ignored what he understood to be the proper sequential development of Christian origins. Whether that observation is accurate or not, Luke's author has a declared concern to lay things out "in order." This has a close parallel to Josephus's concern with changing phases both in the war and in the consitution *(Antiquities)*. For both authors, it would be wrong to pull out one paragraph from some point in the narrative and hold that to represent the author's entire view.

In writing a sequel to his Luke, the author of Acts did what Josephus had done. In Josephus's *Antiquities,* he first reflects on his motives for writing the *War* (*Ant.* 1.1–4) and then slides into the preface for the *Antiquities* itself. Once again he explains why his work is necessary and how it improves on other treatments of Jewish history (1.5–13). Similarly, when he begins the *Against Apion* (1.1–5) he first reflects on his aims in the prior *Antiquities.*

The writer of Acts likewise begins with a glance back at his previous work:

> Formerly I discoursed, O Theophilus, on all that Jesus did and taught from the beginning until the day on which, having given his orders to the apostles, whom he chose through the holy spirit, he was taken up. To them he presented himself alive after his suffering with many sure proofs, through a period of forty days being seen by them and speaking with them about the reign of God. (Acts 1:1–3)

Like Josephus, Luke glides easily from a summary of his earlier work to his present book. Whereas the former history had dealt with Jesus' actions and teachings, this one will recount the actions and teachings of his apostles. These men had already been introduced in the first volume (Luke 6:13–16). Now they are presented as Jesus' chosen representatives who carry on his mission. In particular, they are credible witnesses to his resurrection from the dead (cf. 1:22; 2:32; 3:15). Continuing his demonstration of the systematic development of Christian teaching, Luke insists in this preface that Jesus' resurrection, the basis of the apostles' preaching, was witnessed during a forty-day period—it wasn't an illusion—and was confirmed with many "sure proofs" (*tekmēria*, a technical term in rhetoric for proof).

Luke's reference to Theophilus in both of his prefaces provides another significant parallel to Josephus, who dedicates his later works—*Antiquities, Life,* and *Against Apion*—to one Epaphroditus. Both names are theophoric, which means that they include a god's name: in Theophilus is *theos* (god) + *philos* (friend); Epaphroditus honors the goddess Aphrodite as caregiver of the person named. Such common Greek names carried an implicit appeal to the deity for mercy in the newborn baby's life (in effect: "May God help you"). Since both Josephus's and Luke's addressees appear to have had some social status and wealth, but were unlikely to be highest-ranking aristocrats, they may have been freedmen who had become somewhat successful after gaining their freedom. This is especially likely in the case of Josephus's patron—a prominent man with a Greek name in Rome.

We know of their success because both Josephus and Luke address their patrons as "noblest," or more literally, "strongest, most powerful" (*kratistos: Life* 430; *Ag. Ap.* 1:1; Luke 1:3). Josephus, as we have seen, plainly implies that his patron is a man of some wealth and leisure. This term confirms it, for it was used most typically (cf. Latin *vir egregius*) as the formal address for those who had acquired the status of lower Roman nobility: *equites* (equestrians) or knights. In fact, Luke himself uses the address outside of the prologue only when someone is speaking to the equestrian governors Felix (a freedman, note) and Festus (Acts 23:26; 24:3; 26:25). Luke does not use it to address King Agrippa II or other high officials, apparently indicating its special significance. All of this implies that the Theophilus of Luke-Acts is a successful freedman who has reached Roman equestrian status, like Josephus's Epaphroditus—unless of course he is a purely literary creation to imply that the early Christians have such friends.

We have in Epaphroditus and Theophilus two clear examples of literary patronage. In chapter 3 we observed the general social conditions related to the production of books in Rome. Patronage was an important feature of this climate of intricate social networks. Although patronage was mirrored throughout the Mediterranean world, our language for it comes from Rome, where it was thought to have been formally established by Romulus as constituent feature of the social order (Dionysius of Halicarnassus, *Ant. rom.* 2.9.2–3; 10.4). According to Dionysius, who may have simply created a past for the custom of his own day, the idea was that the very few elite patricians—members of Rome's distinguished founding families—each became "patron" to a large number of poorer plebeian "clients."

Patronage worked in all spheres of society. Patrons were expected to furnish concrete and practical assistance to their clients, in the form of meals, clothing, and other basic necessities of life if needed. At higher levels, patrons might grant their dependent "friends" a regular stipend and a place to live. Once the imperial system had taken hold, from Augustus's time, the emperor *(princeps)* was the ultimate patron, responsible for the benevolent treatment of all Roman citizens. He arranged for such largesse as the grain dole, monumental public buildings, and expensive entertainment for the people. The obligations of clients in this system could not involve reciprocal payment, of course. Their requirements were less tangible: to bring their patrons honor by faithfully attending them, serving as living proof of the patron's virtues. By Josephus's period, although the power of the patricians had long since faded, the basic pattern of patronage, in which each echelon in the social order was expected to behave as a kind of father *(pater)* to those on the next level down, was still fully operative.

Literary patronage was a particular manifestation of this system. It became a prominent feature of Roman life under Augustus, whose close friend the equestrian Maecenas sponsored such poets as Virgil, Horace, and Propertius, who in turn dedicate some of their works to him. He became, in the memory of later authors, the archetypal literary patron: extremely wealthy and generous with his favorites. Some writers, to be sure, were wealthy and established enough in their own right that they did not need wealthy friends. But many others, especially foreign immigrants and those who were not temperamentally suited to the military-political life that was the normal route to success, relied on catching the eye of a patron. What patrons could give writers, in addition to financial support and lodging, was a *hearing.* They could offer their own properties or rent special halls for the purposes of reading, and they could gather a suitable audience through their influence.

By the end of the first century, when Josephus and Luke were writing, Roman society had plenty of wealthy freedmen who could serve such roles, though they had not the singular wealth or power of a Maecenas. They served niche markets, so to speak, lending their support to writers in whom they had some interest, and in turn receiving special mention in the writer's prologue along with the honor attending a generous patron of the arts. A writer could have numerous patrons, as Martial and Statius did in the late first century. Josephus's friend Epaphroditus was apparently not a central figure in Roman society, and yet he helped to gather a circle to support the Jewish writer. Of Luke's Theophilus we know nothing but his name and likely rank. Presumably he arranged for a hearing for Luke-Acts; perhaps he also subsidized the author as he wrote.

Does all this mean that Luke-Acts was written for a Roman audience as Josephus's writings were? At the end of the day, we have no way of deciding with any probability where the first audience was, although both author and audience were evidently somewhat removed from Judea, given the author's defective knowledge of the geography (Luke 5:19; 12:55; 17:11). It does appear that the author implicitly claims to have a Roman equestrian patron, though that is not a certain reading of the address. In any case, by this time there were prominent men living in the provinces who had attained both Roman citizenship and equestrian status. We cannot determine from the address the relationship between the literary addressee and the actual group for whom the author was writing.

A third standard feature of Hellenistic history shared by Josephus and Luke-Acts is the formulation of speeches for the leading characters. Herodotus and Thucydides preserved an important role for speeches in history-writing, and Thucydides explicitly reflected on their use. He observed that speeches could not be reconstructed as accurately as events, so he would try to give the general drift of what was said, being sure to make it fit the occasion and the speaker (*Hist.* 1.22). However, commentators have long since noted that, although Thucydides does give his characters speeches appropriate to the occasion—the arrogant speak arrogantly, statesmen speak like statesmen—the speeches are his own creations. Some may be based on recollection of what was actually said, but they are all ultimately Thucydides's own statements, a means of making his own points and advancing his narrative. A concordance shows that Thucydides does not allow the various characters true independence of vocabulary and style; they all advance his narrative interests. Under the influence of rhetorical training, such speeches became even more essential vehicles for writers of Hellenistic history to put their own themes in the mouths of their characters.[4]

Josephus's *War* provides excellent examples of how such speeches could function. For example, Josephus gives a long oration to Agrippa II, in which the king tries to dissuade the Jerusalemites from rebelling against Rome (2.345–404). On the one hand, the general thrust of the speech accords well with what was clearly the king's political position. On the other hand, it is just as clearly Josephus's composition: it makes his own fully developed case for remaining at peace. In particular, it enunciates Josephus's themes that God is on the Roman's side at present (2.390), and that the temple must be spared at all cost (2.400). The vocabulary and style are typical of Josephus, and the content of the speech is closely paralleled by Josephus's and Titus's later appeals to the tyrants (5.375–419; 6.328–350). In effect, then, he uses the speech as a convenient means of making a systematic argument, which would otherwise be out of place in a historical narrative.

A fascinating specimen of a crafted speech is the one attributed to the rebels at Masada before they take their own lives in the face of sure death from the advancing Roman army. Josephus had spoken vehe-

---

[4] On speeches in Greco-Roman historiography, see most conveniently David E. Aune, *The New Testament in Its Literary Environment* (Philadelphia: Westminster, 1987), 91–93, and bibliography on 113–14.

mently against suicide when he was called on to take his life rather than surrender (*War* 3.362–382). He argued there that suicide violated nature, that no other species voluntarily killed itself, and that only God could take life: soul and body were "fond companions" (3.362). In the mouth of the rebel leader Eleazar, however, he puts an equally philosophical discourse on life, according to which the soul is not at home in the body but always seeks release from it (7.323–387). He provides examples from sleep (in which the soul allegedly ranges freely from the body) and Indian self-sacrifice. This analysis of body and soul fits well with Josephus's language and outlook elsewhere, where he describes the afterlife (cf. *War* 2.154–158). Plainly, Josephus has composed both speeches, but he has cleverly adapted his arguments to suit the occasion. He does not impose a single theory of suicide, but allows Eleazar to speak in a manner appropriate to his role in the narrative.

Notice, however, that Josephus uses both speeches to convey his own main thesis about the war. The rebel leader ends up confessing that their miserable end is a sign of God's wrath "at the many wrongs which we madly dared to inflict upon our countrymen" (7.332). The rebel leader, in other words, serves as a mouthpiece for Josephus's interpretation of the revolt as the product of a few reckless tyrants. Eleazar's confession goes on: "For long since, so it seems, God passed this decree against the whole Jewish race in common, that we must quit this life *if we would not use it aright*" (7.359, LCL). Thus Josephus is not really commending suicide, even though he wrote Eleazar's brilliant speech on the subject. Rather, he sees the rebels' suicide as the fitting end for those who so flagrantly violated Jewish tradition. The rebels die not as heroes for the Jewish cause, but as pathetic individuals who confess their own folly before taking their lives. Josephus had to come up with a speech in defense of suicide that would suit Eleazar's role, and so he did.

To summarize: the challenge of the Hellenistic historian was to create speeches that, on the one hand, were appropriate to the speaker and occasion and, on the other hand, served to advance the author's own narrative aims. Those aims need not have been exclusively earnest, however. They might include large doses of entertainment and wordplay. Ancient readers knew this, and were not expected to believe that such speeches were merely reproductions of what was really said on a given occasion.

The author of Luke-Acts follows the conventions of his day also in the formulation of speeches. There are too many brief speeches in Luke to discuss profitably here, and in Acts he includes at least thirteen significant speeches in a relatively brief narrative:

1. Peter on the selection of an apostle to replace Judas (1:16–22)
2. Peter on the day of Pentecost (2:14–36)
3. Peter before the Jewish council (3:12–26)
4. The Pharisee Gamaliel in defense of Christianity (5:34–39)
5. Stephen facing martyrdom (7:1–53)
6. Peter to Cornelius (10:34–43)
7. Paul in Antioch of Pisidia (13:16–41)
8. James at the apostolic conference (15:13–21)
9. Paul at the Areopagus in Athens (17:22–31)
10. Paul to the Ephesian elders (20:17–35)
11. Paul to the Jews in Jerusalem (22:3–21)
12. Paul before Felix (24:10–21)
13. Paul before Agrippa II (26:2–23).

These speeches, along with many shorter ones, play a crucial role in the development of the plot of Luke-Acts.

In keeping with the expectations placed on Hellenistic authors, the writer of Acts has each of his characters speak in an appropriate way. We have already seen that Paul's remarks to Felix and Agrippa II are carefully chosen to make fun of those rulers' personal lives. Similarly, when Paul is in Athens he quotes from Greek poets rather than from Jewish Scriptures (17:28), which would have meant nothing to his Athenian audience. Gamaliel's defense of Christianity is based on the kind of pragmatic grounds that a Jewish councilor might have advocated; he does not personally confess belief in Jesus or even real enthusiasm for the Christian movement (5:35–39). And again, the proconsul Gallio speaks exactly as a Roman governor might, entirely jaded and caring nothing for the internal disputes of a subject nation (18:14–15). As many studies of Acts have shown, the author satisfies one of the key criteria for Hellenistic history. His writing is plausible; it has a realistic quality about it or "verisimilitude."

It is equally clear, however, that the speeches of Acts are the author's own and serve to advance his narrative aims.[5] To begin with,

[5] The summary in this paragraph is partly adapted from Eduard Schweizer, "Concerning the Speeches in Acts," in *Studies in Luke-Acts* (ed. Leander E. Keck and J. Louis Martyn; Philadelphia: Fortress, 1980), 208–16.

those addressed to Jewish outsiders share a remarkably similar structure, which includes: (a) direct address to the audience ("men of Israel," "men and brothers," etc.); (b) appeal for attention ("lend your ears," "let this be known to you," "hear me"); (c) a keynote quotation from Scripture; (d) summary of the Christian preaching about Jesus; (e) scriptural proof; and (f) final proclamation of salvation. Not only are the overall structures of the speeches similar; the specific content of each structural element is also consistent, no matter who the speaker is. For example, virtually everyone begins his address with the Greek word for "Men!" which is then qualified with "brothers," "Israelites," "Judeans," or whatever is appropriate (2:14; 3:12; 7:2; 13:16). Even the angels (1:11) and Gamaliel (5:35) speak this way.

Similarly, according to Acts, out of all the possible Scriptures that one could cite as proof texts, Peter and Paul choose the same ones and use them in the same way.[6] Their summaries of Christian preaching are likewise similar, even though we know from Paul's letters that he, for one, had quite distinctive language for discussing Christ's work.[7] In his letters, because he writes as the apostle to the Gentiles, Paul spends no time at all proving that Jesus is the Messiah or recounting Israel's history in any connected way. Indeed, the absence of Jewish content in his gospel is what provoked a response from his Jewish-Christian opponents. Romans, with its unique audience, is only a partial exception. Yet Acts depicts Paul, like Peter (2:14–31) and especially Stephen (7:2–50), as rooting his gospel in Israel's history (13:17–37). Like Peter in Acts (2:38; 5:31; 10:43), Paul even preaches "forgiveness of sins" (13:38; 26:18). But this phrase is part of the characteristic vocabulary of Luke-Acts (cf. Luke 1:77; 24:47); it does not appear at all

---

[6]Note especially the use of Ps 16:10 in Acts 2:27; 13:35. Both Peter and Paul understand the line "Thou wilt not let thy holy one see corruption" as a proof text for Jesus' resurrection, identifying Jesus as the "holy one." But the designation of Jesus as the holy one or child of God is part of Acts' special vocabulary (cf. 3:14; 4:27, 30). So the interpretation of this verse by Peter and Paul fits with the author's own perspective.

[7]Almost entirely absent from Paul's speeches in Acts are his distinctive themes, especially being "in Christ," dying and rising with Christ, Paul's sharp distinction between this present evil age and the one about to break in with the return of Jesus, or his flesh/spirit dichotomy. Only in 13:38–39 do references to "freedom from the law of Moses" and righteousness through faith in Christ approach one of Paul's major themes. This parallel reflects the author's effort to make each of his speeches fit the speaker and situation.

in Paul's undisputed letters, where he typically speaks of sin, in the singular, as a power.[8]

The result is that the Paul of Acts sounds remarkably like the Peter and Stephen of Acts. As with Thucydides or Josephus, one does not find here the striking differences of style or personal spoken mannerisms that one would expect in an anthology of speeches from different individuals. Although the author has provided each character with a speech appropriate to the occasion and has even introduced *some* Pauline language into one of Paul's speeches (13:38–39), on the whole the speeches advance the author's own portrayal of Christian origins and belief. They are not mere reproductions of what was actually said.

The apparatus of the preface, the references to patrons, and the carefully crafted speeches are only a few of the most obvious features of Hellenistic history writing that are shared by Josephus and Luke-Acts. Historians of the period were also obligated to make their narratives exciting and "delightful." The story of Paul's shipwreck (Acts 27) is similar to an episode Josephus tells about himself (*Life* 14–16) and reflects the common theme of divine protection at sea. Sea travel was notoriously dangerous in the first century, and the Romans took the matter with great seriousness, sacrificing to the gods before and after voyages, and avoiding any possible offense to the deity while at sea. Stories of both shipwreck and miraculous rescue through divine protection were common. Paul's encounter with the snake (Acts 27), in which he survives what should have been a fatal bite, was a common motif in the literature of the period. The immediate divine punishment of Ananias and Sapphira (Acts 5) and of Agrippa I (Acts 12) heightens the readers' sense of awe; Josephus relates many similar episodes of divine justice (e.g., *Ant.* 4.53–56; *Ag. Ap.* 2.143–44). "Poetic justice," immediate and fitting retribution for sin, was a standard feature of ancient Greek narrative. Further, like all Hellenistic historians, Josephus and Luke detail the human emotions of their characters—jealousy, envy, "fear and trembling," joy, and remorse. We have already noted that Luke's account of Jesus' genealogy (3:23–38) and

[8] Col 1:14 does have a similar phrase, but many scholars doubt that Paul wrote Colossians. In any case, the phrase in Greek there is not exactly the same as the one used in Luke-Acts, which has no definite article. On the question of Colossians, see Steve Mason and Tom Robinson, *Early Christian Reader* (Peabody, Mass.: Hendrickson, 2003).

Coin from the First Jewish Revolt. Photo courtesy of the British Museum.

precocious youth (at age twelve, 2:40–52) were common features of Greco-Roman biography also paralleled in Josephus. These and many other commonplaces situate Josephus and Luke-Acts squarely within the world of Hellenistic historiography.

Yet these two authors also share a certain distance from that world—they are in it but not of it. Several other Hellenistic histories have survived, but most of them are products of the dominant Greco-Roman culture. They deal with the major political theme of the day: the rise of Roman power and various conflicts along the way. Neither Josephus nor Luke writes political history from the center. Following the lead of Babylonian and Egyptian predecessors, who had in the wake of Alexander the Great's conquests written detailed accounts of their native cultures in Greek to help the larger world understand them better, Josephus and Luke write from the margins of the dominant culture.

Both the Jewish and Christian communities faced massive image problems at the end of the first century. The reputation of the Jews, as we have seen, suffered serious injury from the recent revolt in Judea. It is clear from the Romans' production of commemorative coins after the war and from the prominent place given to the arch of Titus that they treated the conflict as a major event. Their victory was a symbolic triumph over a troublesome people. And postwar contempt for the Jews encouraged the revival of slanders about Jewish origins and customs.

To outsiders, the Christians were at first indistinguishable from Jews. By the end of the century, however, many Christian communities were entirely non-Jewish, thanks largely to the missionary efforts of Paul. Almost nothing was known about them in elite Roman circles and what was known was not good. They met at night, in secret, men and women together; they greeted each other with kisses, and shared a common meal of someone's "body and blood." By the middle of the second century, Christians were still widely associated in the minds of elite observers with cannibalism and sexual promiscuity.[9] They were known to worship as "son of God" a man who, far from being a great hero in the classical sense, had recently been crucified by a Roman governor—a punishment for murderers and other troublemakers—in the backwater province of Judea. Moreover, they had no history, no geographical center, no temple or sacrifice, no ancient constitution, and no ethnic base. So they were quite different from the many ethnic religions that thrived in the Greco-Roman world. They resembled a voluntary association or club, of which there were many, but whereas the state had come to recognize many clubs as old and nonthreatening to the social-political order, Christians were newcomers whose real motives were unknown. Roman intellectuals tended to dismiss even the established foreign religions, including Judaism, as "superstitions." But Christianity was doubly disdained because it was a *new* superstition; it had all of Judaism's peculiar ways and "antisocial" behavior, but lacked even "the defense of antiquity."[10]

As in Josephus's case, it is inherently unlikely that Luke intended to reach directly those who either hated or did not care about the Christians with his narrative of origins and values. Even more obviously than Josephus's works, Luke-Acts presupposes a friendly audience, and (unlike Josephus's audience) one somewhat attuned to biblical and Christian themes. Whereas Josephus remains finely sensitive to his Gentile readers, explaining even the most basic customs and describing the founding figures, Luke-Acts mentions Sabbath, circumcision, the law, Abraham, and Moses as if their value and meaning were self-evident to the reader. As we have seen, Luke indicates that Theophilus already knows other accounts of Christian origins. Luke will provide the reliable basis for helping him to sort out the truth in "what you have been instructed" (Luke 1:4). So Theophilus and his circle seem to be in some

---

[9] See Robert L. Wilken, *The Christians as the Romans Saw Them* (New Haven, Conn.: Yale University Press, 1984).

[10] This phrase is from Tacitus, *Hist.* 5.5. He uses it to distinguish between those customs of the Jews that are merely quaint, but deserve respect on account of their age (Sabbath rest and food laws), from those that are "evil and disgusting" (misanthropy, lust, circumcision, and mean-spirited behavior).

way on the edge of Christian faith: very interested outsiders, new converts, or perhaps disillusioned members looking for reasons to stay. Like Josephus (outside of the *Against Apion*), Luke does not explicitly confront outsiders' impressions of the Christians. Rather, he tells a story that removes the ground from any false rumors. Benevolent readers will broker this good news to the larger world.

To impress these readers with the nobility of their communities, both Josephus and Luke must demonstrate both the *antiquity* and the *virtue* of those religions. "Virtue" in this context includes a high communal ethic, but also proven political respectability and cooperation with the Roman "peace." We have seen how Josephus accomplishes these goals. He claims that only a small group of untypical Jews hijacked the conflict in Judea from the aristocracy *(War);* that Jewish tradition goes back to the remotest antiquity and is not a corruption of Egyptian religion *(Antiquities);* and that Moses' constitution, which Jews scrupulously follow, reflects the highest standard of moral philosophy and human aspiration; it is the envy of the world *(Antiquities/Against Apion).*

Luke seems to have an appreciably harder task, since faith in Jesus has not been around for more than a few decades at his time of writing. His strategy, which will be taken over by many of the young church's later spokespersons, is bold. He must plant Jesus' life and Christian origins deeply within the soil of Judaism. In his portrayal, Christianity is not in fact new but is the true descendant of the Jewish heritage.

First, unlike the other gospel writers, he begins his story in Jerusalem, which was famous around the world as the national home of the Jews. The renowned Jewish temple is where the Christian story takes shape (Luke 1:8). Now, Luke's sources tell him that Jesus spent most of his career away from Jerusalem, in the villages of Galilee, and came down to the great city only in the final days of his life (cf. Mark 11:1; Matt 21:1). But Luke gets around this problem by regularly introducing Jerusalem into the narrative before its time. He has Jesus' family visit the temple regularly (Luke 2:41–51), and he has Jesus "set his face toward Jerusalem" early in the narrative (9:51), long before he actually goes there. Indeed Jesus remains in Galilee for most of the story, as in the other gospels (cf. 19:28), but this author keeps reminding the reader that Jesus is on his way to Jerusalem all the while (9:51; 13:33; 17:11; 19:11).

After Jesus' resurrection, similarly, Luke departs from Mark (16:7) and Matthew (28:7, 16) by insisting that the disciples stayed in Jerusalem for Jesus' appearances (Luke 24:13, 18, 33). They are explicitly told to remain in Jerusalem until the Spirit is given, for the gospel will go out from Jerusalem to the ends of the world (Luke 24:47, 52; Acts 1:8, 12). In Acts, Jerusalem is indeed the church's headquarters. The apostles who reside there, having been chosen by Jesus himself, oversee the church's affairs (Acts 8:1, 14; 9:26; 11:22; 15:2; 16:4; 21:17–18). Although Christianity might seem to observers in Rome or Asia Minor like a shadowy and secretive movement, Luke forthrightly claims that it has both a geographical center and an authorized leadership.

More than that, Jesus and the first Christians are solidly rooted in Jewish tradition. Luke's birth narrative is filled with quotations from and allusions to Jewish Scripture. John the Baptist's parents obey all of the laws scrupulously (Luke 1:6), as do Jesus' parents (2:39–42). Jesus himself goes to the synagogue "as was his custom" (Luke 4:16). Only Luke has him eat dinner with a leader of the people who was a member of the Pharisees (Luke 14:1), claimed by Josephus to be the dominant religious group in Jewish life. After his resurrection, Jesus opens the Jewish Scriptures to demonstrate that Moses and the prophets all spoke of him (24:27, 44). The theme that Jesus fulfills Israel's ancient hope is equally strong in Acts (e.g., Acts 2:16, 25; 4:11, 25; 8:35).

Notice that even after Jesus has risen, the apostles continue to attend Jewish temple sacrifices (Acts 3:1).[11] A prominent Pharisaic "teacher of the law" defends the church (5:34–39), and Paul, who emphatically removes himself from Torah observance in his letters (Phil 3:3–11; Gal 3:23–29; 4:21–31), appears in Acts regularly attending synagogue, "as was his custom" (17:2), and taking a Jewish vow (21:20–26). Clearly, Luke wants to impress his readers with the Jewish roots of Christianity. The mission to the Gentiles is for him an *extension* of this Jewish core, maintained by "thousands of Jews" (21:20), and so even Gentiles must observe a few basic Jewish laws (Acts 15:20, 29; contrast Paul, Gal 2:10).

For both outside observers of early Christianity and thoughtful insiders, an obvious question was: "If Christians claim to have ancient roots going back to the origins of Jewish tradition, if they claim the Jewish heritage as their own, why do they not observe the Jewish law?" We see this question posed forcefully, not long after the completion of

---

[11] That is, the disciples are said to go up to the temple "at the hour of prayer, the ninth hour." This was the time of the daily afternoon sacrifice.

Luke-Acts, by Justin Martyr's (fictional?) dialogue partner, Trypho (*Dial.* 46), and by the astute philosopher Celsus (Origen, *Cels.* 1.28; 2.4). But it was also a serious problem internally. Jewish Christians insisted that the law must in fact be obeyed (Eusebius, *Hist. eccl.* 3.27.2) and, on the other extreme, Marcion of Pontus wanted to break all connection between Christianity and Judaism. This was arguably the most basic problem of Christian self-definition through the first two centuries.

Luke's solution to the problem is quite sophisticated. The other gospels had tried to confront the same issue with simpler remedies: either Jesus was alien to his Jewish environment and essentially abrogated the law (Mark, e.g., 7:19; John 1:1–18) or he was Israel's hope and maintained the law fully (Matt 5:17–20). But Luke wishes to preclude the difficulty by showing that, although Christianity began deeply embedded in Judaism (with Jesus, the apostles, and even Luke's Paul), God has showed through a series of revelations that it must open itself also to the Gentiles. And by the end of the story it has become clear that only the Gentiles, by and large, are receptive (Acts 28:23–28).

Alongside this motif of sequential development, which seems to be the main thesis of the narrative, Luke repeatedly shows that the Christian view is credible because the church's leaders had absolutely no choice in the matter. It is not, as Celsus implied, a matter of their own wishes. To the contrary, after Jesus' resurrection the apostles plead that they must obey God, no matter how impressive the Jewish authorities are (Acts 4:19–20). Peter, for his part, is adamantly opposed to the de-Judaization of the faith, and has to be forced into compliance. When he refuses to eat "unclean" food, God censures him for what was now an act of disobedience (10:14–16). And Luke's whole portrait of Paul draws its force from the fact that Paul was the most unlikely missionary to the Gentiles. He was a zealous Pharisee and an active persecutor of the Chirstians. He had to be literally compelled—in a story that Acts tells three times—to follow God's orders. He could not be disobedient (9:1–19; 22:1–21; 26:4–18).

This theme of unwilling compliance both supports the Christian claim to truth and resolves the related question: "If what you Christians are doing is right, why do most Jews not follow you?" Luke appeals here to common human psychology, which tends to reject what seems new and different. This appears to be the reason for the otherwise puzzling speech he crafts for Stephen in Acts 7, which seems to dwell on ancient

Jewish history for too long. But that speech highlights Moses' own difficulty in gaining acceptance at first. The point is to show that Stephen's present accusers should be forgiven, since it is only natural that they fail to see what God is doing in the church.

Like Josephus, Luke must also show that his religion is not opposed to Roman order, though it seems to be from the outside. Whereas Josephus has to account for the Jewish revolt, Luke has to explain why Christians revere someone who was punished with death by a Roman governor. Luke's strategy is clear. He presents the Roman authorities as consistently friendly to the young church. In the trial of Jesus, Pilate insists three times on Jesus' innocence; he finds no "cause of death" in him (Luke 23:4, 14–15, 22). In the end, he merely capitulates to the clamor of the "chief priests and scribes," who vehemently accuse Jesus. Notice, however, that in the retelling of the story Pilate's role all but drops out. In Acts, the writer flatly claims that *the Jews* crucified Jesus (2:23; 3:15; 4:10). He goes as far as to claim that the Jewish leaders killed Jesus "by hanging him on a tree" (5:30). Thus the (actual) Roman crucifixion has shaded into a Jewish lynching, the effect of which is to remove the Roman authorities from the scene altogether. Similarly, in Paul's case, it is the Jews who relentlessly oppose him, but the Roman officials who spirit him to safety (Acts 17:12–17; 22:22–29; 23:10, 16–35).

An interesting case in point is Paul's trip to Cyprus in Acts 13:6–12. There he is welcomed by the Roman proconsul, a "man of intelligence," who wants to hear the word of God (13:7). But Paul's mission faces interference from a Jewish magician named Elymas. Paul has to confront this man, a "son of the devil, enemy of all righteousness, full of all deceit and villainy," and have him struck blind (13:10). This Jew anticipates the many others who will meddle in the gospel to the Gentiles later in the narrative (Acts 13:45, 50; 14:19; 17:5; 18:6; 19:9; 21:27).

So Luke's method of presenting Christianity as cooperative with Roman life and order is, on the one side, to portray Roman authorities as well disposed to Jesus and the Christians. On the other side, to explain how the Christians ran into trouble with the authorities, he consistently blames the temple authorities in Jerusalem. Although the theme of Jewish obstinacy was present in Christian writings from the beginning (cf. 1 Thess 2:14–16), it must have taken on special significance after the revolt. While charges of Jewish "hatred of humanity" and resistance to legitimate authority were in the air, Luke's presentation would presumably have been expected to resonate with non-Jewish readers' assumptions. Both Josephus and Luke must show how, in spite of appearances, their groups pose no threat to Roman order. Josephus tries to obliterate the equation of "Jew" with "rebel," whereas Luke depends on that link for his appeal.

As far as Christian teaching goes, Luke knows full well that the central claim concerning Jesus' bodily resurrection is difficult for many readers to accept. We know this also from second- and third-century writers on Christianity.[12] But Luke faces the problem squarely and insists that the event is nevertheless undeniable because of ample eyewitness evidence. That is the basis of the apostles' office: they are witnesses to the resurrection. As for moral teachings and lifestyle, the church appears very much like the Essene community of Josephus—sharing all things in common, expressing great love for one another, and living upright lives. Like the Essenes, they pose no political threat.

In arguing for the established and orderly character of their respective constituencies, both Josephus and Luke idealize the real situation. We have seen that one of Josephus's major themes is the "harmony" of Judaism: Moses delivered a comprehensive constitution; it has been carefully preserved by the priesthood, under the supervision of the high priests, whose succession can be traced all the way back to Aaron; all Jews study the laws with devotion, are ready to die for them if necessary, and refuse to change a word. Yet Jewish life was never so serene. From at least 200 B.C.E., we see major divisions shaping up in the community over the question of who truly represents the Jewish tradition. The Maccabean revolt, which began in 167 B.C.E., was evidently as much a civil war over the proper course of the Jewish state as it was a conflict with the Seleucid regime of Antiochus IV. Our impression of a broad spectrum of Jewish belief and behavior was beginning to emerge even from the traditional sources—1 and 2 Maccabees, Josephus himself, Philo, and others—but it has been placed beyond doubt by the publication of the Dead Sea Scrolls and archaeological finds demonstrating the diversity of lived Judaism. All of these attest to a wide variety of Jewish perspectives, which were often in conflict. But this means that Josephus has, in order to enhance his portrayal of Judaism's virtues, exaggerated and idealized. Cicero could do the same for Rome (see chapter 3).

---

[12] In particular, Celsus (second century) and Porphyry (third century). See Wilken, *Christians,* 94–163. See also 1 Cor 15:12, 35–51.

We see a similar phenomenon in Luke-Acts. Careful study of Paul's letters reveals fundamental divisions among the first generation of Christians. He condemns Peter for perceived misconduct (Gal 2:11) and regularly denounces Christians who disagree with him, no matter what their status, as servants of Satan and workers of evil (2 Cor 11:4, 15). He even pronounces a solemn curse on some of them (Gal 1:8; 5:10). These rifts were deep, as Christians debated with each other what it really meant to be a follower of Jesus. A major division was between those who saw Christian faith as continuous with Judaism and those who did not. But Christians also debated whether Jesus' primary work was already completed, so that one could enjoy new life now, or whether new life lay mainly in the future, so that one should invest little in this present age, waiting rather for Jesus' return (1 Cor 4:8–11).

Little or no trace of these sharp divergences can be found in Luke-Acts. To be sure, the dispute over Gentile Christianity is the subject of some discussion (Acts 11:2; 15:1) as is Paul's stance toward Judaism (21:21). But in keeping with Luke's portrayal of a central authority in Jerusalem, these disagreements are resolved amicably through the counsel of the universally respected elders. Paul dutifully receives instruction from Jerusalem, even if it means taking a Jewish vow (21:22–26). But the friendly relations pictured in Acts seem to minimize some of the conflicts that we see in Paul's own letters, in which he insists on his utter independence from Jerusalem (Gal 1:12, 17; 2:1) and his disregard for the reputation of the Jerusalem apostles (Gal 2:6). It seems therefore that Luke idealizes his portrayal of early Christian relations, just as Josephus does for Judaism. In both cases, the idealization arises from a concern to present the group as worthy of respect.

So far, we have seen that Josephus and Luke-Acts share the same broad literary type. To be sure, there are important differences between them. Luke's Greek style is much more consistent than Josephus's: the Jewish historian reaches higher, in imitation of fashionable trends, but sometimes falls lower, as in the tangled prose of *Ant.* 17–19. Josephus has nothing really parallel to the gospel of Luke, with its many short sayings of Jesus. Nevertheless, both writers consciously develop their accounts with the conventional tools of Hellenistic historiography. In this respect, they are like numerous other writers of the period.

Yet Josephus and Luke also stand out from most other Hellenistic historians because they are both aliens, trying to mediate healthy portraits of their communities via friendly parties in the larger culture. For this purpose, the points that they need to make are similar: they must show that their groups are worthy of respect because, contrary to first impressions, they are well established in remotest antiquity, possess enviable moral codes, and pose no threat to Roman order. In the event, both writers will lay claim to the great heritage of Judean culture. But to explain popular misconceptions, they must also drive a sharp wedge between true representatives of the tradition and the troublesome renegades who have created bad impressions. For Josephus, the troublemakers are those who rebelled against Rome: they betrayed the heritage of their nation. For Luke, and this is his boldest claim, it is those Jews who do not believe in Christ (the vast majority, whom Josephus was defending!) who have departed from the tradition.

COMMONLY REPORTED EVENTS

The main reason for scholars' speculation about the relation between Josephus and Luke-Acts is the remarkable number of incidents reported by Luke, in both the gospel and Acts, that have parallels in Josephus. More than any other gospel writer, Luke includes references to the non-Christian world of affairs. Almost every incident of this kind that he mentions turns up somewhere in Josephus's narratives. Yet Luke and Josephus differ significantly in their reporting of these common events. So, although the correspondences are tantalizing, the differences appear at first to preclude any direct use of one author's work by the other. Some scholars have proposed, nevertheless, that Luke knew Josephus's work but remembered it imperfectly or, in some cases, deliberately altered it to suit his story. In this chapter, we can discuss only the most significant points of intersection.

The Census Under Quirinius

We turn first to the whole complex of persons and events associated with the census under Quirinius. Recall that this census plays a crucial role in both the *War* and the *Antiquities*. Josephus relates that with the removal of Herod's incompetent son Archelaus as ethnarch of Judea in 6 C.E., the Romans incorporated the Jewish heartland as a province. Whereas they had ruled it only indirectly as a client kingdom under Herod's family, they now sent their own governor to manage its affairs. But direct administration inevitably meant direct taxation, and for that purpose the new governor of neighboring Syria conducted a census of property, both in his existing territory and in the newly acquired province. It was this census, and the submission to Rome which it symbolized, that led Judas the Galilean (or Golanite) to call for the creation of an independent Jewish state (*War* 2.117–118; *Ant.* 18.1–5).

Josephus places great emphasis on this early rebellion as a prototype of the later revolt: "They sowed the seed from which sprang strife between factions and the slaughter of fellow citizens" (*Ant.* 18.8, LCL). Judas and his followers set in motion a disastrous freedom movement that ended with the destruction of the "very temple of God" two generations later (*Ant.* 18.8–9). Indeed, the sons of Judas will be crucified as rebels in the 40s, and Josephus claims that one of the key leaders of the final revolt (Menahem) was also a son of Judas, "that redoubtable doctor who in old days, under Quirinius, had upbraided the Jews for recognizing the Romans as masters" (*War* 2.433, LCL). His emphatic repudiation of this mindset leads Josephus in both the *War* and the *Antiquities* to include his famous descriptions of the three normal "philosophical schools" among the Jews, by way of contrast. Finally, Eleazar ben Yair, rebel leader at Masada, was also from Judas's family (*War* 2.447). So the census is not mentioned in passing by Josephus; it is for him a watershed event in recent Jewish history.

Before turning to Luke, we should note briefly that this analysis seems to be part of Josephus's peculiar way of seeing things. Recent historical scholarship has cast serious doubt on the notion that there was anything like a unified "zealot" faction, or "fourth philosophy" as Josephus calls it, in first-century Palestine. There seem to have been all sorts of peasant movements, perhaps also aristocratic ones, that were opposed to Roman rule for a variety of economic and political reasons.[13] It appears, therefore, that Josephus has exercised a strong hand in making his point about the rebels: he has welded them into a single, aberrant "school of thought," which he traces back to the census under Quirinius. But this means that it is Josephus who gives the census its crucial function, because of his own literary aims. A writer with a different viewpoint might not have seen so much significance in the census and its aftermath.

---

[13] See Richard A. Horsley with John S. Hanson, *Bandits, Prophets, and Messiahs: Popular Movements at the Time of Jesus* (San Francisco: Harper & Row, 1985), xi–xxviii.

It is noteworthy, therefore, that the census under Quirinius also appears in Luke's gospel as a watershed event. Luke knows about the kind of political significance attributed by Josephus, as we shall see, but he uses the census mainly as a means of explaining how "Jesus of Nazareth" came to be born in Bethlehem. Luke's account begins as follows:

> Now it happened in those days that a decree was issued by Caesar Augustus that the entire civilized world should be enrolled [for taxation]. This, the first census, occurred while Quirinius was governor of Syria. And everyone was traveling to be enrolled, each to his own city. (Luke 2:1–3)

Because Joseph was a descendant of David, Luke continues, he had to leave Nazareth with the pregnant Mary and travel to Bethlehem, the city of David's origin. That is how Joseph and Mary came to be in Bethlehem when Jesus was born. Two weeks later, they would return to Nazareth along with the newborn Jesus (2:22, 39; cf. Lev 12:1–8). So the census is critical to Luke's story because it provides the context for Jesus' birth.

Yet Luke's portrayal offers numerous well-known difficulties. (a) Luke puts Mary's pregnancy under the reign of Herod the Great, who died in 4 B.C.E. (Luke 1:5), in agreement with Matthew (Matt 2:1). So he seems to think that Quirinius was governor of Syria while Herod was still alive. But according to Josephus, Quirinius only arrived in Syria in 6 C.E., after the deposition of Herod's son Archelaus in Judea. It is impossible to modify Josephus's dates by more than a year either way without pulling down his whole elaborate chronology of the period. Further, it is not clear how there could have been a census of Judea under Herod's rule, since the territory was not yet subject to direct Roman taxation. According to Josephus, it was the removal of Herodian family rule after Archelaus that brought about the need for a census and direct Roman rule.

(b) The census described by Josephus was conducted only in Syria and Judea, for taxation purposes. There is no record anywhere of a worldwide census such as Luke reports in this period. And such an event, as described by Luke, would have caused massive upheaval, with each person returning to his or her ancestral home. This would mean that all the Jews of the Diaspora—nearly one million in Egypt and tens of thousands in all the major cities of the empire—would have had to return to Judea. Throughout the Roman empire, virtually everyone would have been in transit somewhere!

(c) There were two kinds of census in the Roman world. One was the regular Roman census conducted by the "censors" for the purposes of maintaining the list of Roman male citizens around the world. Under Augustus (ruled 31/27 B.C.E. to 14 C.E.), for example, there was such a census in 28 B.C.E., 8 B.C.E., and 14 C.E. Male citizens had to declare their family lines, age, occupation, place of residence, and the value of their possessions for taxation purposes. The other kind of census came about only very gradually, as the provinces were organized for taxation, such as the one in Judea in 6 C.E. This was conducted by the provincial governor and his aides, mainly for the purpose of registering property for the purpose of taxation. In neither case, however, did it make any sense for the person being enrolled to travel to some distant ancestral home, far from their place of residence and property possession. No such movement is recorded, and it would make little practical sense.

Joseph was separated from David by about one thousand years. Was everyone, then, supposed to figure out who his ancestor was a thousand years before and track down the ancestor's town, if it still existed? And how was this possible? Since both ancestors and descendants grow exponentially, it takes only twenty generations (500–600 years) for one to have one million ancestors from a given time period. Josephus was a descendant of most of David's contemporaries. Which ancestor and town should one choose? Given that David's son Solomon had one thousand wives and concubines (1 Kgs 11:3), who was *not* a descendant of David after a thousand years?

Some scholars have tried to solve the first problem by proposing that there was an earlier census, also by Quirinius, while Herod was still alive—different from the one mentioned by Josephus in 6 C.E. But Josephus and Luke both make it clear that this census under Quirinius was the "first" census. That point is indispensable to Josephus's whole portrayal of Judas's campaign, for if there had been a census ten years earlier, the rebels' complaints would have been poorly timed. In any case, Luke himself later refers to "Judas the Galilean," who "arose in the days of *the census*" (Acts 5:37). It is clear that he thinks of one famous census under Quirinius, the one in which Judas initiated a rebel movement. And however one resolves the first problem, the equally serious second and third remain.

Here, then, is the issue. In the few but important lines that he devotes to the census, Luke manages to associate it with both Quirinius, governor of Syria, and Judas the Galilean. These points agree with

Josephus's presentation in a conspicuous way. Because of his literary aims, Josephus is the one who makes the point that the census symbolized Roman occupation and so was opposed by the arch rebel Judas the Galilean. We suspect that other writers would not have given the census such prominence or made such connections with the rebel psychology. These observations suggest that Luke was familiar with Josephus's work. Otherwise, it would be a remarkable coincidence that he also chooses to feature the census and to mention its connection with Judas the Galilean. If Luke knew Josephus's accounts, admittedly, it is difficult to see how he could have imagined a worldwide census requiring the return to one's ancestral home, or why he would date the census under Quirinius also to the time before Herod's death in 4 B.C.E. Given what we have just said, however, these changes might best be explained if Luke knew some highlights of Josephus's narrative but did not recall, or was not concerned with, the details.

Judas the Galilean, Theudas, and the Egyptian Prophet

In support of this conclusion, we may note that Luke knows about Josephus's three most important rebel figures from the prewar period: Judas the Galilean, Theudas, and the Egyptian prophet. We have seen that Josephus makes Judas a kind of rebel patriarch: some of his sons are crucified by the governor Tiberius Julius Alexander (46–48 C.E.; *Ant.* 20.102), and another becomes an early leader of the great revolt. Theudas appears in the period 44–46 C.E. Josephus describes him as an impostor, or perhaps wizard *(goēs)*, who deceived "the majority of the masses" (*Ant.* 20.97). Claiming to be a prophet, he persuaded his followers to accompany him to the Jordan river, which he promised to part before their eyes (in imitation of Joshua). But the governor's soldiers killed or dispersed his followers, and Theudas himself was beheaded. Finally, under Felix (52–59 C.E.), the false prophet from Egypt, who is also called an impostor or wizard, appeared in Judea. In the *War*, Josephus claims that he had a following of about thirty thousand, with which he proposed to force his way into Jerusalem and overcome the small Roman garrison. In the event, most of his followers were killed or captured, though he escaped (*War* 2.261–263). In the *Antiquities*, by contrast, the Egyptian promises only that the walls of Jerusalem will fall miraculously; only four hundred of his followers are killed, and two hundred taken prisoner (*Ant.* 20.171). The smaller numbers implied may account for the expectation of a miracle rather than a seizure of Jerusalem by force.

Notice, however, Josephus's repeated assertion that there were *numerous* impostors, false prophets, and wizards around in the period before the revolt. These unnamed popular leaders typically led the masses out into the desert, promising them miraculous signs of imminent salvation: "Deceivers and impostors, under the pretence of divine revelation fostering revolutionary changes, they persuaded the multitude to act like madmen, and led them out into the desert" (*War* 2.259; cf. 264; *Ant.* 20.160, 188, LCL). In both of his major works, he presents the Egyptian as only one among *many* anonymous troublemakers at the time (*War* 2.261; *Ant.* 20.167–169). Notice also that Josephus distinguishes between these false prophets, whom we might call religious impostors, and the more militant popular leaders who engaged in guerrilla warfare. In particular, a group known as the *sicarii* emerged in the time of Felix. These men would conceal short daggers *(sicae)* under their clothing, mingle in a dense crowd, then dispatch their enemies with impunity (*War* 2.254–257; *Ant.* 20.164–165). Their methods struck terror into the moderate and pro-Roman factions. Josephus abhors both the false prophets and the guerrillas, and only distinguishes them in order to say that, between them, the country was in chaos (*War* 2.264). Interesting for our purposes is that in both of his works, he introduces the (political) *sicarii* immediately before his discussion of the (prophetic-religious) Egyptian. This is his unique narrative arrangement.

When we turn to Luke-Acts, we are struck by two facts: (a) the author happens to mention the same three figures who are featured by Josephus, and (b) he associates them in ways reminiscent of Josephus's narratives. Judas and Theudas appear together in the speech of Gamaliel, in which he advises the Jewish council to leave the Christians alone:

> For before these days Theudas arose, professing to be somebody, and he was joined by men numbering about four hundred; he was killed, and all those who followed him were dispersed and came to nothing. After this man, Judas the Galilean arose in the days of the census and inspired rebellion in the people who followed him. That one too was destroyed and all those who followed him were scattered. (Acts 5:36–37)

Taken individually, Luke's remarks about these two figures match Josephus's accounts fairly well. Admittedly, Theudas's following of four hundred hardly captures Josephus's claim that he persuaded the majority of the masses, and Josephus does not mention Judas's death as Luke does. But numbers are notoriously fluid in ancient texts (Compare Josephus's own differences with himself on the size of the Egyptian's following!), and Luke's statement that Judas was "destroyed" is quite vague.

The most obvious difficulty is Luke's order: he asserts that Judas's revolt and the census, placed by Josephus in 6 C.E., took place *after* the Theudas incident, which Josephus dates to about 45 C.E. An easy solution is to suggest that there was another false prophet named Theudas before Judas, but we do not know of such a person from any other source, and the coincidence—that Luke would just happen to mention another rebel with the same name as one of Josephus's featured figures—would be uncanny. It seems more likely that Luke has reversed the order of the two characters. Indeed, if the author wanted to mention Josephus's Theudas, he would face the problem that the speech of Gamaliel (Acts 5) occurs before the conversion of Paul (Acts 9), and therefore in the early 30s, at least a decade before Josephus's Theudas was killed. So if Luke wanted Gamaliel to cite Theudas as an example of a failed popular leader, he would be forced to redate this figure. But that raises a critical question for our study: why, if there were so many other popular leaders around, did Luke find it necessary to use Theudas—even rearranging the chronology to do so—rather than choosing some other figure? It seems that Luke could not draw on other figures, and this means either that Josephus misrepresented things entirely—that there really were no other suitable characters—or that Luke's knowledge is limited to the individuals mentioned by Josephus.

Perhaps Luke simply did not have a clear idea of when Theudas lived: as with the census, he knew of a significant event that he could use in his narrative but did not know the details. Yet that possibility also suggests that he knew of these events from having read or heard Josephus at some time, for Josephus is the one who isolates Judas and Theudas from among the many popular leaders of the time. Moreover, Josephus links the two characters in his story. Immediately after describing the fate of Theudas under Cuspius Fadus (*Ant.* 20.97–99), he summarizes the governorship of Tiberius Julius Alexander. Alexander's main claim to fame was that he crucified the sons of Judas the Galilean (20.100–102). In describing this action, Josephus reminds the reader about Judas, who incited the people to revolt during the census of Quirinius. The description of Judas here ("incited the people to revolt") is very close to the construction in Acts 5:37, quoted above. As several scholars have suggested, therefore, it may be that Luke's order, Theudas then Judas, was suggested by his memory of this passage from Josephus. Since Josephus links Theudas and Judas in this order for his own narrative purposes, the reproduction of this connection in Acts is either another noteworthy coincidence or the result of Luke's knowledge of Josephus.

Luke's reference to the Egyptian false prophet also recalls Josephus's narrative. In Acts 21, Paul is rescued from a Jewish mob by the Roman tribune, who whisks him to safety in the military garrison. When Paul addresses the tribune in Greek, the latter responds:

> You know Greek? Aren't you, then, the Egyptian, who stirred up trouble some time ago and led the four thousand men of the *sicarii* out into the desert? (Acts 21:38)

Paradoxically, it is the differences between this remark and Josephus's account that suggest Luke's awareness of Josephus. The similarity is clear enough: Paul is arrested while Felix is governor, and that is also the period to which Josephus assigns the Egyptian. But Josephus stresses that the Egyptian was not a member of the *sicarii;* they were guerrillas, whereas he was a religious-prophetic figure (*War* 2.258). Acts has him leading the *sicarii.* Josephus also claims that the Egyptian led his men to the Mount of Olives to prepare for the seizure of Jerusalem, whereas Acts has him leading men out into the desert. And, given the *sicarii* mode of operation, mingling with crowds to dispose of enemies, it is not clear why they would head for the desert. Further, whereas Josephus gives the Egyptian about thirty thousand men in the *War,* rather fewer in the *Antiquities,* Acts has only four thousand.

Are these discrepancies best explained by Luke's knowledge of Josephus, or by his use of another source or oral tradition? Notice first that, like Josephus, Luke knows the man only by his place of origin. Presumably, his parents did not call him "the Egyptian," but gave him a personal name. It is easy enough to understand why Josephus should have chosen the geographical epithet alone, given his hostility toward Egyptians. It is harder to explain Luke's use of this term, rather than a personal name, if he had independent access to information. There were many Jews from Egypt in Judea.

Second, although Josephus does not make the Egyptian's followers *sicarii,* he mentions both groups in the same breath. As we have seen, he discusses the Egyptian immediately after describing the daggermen (*War* 2.261; *Ant.* 20.167–169). But this is clearly part of his literary artistry. How did Luke, then, come to associate the Egyptian, incorrectly, with the *sicarii?* If he did so independently of Josephus, the coincidence is remarkable. It is even more remarkable because *sicarii* is a Latin term for assassins. In Roman law and literature, *sicarii* were a well-known problem. One of the eight standing courts established in the capital was to hear charges of assassination *(quaestio inter sicarios),* and one of Cicero's most famous early cases involved defending a man before this court *(For Sextus Roscius Amerinus).* It is most unlikely that the Judean group in question called themselves by this Latin title; it seems entirely likely that "official" outsiders such as Josephus applied the title to them. How, then, did Luke, who also writes in Greek, happen upon the Latin word? That he derived it from a source is clear because he uses it casually, without betraying any knowledge of its significance as a reference to assassins who carried concealed daggers. So who was his source? It is easiest to suppose that he had some knowledge of Josephus, and that he linked the Egyptian with the *sicarii* because Josephus's account had done so.

Similarly, although Josephus has the Egyptian leading his men to the Mount of Olives (*War* 2.261–262; *Ant.* 20.169), he introduces this figure with a more general statement about impostors of this kind, that they "persuaded the multitude to act like madmen, and *led them out into the desert* under the belief that God would there give them tokens of deliverance" (*War* 2.260; cf. *Ant.* 20.167). Once again, Luke's claim that the Egyptian led his followers into the desert, though it does not match Josephus's exactly, seems easily explained on the hypothesis that he imperfectly remembered Josephus and so ran together Josephus's distinct statements. His placing of either the Egyptian or the *sicarii* in the desert is harder to explain if Luke knew the story from another source, perhaps from an independent oral tradition, which would not have included Josephus's general statement about impostors in the desert.

Luke's placing of the *sicarii* in the desert indicates that he knows their name but is not clear about what they do. This confusion is best explained if he is relying on a source that led him to link the *sicarii* with the Egyptian, and the Egyptian with the desert. Luke's use of this group is symptomatic of his general relation to non-Christian affairs. Like Judas and the census, Theudas, and the Egyptian, the *sicarii* lend an air of realism to Luke's narrative—an important quality in Hellenistic history-writing. He does not match Josephus in details, but the particular ways in which he disagrees suggest that he knew a narrative much like that of Josephus. His references to political events in Judea are understandable if he had read portions of Josephus or had heard the Jewish historian recite,[14] then later recalled some of this material for his own story. If Luke did not know Josephus, we are faced with an astonishing number of coincidences: he links Judas and the census as a watershed event, connects Judas and Theudas, connects the Egyptian with the *sicarii,* connects the Egyptian with the desert, and selects these three figures out of all the anonymous guerrillas and impostors of the period.

Minor Parallels

Space does not permit a complete inventory of the parallels between Luke-Acts and Josephus. Some of these have been considered in earlier chapters. We have seen, for example, that Luke's portrayals of King Agrippa's death, of the governor Felix and Drusilla, and of Agrippa II and Berenice all dovetail with Josephus's account very well. This means that Luke must have had, in each case, an account *like* Josephus's in his memory. Many scholars have pointed out the clear differences between Luke and Josephus in relation to the episodes considered in this chapter and have concluded that Luke could not have known Josephus's work. I would propose, however, that even these differences require that Luke knew a source like Josephus. Most of the differences are best understood as conflations of closely related elements of Josephus's narrative structure. It would be far more difficult to explain the differences if Luke did not know something like Josephus's work.

In addition to the parallels considered in this and earlier chapters, several less significant ones may be mentioned: (a) Luke's mention of "Lysanias, tetrarch of Abilene" (Luke 3:1; cf. *War* 2.215, 247; *Ant.* 19.275); (b) Luke's parable of the man who traveled to another country to receive his kingship, but was hated by his own people, whom he punished with death, which seems like a thinly veiled reference to the family of Herod as described by Josephus (Luke 19:12–27; *War* 1.282–285); (c)

---

[14] Recitation by the author was the common mode of publishing a new work. See chapter 3.

Luke's description of the siege and destruction of Jerusalem, including a reference to the slaughter of children (Luke 19:43–44; cf. *War* 6 in general); and (d) Luke's reference to a famine during the reign of Claudius, in which Barnabas and Saul brought relief to Jerusalem from Antioch (Acts 11:28–29; cf. *Ant.* 3.320; 20.51–53, 101). Although they do not seem at first to describe the same incident, (e) Luke's reference to Pilate's attack on some Galileans (Luke 13:1) sounds somewhat like Josephus's account of Pilate's dealings with some Samaritans at Mount Gerizim (*Ant.* 18.85–87). By themselves, these parallels are too vague to establish a relationship between the texts.

Nevertheless, the affinities discussed above and in earlier chapters do indicate such a relationship. In any given case—say, the connection of the Egyptian with the *sicarii* or with the desert—one might be content to dismiss the affinity with Josephus as a coincidence. But a series of half a dozen such coincidences of narrative detail, combined with the coincidence that Luke happened to include some key features of Josephus's story (the census, the three rebel figures), makes the hypothesis that Luke had some knowledge of Josephus more likely than not.

AGREEMENTS OF THEME AND VOCABULARY

In assessing the relationship between Josephus and Luke-Acts, scholars have often neglected to compare the two authors' specific aims. Yet this may produce the most telling evidence of all. To be sure, the neglect results from understandable causes: the literary aims of Josephus have until recent years been largely ignored, while those of Luke have been hotly debated. Since I have already revealed my hand on both issues, I can have no qualms about going further, to point out specific thematic and verbal parallels.

We have seen (chapter 3) that a major part of Josephus's appeal to his Roman audience involves the presentation of Judaism as a national philosophy. Moses is the founding teacher, and his teachings have been handed down intact by a "succession" of high priests. Like other philosophies, Judaism offers "well being" *(eudaimonia)* to those who carefully observe the teachings of Moses. Like other philosophies it teaches virtue, which means piety toward God and justice toward one's fellows. Prominent figures from Israel's past, such as Abraham and Solomon, in addition to Moses, were philosophers as well as great leaders. And like

Greco-Roman society, Jewish culture has traditional schools *(haireseis;* singular *hairesis),* which debate philosophical issues like the immortality of the soul or the roles of fate and free will in human actions. Josephus explicitly compares the Pharisees to Stoics and the Essenes to Pythagoreans; he insinuates that the Sadducees are Jewish equivalents of the Epicureans. His bid to make Judaism a philosophy is already implicit in the *War,* but is fully developed in the *Antiquities* and *Against Apion.*

We also noted in chapter 3 that Judaism appeared as a philosophy to its earliest outside observers. One can speculate about the reasons for this. On the theoretical level, it had no images of God, unlike all other cults, but considered the Deity invisible and indescribable, just as the philosophers did. On the practical level, outside of Judea the Jews had no temples and performed no sacrifices, in contrast to other cults. Rather, they met to study revered books, hear moral exhortation, and pray. Converts to Judaism adopted an entirely new lifestyle in accord with a comprehensive code. To outsiders, this kind of activity might have seemed more typical of a philosophical school than of a religious group. Nevertheless, by the Roman period, most non-Jewish writers saw Judaism primarily as the religion or "superstition" of the Judeans, sometimes as a corruption of originally noble philosophical ideas. Several Jewish writers before Josephus had invoked current philosophical language to describe aspects of Jewish thought, but Josephus offers by far the most comprehensive attempt to interpret the whole of Jewish culture—its origins, history, leading figures, ethics, and religious groups—in philosophical terms.

It is another noteworthy coincidence, then, that Luke seems to present early Christianity as a philosophical school within the Jewish orbit. While he does not make the claim explicit, much of his language has philosophical overtones, and its cumulative effect is strong. His portrayal of Christianity thus intersects precisely with Josephus's portrayal of Judaism as a philosophy. It fits with Luke's goal of rooting Christianity in Jewish history that he should try to make it another "school" *(hairesis)*—one founded by Jesus—in addition to those mentioned by Josephus. Consider some of the evidence.

In the preface to his gospel, Luke uses two standard terms from the vocabulary of philosophical schools. First, he speaks of a succession of teaching from the teacher. He will record the deeds of Jesus, "even as those who from the beginning were eyewitnesses and servants of the word *handed* them *down* to us" (Luke 1:2). This word is the same one that Josephus used to describe Moses' "handing down" of the laws to the succession of priests, and the Pharisees' tradition, which was "handed down" from the fathers. By Luke's time of writing, the deeds of the revered founder of Christianity have become a tradition that must be carefully guarded from error. This recalls the concern of the Greco-Roman philosophical schools to preserve their various traditions through successions of teachers.

Another interesting term in Luke's preface is *asphaleia:* Luke writes so that Theophilus might come to realize the "secure basis" of what he has been taught. Although this word is characteristic of historical prefaces, as we have seen, philosophers also used the term to describe their efforts. Their goal was to provide a sure basis for ethical action. The philosopher Plutarch (ca. 100 C.E.) distinguishes philosophy from superstition on the ground that only philosophy offers a way of seeing the world that is "secure" (*Superst.* 171E). Justin Martyr (mid-second century), having set out to find a "philosophy which is secure and profitable" (*Dial.* 8.1), finally became a Christian. Although he uses a different Greek word, Justin's contemporary Lucian has one of his characters turn to philosophy in order to find a "plain, solid path in life" (*Men.* 4). These words had numerous other applications, but their appearance in the preface to Luke fits the notion that he wanted to present the religion of Jesus as a philosophy.

Second, Luke-Acts devotes considerable space to a critique of wealth, luxury, and the hypocrisy of the powerful. Yet these themes were staples of Greco-Roman philosophy. Virtually all philosophical schools agreed that the simple life, perhaps even poverty, was most conducive to the purity of the soul. Thus Paul's contemporary Seneca, though wealthy himself, says: "Riches have shut off many a man from the attainment of wisdom; poverty is unburdened and free" (*Ep.*17.3). He summarizes the heart of his teaching:

> We talk much about despising money, and we give advice on this subject in the lengthiest of speeches, that mankind may believe true riches to exist in the mind and not in one's bank account, and that the man who adapts himself to his slender means and makes himself wealthy on a little sum, is the truly rich man. (*Ep.* 108.11, LCL)

He claims that when the philosophers utter proverbs against greed, such as "The poor lack much; the greedy man lacks all" or "He needs but little who desires but little," the crowds break out in thunderous applause—even the wealthy and the greedy (*Ep.* 108.9, 11–12)! Another philosopher sounds very modern when he says of happiness: "It is not in possessions. If you doubt that, . . . look at the rich nowadays, the amount of lamentation with which their life is filled" (Epictetus, *Diatr.* 3.22.27, LCL).

As for hypocrisy, Seneca devotes one of his moral epistles to the theme of "practicing what you preach." He says:

> Philosophy teaches us to act, not to speak; it exacts of every man that he should live according to his own standards, that his life should not be out of harmony with his words. . . . This, I say, is the highest duty and the highest proof of wisdom,—that deed and word should be in accord. (*Ep.* 20.2, LCL)

Lucian scorns teachers who fail to live by their own principles (*Men.* 5), and Epictetus mercilessly satirizes philosophers who spout lofty wisdom but do not put it into practice (*Diatr.* 2.9.13–22). Ever since Socrates, the image of the philosopher as "gadfly," relentlessly challenging the established order and especially those in power, had been basic to the enterprise of philosophy.

If we now return to Luke-Acts we find that Jesus and his followers represent these standard features of moral philosophy. In Luke's narrative, Jesus is born in an animal's stable (2:7, 16). As his poor parents lack the influence to find more fitting accommodation, they also lack the resources to present a sacrificial lamb at the temple; they can give only a pair of birds (2:24). Jesus' keynote address promises especially good news for the poor (4:18), and Luke's version of the beatitudes bears this out: it is the truly poor, not Matthew's "poor in spirit," who receive the reign of God. Only Luke includes alongside the good news of the beatitudes *bad news* for the rich and complacent (6:20–26; cf. Matt 5:3–11). In this story, even John the Baptist offers advice to the crowds about how to live simply (3:10–14). Jesus' only lethal conflict, accordingly, is reserved for his encounter with the supremely powerful, the Jerusalem priestly aristocracy.

Much of the material found only in Luke underscores Jesus' concern for the poor and disdain for the rich. Only Luke's Jesus tells the story of the foolish man whose prosperity drove him to tear down his barns and build bigger ones, to find security in his wealth (cf. *Gos. Thom.* 63). Like other philosophers, Jesus declares that a man's wealth does not consist in the amount of his possessions (12:13–21). Only

Luke has Jesus castigate the well-to-do host of a banquet for inviting only friends and rich neighbors, not the poor and destitute (14:1–14). It is in Luke that we find the poignant story of the rich man who dies and then longs for relief from his torment, while poor Lazarus, who had lived in abject suffering and poverty, is consoled in Abraham's bosom (16:19–31). Only Luke tells of the self-critical and repentant tax-collector, who is justified ahead of the complacent religious authority (18:9–14). Luke's Jesus sides with the defenseless widow who makes a nuisance of herself pleading for justice from a callous judge (18:1–8).

In Luke, then, Jesus is pitted against a smug, privileged establishment, whose representatives are "lovers of money" (16:14). Although highly trained in intellectual matters, like the logic-choppers and rhetoricians denounced by Seneca and Epictetus, they are incapable of offering real help to those in need. Jesus appears as a gadfly, to use Socrates's image, castigating these leaders for their misplaced values. Accordingly, as one scholar has recently shown, Luke portrays Jesus' death in a way that recalls the death of Socrates in Plato's *Phaedo.*[15] In keeping with his portrayal of Jesus, Luke goes on to claim that Jesus' followers shared all of their goods in common. They "sold their property and possessions and distributed the proceeds to everyone, according to a person's need" (Acts 2:44–45; 4:32–35). This idyllic portrayal of the Christian community recalls both the legendary followers of Pythagoras and Josephus's Essenes—a Jewish philosophical school.

Third, in his famous Areopagite scene at Athens (Acts 17:16–34), Luke deliberately places Paul in dialogue with Stoics and Epicureans (17:18) as a competitor in the philosophical marketplace. In keeping with his obligation to craft plausible speeches, Luke does not have Paul appeal to Scripture to support his claims, for that would mean nothing to his Greek audience. Rather, Paul begins in a philosophical tone by arguing that there is one God behind all of the religious aspirations of different nations. In support of his assertion that God is "not far from each one of us," he cites two noted Greek authors to the effect that "In him we live and move and have our being" and "We are all God's offspring" (Epimenides and Aratus, respectively). But these slogans were precisely what the Stoics believed—that there was one divine spirit animating all of life. Luke's Paul here anticipates Christian apologists such as Justin

[15] See John S. Kloppenborg, "*Exitus clari viri:* The Death of Jesus in Luke," *Toronto Journal of Theology* 8/1 (1992): 106–20.

Martyr. Justin will connect Christian teaching with the best of Greco-Roman philosophy on the ground that the one principle of truth *(logos)*, though most clearly embodied in Christ, was already given to those of all times and places who "lived reasonably" (*1 Apol.* 1.46). Thus Paul's Areopagite address strengthens Luke's presentation of Christianity as a philosophy.

Fourth, one of the goals of philosophers in the first century was bold, fearless, frank speech *(parrhēsia)*. This frequently got them into trouble, especially if their audience included a humorless emperor. Several famous philosophers in the later first century, especially under Nero and the Flavian dynasty, faced death or exile for their endless moral prattling. One reporter complains that the offenders behaved "as if it were the function of philosophy to insult those in power, to stir up the multitudes, to overthrow the established order of things" (Dio Cassius, *Hist. rom.* 65.12.2). As Epictetus said before he was exiled by Domitian, "Tyranny hates wisdom" (*Diatr.* 1.29.10). The mark of a true philosopher therefore was a determination to speak with *parrhēsia*, without regard for the consequences. This is exactly what we find among the early Christian preachers, according to Luke.

The word occurs only five times in Acts, but at strategic places. In his opening address, Peter sets the tone by claiming to confront the Jews on the issue of Jesus' resurrection with *parrhēsia* (2:29). In the repeated conflicts of chapter 4 between the apostles and the aristocratic magistrates, the word appears three times: first, the judges are amazed at the *parrhēsia* of these unschooled men; then the disciples pray for the ability to continue their *bold* manner of confrontation (4:29); and finally, their prayer is answered so that they once again speak with *boldness* (4:31). The importance of this theme is clear from the fact that Acts closes with the statement that Paul, though under house arrest in Rome, was "preaching the kingdom of God and teaching about the Lord Jesus with all *parrhēsia*, unhindered (28.31)." Just as Jesus appeared in the gospel of Luke as a tenacious critic of the wealthy and powerful, so his followers now appear as a fearless but persecuted, truth-loving minority.

It is truly remarkable that Acts takes over Josephus's classification of the Pharisees and Sadducees as "philosophical schools" (*haireseis;* 5:17; 15:5; 26:5), as if this terminology were self-evidently appropriate. The powerful "school of the Sadducees" opposes Jesus' followers (Acts 5:17), and some believers who belong to the "school of the Pharisees" insist on circumcising Gentile converts (Acts 15:5). Luke's Paul even calls the Pharisaic group the "most precise school" among the Jews (Acts 26:5). This is a triple coincidence because: the school language is part of Josephus's presentation; "precision" *(akribeia)* is also one of Josephus's key terms; and Josephus routinely claims that the Pharisees are reputed to be the most precise of the schools (*War* 1.110; 2.162; *Ant.* 17.41; *Life* 189). We do not know of any author but Josephus who called the Pharisees and Sadducees "philosophical schools" or the Pharisees the most precise school, yet we do know that this presentation fits with Josephus's carefully developed defense of Judaism. If Luke did not know of Josephus's work, how did this language suggest itself to him?

Still more interesting is that Acts presents the Christian faith as yet another Jewish school *(hairesis)*. The Jews who accuse Paul claim that he is a ringleader of the "school of the Nazarenes" (24:5). In his defense, Paul prefers to call Christianity the Way (or Path) but admits that *they* call it a "school" (24:14). When Paul speaks with the leaders of the Jewish community in Rome, they too have heard of this "school," and that it is spoken against by everyone (28:22). By applying the title "school" to Christianity, Acts implicitly places it within the world of Judaism, alongside the Pharisees and Sadducees.

It has been objected, against this interpretation, that the designation of the church as a school is rejected by Luke's Paul (24:15) and elsewhere appears only on the lips of Jews (24:5; 28:22). But this objection misses the point. Luke's Paul disdains the title of "school" not because he wants to dissociate Christianity from the established Jewish system, but rather because he thinks that the Christian "way" is for *all* Jews. He does not want the Christian truth claims to be seen as matters of dispute like the mundane issues that divide the other schools. Nevertheless, although Luke and his Paul would prefer that all Jews recognized Jesus as Messiah and Lord, he is quite happy to concede that, until then, they do at least recognize the church as one school within the Jewish community. By placing this acknowledgment matter-of-factly on the lips of the Jewish leadership, he cleverly avoids the impression that it is *he* who is bidding to bring the church under the sociopolitical shelter of Judaism. He can have his cake and eat it too.

In the interest of the church's social survival, then, Luke will tolerate the status of "Jewish philosophical school" until a better alternative comes along. This option will not be so readily available to later Christian apologists, because of the obvious distance between Judaism and

Christianity by the mid-second century. But Luke is keenly aware of the charges of "novelty" that plague the church. His only recourse at the end of the first century is to ground the Christian Path solidly in Jewish history. He wants to show that the young church, though viewed by established Judaism (he claims) as merely one of its several schools, is really a victim of the Jews' legendary intransigence—from the Roman perspective, after 70.

Now we must ask how Luke came to settle on the approach of presenting Christianity as a philosophical school, founded by Jesus, but solidly within Judaism. It is possible, of course, that many of the factors that led Josephus to present Judaism as a philosophy independently led Luke to the same strategy. Like Judaism, Christianity differed markedly from the ordinary religions of the Greco-Roman world. It was an international body that had no ethnic base, no temple, no images of its God, and no sacrifice. Instruction and moral exhortation formed a large part of its communal life, in addition to rituals of a nonsacrificial nature. Conversion to Christianity required a radical change of lifestyle.

These factors might indeed account for Luke's decision to portray Christianity as a philosophy, as his second-century successors—Justin Martyr and Athenagoras—would later do even more forcefully. But these general social conditions do not explain the marked similarities of language to Josephus's narrative, especially the description of Pharisees and Sadducees as philosophical schools and the insinuation of Christianity as their partner within Judaism. It seems more likely that Luke is building directly on Josephus's portrayal of Judaism as a philosophy by firmly embedding the church within that context. Thus, the Christians, though scarcely mentioned by Josephus, constitute yet another school within Judaism. Their denigration by the Jews results only from their fearless "gadfly" activity, confronting the complacent majority with their truth and superior "way."

This hypothesis also explains why Luke, if he is drawing details of Jewish life from Josephus, makes no mention of the Essenes, whom Josephus admires so greatly. The obvious explanation for this omission is that in Luke's portrayal the Christians take the place of the Essenes. Recall that Josephus had depicted that group as the most philosophical of all Jews, sharing everything in common, living peaceful and disciplined lives, and accordingly having powers of healing and prophecy. In Acts, it is the school of the Nazarenes, or Christians, that fulfills this role. They share their goods, live in peace, practice healing, exorcism, and prophecy, and shame all other Jews with their love of the truth. To include the Essenes in his narrative would have caused needless problems for the author of Acts, for that group would have been in direct competition with the Christians!

So it seems that the author of Luke-Acts tries to do for Christianity much of what Josephus has done for Judaism. He completes Josephus's picture of an idyllic philosophical nation, with three recognized schools, by making Jesus and the Christians the most sincere philosophers of all: they challenge the complacent establishment, which explains why the Jews dislike them.

CONCLUSION

In this chapter we have seen that Luke-Acts is unique among the NT writings in the extent of its affinities with Josephus's narratives. To begin with, both authors employ the same genre or literary type to convey their message: they both consciously adopt the forms of Hellenistic history. They have good reason to do so, since they want to make their groups seem part of the established order. Yet that very goal sets them apart from other Hellenistic histories, for they both write as outsiders, trying to commend their causes to the world. In attempting to legitimate their respective faiths, both writers had one eye on their own membership; Luke may even have had new Christians as his primary intended audience.

These similarities of literary type do not require that "Luke" knew Josephus's work. It is true that they resort to similar techniques. They go to great lengths to demonstrate that their communities are friendly to Rome, have ancient traditions, and espouse the highest moral ideals. Both authors minimize internal conflicts in their desire to portray unified, centrally administered, disciplined bodies. But these generic agreements may result only from the similar pressures that they faced: the Jew and the Christian had to show that their constituencies, which seemed troublesome to the Romans in view of the revolt, Jesus' crucifixion, and withdrawal from normal civic-religious life, were in fact respectable and politically harmless components of the empire.

More suggestive of a relationship between the works is the striking number of incidents reported in common. In several cases—Agrippa I's death, Felix and Drusilla, Agrippa II and Berenice—Luke's narrative seems to depend squarely on such information as Josephus presents. In other cases—the complex of events associated with the census and ensuing rebel movements—Luke regularly differs from Josephus in specifics. But his disagreements can be readily understood as conflations of Josephus's narrative, resulting from imperfect memory or deliberate schematization. Since the conflated elements lie together only in the narrative that Josephus constructed, as far as we know, Luke's product is much more difficult to explain if he had no knowledge of Josephus.

Most telling, however, is Luke's presentation of Christianity as a "philosophical school" within Judaism, alongside the other schools but based on the teachings of its founder Jesus. To my knowledge, Josephus is the only Jewish writer who undertook a systematic account of the Pharisees, Sadducees, and Essenes as "schools," and of the Pharisees as reputedly the "most precise school." Although Luke might have been moved to adopt the theme "Christianity as philosophy" independently, his agreement with peculiar features of Josephus's narrative suggest that he was building directly on the more famous work of the Jewish historian. He was saying, in effect: You know what Josephus said about the nobility of history and tradition. Well, we Christians are part of the same culture; we are another school, alongside the Pharisees and Sadducees. We agree in many respects with the Pharisees (cf. Acts 23:6–9), but the obstinate Jewish leadership (witness the recent war) finds us troublesome because of our devotion to truth.

I cannot prove beyond doubt that Luke knew the writings of Josephus. If he did not, however, we have a nearly incredible series of coincidences, which require that Luke knew something that closely approximated Josephus's narrative in several distinct ways. This source (or these sources) spoke of: Agrippa's death after his robes shone; the extramarital affairs of both Felix and Agrippa II; the harshness of the Sadducees toward Christianity; the census under Quirinius as a watershed event in Palestine; Judas the Galilean as an arch rebel at the time of the census; Judas, Theudas, and the unnamed "Egyptian" as three rebels in the Jerusalem area worthy of special mention among a host of others; Theudas and Judas in the same piece of narrative; the Egyptian, the desert, and the *sicarii* in close proximity; Judaism as a philosophical system; the Pharisees and Sadducees as philosophical schools; and the Pharisees as the most precise of the schools. We know of no other work that even remotely approximated Josephus's presentation on such a wide range of issues. I find it easier to believe that Luke knew something of Josephus's work than that he independently arrived at these points of agreement. Nevertheless, further study may provide alternatives.

Of course, if Luke did know Josephus, then we can fix the date of Luke in the mid-90s or later, for Josephus finished the *Antiquities,* the major work in question, in 93. Luke may have heard an earlier version or only a part of the work recited, perhaps in 90 or so. But a date of 95 or later for Luke would seem most plausible if he knew *Antiquities* 18–20. Although such a late date may seem troubling at first, I see no cause for concern. Even without the hypothesis that Luke knew Josephus, most scholars date Luke-Acts to the 80s or 90s or even later, on entirely different grounds. Most important, he reflects a period when the era of the apostles was seen as a bygone "golden age" of serenity; the sharp intramural conflicts of Paul's letters appear only as mild disputes, resolved with good will. Furthermore, the author assumes that a high degree of church structure is normal. So the acceptance of Luke's knowledge of Josephus would not have radical implications for dating Luke-Acts.

FOR FURTHER READING

Perhaps the most efficient way to get a sense of ancient historiography is to peruse the short work, *How History Should be Written,* by Lucian of Samosata in the middle of the second century. Lucian collects the commonplace views of history-writing from Josephus's time and later. For an analysis of Lucian in relationship to practicing ancient historians, see:

- G. Avenarius, *Lukians Schrift zur Geschichtsschreibung* (Meisenheim am Glan: Anton Hain, 1956).

Readable introductions to ancient historiography include:

- J. B. Bury, *The Ancient Greek Historians* (New York: Dover, 1909; repr. 1958).
- Arnold J. Toynbee, *Greek Historical Thought: From Homer to the Age of Heraclitus* (New York: New American Library, 1952).
- Michael Grant, *The Ancient Historians* (London: George Weidenfeld & Nicolson, 1970).
- Arnaldo Momigliano, *The Classical Foundations of Modern Historiography* (Berkeley: University of California Press, 1990).

- John Marincola, *Authority and Tradition in Ancient Historiography* (Cambridge: Cambridge University Press, 1997).
- Ronald Mellor, *The Roman Historians* (London: Routledge, 1998).
- Christopher Pelling, *Literary Texts and the Greek Historian* (London: Routledge, 2000).

On Luke-Acts in its historical environment, the classic study is:

- Frederick J. Foakes Jackson, Kirsopp Lake, and Henry J. Cadbury, *The Beginnings of Christianity*, vol. 1, *The Acts of the Apostles* (5 vols.; London: Macmillan, 1920–1933).

This has been updated in recent years by the new multivolume project:

- Bruce Winter, ed., *The Book of Acts in its First Century Setting* (6 vols.; Grand Rapids: Eerdmans/Carlisle: Paternoster, 1993–1998).

Other studies of Luke-Acts that pay particular attention to its historiographical and literary associations include:

- Robert L. Brawley, *Luke-Acts and the Jews: Conflict, Apology, and Conciliation* (Atlanta: Scholars Press, 1987).
- Martin Dibelius, *Studies in the Acts of the Apostles* (trans. Heinrich Greeven; London: SCM, 1956).
- Leander Keck and J. Louis Martyn, *Studies in Luke-Acts* (Philadelphia: Fortress, 1980).
- Heinz Schreckenberg, "Flavius Josephus und die lukanischen Schriften," in *Wort in der Zeit: Neutestamentliche Studien: Festgabe für Karl Henirich Rengstorf zum 75. Geburtstag* (ed. W. Haubeck and M. Bachmann; Leiden: Brill, 1980), 179–209.
- Charles H. Talbert, ed. *Luke-Acts: New Perspectives from the Society of Biblical Literature Seminar* (New York: Crossroad, 1983–1984).
- Richard Pervo, *Profit with Delight: The Literary Genre of the Acts of the Apostles* (Philadelphia: Fortress, 1987).
- Jack T. Sanders, *The Jews in Luke-Acts* (London: SCM/Philadelphia: Fortress, 1987).
- David E. Aune, *The New Testament in Its Literary Environment* (Philadelphia: Westminster, 1987), 77–157.
- John A. Darr, *On Character Building: The Reader and the Rhetoric of Characterization in Luke-Acts* (Louisville: Westminster John Knox, 1992).

- John S. Kloppenborg, "*Exitus Clari Viri:* The Death of Jesus in Luke," *Toronto Journal of Theology* 8/1 (1992): 106–20 = John S. Kloppenborg and Leif E. Vaage, *Scriptures and Cultural Conversations: Essays for Heinz Guenther at 65,* forthcoming.
- Gregory E. Sterling, *Historiography and Self-Definition: Josephos, Luke-Acts and Apologetic Historiography* (Leiden: Brill, 1992).
- Loveday Alexander, *The Preface to Luke: Literary Convention and Social Context in Luke 1:1–4 and Acts 1:1* (Cambridge: Cambridge University Press, 1993).

For the problems of Christian self-definition over against Judaism and in relation to Hellenistic-Roman culture, see:

- Hans Conzelmann, *Heiden—Juden—Christen* (Tübingen: Mohr Siebeck, 1981).
- E. P. Sanders, Ben F. Meyer, et al., *Jewish and Christian Self-Definition* (3 vols.; London: SCM, 1980–).

Conclusion

The Significance of Josephus for New Testament Study

I wrote this book in order to introduce the NT reader to the most significant nonbiblical writer for NT interpretation. Although Josephus's name is widely known, his writings seem bewildering and impenetrable on a first approach. My goal therefore was to sketch out a map of this territory, to indicate some highlights and features "not to be missed." If successful, this tour guide will have left more questions than answers, along with a desire to explore the territory for oneself. As the reader probes more deeply, even the information offered here may seem not to be information at all, but only my faulty interpretation of the data. Some readers may ultimately decide that Josephus had no sincere interest in promoting his nation, that John the Baptist consciously declared Jesus to be Messiah, or that Luke could not possibly have known Josephus's writings. I am willing to take that risk. All history is, at bottom, someone's formulation of the past. It usually happens that we find the first maps offered to us defective: as we experience the territory in question, we see things that were not on the map and routes that are no longer open. But none of this diminishes the need for a map in the first place.

Before summarizing the results and implications of this book, it may be helpful to recall what we did not set out to do. This study was not intended to be an exhaustive analysis of the relationship between Josephus and the NT. The areas that were not discussed far outnumber those that were. We said almost nothing, for example, about the versions of the Bible used by Josephus and the NT authors, about Josephus on the historical geography of Palestine, the temple and its service, the economic and social conditions of Jerusalem, Galilean history and geography, the Samaritans, the Jewish communities of the diaspora, or about numerous other topics that are pertinent to the study of the NT. These are the kinds of issues usually taken up in reference works and studies of "NT backgrounds." The fact is that virtually every line of Josephus's copious work is relevant in some way or other to NT interpretation. We have merely sighted and described the proverbial tip of the iceberg.

We have looked first at Josephus on his own terms (chapters 1–3). That phrase, "on his own terms," is admittedly deceptive, because we do not have immediate or objective access to his life; we can only *interpret* what he has left behind. Nevertheless, we can resolve to avoid some of the most obvious errors of the past. We can at least make it our goal to understand him *in his world,* recognizing that he did not write some kind of "fact book" from which we can cut and paste, and that he did not intend to be a witness to the truth of Christianity. He was a man of at least moderate intelligence who wrote because he had important stories to tell. So our questions were: Who was this man? What did he do? What are his writings about?

Pursuing these questions, we found an apparently sharp conflict between the common view of his biography and his major writings. His biography, on the one hand, especially the period from his assumption of "command" in Galilee to his surrender to the Romans, is filled with contradictions and unanswered questions. It may well seem, though we cannot be certain, that he has a great deal to hide. Moreover, the rest of his life story is told in such thoroughly rhetorical terms that we can learn little about it. His major writings, on the other hand, are bold attempts to defend and even commend Jewish culture in the Greco-Roman world. In the face of anti-Jewish government policies, widespread popular resentment, and violence after the failed Judean revolt, he goes to incredible lengths to argue before his circle of benevolent readers that Jews are typically cooperative with those in power *(War),* that they have an ancient and respectable history, and that their influence on the world is thoroughly beneficial *(Antiquities, Against Apion).*

Although we might wish to make a final decision about Josephus's character, on the basis of his career, I have argued that several factors prevent us from doing that responsibly. (a) Any account of his personal life must be hypothetically reconstructed, and no reconstruction has yet won widespread acceptance. By contrast, we know what he wrote in defense of Judaism. (b) He seems deliberately to play up his own duplicity and deviousness, for rhetorical effect. (c) Like any political figure, especially an aristocrat involved in a war, not least in the Middle East, Josephus must have had all sorts of genuinely divided loyalties; we cannot assume that he always had a clear direction of any sort. And (d) even if he did fail morally, people cannot be so easily separated into the good and the bad. If we removed all moral failures from the ranks of the great, those ranks would be sorely depleted.

Armed with some initial awareness of (my interpretation of) Josephus's life and writings, we proceeded to consider his direct relevance for the study of the NT. We looked first at his accounts of some key figures in the background of the NT—the family of King Herod, the Roman governors of Judea, the high priesthood, and the religious groups in Palestine. In each case, our goal was to understand these groups as they function in Josephus's own narratives. What this showed was that everyone who recounts the past necessarily interprets it. This means that the historical questions "What really happened? What were these people *really* like?" so far remain largely unanswered. To answer them would require further investigation, which would develop hypotheses to explain the accounts in Josephus and the NT as well as other written sources and, in some cases, archaeological evidence. We must accept that, in the end, some of these questions may not be answerable with historical probability. Our goal was much more limited, namely, to understand how an important author of the period integrated these figures of interest to the NT reader into his writings, which are quite different in outlook from the NT texts.

Chapter 5 examined what Josephus has to say about figures from the Christian tradition. He mentions only three—John the Baptist, Jesus, and James—and these very briefly. In the case of John the Baptist, Josephus provides a crucial perspective from outside the NT. In that single case, I made bold to proceed to a historical hypothesis about the real Baptist, to illustrate how Josephus's accounts might be used in historical reconstruction. But that exercise also highlighted the degree to which Josephus, as much as any other writer, interprets the past and does not simply report it. His account of Jesus is filled with textual problems, and the investigation of those was a welcome reminder of the distance between ancient texts and our modern English translations.

Finally, his note about the death of Jesus' brother James, in spite of its brevity, provided a valuable supplement to the NT's few references to this prominent but little-known figure.

It seemed advisable to devote a separate chapter (6) to the relationship between Josephus and Luke-Acts. Regardless of how one settles this famous problem, the parallels of genre between the two works illuminate the interpretation of Luke-Acts. We see here a two-volume history written according to current conventions, which shares with Josephus's works the goal of explaining the culture and values of a minority community to a small circle of more influential friends. But it seems that we can go further. Close inspection of the many affinities between Josephus and Luke-Acts indicates that Luke probably knew—in some way or other—the writings of his famous Jewish contemporary. He appears to build his case for Christianity squarely on the foundation of Josephus's case for Judaism. If he is not doing so, the coincidences are remarkable.

What, then, is the significance of Josephus for NT interpretation? On the one hand, a few particular points emerge from this study. (a) Josephus wrote as a bold advocate of what he considered the finest constitution and noblest culture known to the world. (b) Therefore, although Josephus is the most valuable nonbiblical source for understanding the NT, his outlook was fundamentally at odds with that of Paul and most other NT writers, who believed that Judaism per se had been made obsolete with the coming of Christ. (c) His aim was ignored by later Christians, who used him as a witness against Judaism. (d) To understand any given passage in Josephus, one must recognize that it is part of a larger story, and attempt to understand the passage within the terms of that story. The NT reader in particular must resist the temptation to assimilate Josephus too quickly to the NT environment. (e) Nevertheless, since he often includes significant accounts of people, places, and events that intersect with the NT world, his portrayal offers us an invaluable "outside" perspective.

On the other hand, our analysis of Josephus and the NT has direct implications for the relationship between faith and history: What role can history play in Christian (or other) faith? History is popularly considered to consist of the mass of established facts about the past, as a set of known events written down somewhere. With this view in mind, many NT readers profess an interest in "the history of the period," by which they mean the *background* of the NT, the manners and customs of first-century Jews, the religious, social, political, and economic world in which Christianity was born. The NT stood by itself as a serene island of divine revelation, while "history" swirled around it.

But we have seen that such history, comprising pure facts about the past, does not exist anywhere. By definition, the past—Vespasian's campaign against the Jews, the career of Josephus in Galilee, or the aims of John the Baptist—no longer exists. So it is not immediately accessible to us. We have only traces of the past: occasional physical remnants, like a piece of pottery or papyrus, and literary interpretations of certain periods in texts such as Tacitus's, Josephus's, and Luke's. And these people did not write about their times merely to generate chronicles of facts; they carefully selected episodes that would help them make their points. Their accounts are thoroughly conditioned by: (a) the limited information available to them; (b) their assumptions and values; (c) their habits of thought and speech; and (d) their conscious literary purposes. Indeed these same factors affect even our television news. It is also a product of someone's conscious and unconscious perspective—decisions about what *is* news, limitations of camera angles, choice of how much context to supply, commentators' choice of vocabulary. If perspective is unavoidable even where we have video cameras and satellite relays, how much more does it figure in any text from the Greco-Roman world?

History, therefore, is not simply a matter of reading whatever portrayals of the past happened to survive. It is a much more active enterprise, a kind of detective work requiring the interpreter to try to recreate the past. Such a re-creation can only be hypothetical: the historian sets out to develop the hypothesis that will best explain all of the available evidence. Strictly speaking, then, there are no historical facts—in the simple sense of self-evident truths about the past—but only hypotheses that range from highly probable to scarcely conceivable. We have one portrait of John the Baptist in Mark, another in Josephus, another in John, and perhaps another in Q. Which one does the historian accept? He or she appreciates all of them, but must then go on to develop a hypothesis that will explain all of them. This activity produces still another interpretation, but one that will be more plausible because it explains more of the surviving evidence. So the historian is a detective who listens carefully to each surviving witness, but then proceeds to create a new and independent hypothesis on a given question.

Once we read Josephus historically, we are compelled to read the NT, written by his contemporaries, in the same way. When we become sensitive to his perspectives, we want to know those of the NT authors. When we see how the census under Quirinius functions in his narrative, we want to know how it serves Luke's story. When we see how he chooses Pontius Pilate to mark a shift toward unbearable and incompetent Roman rule in Judea, we become more aware of the gospel writers' limitations and biases. Similarly, his discussions of the Pharisees and Sadducees, the high priesthood, or any other element of Jewish culture, force us to ask how the NT writers present them. In other words, history is not something behind and outside of the NT, its background, but the NT texts themselves must become subject to historical analysis if we are to rediscover something of first-century realities.

Index of Subjects

Abraham, 103, 114, 283
Adiabene, 115–16, 237
Aelia Capitolina, 24
Against Apion, 11, 65, 103, 132–40, 267, 280
Agapius, 230–31, 234
Agrippa I, 9, 118, 152–53, 155, 158, 163, 282, 291–92
Agrippa II, 9, 76, 86, 95, 98, 118, 129–30, 138, 153, 155, 158, 163–64, 170, 186, 237–38, 240–41, 244–45, 260; incest, 158, 164, 282, 291–92
Albinus, 170, 175, 239, 244–45
Alexander Janneus, 198
Alexandra Salome, 117, 198–99
Alexandria, 52, 60, 104, 158
Antiochus Epiphanes, 134, 271
Antipater, 154, 156, 165
Antonia fortress, 91
Antonius Felix, 97, 165, 170, 174, 176, 191, 251, 258, 277–78
Antony, 73
Apion, 104, 133, 137
Apollonius Molon, 133
Apollonius of Tyana, 39
Arch of Titus, 265
Archelaus, 9, 152, 160, 165, 197, 273, 275
Aretas IV, 214
Aristobulus I, 74, 108, 198
Aristocracy. See Jewish or Roman.
Aristotle, 80, 105, 133, 240
Athenagoras, 290
Augustus, 57, 73, 97, 106, 182, 242, 259, 276

Bandits. See tyrants.
Bannus, 39, 41, 195, 204
Berenice, 118, 158, 164, 282
Bethlehem, 160, 275
Books, 66, 94–96, 136, 199, 253, 258–59, 282

C. Cassius Longinus, 73, 97
Caesarea Maritima, 52, 163, 166, 170
Cannibalism, 11, 14, 84, 93
Cato, 69
Celsus, 22, 62
Census, 160, 172, 273–76, 279, 282, 292, 302
Cestius Gallus, 18, 98
Chief priests. See high priests.
Christians, 10, 180, 218, 231, 258, 266, 272; and Jews, 20, 229, 251, 267, 290, 292; misuse of Josephus, 10, 17, 19–20, 22, 141, 172, 228, 232, 300
Cicero, 57, 61–62, 69, 105–7, 111, 115, 118, 271, 281
Claudius, 155, 169, 237, 283
Cleopatra, 73
Coliseum, 61
Coponius, 166
Critolaus, 71
Cumanus, 169, 173, 178
Cuspius Fadus, 172, 279

Daniel, 49, 50, 92–94, 115, 120–21, 138, 223–24
Dead Sea Scrolls, 120, 223, 271
Democracy, 78, 109
Diaspora, 13, 298

Dio Cassius, 59, 80, 288
Dio Chrysostom, 69
Diocletian, 57
Diogenes Laertius, 112
Dionysius of Halicarnassus, 80, 99, 104, 258
Domitia Longina, 126
Domitian, 8, 47, 53, 61–62, 66, 86–88, 106, 126, 288

Egyptian false prophet, 277–78, 280–83, 292
Eleazar ben Yair, 274
Eleazar son of Simon, 79, 98
Epaphroditus, 95, 132, 136, 257–59
Epictetus, 59, 111–12, 286–88
Essenes, 89, 96, 115, 155, 166, 194–97, 204, 207, 215, 284, 287, 290–91
Eusebius, 8, 15–17, 19, 39, 230–32, 234

Fourth philosophy, 194, 274
Fortune, 71–72, 89

Gaius Caligula, 109, 117–18, 158, 168
Galba, 48, 80–81
Galilee, 96, 123, 131, 206, 267, 298
Gamala, 91, 98
Gessius Florus, 75–76, 171, 175, 183, 237
Gischala, 98
Greek culture, 55

Hadrian, 24
Hairesis (philosophical schools), 284, 288–90, 292
Hasmoneans, 30, 72–74, 89, 96, 98–99, 108–9, 117, 164–65, 186, 198–99, 204
Hegesippus, 17
Hellenistic history, 252–53, 260–61, 264–65, 272, 282, 291
Herod, 9, 26, 29, 39, 65, 73–74, 89, 96, 98–99, 109, 117–18, 152, 154, 156–57, 159–60, 197, 202, 214, 242, 284; ally to Roman leaders, 59, 73–74; client-kingship, 74, 156, 165, 273; death, 75, 152, 275; descendants, 118, 152, 299
Herod Antipas, 9, 152–53, 157, 161, 214, 216–17, 225
Herodias, 152, 157, 161
Herodotus, 103, 105, 133, 253, 260
High priests, 74, 77, 93, 96, 107–8, 237, 299, 302; Aaron, 107, 181, 185, 271; Ananias, 183, 186, 191; Ananus II, 67–68, 77–79, 98, 180–81, 183–88, 197, 203, 238–47; Annas (Ananus I), 9, 188, 191, 240; Caiaphas, 9, 188, 190, 192; Eleazar son of Ananias, 102, 107, 240, 242; Ishmael son of Phabi, 238; Jesus, 67–68, 77–79, 98, 184, 186; Jonathan, 174; Joseph Kabi, 238; Onias II, 186; Simon son of Gamaliel, 43; Zadok, 181
History, ancient, 66, 259, 260–64
Homer, 37, 46, 231

Idumeans, 79, 67–68, 79, 184, 240
Impietas, 57

James, brother of Jesus, 9, 12, 15, 17, 175, 186, 213, 228, 233, 236–37, 239, 242–43, 246–47, 299–300
Jeremiah, 92–93, 120–21, 138
Jerome, 230–31, 234
Jerusalem, 39, 59–60, 72, 78–79, 90, 96, 267–68, 283, 298; destruction of, 21–23, 52, 60, 63, 69, 83, 85, 88
Jesus, 9, 14, 23–24, 37, 39, 130, 152, 177–80, 189, 206–7, 213, 217–18, 220–22, 226, 228, 232–33, 243, 256–57, 267–69, 271, 275, 286–87, 290, 299
Jewish: antiquity, 103–4, 229, 267; aristocracy, 69, 74–77, 81, 89–93, 108, 168–70, 244; civil war, 104–5, 107–8, 180, 229, 237–38, 267, 271, 300; law, 166, 168–69, 241, 246; military, 89–91; revolt against Rome, 60, 76, 98, 180, 224, 254, 265
Jewish Antiquities, 11, 26, 29, 41, 99–100, 102–3, 107–8, 113, 115–16, 120–21, 129, 155, 158–59, 172, 184–87, 194, 198–99, 213, 215, 226, 238, 242, 284, 293; aristocracy, 108–9, 244; census, 273–74, 279; Essenes, 115, 194–95, 197; Herod, 117–18, 155–58, 160, 202; James, 213, 225, 233, 237,

239, 242; Jesus, 213, 225, 227, 233; Jewish constitution, 103, 105–7, 114, 155, 158, 237, 267; Pharisees, 115, 193–94, 196, 198–99, 202–3, 205; philosophy, 103, 111, 185, 194, 208, 274; Roman governors, 171–75, 238, 245; Sadducees, 115, 193–94, 196–97, 199, 205, 241, 284
Jewish War, 8, 11, 14, 26, 29, 36, 41–42, 47, 63–67, 78, 86, 88–89, 129, 154, 159, 183–84, 188, 198, 273–74; cannibalism, 11, 14, 84, 93; Essenes, 155, 194–95, 197, 207, 215; governors, 172, 174–75; Pharisees, 193–95, 198, 202, 244; Roman audience, 94–98; Roman propaganda, 65, 68, 88, 92, 100; Sadducees, 193–94, 284; Titus's clemency, 82–85, 88
Jews, 58–59, 178; as a tribe, 232; "atheists," 60, 214; "Christ killers," 22–23, 25; hostility towards, 60, 62–64, 265; "misanthropes," 60, 62, 138, 195, 214, 270
John, gospel of, 179, 192, 218, 246, 256
John Hyrcanus, 38, 108, 183, 197–99, 202
John of Gischala, 42–43, 79, 83, 98, 124, 127, 203
John the Baptist, 9, 12, 152, 160–61, 208, 213–24, 299, 301
Josephus, 8, 9, 11, 20, 24–28, 30–31, 38–39, 41, 44, 52–53, 63–64, 68, 70, 72, 82, 93, 95, 114, 118–20, 131, 135, 141, 154, 158–59, 202–3, 214–15, 226, 231–32, 252, 254, 264, 271, 273, 283, 299; aristocrat, 55, 77, 88, 131, 206, 299; census, 274–75, 279, 292, 302; Christianizing of, 8, 17, 229, 234; divine mission, 45, 47, 52; education, 40–41, 70; Essene involvement, 30, 39, 41, 194, 204; fate, 28, 114, 156, 284; general, 42–43, 70, 77, 84–85, 89, 98, 165, 203, 298, 301; Hasmonean descent, 30, 38, 72, 183, 197–99; Herodian history, 153, 156, 159–61; historian, 70, 252, 254; Palestinian geography, 9, 10, 79, 298; Pharisee, 29–30, 39, 41, 196, 198, 199, 204–6, 302; philosophy, 113, 194–95, 205, 274, 292; prediction of Vespasian's rule, 47–48, 50, 182; priestly heritage, 38, 52, 70, 74, 180–82, 206; prophet, 20, 47, 139; rhetoric, 36, 46, 53, 141, 159, 240–41, 298–99; Sadducees, 30, 39, 41, 196–97, 202, 204, 302; speeches, 259–61; surrender at Jotapata, 44–46, 72, 98, 182, 298; traitor, 24–26, 52, 100, 141; trip to Rome, 39, 126, 130
Josippon, 26
Jotapata, 44–46, 51–52, 90, 129
Judah the Maccabee, 72, 98
Judaism, 11–12, 24, 58–59, 223–24, 228, 266, 284, 301; as a philosophy, 113, 185, 283–84; constitution of, 11, 13, 114, 229, 267, 300; conversion to, 58–59, 229; prohibition of images, 58, 96, 167, 284; Sabbath, 58–59, 266
Judas the Galilean, 274, 276–77, 279, 281–82, 292
Judea, 28–29, 58, 74, 96, 139, 154, 165, 238, 241, 273, 284
Judea Capta coins, 60, 265
Judeophiles, 132
Judith, 46
Julian, 57
Julius Caesar, 73, 84
Justin Martyr, 269, 285, 288, 290
Justus of Tiberias, 43, 101, 122, 129, 131, 137, 158
Juvenal, 59

L. Cornelius Alexander, 58
Licinius Crassus, 97
Life of Josephus, 36, 42, 101–2, 122–31, 195, 204; appendix to *Antiquities,* 102, 122, 131; aristocratic character, 37–38, 122, 125, 130–31; moral lessons, 125, 130–31; philosophical schools, 194, 274, 294
Livy, 66, 80, 94, 104
Lucian, 285–86, 293
Luke-Acts, 152, 160, 163–64, 177, 191–92, 207, 209, 215–16, 248, 252–54, 256–57, 264, 266–70, 272, 284, 286–88, 290, 293, 302;

Antipas, 153, 161, 178, 251; audience, 177, 259, 266; census, 275–76, 279, 292, 302; Christianity as a philosophical school, 285, 288–89, 290, 292; death of Agrippa, 163, 291–92; Felix and Drusilla, 177, 282, 291–92; Jesus, 256, 268, 275, 287; John the Baptist, 216–18, 220, 286; Josephus as a source, 164, 178, 251, 273, 277, 278–83, 289–93, 300; Pharisees, 208, 268, 288–89; Sadducees, 207, 246, 251, 288; speeches, 261–63

Maccabean revolt, 271
Manetho of Egypt, 133, 136–37
Marcion of Pontus, 269
Marcus Vipsanius Agrippa, 97
Mariamne, 154
Mark, gospel of, 130, 153, 161, 178, 190, 192, 206–8, 216–17, 246, 256
Martial, 86, 259
Martin Luther, 14
Masada, 51, 67, 76, 86, 260, 274
Matthew, gospel of, 120, 153, 160, 178–79, 190–92, 205–6, 208, 215–16, 218–19, 246
Melito, 12, 14, 23
Michael, patriarch, 230, 234
Monarchy, 74, 154
Moses, 39, 58, 105, 107–8, 110, 114–15, 134, 140, 196, 229, 270–71, 285; laws of, 202, 204, 207, 226, 246, 267, 283

Nazareth, 160, 275
Nero, 39, 47–48, 50–51, 80, 97–98, 126, 174, 239, 288
New Testament, 139, 160, 216, 221, 291, 300–302; Herodian family, 153, 159; James, 246–47; Jewish leadership, 187, 192, 246, 299, 302; John, 223; Pharisees, 187, 205, 207, 302; Pontius Pilate, 177; Sadducees, 187, 302
Nicknames, 228
Nicolaus of Damascus, 159

Old Testament, 139–40, 217, 252
Onias, 67, 96
Origen, 8, 11–12, 13, 17, 22, 229, 269
Otho, 48, 80–81

Parthians, 65, 67
Passover, 67, 96, 169, 177–79
Patron-client relationship, 95, 258–59, 264
Paul, 120, 130, 191, 206–7, 209, 247–48, 262–65, 269, 272, 279–80, 287–89, 293, 300
Pharisees, 9, 27, 28, 43, 96, 115, 187, 193–94, 196–99, 202–8, 244, 284, 289, 292, 302
Philip, 152, 161
Philo of Alexandria, 35, 120, 168, 232, 271
Philosophy, 111–12, 285–86, 288
Pietas, 57
Polybius, 44, 57, 69, 71, 74, 80, 105, 107, 240, 253
Pompey, 97–98, 109, 134, 164
Pontifex Maximus, 56
Pontius Pilate, 22–23, 75, 165–68, 172, 176–79, 190, 225–26, 283, 302
Poppaea, 126, 130
Plato, 80, 105, 107, 111, 114, 209, 287
Pliny the Younger, 10, 69, 245
Plutarch, 37, 44, 69, 71, 73–74, 80, 111, 119, 285
Porcius Festus, 165, 170, 174, 186, 238–39, 258
Pseudo-Hegesippus, 18–20
Ptolemais, 51, 168
Pythagoras, 39–40, 115, 133, 284, 287

Quintilius Varus, 98, 130, 134
Quirinius, 172, 273–76

Rabbinic movement, 37, 101
Revelation, 223
Rhetoric, 36, 39
Roman: aristocracy, 69–70, 103, 106, 109, 182, 245; civil war, 67, 69, 73, 80–81, 97, 106; constitution, 106, 109; education, 40, 69; governors, 164, 166, 168–75, 238, 245, 299; military stratagems, 63, 84, 88, 91; religion, 56–58, 94, 182
Rome, 56, 69

Sacrifice, 76, 96, 183, 243, 268
Sadducees, 9, 96, 115, 187, 193–97, 199, 202, 204, 207–8, 241, 244, 251, 284, 288–89, 292, 302
Sallust, 69, 80, 119
Samaritans, 9, 169, 172, 177–78, 226, 237, 283, 298
Sanhedrin, 186, 197, 207, 241, 246
Scriptoria, 8
Seneca, 36, 40, 111, 285–87
Senate, 56, 60, 94, 155
Septuagint, 93, 119
Sicarii, 174, 278, 280–81, 283, 292
Siege of Jerusalem, 12–14, 52
Simon son of Giora, 79, 98
Socrates, 111, 114, 286, 287
Solomon, 115, 283
Solomon's Temple, 21, 92, 100, 181
Sossius, 98
Source critical analysis, 29–30
Stasis, 69, 78–81, 85
Statius, 86, 259
Stoicism, 114, 284, 287
Suetonius, 59, 119
Suicide, 45, 90, 261
Sulpicius Severus, 82
Sibylline Oracles, 225

Tabor, 98
Tacitus, 40, 50, 59, 62, 69, 82, 86, 115, 119, 123, 136, 138, 174, 245, 266
Tarichea, 91, 127
Temple, 9, 21, 61, 67, 75, 79, 81–82, 84–86, 92, 94, 96, 100, 168, 267, 274, 298
Temple in Egypt, 67, 96
Temple of Peace, 61, 64, 67, 81
Tertullian, 23
Testimonium flavianum, 225, 227, 229–35
Theocracy, 134
Theophilus, 257–59, 285
Theudas, 172, 276, 278–79, 281–82, 292
Thucydides, 80, 239–40, 253, 260, 264
Tiberias, 127, 129, 168
Tiberius, 158, 168, 176
Tiberius Julius Alexander, 173, 276, 279
Titus, 9, 47, 51–52, 60–63, 69, 72, 81–86, 88, 90–92, 96, 98, 173, 260
Tobit, 37
Torah, 21, 207
Tyrants, 79–80, 85, 92–93, 154, 182, 238, 243, 254, 260

Vallerus Flaccus, 86
Vespasian, 9, 37, 44–45, 47–48, 50, 51–53, 64, 72, 79, 81–83, 87, 90–91, 96, 98, 173, 182, 301
Virgil, 37, 104
Vitellius, 48, 80
Voluntary association, 266

Yochanan ben Zakkai, 48

Zealots, 67–68, 78–79, 184, 240, 274

Index of Ancient Sources

OLD TESTAMENT

Genesis
39:6–20 119

Exodus
20:4 167
25:22 181
29:9 228
29:44 181

Leviticus
10:8–11 181
12:1–8 275
16:2–5 181
18:16 157

Numbers
18:36–38 157
19:11–16 157
22–24 114

Deuteronomy
17:14–20 181
18:15–22 181
21:6–9 178
28 110
31:9 186
31:25 186

1 Samuel
10:1 228

1 Kings
11:3 276

Nehemiah
9:12–37 21
10:30 21

Psalms
16:10 263
119 21

Isaiah
40:3 217
45:1 50

Jeremiah
7:9 93
7:11 93
7:34 93
17:1–4 21
17:21–27 21

Lamentations
2:20 93
4:10 15

Ezekiel
18:20 23
20:4–44 21

Daniel
1:17 94
1:20 93, 94
2 224
2:21 93
2:30 94
2:31–45 49
2:34 94
2:45 94
2:47 94
2:48 93
3:30 93
4:14 93
4:22 93
4.29 93
5:11–12 94
6:29 93
7:7 50
7:9–11 223
8:14 93
8:25 94
9:4–14 21
9:24–27 49
9:26 50
11:33–35 94

Malachi
3:1 217
4:5 218

NEW TESTAMENT

Matthew
1–2 160
1:2–17 37
1:23 120
2:1 275
2:1–19 152
2:23 120
3:3 217
3:7 208
3:7–10 215–16
3:10 223
3:11–12 224
3:12 222–23
3:14–15 222
5:3–11 286
5:17 139
5:17–20 269
5:20 205
7:12 139
9:11 246
9:14 246
9:34 246
11:2–6 220–21
11:11 218
11:13 218
11:14 218
11:16–19 218
11:18–19 219
12:2 246
14:1 152, 153
14:3–4 152
14:4 216
14:5 161
15:1 246
15:12 246
16:1 208
16:6 246
16:12 208
16:21 180
20:18 180
21:1 267
21:23–27 218
22:15 246
23:2–3 206
23:13–36 246
26:55–58 190
27:15 179
27:19 178
27:24 178
27:25 179
28:7 267
28:16 267

Mark
1:2–3 217
1:7–8 217
1:14 218
2:16 246
2:18 219
2:24 246
3:6 178, 246, 256
3:19–31 248
5:22–43 130
6:1–6 248
6:14 161
6:14–29 153
6:17 161
6:17–18 152
6:18 216
6:20 161
6:21–29 161
7:1 246
7:3 206

7:19 269
8:11 208
8:15 208
8:31 180
11:1 267
11:17 93
11:27 187
12:13 246
12:18–27 207
14:1 178, 187
14:43 178
14:48–54 190
14:53 22
14:53–64 180
14:54–15:1 190
14:59–65 178
14:67 192
15:1 22
15:5 178
15:6 179
15:9 178
15:10 178
15:14 178
15:15 178
16:7 267

Luke
1:1–4 254–55
1:2 252, 284
1:3 257
1:4 266
1:5 152, 275
1:6 268
1:8 267
1:12–17 218
1:36 218
1:41–42 218
1:77 263
2:1–3 275
2:1–39 160
2:7 286
2:16 286
2:21 256
2:22 275
2:24 286
2:39 275
2:39–42 268
2:40–52 265
2:41 256
2:41–51 267
2:49 256
3:1 152, 282
3:2 188, 191
3:4 217
3:7 208
3:7–9 215–16
3:9 223
3:10–14 216, 286
3:17 222–23
3:19 152, 153, 161, 216–17
3:23–38 37, 264
4:16 268
4:18 286
5:19 259
6:13–16 257
6:20–26 286
7:18–23 220–21
7:28 218
7:36 246
9:22 180
9:51 67, 267
9:51–56 177
9:54 178
11:37 246
12:13–21 286
12:55 259
13:1 178, 283
13:31 152, 161, 246
13:33 267
14:1 246, 256, 268
14:1–14 287
16:14 208, 287
16:17 218
16:19–31 287
17:11 259, 267
18:1–8 287
18:9–14 287
19:11 267
19:12–27 282
19:28 267
19:43–44 283
19:47 180
22:54 191
23:4 270
23:5 178
23:6–12 152, 161
23:14–15 270
23:15 176
23:18 179
23:22 176, 270
24:13 268
24:18 268
24:27 268
24:33 268
24:44 139, 268
24:47 263, 268
24:52 268

John
1:1–18 269
1:6–8 218
1:21 218
1:24 246
1:31 218
1:37 218
1:45 139
3:22–23 218
3:30 218
4:1 246
5:18 256
7:2–5 248
7:32 180, 246
7:45 246
9:16 246
11 67
11:47–53 180
11:51 192
12:10 180
12:42 246
18:2–3 179
18:12–28 188
18:13–24 192
18:31 179
18:35 179
18:38 179
18:39 179
19:8 179
19:12 179
19:16 179

Acts
1:1–3 257
1:5 218
1:8 67, 268
1:11 263
1:12 268
1:16–22 262
1:22 257
2:14 263
2:14–31 263
2:14–36 262
2:16 268
2:23 270
2:25 268
2:29 288
2:32 257
2:36 217
2:38 263
2:44–45 287
3:1 268
3:12 263
3:12–26 262
3:14 263
3:15 257, 270
4:1–2 246
4:6 188, 191
4:10 270
4:11 268
4:18 256
4:19–20 269
4:25 268
4:26 217
4:27 263
4:29 288
4:30 263
4:31 288
4:32–35 287
4:33 217
5 264, 279
5:17 288
5:17–18 246
5:21–39 187
5:30 270
5:31 263
5:34–39 246, 262, 268
5:35 263
5:36 172
5:36–37 278
5:37 276, 280
7:1–53 262
7:2 263
7:2–50 263
7:59 217
8 256
8:1 268
8:14 268
8:35 268
9 279
9:1–19 269
9:26 268
9:29 255
10–11 256
10:14–16 269
10:34–43 262
10:43 263
11:2 272
11:16 218
11:22 268
11:28–29 283
12 264
12:1 153
12:2–19 153
12:3 163
12:17 248
12:20–23 251
12:21 163
12:22 163
12:23 163
13:6–12 270
13:15 139
13:16 263
13:16–41 262
13:17–37 263
13:38 263
13:38–39 263, 264
13:45 270
13:50 270
14:19 270
15 256
15:1 272
15:2 268
15:5 288, 289
15:13–21 262
15:13–22 248
15:20 268
15:29 268

16:4 268
17:2 268
17:5 270
17:12–17 270
17:16–34 287
17:22–31 262
18:6 270
18:14–15 262
19:1–5 219–20
19:9 270
19:13 255
20:17–35 262
21:17–18 268
21:18 248
21:20–26 268
21:21 272
21:22–26 272
21:27 270
21:34 255
21:38 163, 170, 280
22:1–21 269
22:3–21 262
22:22–29 270
22:30 255
22:30–23:10 187
23:2 191
23:6–9 292
23:6–10 246
23:8 207
23:9 207
23:10 270
23:16–35 270
23:26 258
24:1 191
24:2–3 176
24:3 258
24:5 289
24:10 176
24:10–21 262
24:14 139, 289
24:15 289
24:19 176
24:24 176
24:25 177
24:26 177
25:13 153, 164
25:13–26:32 153, 163
25:16 176
25:23 164
25:25 176
25:26 164, 255
26:2–3 164
26:2–23 262
26:4–18 269
26:5 288, 289
26:18 263
26:25 258
26:26–27 164
26:30 164
27 264
28:22 289
28:23 139
28:23–28 256, 269
28:31 288

1 Corinthians
1:2–3 217
1:7–8 217
4:8–11 272
8–10 130
9:5 247
15:7 248
15:12 2712
15:35–51 271

2 Corinthians
11:4 272
11:15 272

Galatians
1:8 272
1:12 272
1:14 206
1:17 272
1:18–19 247
2:1 272
2:6 272
2:6–10 247
2:10 268
2:11 272
2:11–14 247
3:10–14 120
3:23–29 268
4:21–31 120, 268
5:10 272
6:13 247

Philippians
3:3–11 268
3:5 206

Colossians
1:14 264

1 Thessalonians
1:1 217
1:3 217
2:5 209
2:9 209
2:14–16 270

Hebrews
5:10 180
7:26 180

James
1:1 217

1 Peter
1:3 217

Revelation
20:10 223

JOSEPHUS

Jewish War
1–2.275 237
1.1 95, 254
1.1–30 66
1.2 254
1.3 36, 64, 74, 77, 136, 182, 254
1.4 81
1.4–6 254
1.5 72
1.6 36, 64, 136
1.6–8 254
1.8–9 89
1.9 93
1.9–10 74, 78
1.10 81–82, 85, 254
1.11–12 72
1.12 93
1.13 95
1.13–16 135
1.16 36
1.17–30 97
1.23 72, 81
1.24 78
1.25 78
1.27 78
1.31 78, 96
1.31–33 67
1.31–122 73
1.33 96
1.36 74, 201
1.36–37 96
1.36–39 89
1.38 72
1.43–44 89
1.48 72
1.53 74, 89
1.67 199
1.68 74
1.69 74, 183, 198
1.77 198
1.78–80 197
1.81 198
1.91 198
1.97 198
1.108 198
1.109 76, 198
1.110 289
1.110–111 198
1.110–114 198
1.113–114 198
1.117 198
1.118 97
1.127 97
1.170 74
1.175–182 67
1.179 97
1.180 97
1.181 97
1.183 97
1.184 201
1.187 73
1.201–203 154
1.208 154, 156
1.212 154
1.221 73
1.237–238 67
1.242–244 73
1.248–269 67
1.263–267 154
1.264–266 67
1.270 96
1.282 73
1.282–285 282
1.286–294 67
1.288–291 67
1.295 154
1.331 154
1.341 154
1.344 201
1.354–357 154
1.369–385 154
1.380–385 89
1.386–393 73
1.429–430 154
1.433–434 156
1.463 76
1.571 202
1.649–650 159
1.649–651 76
1.650 96
2–3 123
2.1–110 154
2.2 96
2.10 96
2.10–11 179
2.10–30 67
2.20–38 153
2.22 74
2.25 242
2.37–38 242
2.39–79 75
2.42 179
2.55 242
2.56–60 242
2.56–65 154
2.73 154
2.80–92 74
2.84–86 159
2.84–89 154
2.93–100 153
2.94–98 152

2.117–118 166, 274
2.117–183 29
2.118–162 96
2.118–166 155
2.124 207
2.137–142 41
2.139 215
2.140–142 166
2.150–153 89
2.154–158 261
2.157 196
2.160 195
2.162 196, 289
2.162–166 194
2.164 196
2.165 196
2.166 196
2.169–177 166
2.169–277 75
2.170 96
2.174 167
2.184–187 168
2.201–202 168
2.204–213 155
2.214–222 153
2.215 282
2.220 169
2.223–284 153
2.224 179
2.224–227 169
2.225 76
2.228–231 169
2.229–230 67
2.232 169
2.232–234 179
2.232–292 75
2.236 169
2.237 170
2.238 170
2.240 189
2.243 189
2.245–246 170
2.246 97
2.247 282
2.253–265 170
2.254–257 278
2.258 280
2.259 278
2.260 281
2.261 278
2.261–262 281
2.261–263 277
2.262 170
2.264 278
2.270 170
2.271 170
2.274 171
2.275 171
2.275–276 79
2.277 175
2.277–343 171
2.286 76
2.287–288 75
2.293–306 171
2.295 75
2.301 183
2.304 75
2.306–308 75
2.308 171
2.313 96
2.318–324 183
2.318–329 171
2.322 76
2.337 76
2.343–357 171
2.345–404 155, 260
2.350 76
2.352 76, 165
2.358–359 138
2.366 232
2.379 232
2.390–393 224
2.390–395 86
2.393 171
2.398–399 121
2.400 93
2.405 67
2.409 240
2.409–410 76, 243
2.409–442 189
2.410 171, 183
2.411 187, 195, 196, 244
2.412–414 171
2.414 183
2.417 183
2.418 76
2.426 183
2.427 39
2.433 79, 274
2.441 183, 188
2.442 79
2.447 79, 274
2.455 93
2.457–486 60
2.513–555 77
2.531 18
2.539 18, 86
2.540–555 92
2.556 77
2.559 60
2.562 166
2.562–568 123
2.562–582 42
2.563 189
2.567 166
2.569–582 89
2.583 42
2.585 42
2.585–646 89
2.595 76
2.595–596 123
2.595–607 121
2.614–625 127
2.624–626 127
2.626–629 124
2.648–653 189
2.651 78
3 128
3.7 47
3.11 197
3.35–58 96
3.56–57 153
3.68 155
3.70–109 89
3.108 65
3.127–131 45
3.136–137 121
3.137 52
3.137–138 45
3.149 90
3.153–154 90
3.193–201 25
3.193–202 121
3.200 45
3.202 45
3.229–220 90
3.236 90
3.263 93
3.341 45
3.351 45
3.351–352 129
3.352 49, 182
3.354 45, 72, 232
3.359 72
3.362–382 261
3.362–386 45
3.389 121
3.396 72
3.400 25, 45
3.400–402 47
3.403 48
3.404 48
3.406 51, 183
3.438 25
3.439 52
3.472–484 91
3.487–488 91
3.501 93
4.39–48 91
4.84–120 83
4.104 84
4.128 93
4.147–325 183
4.148 183
4.151 79
4.155 189
4.155–157 184
4.158 79
4.160 184
4.163 184
4.166 79
4.177 79
4.208 79
4.224–304 68
4.225 79
4.242 184
4.305–365 67
4.316–317 184
4.317 96
4.318 68
4.319 78
4.326–327 68
4.334–344 242
4.347–352 79
4.353 68
4.356–365 79
4.366–376 79
4.388 79
4.397 79
4.401 79
4.412 93
4.451–485 96
4.496 81
4.502 81
4.545–548 81
4.564 79
4.566 79
4.569 79
4.570–584 79
4.573 79
4.616–617 173
4.622 72
4.623–629 51
4.629 51
4.655 48
5.2 79, 121
5.5–20 79
5.20 93
5.41 92
5.45–56 173
5.71–84 90
5.85–97 90
5.88 72
5.104–105 79
5.114 25
5.120–124 91
5.136–183 96
5.184–247 96
5.236–243 82
5.256–257 74
5.277–278 91
5.287–288 91
5.305–306 90

5.316 47, 84
5.319 47
5.329 84
5.360–362 25
5.367–368 86
5.375–419 260
5.378 86
5.391–393 93
5.399 73
5.400 94
5.402 93
5.408–412 86
5.409 47
5.409–411 87
5.411 93
5.418 93
5.419 52
5.442–445 86
5.515 93
5.566 86
6 283
6.7 93
6.12 84
6.29–32 84
6.33 90
6.33–53 91
6.39–40 86
6.46–52 92
6.50 92
6.57 72
6.78–79 84
6.96–111 93
6.104 93
6.114 183
6.126–128 86
6.147–148 90
6.152–156 84
6.190 84
6.193–213 93
6.201–213 11–12
6.214–227 84
6.228 84
6.233 67
6.236–243 84
6.250 84
6.251 86
6.252 86
6.254 84
6.259 67
6.266 82
6.267 93
6.268 93
6.271–274 93
6.285 91
6.285–287 79
6.288–309 16
6.294–300 136
6.299–300 16
6.300–309 188
6.301 93
6.312 49
6.313 50
6.328–350 260
6.353 85
6.354 39
6.356 85
6.392 17
6.407 17
6.408 72
6.411–413 72
6.413 72
6.421–431 67
6.423–425 169
6.437 93
6.439 93
7.37 66
7.75–88 87
7.84–88 47
7.85–88 66
7.87 88
7.88 88
7.105 67
7.143 63
7.152 66
7.157 67, 81
7.158 64
7.158–162 61
7.203 72
7.221–224 67
7.237 67
7.255–406 67
7.261 80
7.267 68
7.323–387 261
7.327 232
7.331–333 86
7.332 261
7.359 261
7.360 86
7.367–368 60
7.420–436 67
7.447–450 25

Jewish Antiquities
1–10 100
1–11 29
1–16 26
1.1–4 66, 256
1.1–6 102
1.1–26 100
1.5 99, 103, 105
1.5–13 256
1.8 102
1.9 99, 102
1.10–12 107
1.11 102, 112
1.13 105
1.14 99, 110, 113
1.15 105
1.17 119
1.18 107
1.18–19 114
1.18–25 110
1.20 99, 110, 113
1.22–24 114
1.25 114
1.27 103
1.34 114
1.41–59 119–20
1.53 117
1.60–61 117
1.66 117
1.69 114
1.72 117
1.85 113
1.121 135
1.155–156 114
1.158–160 103
1.161 114
1.166 114
1.167–168 114
1.256 117
1.346 117
2.43 154
2.53 154
2.177 104
2.185–187 174
2.188 174
2.198–204 117
2.229–230 114
2.259 174
2.271 174
3.80–82 105
3.84 107, 114
3.151–192 185
3.159–187 107
3.213 107
3.214 107
3.224–286 107
3.320 283
3.322 107
4.12 110
4.14–19 110
4.20 110
4.37 110
4.45 107
4.53–56 264
4.114 114
4.115–116 114
4.152 108
4.184 107
4.186 108
4.191 107
4.193–195 107
4.196 119
4.196–198 107
4.199–319 107
4.214–222 107
4.218 108
4.219 154
4.220 108
4.223 108, 109
4.238–253 120
4.255 108
4.256 108
4.302 107
4.304 107, 186
4.310 107
4.312 107
4.325 108
4.326 115
4.327–331 117
4.328 115
5.15 108, 185
5.43 108, 185
5.55 108
5.55–57 185
5.98 107
5.117–118 117
5.135 108
5.179 107
5.253 117
5.317 117
5.318 108
6.3 113
6.36 108
6.122 108
6.166 117
6.242 108
6.292–294 117
6.343–350 117
6.378 117
7.37–38 117
7.194–196 110
7.338 215
7.342 215
7.356 215
7.374 215
7.384 215
7.390–391 117
8.42 115
8.44–49 115
8.53 233
8.146 113
8.211 117
8.318 154
9.182 233
9.236 215
10.35 233
10.79 120
10.79–80 121
10.89 121
10.90 121
10.114 121
10.119 121
10.126 121
10.129–130 121

10.139 121
10.150–152 108
10.151–153 108
10.186 121
10.189–190 121
10.193 115
10.194 115, 121
10.207 121
10.210 121, 224
10.237 233
10.266 49, 120
10.266–281 103
10.276 49
10.276–281 99
10.277 113
10.277–280 114
10.277–281 120, 195
11 99
11–20 100, 117
11.1–3 103
11.73 108
11.90 108
11.111 108
11.331–339 103
12–20 237
12.63 233
12.138 108
12.142 108
12.158 186
12.230–300 201
12.265 201
12.282 113
12.285 201
12.304 113
12.373 201
12.434 201
13–14 99
13–16 129
13.1–200 201
13.10–11 201
13.166 108
13.169 108
13.171–173 115, 194, 199
13.173 102
13.235 201
13.288 110
13.288–298 194, 199
13.293 197
13.293–296 239
13.293–298 241
13.296 197
13.297 206
13.297–298 202, 204
13.298 102, 197
13.300–301 108
13.300–319 186
13.301 38
13.301–319 201
13.309 201
13.318–319 117
13.320–404 201
13.323 201
13.371–373 115
13.380–383 117
13.399–400 198
13.399–432 201
13.401 110
13.407 198
13.408 201
13.411–417 198
13.417 198
13.423 198
13.426 199
13.430 198
13.430–431 154
13.430–432 117, 199
13.431–432 186
14–17 29, 99, 155
14–20 118
14.2 116
14.8–18 156
14.41 109
14.71 201
14.91 109
14.125 201
14.172 156
14.176 203
14.185–267 118
14.223 60
14.226 239
14.230 60
14.400 199
14.403 109, 118, 156
14.430 118
14.442–444 118
14.462–463 118
14.482–483 118
14.487–490 201
15 242
15.3 203
15.8–10 156
15.51–56 201
15.98 154
15.121–154 118
15.165–182 118
15.174 159
15.182 156
15.219 154
15.247–252 201
15.254 107
15.267 156
15.267–276 118
15.281 107
15.305 118
15.328 156
15.371 115
15.371–379 197
15.375–376 118
16.1–4 118
16.42 215
16.150–159 118, 156
16.160–178 118
16.172 60
16.179–187 118
16.179–188 156
16.184 159
16.187 30
16.188–189 118
16.395–404 114, 118, 156
16.396–399 196
16.398 113
17–19 239, 272
17.19 233
17.32–40 202
17.41 202, 289
17.42 202
17.43 202
17.45 202
17.81 233
17.150–152 157
17.151 118
17.168–171 118
17.180–181 118
17.191 156
17.191–192 118
17.341 189
17.346 197
17.351–353 154
18–20 29, 99, 213
18.1–5 274
18.2 172
18.3–6 110
18.4 196
18.6–8 196
18.7 233
18.8–9 274
18.9 107, 194
18.9–10 110
18.11–23 194
18.12 208
18.12–20 115
18.15 29, 110, 196, 199, 205
18.16 115, 196
18.17 29, 110, 196, 197, 205, 241
18.20 195, 196
18.23 196
18.24 194
18.26 189, 240
18.30–35 172
18.34 189
18.35 189, 225
18.39 233
18.55–59 225
18.56 172
18.60–62 225
18.63–64 172, 225, 226, 227, 243
18.65 227, 233
18.65–80 226
18.80 233
18.81 59
18.81–84 226
18.85–87 172, 226, 283
18.88–89 226
18.95 189
18.99 233
18.109–124 157
18.116–119 157, 214, 225
18.117 215
18.121 233
18.123 189
18.128 157
18.143–204 158
18.172 176
18.257–259 104
18.297–301 158
18.310–379 116
18.376 233
19.15–16 117
19.28–92 60
19.161 109
19.162–164 109
19.167–184 109
19.178 109
19.202 109
19.208–209 117
19.275 282
19.278 233
19.279 158
19.288 158
19.292–352 153
19.297 189
19.299–311 158
19.310 60
19.313 189
19.316 189
19.325 113
19.331 158
19.342 189
19.343–352 158
19.366 172
20.1–159 237

20.2 239
20.5 172
20.16 189
20.17 116
20.48 116
20.51–53 283
20.97 277
20.97–99 279
20.99 172
20.100 173
20.100–102 279
20.102 173, 277
20.103 189
20.104 153
20.108 173
20.110 173
20.111 173
20.113 239
20.116 173
20.118–136 173
20.131 189
20.138–140 153
20.143 174
20.144 174
20.145 158
20.160 110, 238, 278
20.160–178 238
20.162 174
20.164–165 278
20.166 175
20.167 110, 243, 281
20.167–169 278, 281
20.169 243
20.171 279
20.172 110
20.179 189, 238
20.180 238
20.180–181 175
20.182 174
20.188 278
20.189–193 238
20.191 158
20.194 189
20.194–197 238
20.195 59
20.196 189
20.197 174, 189
20.197–198 188
20.197–203 238–39
20.198–199 240
20.199 186, 197
20.200 228, 233
20.200–201 15, 175
20.200–203 186
20.203 189
20.204 175
20.205 188
20.206–207 186
20.208 240
20.211 240
20.213 186, 189
20.214 186
20.215 175
20.216 239, 241
20.218 186
20.223 189
20.224–251 108, 185, 237
20.227 189
20.229 105
20.250 82
20.251 105
20.252–258 237
20.253 175
20.254 175
20.257 171
20.259 103
20.259–266 122
20.259–268 237
20.261 105, 185
20.262 99
20.262–263 135
20.263 36
20.266 121
20.267 103

Life of Josephus
1 108, 125
1–6 37
1–11 123, 126
1–12 131
2 30
2–6 38
6 126, 129
7–12 39
8–10 121
10–11 40, 195
10–12 113, 194
10–12a 204
11 195
12 40–41, 115, 125
13 174
13ff 204
13–16 39, 126, 130
14–16 264
15 127
16 125, 126
17–22 87
17–412 126
20 121
21 187, 195, 244
22 124
27 124
28–29 123
29 42
31 129
36–42 129
37–40 124
40 25, 87, 122, 135
43 43
45 43
48–49 123
62–63 129
64–69 129
66 123
68 158
70–72 124
70–73 123
73 42
75 25
77 43
78 42
79 25
80 129, 199
80–86 130
84–103 127
85 199
85–87 87, 124, 127
85–103 127
89 123, 127
92 127
93–94 127
96 127
97–100 127
99–103 85
101 127
112–13 130
122 199
126–127 123
126–144 87
128 158
128–131 25
130–131 124
137 25
138–144 124
141–142 25
141–144 42
148 85
149–153 130
157 239
163 85, 87, 123
169 85
169–173 43
175–178 87, 124
179 123
179–181 130
189 289
189–198 43, 244
189–205 124
190 203
191 203
193 186, 188, 203
193–197 187
195 203
196 186, 203
204 199
204–207 128
208–209 128
210–211 128
216 203
217–218 87
233 203
236 239, 241
237 203
245 203
259 129
261 25, 203
265 85
266–268 129
271–308 127
272 127
274 203
281 203
284 25
290 203
292 127
296 129
297 127
301–303 203
302 25, 43
304 127
305–308 127
307 85
309 239
310 42
329 85, 127
331 127
335 127
336 25
336–337 137
336–367 122
336–376 129
338 122
340 43, 122
341 42
344 123
355–356 129
357 46, 99
360–362 8
361 64
361–362 96
361–363 95
363–366 163
364 158
365–366 95
368 239, 241
368–389 127
369–372 127
375 85

379 85
385 85
388 85
391–393 129
407–409 130
412 124
413–430 126
414 52
414–430 131
422 126
423 53, 126, 199
424 52
424–425 126
425 25, 53, 127
426 52
428–429 8
429 53, 126
430 38, 121, 122, 257

Against Apion
1.1 257
1.1–5 132, 256
1.6–56 132
1.12 132, 135
1.15–16 135
1.17 139
1.20–21 135
1.22 96
1.23–27 135
1.29 185
1.34–35 134
1.35 52
1.36 185
1.37–41 138
1.42–43 89
1.44–46 135
1.47 36
1.47–56 102, 132
1.50 8, 64, 96
1.50–51 96
1.51 95
1.53 36
1.53–56 99
1.54 113, 122
1.58–59 133
1.59 137
1.66 135
1.69–218 132
1.72 137
1.91 137
1.135–141 137
1.146–153 137
1.162 134
1.166–167 134
1.175 134
1.179 112
1.182 134
1.190 134
1.219–2.144 132
1.223–226 133
1.225 137
1.228 137
1.229 137
2.115 137
2.127 138
2.143–144 264
2.144 137
2.145–296 106
2.146–147 134
2.164 108
2.165 134
2.168 134
2.171–172 107
2.179–181 134
2.180–181 114
2.184–187 185
2.185 108, 134
2.196 132
2.201 154
2.209 112
2.209–210 134
2.211–217 134
2.218 196
2.220–231 134
2.232–233 134
2.257–261 134
2.271–275 134
2.276–278 134
2.279–286 140
2.282–283 132
2.287 105
2.318 137

OTHER EARLY JEWISH WRITINGS

1 Enoch
90.26 223

1 Maccabees
8 72
8:1–32 59
16:16 201

1QHa
3.27–32 223

'Abot of Rabbi Nathan
4.5 48

b. Gittin
56a–b 48

Genesis Rabbah
33 37

Philo

Hypothetica
11.14–17 195

On the Embassy to Gaius
302 168

Sanhedrin
1:4–5 22

m. Ta'anit
68d 37

y. Ta'anit
4:5 37

Tobit
5:11–14 37

OTHER EARLY CHRISTIAN WRITINGS

Eusebius

Ecclesiastical History
1.7.13 39
1.11 230
2.1.4 248
2.2.1 23
2.23.20 17
3.5.2 16
3.5.3 13
3.5.4 16
3.5.6 17
3.5.7 16
3.6.20–28 16
3.7.1 16
3.7.8–9 16
3.9.2 8
3.9.4 103
3.10 122
3.27.2 269

Proof of the Gospel
3.5 230

Gospel of Peter
1–24 23
46 23

Gospel of Thomas
63 286

Justin

Apology
1.46 288

Dialogue with Trypho
8.1 285
46 269

Melito

Passover Sermon
43 12
52 15
92 23
99–100 12

Origen

Against Celsus
1.16 103
1.28 269
1.47 15, 229
2.4 269
4.22 12–13
5.41 63

Commentary on Matthew
10.17 229

Fragments on Lamentations
105 15
109 16

Secret Book of James
1 248

Tertullian

Apology
5.2 23
21.24 23

GRECO-ROMAN AUTHORS

Aristotle

Nicomachean Ethics
10.6.1 111

Politics
3.5.1–2 105

Rhetoric
1.2 123

Catullus
64 103

Cicero

Divination
2.2.4 103

For Flaccus
28.69 60
69 62

On Fate
39 115, 194

On Laws
1.5.17 111
1.6.20–12.34 105
2.5.13 105
2.7 57
2.12.31 106

On Pompey's Command
36–48 125

On the Classification of Rhetoric
75–82 125

On the Orator
2.156 113

Republic
1.27–28 107
1.40.62 106
1.42.65 109
2.1.3 105
2.2.4 104
2.5.10 106
2.9.15–16 106
2.10.17 106
2.11.21–22 107
2.13–14 106
2.14.28–29 106
2.22.39 105
2.30.52 106
2.42.69 106
3.3 112

Dio Cassius
65.1.4 48
65.12.2 288
67.2–3 59
67.13.2 112
68.1.2 59

Diodorus Siculus
34.1.2 59
40.3.4 113

Diogenes Laertius
Lives of Eminent Philosophers
1.16 194
4.16 112
5.22.12 112

Dionysius of Halicarnassus
Roman Antiquities
1.4.1–11.4 104
2.9.2–3 258
2.58–66 106

Epictetus
Discourses
1.4.32 111
1.6 114
1.16 114
1.29.10 288
2.9.13–22 286
2.9.20 59
3.17 114
3.21.20 112
3.22.27 286
23.37 112

Herodotus
Histories
3.80 80

Hesiod
Works
105–199 103

Hippolytus
Against the Jews
7 12

Homer
Odyssey
4.60–64 37
4.147–54 37
13.250–301 46
14.264–69 37

Horace
Odes
3.6 103

Isocrates
Antidosis
278 123

Juvenal
Satires
3.268–314 103
5.14.96–106 59
6.158 164

Livy
History of Rome
1.pref.6–9 103
1.pref.10–12 107
1.6.1 80
29.8.8–11 94

Lucian
Menippus
4 285
5 286

Wisdom of Nigrinus
1 112
35–37 112

Martial
Epigrams
3.9 53
4.27 53
7.72 53

Minucius Felix
Octavius
8–10 10
10 62
33 62

Philostratus
Apollonius of Tyana
5.33 63

Plato
Republic
3.386–417 114
5.473b–d 111
8.543–9.576 105

Pliny
Epistles
5.10 102
7.29 97
8.6 97
10.79.3 244
10.96 10

Plutarch
Cato the Elder
1.3–4 107
2.1 107
2.3 107
2.3–4 111
8.2 154

Life of Caesar
4.8 80
6.3 80

Moralia
814c 73
815d 77

On Superstition
171E 285

Philopoemen
17.3–4 71

Titus Flamininus
11.7 74

Polybius
6.1.4–5 105
6.4.4 78
6.7.5–8 107
6.9.8–9 109
6.18 105
6.47.7–10 107
6.48.2 105
6.56.9–12 57
24.11–13 71
38.12–13 71
38.20.1–21.1 71
44.9 109
48.3 107
56.1–5 107

Porphyry
On Abstinence
2.26 113

Pseudo-Hegesippus
De excidio Hierosolymitano
1.1 18
1.3 18
2.12 18
2.15 19

Quintilian
1.pref.1 102
11.1.35 112

Sallust
Catilinarian Conflict
5.1–8 119
5.4–6 80
5.9–13.5 103
11–13 107
14.1–6 119

Jugurthine War
95.3–4 119

Seneca the Elder
Controversies
1.pref.1 102

Seneca the Younger
Epistles
5.2 112
5.56 112
15.1 111
17.3 285
20.3 286
108.9 286
108.11 285
108.11–12 286
108.22 112

Sililus Italicus
Punica
3.605–606 62

Strabo
16.2.35 113

Suetonius

Claudius
25.4 228
28–9 97

Divus Titus
1.6–7 63

Domitian
2 87
14 59

Vespasian
4–5 48
12 37

Sulpicius Severus

Chronica
2.30.6–7 82

Sybilline Oracles
4.162–178 224–25

Tacitus

Agricola
1.1–3 86
1.3 123
2.3 109
4.1 37
4.3 40, 112, 113

Annales
12.53 97

Histories
1.4 109
1.6.7–10 119
1.13–14 119
1.22–23 119
1.32 109
4.75–85 87
5.1–4 104, 136
5.1–13 62, 138
5.5 59, 116, 266
5.9 174
5.12 60
5.13 50, 136

Thucydides

History of the Peloponnesian War
1.22 260
3.82.2–3 110

Valerius Flaccus

Argonautica
1.12–14 61

Virgil

Aeneid
6.761–895 37

INTRODUCTION

Welcome to the rest of your life! Easy for us to say. We've been in your shoes and have made it through to the other side—into adulthood, that is—still alive and breathing.

It wasn't that long ago that we too were forging through adolescence, making plenty of mistakes, watching our bodies change, and plowing through mounds of school work. Both of us loved our parents and stayed tight with them throughout the teen years, but friends became the center of the social universe while boys acted like gravitational pulls, distracting our attention every time they entered our galaxies. To top it all off each of us was one of the only African American girls in our schools and neighborhoods. To say the least, our teenhoods were filled with confusion, loneliness, and excitement, in other words, all the normal feelings of adolescence.

It wasn't until we got older that we realized we weren't the only ones having a tough time through those years. Each of us honestly thought that nobody else was going through such difficulties on the inside, and having to act "normal" on the outside. Part of becoming an adult was learning how to face the painful and embarrassing moments of the teen years with compassion and a sense of humor. (We can both finally laugh now at some of the hideous clothes we used to wear that we thought we looked so hot in.)

Best of all, we're able to say we learned some of our most important life lessons during that time, like setting goals for ourselves for the long term, believing in our own intelligence—despite what anyone else has to say about it—and taking care of ourselves. These lessons came out of years of experience, trying to get to know ourselves and our worlds better. Out of every mistake or pain came new growth, out of new growth came strength.

We also noticed that the only way we were ever able to learn a lesson was if we listened to that little voice inside. We all have it. It's that same voice that gives you a "creepy" feeling about someone, sets off a creative light